STUDY TEXT

LAND LAW

STUDY TEXT

LAND LAW

Roger Sexton LLM, PhD
Senior Lecturer, Nottingham Law School

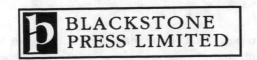

First published in Great Britain 1996 by Blackstone Press Limited,
9–15 Aldine Street, London W12 8AW.   Telephone 0181–740 1173

ISBN: 1 85431 525 0

British Library Cataloguing in Publication Data
A CIP catalogue record for this book is available from the British Library.

Typeset by Style Photosetting Limited, Mayfield, East Sussex
Printed by Livesey Limited, Shrewsbury, Shropshire

FOREWORD

All law students are aware that if they are to succeed in their studies they will need commitment and determination. In addition to this they must be provided with good teaching and good materials, and whilst this is normally the case with the teaching it is not always true of the material.

However, help is at hand. Blackstone Press, in association with Nottingham Law School, have developed a unique series of Study Manuals which it is hoped will assist hard-pressed students to achieve their ultimate goal.

The authors consider all the problems encountered by 'traditional' students and attempt to solve these as well as the problems specific to a distance learning course. The whole philosophy behind the series is the concept of studying effectively in your **own time**, at your **own pace**, in your **own place**.

The Study Text is like a traditional textbook, but also takes the place of a tutor, while the companion Cases and Materials volume will act as your own portable source of reference, available whenever and wherever you need it.

The content of the Study Text reflects the typical syllabus found in most English University Law departments. Each chapter contains a list of Learning Objectives which indicate what you should be able to do by the time you have finished studying a chapter. If you cannot meet these objectives, then your knowledge and understanding are not yet complete.

The Activities in each chapter of the Study Text require you to read a case, a statutory provision, or a commentary in the companion Cases and Materials volume. The chapters also include Self Assessment Questions (SAQs) to ensure that you have understood the relevant points. Some of the chapters also include an End of Chapter Assessment Question, which is of examination standard. Suggested answers are found in the companion volume of Cases and Materials.

Although the Study Text can stand alone, buying both volumes ensures that you get the whole picture and have access to all the cases and materials needed at any time.

The books are designed to be interactive — you do not learn passively, but are able to assess continually what you have learned. The books have been written by experts in their particular areas of the law, and will help you formulate the '**own time, own pace, own place**' method of study which is the key to success on all law degree courses, both full and part-time.

Work wherever, whenever and however it suits you best.

CONTENTS

PREFACE

Land law has a reputation for being a difficult and complex subject – a reputation that is only partly deserved. While part of land law is case-law derived, it has nothing like the number of cases encountered in subjects such as criminal law or tort.

The main problem with land law is that it is statute based, and most of the statutes derive from 1925. But society has radically changed since then. There has been quite a bit of piecemeal legislation over the last 70-odd years, but I firmly believe that the law needs another total revamp. 'We need another 1925.'

In preparing this book my prime aim has always been to give a clear explanation of the subject, rather than a mass of detail. To cope with the difficulties of land law, I have divided the book into 33 chapters. Not all chapters conclude with an assessment question. Within the chapters I have included a lot of *short* self-assessment questions and activities. Some of my activities ask that you read extracts in the companion *Cases and Materials* volume, but others are in effect saying, 'No need to read anything; just pause a minute and think about such-and-such.'

In some universities, land law is a first-year subject, while in others it is taught in the second or even third years. At my own university, it is a second year subject on the LLB (Distance Learning), but a first-year subject on most of our other degrees. I hope the more 'senior' students will forgive me when I say that I have written this book so that it can be used by first-year undergraduates. I have assumed that the reader is in the process of studying contract, and has no knowledge of the law of trusts.

I firmly believe that land law can be fun, and I hope that my enthusiasm for this subject (which I have taught for more than 25 years) is apparent in the pages of this book. A lot of the enjoyment of any legal subject comes through discussion of the knottier points so I would like to thank all those colleagues *and students* (past and present) who, with their ideas or their interest, have indirectly contributed to the content of this book. It would be impossible to name them all, so I shall not name anybody.

Land law used to be a subject which, in comparison to other legal subjects, changed only slowly. Unfortunately, this seems no longer to be true. I must therefore stress that, subject to one exception, I have endeavoured to state the law as of 1 December 1995. The exception is the important decision regarding mortgagees' taking possession, *Cheltenham and Gloucester Building Society* v *Norgan*. I have managed to work this case (decided on 5 December) into Chapter 30.

Roger Sexton
Nottingham Law School

TABLE OF CASES

TABLE OF STATUTES

CHAPTER ONE

INTRODUCTION TO THE TYPES OF PROPERTY RIGHTS IN LAND

1.1 Objectives

By the end of this chapter you should:

- have some appreciation of the enormous variety of property rights which can exist with respect to land;

- be able to explain in outline the fundamental concept of the 'fee simple estate';

- be familiar with the concept of a lease;

- be able to recognise the important types of property right which can exist in favour of third parties against land the fee simple in which is owned by someone else.

1.2 Introduction

In this chapter I aim to give you an **introduction** to certain basic concepts of land law. I should stress that you are not expected at this stage to learn the detailed rules governing (say) leases, easements, or restrictive covenants. Rather, I am trying to give you a broad overview of those property rights in land which are so important that we will be meeting them constantly throughout this text.

Before embarking on this broad overview, there is just one other preliminary point. In English law, 'land' includes not just the surface of the earth, but also buildings and things 'underground' as well. If you own an open site upon which a house is then built, the house becomes part of the land and is therefore yours.

Read *Berkley* v *Poulett* (1976) EG 911 in *Cases and Materials* (1.1). Why was the plinth part of the land, but the statue resting on the plinth not part of the land?

The plinth had become embedded in the surface of the land, while the statue rested on the plinth by its own weight.

1.3 Property Rights which Give Immediate Use and Enjoyment of Land

If a man is occupying land which he regards as 'his', this will almost certainly be because either:

(a) he owns a **fee simple** estate in that land; or

(b) he holds a **lease** of that land.

(There are other possibilities which need not concern us yet.)

1.3.1 FEE SIMPLE ESTATE

In everyday conversation we say things like, 'Farmer Giles owns all those fields over there'; 'Fannie Bloggs owns that cottage'; 'Big Company plc owns that hideous looking factory'. As a matter of strict legal theory such statements are incorrect. Ever since the Norman Conquest (1066), all English (and Welsh) land has been vested **theoretically** in the Crown (the monarch for the time being)!

The persons who are colloquially referred to as 'owners' of a piece of land (Giles, Fannie, Big Company) technically own not the land itself but a 'fee simple estate' in the land. They hold this fee simple estate from the Crown under **freehold tenure**. (We might sometimes say in ordinary conversation things like, 'Fannie owns the freehold to her cottage' or 'Giles has got the freeholds to [of/in] those fields'.)

Nowadays the idea that everybody holds 'their land' off the Crown is nothing more than an amusing historical relic. Since 1925 there has been no practical difference between ownership of a fee simple estate in land and ownership of all other types of property, such as furniture, jewellery, other types of goods, money, stocks and shares, bank accounts, etc. Ownership of a fee simple does not now involve performing any special obligations to the Crown.

Ownership of a fee simple, just like ownership of goods and chattels, money, etc., is in principle perpetual. There is just one problem which occurs very occasionally. If an owner of property dies intestate (i.e. without having made a will), all his property passes (after debts etc. have been paid) to his **statutory next-of-kin**. The deceased's widow(er) and children obviously qualify as 'statutory next-of-kin'. Failing them, other close blood relatives such as parents, siblings, uncles/aunts and first cousins qualify as 'statutory next-of-kin'. If, however, the deceased left no close relatives, his property is in effect now without an owner. We use the Latin phrase *Bona Vacantia* to describe such property. *Bona Vacantia* (ownerless property) passes to the Crown.

SAQ 1

Jack owns the fee simple estate in a 5,000 acre farm, 'Bigtrees'. He is a bachelor and has no close relatives whatsoever. He is 30 years old and in excellent health. Why should he make a will?

Recent surveys show that two-thirds of people die intestate. For people who own very little property this perhaps does not matter. But if Jack dies intestate, the valuable fee simple in Bigtrees (together with all other property he owns) will pass to the Crown. I think Jack would prefer his wealth to go to his friends and/or his favourite charities.

1.3.2 LEASES

If somebody has a lease over a piece of land then he has the right to use and enjoyment of that land for the duration of his lease. It must be stressed that a lease is itself a property right. Leases can (as a general rule) be bought and sold, given away, or left by will.

SAQ 2

If an owner of a lease died intestate, what would happen?

Like the rest of his property, the lease would pass to his statutory next-of-kin.

A lease may (depending on the circumstances) be extremely valuable. Suppose you owned a 999-year lease of a 5,000 acre farm; the rent payable is just one pound per year; there are no other obligations on you, the lessee. You would consider yourself quite a wealthy person!

Leases are basically of two types:

    (a) fixed term; and

    (b) periodic tenancies.

1.3.2.1 Fixed term leases

A fixed term lease may be for any period of time, provided the maximum duration is fixed. Thus, for example, one could have a lease for one day, one week, five years, 21 years, 99 years, 999 years or any other **definite** period. (Very short fixed term leases are, however, unusual.)

You cannot create a lease for an uncertain period such as 'so long as there is a Conservative Government', or 'while Manchester United play in the Premier Division'. However, a fixed term lease often includes a forfeiture clause entitling the lessor to terminate the lease prematurely if the lessee breaks any terms of the lease (e.g., fails to pay the rent). Such a clause does not infringe the rule that a lease must have a definite maximum duration.

1.3.2.2   Periodic tenancies

These comprise, for example, weekly, monthly, quarterly or yearly tenancies. A periodic tenancy is technically a lease for one period, which goes on extending itself automatically until either landlord or tenant gives notice to terminate the tenancy. (The period of notice is usually one period.)

Suppose you have a monthly tenancy of the private lock-up garage in which you keep your car. As a matter of **technical law** you have a lease for one month, then another, then another . . . and so on, until either you or your landlord give one month's notice to terminate the arrangement. In **practical terms**, however, a periodic tenancy goes on indefinitely until one or other party gives notice.

1.4   Property Rights Against Land Owned by Other People

One of the factors which makes land law both interesting and complicated is the fact that while Bloggs may own the 'fee simple estate' in a piece of land, 'Blackacre', all sorts of other people may have rights against that fee simple. We have just mentioned leases. But there are all sorts of other property rights which could affect the fee simple in Blackacre. One practical effect of the existence of a lot of 'third party' rights against a fee simple would be to reduce the value of that fee simple.

The first of these 'third party' rights is one with which many of you (particularly older readers) may have **some** acquaintance.

1.4.1   MORTGAGES

How many times have you heard a couple (call them Mr and Mrs Average) say something like, 'We are buying our house with the assistance of a mortgage given us by the Bruddersford Building Society'? You may have said it yourself. If you have, you were wrong, but I will forgive you. The correct legal analysis is as follows:

Mr and Mrs Average own the fee simple estate in the house. In order to finance their purchase they borrowed a lot of money from the Building Society. The moment they acquired the fee simple in the house the Averages **granted to the Building Society** a mortgage, i.e. the Averages are the **grantors** of the mortgage; they are the **mortgagors**.

The Building Society did not 'give' the mortgage. It lent the money, and **was granted** the mortgage. It is the **mortgagee**. The Building Society does not own the fee simple in the house; it owns its 'mortgage'. The mortgage gives the Building Society security. If the Averages fail to repay the loan the Society can enforce its mortgage. This will usually involve taking possession and selling the house over the heads of the Averages. (Mortgages may of course exist with respect to all types of property, not just houses. Any person, not just Building Societies and Banks, can be a mortgagee.)

Adverts in banks often say 'mortgages available here'. What is really meant by such advertising?

Such advertising should not be taken literally. The bank is really saying, 'We are willing to lend you (our customers) money provided **you grant us** a mortgage of your house (or other property) to secure the loan'.

1.4.2 RESTRICTIVE COVENANTS

This is another type of right in land which you may have already come across, particularly if your house is in a relatively 'posh' area. A restrictive covenant is a promise by one landowner in favour of a neighbouring landowner(s) that he will **not** do certain things upon his land. For example, a farmer promises a neighbouring farmer not to develop his own land but to keep it for agricultural purposes only; or a shopowner promises a neighbouring house-owner that he will not sell takeaway food. In each of these two cases the land restricted is the **servient** land; the land benefited is the **dominant** land.

A more complicated example is as follows. A developer sells off a new housing estate. Each house on the estate is subject to a set of similar restrictive covenants:

(a) Houses shall not be used for any trade, profession or business.

(b) Front fences must not be more than one foot high.

(c) Caravans and boats must not be kept on the properties.

(d) There must be no outside TV aerials or satellite dishes.

Each purchaser is granted (by the developer) the right to enforce these covenants. Thus every house on the estate is both servient and dominant.

1.4.3 EASEMENTS

Only a very vague definition of this concept is possible. An easement is a right of one landowner to make use of another nearby piece of land for the benefit of his own land. A mere glance at any textbook's chapter on easements will show that a wide variety of rights come under that general heading.

The most commonly encountered kind of easement, and the one which is easiest to envisage, is the private right of way. For example, Farmer Smith, current owner of High Farm, has the right to use a track across Farmer Brown's Low Field in order to get from the public road to High Farm. We say that the easement is 'appurtenant' to High Farm: High Farm is the **dominant** land; Low Field is the **servient** land.

Another easement of considerable modern importance relates to drains. There may be a right 'appurtenant' to a building to run the drains from that building under neighbouring land (owned by someone else) to the public sewer. Similar easements can exist in relation to gas-pipes, electric and telephone cables, etc.

1.4.4 PROFITS À PRENDRE

A quite extraordinary mixture of rights come under the general heading of profits à prendre ('Profits'). A loose definition of a 'profit' is a right to go on to somebody else's land and to remove from that land something which exists there naturally.

The concept of a 'profit' includes, for example:

(a) a right to extract minerals such as gravel or chalk;

(b) a right to cut peat;

(c) a right to go hunting or shooting over somebody else's land;

(d) a right to fish in someone's lake/river/pond;

(e) a right of a farmer to graze sheep or other animals on land which does not belong to him.

We have already noticed that with easements and restrictive covenants, in addition to the **servient** land over which the right exists, there must also always be **dominant** land benefited by the right. A profit can and usually does exist 'in gross', i.e. as a totally separate right not attached to any dominant land. A profit may, however, exist 'appurtenant' to dominant land, and one important example should be mentioned. The fee simple estates in our great moorlands such as Dartmoor, the Northern Peak District, etc. belong not to the government but usually to some big private landowner. The sheep (and possibly other animals) which we see grazing on the moors do not (normally) belong to that 'big private landowner'. Rather, they belong to farmers who own farms on the edge of the moor.

If I bought a farm on the edge of (say) Dartmoor, what sort of 'profit' would almost certainly be an automatic part of my purchase?

I would expect that 'appurtenant' to the farm would be a right to graze a fixed number of sheep (or other animals) upon the moor.

1.4.5 RENTCHARGES

This is a type of property right which many find difficult to understand. Rentcharges, for historical reasons, are very common in the Manchester and Bristol areas, but are relatively uncommon in all other parts of the country.

If you own a rentcharge, you have the right to receive payment of a regular (usually annual) sum of money. That sum of money is charged upon a fee simple estate in a piece of land. You are **not** landlord of that land. Now this probably does not mean much to you. Things should become clearer if I explain what used to happen in the Bristol area from (about) 1950 to 1977 on the sale of new houses.

Imagine it is 1960. Bloggs is a builder of houses operating in the Bristol area. He builds new houses on land which he owns. He then sells each house for £10,000 **and** a perpetual rentcharge of £100 per annum. (These figures are realistic.) Smith buys one of these new houses from Bloggs. He pays £10,000 and acquires the fee simple estate in his house. Despite having the freehold, not a lease, Smith must still pay £100 per annum to Bloggs. If Smith sells the house to Thompson, Thompson must now pay the £100 per annum.

What happens if Thompson now sells the fee simple in the house to Unwin?

Bloggs has a property right in the house – the right to £100 per annum – which he can claim from the current owner of the fee simple. So Unwin must pay the rentcharge, until he, Unwin, disposes of the fee simple in the house.

Rentcharges have never been popular with the ordinary public. The Rentcharges Act 1977 did not abolish them, but:

(a)   (subject to exceptions) it prohibited the creation of new ones;

(b)   it provided that existing rentcharges (which usually are perpetual, i.e. for ever) should terminate after a further 60 years.

1.4.6   RIGHTS OF OCCUPATION UNDER THE MATRIMONIAL HOMES ACTS

These rights are commonly referred to as 'Class F land charges', for reasons which will emerge later in this text at **8.3.3.3**.

Where one spouse has sole legal title to the matrimonial home (whether he/she has a fee simple or a lease), the other spouse has a statutory right to occupy the home. This kind of property right was created by Parliament in 1967. It has no application where the legal title to the home is in the joint names of both husband and wife.

It must be emphasised that the Matrimonial Homes Acts do not apply to cohabitees. They apply only to couples who have had a proper ceremonial marriage. It should also be stressed that people who call themselves 'common law husband and wife' are cohabitees and are outside the provisions of the Acts.

A further point of extreme importance is that the rights of occupation under the Matrimonial Homes Acts are entirely independent of any equitable share in the home which the spouse without legal title may have by virtue of a constructive trust.

1.4.7   INTEREST UNDER A CONSTRUCTIVE TRUST

Detailed examination of constructive trusts forms part of the law of trusts. For present purposes you need only a basic understanding of the one aspect of constructive trusts which affects land law. This point is best explained by reference to an example.

Alfred owns the fee simple in a house, Chenu. Bertha makes substantial contributions to Chenu in one or more of the following ways:

(a) she directly pays a large part of the price of Chenu;

(b) (the most likely possibility) Chenu is bought with the assistance of a mortgage, and Bertha contributes substantially to the mortgage repayments;

(c) Bertha makes substantial improvements to Chenu, e.g., by personally renovating the house, or by paying for contractors to build an extension.

In this sort of situation the courts will normally infer that Bertha was intended to have a share in the property approximately proportionate to her contributions. Suppose in (a) above the house cost £90,000. Alfred paid 'cash down', i.e. he did not have to borrow. £30,000 was in fact provided by Bertha. In principle Bertha will acquire a one-third (equitable) share in the property under a constructive trust. Calculating the size of Bertha's share is going to be more difficult in situations (b) and (c) above; for the purposes of our **land law** course, we need not worry about this problem.

You may have noticed that I have not told you whether Alfred and Bertha are married. It does not matter! Nor would it matter if Bertha had the legal title to the property and it was Alfred who made substantial contributions. Nor would it matter if the property were not a house but some other kind (say a farm).

In *Lloyds Bank* v *Rosset* [1990] 1 All ER 1111, the husband had been given money to buy a derelict house on the understanding that the house should be in his name alone. The wife did a limited amount of work helping the renovation of the house; in particular she helped with the interior decorations. The vast bulk of the work was done by contractors employed and paid for by the husband.

Read the relevant parts of *Lloyds Bank* v *Rosset* in *Cases and Materials* (1.3.7), and consider why Mrs Rosset did not get a constructive trust interest. What sort of activity would have given rise to a constructive trust interest in the property?

Horace and Wendy were married in 1950. They have always lived in Grey House. Horace is sole owner of the fee simple in Grey House. Wendy has just come into your office in great distress. Between sobs she explains that Horace has just left her. Consider the land law aspects of this situation. She certainly has one, perhaps two, property rights against the home.

You should have concluded that Wendy will **automatically** have her rights of occupation under the Matrimonial Homes Act, and this will be so even if her role throughout the marriage has been purely as a housewife making no financial contributions to the family income.

She **may** also have a constructive trust interest, but that would (normally) depend upon her having made a substantial contribution to the acquisition or improvement of the house.

1.4.8 LICENCES BY ESTOPPEL

In *Inwards* v *Baker* [1965] 1 All ER 446 the Court of Appeal (led by Lord Denning) appeared to invent a new type of property right in land, i.e. licences by estoppel (sometimes called 'proprietary estoppel').

Baker junior was keen to build himself a bungalow, but he could not afford the price of an empty site. His father had some spare land. Baker senior said to his son, 'Why not put the bungalow on my land and make the bungalow a little bigger?'. Baker junior did exactly that, and made the bungalow his permanent home.

Baker senior retained ownership of the fee simple to the land, and so the house also became **Baker senior's** property. All was well while both senior and junior were still alive, but when Baker senior died his will (made long before the bungalow was built) left the land in question not to Baker junior but to Inwards. Inwards brought proceedings to recover possession of the bungalow. These proceedings failed.

The Court of Appeal held that where a landowner (L) encourages a third party (T) to expend money and/or effort on L's land, and T reasonably assumes that he will have some degree of permanence on the land, T acquires some sort of right with respect to the land. This right is (in principle) binding on third parties.

There have been many other cases since, but the exact nature of the proprietary estoppel right is still subject to much debate. It seems that T acquires such right in the land as the court thinks just in all the circumstances. In *Inwards* v *Baker* the son was allowed to live (rent-free) in the bungalow for the rest of his life.

1.4.9 ESTATE CONTRACTS

As anyone who has bought a house or other land may well know, the purchase of a piece of land **may** be a long-drawn-out process. From a legal point of view, the purchase of a piece of land normally takes place in two stages:

(a) The vendor and the purchaser enter into a contract under which it is agreed that the land should be sold by V to P (the 'contract stage').

(b) The vendor transfers the fee simple in the land to the purchaser by conveyance or land transfer (the 'completion stage').

The time interval between stages (a) and (b) is normally only a few weeks. The important point to remember is that, during this time interval, the purchaser does not own the fee simple in the land. But he does own an interest in the land known as an **estate contract**.

1.4.10 OPTIONS

An option is a right under which the grantee (i.e. owner) of the option can at any time during a fixed period (not exceeding 21 years) exercise the option and insist that the land the subject matter of the option is sold to him.

Suppose, during my travels, I come across Purple House, a very attractive country residence. I immediately react, 'What a smashing place; one day I might want to buy it!'. I approach Valerie, the owner of Purple House, and we do the following deal.

Valerie grants to me an option exercisable at any time within the next 10 years. I pay her £5,000 **for the option**. The option agreement includes a clause that should I exercise the option the price for Purple House itself is to be negotiated between us. If we cannot agree a figure, the price is to be fixed by an arbitrator appointed by the President of the Royal Institution of Chartered Surveyors.

It is important to note the following points:

(a) If at any time in the next 10 years I exercise the option, Valerie cannot turn round and say, 'But I don't want to sell'. I can sue if she refuses to comply.

(b) Valerie has in effect granted me a valuable right over Purple House. Hence the price of £5,000 which I paid **for the option**.

(c) An option should not be confused with **a right of first refusal** (sometimes called a right of pre-emption). A right of first refusal is much less valuable than an option. Suppose that Valerie had granted me a right of first refusal instead of an option. All that would mean is that **if she decided to sell** she would have to offer the property to me before she put it on the open market. I don't think that I would pay very much for a right of pre-emption over Purple House.

(d) The clause in the option agreement regarding the fixing of the price if I do exercise the option reflects standard modern practice.

1.5 Conclusion

If somebody is occupying a piece of land, his right to be there will (normally) stem from the fact that he either owns the fee simple ('freehold') in the land, or he has some form of lease (fixed term or periodic) over the land.

Fees simples and leases are not, however, the only property rights which can exist in land. There is a wide variety of property rights which people can enjoy over land which they do not themselves in any sense 'own'. Some of these rights, e.g., restrictive covenants and options, can come about only as a result of some formally agreed transaction. But others, notably interests under constructive trusts and licences by estoppel, can arise informally as a result of a course of conduct. As you will see as you work through this text, much of the difficulty (but also the fascination) of land law lies in the rules governing rights against other people's land, whether those rights are created formally or informally.

CHAPTER TWO

SOME BASIC CONCEPTS OF PROPERTY LAW

2.1   Objectives

By the end of this chapter you should:

- be familiar with the basic features of a trust;

- be aware of the types of trust which can exist with respect to land;

- be able to explain the fundamental differences between unregistered and registered title;

- be able to explain what are 'title deeds';

- be able to distinguish between 'real property' and 'personal property'.

2.2   Introduction

This chapter is necessarily something of a miscellany. In it we will examine in outline three matters of which you need some basic understanding before we proceed further with land law. These three matters are the concept of the trust and how it applies to land law; unregistered and registered title; and the (fortunately now relatively unimportant) distinction between real and personal property.

2.3   The Trust

2.3.1   THE CONCEPT OF THE TRUST

The concept of the trust is fundamental to English property law, and has been so for hundreds of years. You have probably already learnt that historically the **common law** had the biggest influence on the evolution of English law. But the system of rules known as **equity**, developed by the Court of Chancery, has also been and remains of profound importance. The concept of the trust is equity's biggest contribution to the English legal tradition.

A trust normally involves three parties or groups of parties:

(a)   the **settlor** who creates the trust;

(b)   the **trustees** who manage the trust property but do not keep any income (rents, interest, dividends etc.) derived from the property;

(c)   the **beneficiaries** who are entitled to the income from the trust property.

The structure of a trust is illustrated by **Figure 1**.

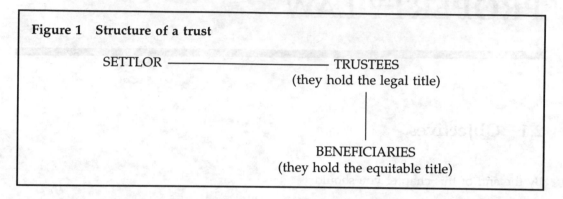

Figure 1   Structure of a trust

SETTLOR ———————————— TRUSTEES
(they hold the legal title)

BENEFICIARIES
(they hold the equitable title)

The references in **Figure 1** to 'legal title' and 'equitable title' can be properly explained only by going back a long way in history to about 1300. The following story is typical of that era.

Sir Richard Goodbody is going abroad for a long period of time, quite probably on a Crusade or some other warlike activity. He is concerned that, in his absence:

(a)   his land ('Widetrees Manor') should be properly managed;

(b)   the income from the land should be used to support his wife and children.

He makes the following arrangement with Thomas and Terence, two old friends whom he thinks he can trust:

(a)   He transfers the ownership (i.e. the 'fee simple') in Widetrees Manor to Thomas and Terence.

(b)   They agree –

(i)   to manage the land;

(ii)   to pay the income from the land to Lady Goodbody and the children;

(iii) to transfer the land back to Sir Richard on his return;

(iv) should Sir Richard be killed, to transfer the land to Sir Richard's eldest son Stephen on his attaining the age of 21.

Now, with the vast majority of trusts created over the last 600 years, the trustees faithfully carry out their trust and the beneficiaries are perfectly happy. You have, however, perhaps already guessed that Thomas and Terence turn out to be a couple of rogues. They manage Widetrees Manor, but keep all the profits from the land for themselves. Lady Goodbody and the children (the 'beneficiaries') are left destitute. They resort to litigation.

Lady Goodbody first tries to bring proceedings against Terence and Thomas in one of the common law courts (the Court of King's Bench, Common Pleas or Exchequer). These proceedings are dismissed. The court rules that, under the common law, Thomas and

Terence are the **legal** owners of Widetrees Manor, and they can do what they like with the land. The claims of Lady Goodbody and the children are purely **moral** ones.

Lady Goodbody now goes to the Lord Chancellor, who until about 1550 was usually a distinguished clergyman rather than a lawyer. He is very concerned that Thomas and Terence carry out their moral obligations. He thus orders them to carry out the terms of the trust, and to pay the profits from the land to the Goodbody family. If they disobey his order, they are locked up for contempt of court, the 'court' being the Court of Chancery.

As a result of many cases similar to the example we have just considered, it became apparent that where a trust is created:

(a) the trustees (Thomas and Terence in my example) are recognised **by the common law** as the owners of the property – they are the **legal** owners of the property;

(b) the beneficiaries (the Goodbody family in my example) are recognised **by equity** as the owners of the property – they are the equitable owners. Each beneficiary has a separate equitable interest in the trust property.

Until the reorganisation of English courts in 1875, if trustees committed a breach of trust, the beneficiaries could not bring a successful claim in a common law court. They could only enforce their claim in the Court of Chancery. Although the courts were merged in 1875, the distinction between common law and equity has continued. In particular, it is still correct to refer to trustees as **legal owners** and to beneficiaries as **equitable owners.**

SAQ 7

Imagine that it is 1850. Tim and Tom hold a large farm, Blackacre, in trust for Anne, Betty, and Cath. Tim and Tom are in breach of trust by keeping the profits from Blackacre for themselves. In which court should the women commence proceedings?

Since the example occurred before 1875, they would of course sue in the Court of Chancery. If the example happened today, they would sue in the High Court. But note that the case would be allocated to the Chancery Division of the High Court!

2.3.2 MODERN TRUSTS

2.3.2.1 The trust property

Any type of property can be subjected to a trust, even items such as antiques or valuable paintings. As we shall see later at **2.4**, land is still often subjected to a trust. However, in most modern trusts the trust property is stocks and shares, or other investment assets such as company debentures or government bonds. (Usually trustees of investment assets are given wide powers to vary the investments.)

2.3.2.2 The settlor

The settlor's motivation in creating the trust may well even today be to benefit members of his family, or perhaps his friends or employees; or he may wish to benefit 'charity'. With a charitable trust the trust has charitable purposes; there are no human beneficiaries.

Trusts may be created **'inter vivos'**, i.e. while the settlor is still alive. Alternatively, a settlor may create a trust by his will, though I must stress that a will only takes effect when the testator (the person who has made the will) actually dies.

(It is usual to think of the settlor, trustees and beneficiaries, as three distinct persons or groups of persons. This is not always the case. For example, a settlor may appoint himself as one of the trustees, or, rather paradoxically, some of the beneficiaries may also be trustees.)

2.4 Trusts of Land

Basically trusts of land come in three forms:

(a) Strict settlements.

(b) Trusts for sale.

(c) Bare trusts.

2.4.1 STRICT SETTLEMENT

This is a type of trust which can be applied only to land. Strict settlements used to be extremely important. It is estimated that even as late as the end of the nineteenth century, 50 per cent of all land in England was subject to a strict settlement! Nowadays strict settlements are rare but not unknown. For reasons which will emerge later in this text, modern lawyers discourage their clients from creating strict settlements.

A strict settlement was usually created where the settlor hoped that the land would remain 'in the family' from generation to generation, e.g., land was granted to A for life, remainder to A's eldest son (B) for life, remainder to A's eldest grandson (C) in fee simple.

Do not worry at this stage about the technical word 'remainder'. What is important is to understand:

(1) that A, B and C are the beneficiaries of a trust;

(2) that A enjoys the benefits from the land for his lifetime;

(3) that on A's death the right to enjoy the benefits from the land passes to B for his lifetime;

(4) that on B's death, C becomes entitled to the land outright, and can do what he likes with the land.

You may well be asking the question, 'If a strict settlement is a form of trust, and A, B and C are the beneficiaries, who then are the trustees of the land?'. I have to answer that strict settlements are such a big anomaly in this respect when compared to all other trusts that it is better not to try and answer this question **at this stage**!

2.4.2 TRUST FOR SALE

Almost all trusts of land in existence today are trusts for sale. For example, Greenacres is conveyed by X to Tim and Tom as trustees with a direction that they must sell the property and invest the proceeds; the investments are to be held in trust for X's children.

You will no doubt immediately realise that:

    (a)   X is the settlor;

    (b)   Tim and Tom are the trustees;

    (c)   X's children are the beneficiaries.

What is rather more surprising is the fact that Tim and Tom do not in fact have to sell the land immediately. Trustees for sale nowadays invariably have 'a power to postpone sale'. This means that they can put off selling the property indefinitely. This is an important, if rather paradoxical, point which you will have to get used to!

One other point to make at this stage is that while a strict settlement can be applied **only** to land, any type of property can be made the subject of a trust for sale.

In the example above of a trust of Greenacres, who holds the legal title to the land, and who owns equitable interests under the trust?

I hope you found this question very easy. Tim and Tom hold (jointly) the legal title, while X's children own equitable interests under the trust.

2.4.3 BARE TRUST

This is also a form of trust which can be applied to any type of property. It is rare in practice. A bare trust is any trust where the legal ownership of the property is vested in trustees, but:

    (a)   there is only one beneficiary;

    (b)   he/she is of full age; and

    (c)   he/she is entitled to all the benefits from the trust property.

2.5 Proof of Title to Land

2.5.1 IMPORTANCE OF PROOF OF TITLE

As you probably already know, buying a piece of land (be it a house, field, factory or anything else) can be a painfully slow process. One of the reasons for the slowness is that the purchaser needs to make all sorts of enquiries about the land he is intending to buy.

Above all, if you are buying a piece of land from (say) Victor, you want to be absolutely sure that Victor does in fact own the land in question. In technical terms, you want to be sure that Victor has a 'good title' to the 'fee simple' in the land which you are buying. Think what a disaster it would be if you paid Victor £300,000 for the house of your dreams, only to find out later that Victor was a fraudster and the house really belonged to somebody else.

2.5.2　METHODS OF PROVING THAT A VENDOR HAS GOOD TITLE

In the English legal system it is up to the vendor to prove to the purchaser that he has got a 'good title' to the land being sold. All fees simple in England and Wales (also all leases over 21 years) are either **unregistered** title or **registered** title.

Until 1897 unregistered title was the only system operating in this country. It can be fairly described as the 'traditional system' for proving that a vendor has a title to his land.

2.5.2.1　Unregistered title

Title deeds

Where land is unregistered title, the vendor produces 'title deeds' to the purchaser. That sounds rather mysterious, but the basic idea is really quite simple. The title deeds are simply those documents which have been used in the past to carry out transactions with the land. The popular conception of 'title deeds' is as a bundle or pile of old, perhaps even ancient, documents. Subject to the point about 'root of title' which I will explain later, this popular conception is correct.

When a vendor produces title deeds to a purchaser, the vendor is demonstrating that he and his **predecessors in title** have been in control of the land for such a long time that no one could possibly dispute their claim to ownership. By 'predecessors in title' I mean the person (let's call her Penny Predecessor) from whom the vendor obtained the property, the person from whom Penny obtained the property, and so on back in time.

Title deeds will include:

(a) **Conveyances**, 'conveyance' is the name given to the formal document, which must be a deed, which is used to transfer a fee simple from one person to another, whether the transfer is a sale or gift.

(b) **Legal mortgages**, even after the mortgage has been paid off. (Do not worry about the complex historical reasons why mortgages form part of the title deeds.)

(c) **Grants of probate** to executors.

(d) **Grants of letters of administration** to administrators.

(e) **Assents** from personal representatives.

Devolution of ownership on death

The matters mentioned in (c), (d) and (e) above have probably left you rather puzzled. They are all to do with what happens to a person's property on his or her death. After a person dies there will be a need for **personal representatives** (who may be either

executors or **administrators**) to wind up the deceased's affairs. There are three possibilities:

(a) The deceased has made a will (we say he has died 'testate'), and that will appoints executors who are able and willing to act. The executors will obtain from the court a grant of probate and then –

   (i)   gather together all the deceased's property;

   (ii) from that property pay any debts owed by the deceased;

   (iii) pay any inheritance tax or other taxes which become payable on the deceased's death;

   (iv) (once they are sure that all debts and taxes have been paid) distribute the property according to the terms of the deceased's will.

(b) The deceased died **'intestate'**, i.e. without making a will. In such a case close relative(s) of the deceased obtain **letters of administration**. The administrators (as they are called) then proceed as in (a) above, except that when they get to stage (iv) they transfer the deceased's property to his **statutory next-of-kin**.

(c) The deceased made a valid will, but that will either fails to appoint executors, or those appointed are either unable or unwilling to act. In such a case close relative(s) of the deceased obtain **letters of administration with the will annexed**. The administrators then proceed exactly as in (a) above.

Assent

Here we have a rather awkward example of the law taking a perfectly ordinary little English word and giving it a technical meaning. In the context of documents relating to land, an 'assent' is the document signed by executors or administrators transferring the land to the person entitled, either under the deceased's will or as statutory next-of-kin.

Investigating title deeds back to the root of title

As we shall learn later when we come to consider the topic of **adverse possession** (see **Chapter 21**), if somebody (and/or his predecessors) has been in control of a piece of land for a long period of time (usually 12 years is enough), all rival claims to the land are automatically destroyed by lapse of time. In investigating title deeds it is not therefore necessary to wade through huge mountains of paper right back to the proverbial 'year dot'.

Normally the purchaser investigates only as far back as the 'root of title'. Usually the root of title is the most recent conveyance which is at least 15 years old. For example:

■ In 1937 A conveyed Purpleacre to B.

■ In 1983 B conveyed Purpleacre to C.

■ In 1988 C conveyed Purpleacre to D.

■ D is now selling Purpleacre to E.

The 1937 conveyance from A to B will be the root of title.

What if in the above example the conveyance from B to C had been six years earlier, in 1977?

That conveyance would be the root of title, as it is the most recent conveyance which is at least 15 years old.

(The **Land Charges Register**, which is kept on a computer situated at Plymouth, is an adjunct to the system of unregistered title. It is not to be confused with the Register of Title, which we consider in **2.5.2.2**.)

2.5.2.2   Registered title

The vendor proves his title to the purchaser by reference to a register kept by the government at various centres. Registered title is gradually taking over from unregistered title. Compulsory registration of title started in Central London in 1897. It was extended to the rest of (modern) London in 1926. In the 1950s it was extended to parts of the South-East of England south of the Thames. In the 1960s and 1970s it was extended to **most** of the heavily populated areas of the country. There was then a lull from 1978 to 1985. From 1985 to December 1990, new compulsory areas were created every six months, and the whole country is now covered.

The Land Registry has had to be considerably expanded to meet the growth of registration of title. The registers are kept at 18 District Registries scattered around England and Wales.

The fact that the whole country is now 'compulsory' does not mean that all titles to land are now in fact registered. When an area was designated 'compulsory' that did not mean that everybody had immediately to rush off to the District Registry and register the land they owned. That would have been hopelessly impractical. Ever since 1897 the basic principle has been that a title to land must be registered the first time it is **sold** after the area in which it is situated is designated a compulsory area. This point will become even clearer if I tell you that there is in Central London ('compulsory' for nearly 100 years) a large amount of land the fee simple titles to which have not been registered.

Why do you think there is a lot of unregistered land in Central London?

As you may well know, a lot of land in London is owned by long-established companies, the government, the Church, big charities and family trusts of people such as the Duke of Westminster. Such people/organisations may own the fees simple for (literally) hundreds of years.

It is worth noting that the Land Registry in November 1992 **proposed** that registration should be compulsory where a fee simple passes **by a gift, by a will, or on an intestacy**.

If this proposal is enacted, will it ensure that all fees simple are registered within (say) 100 years?

Unfortunately not. It will not affect land owned by charities, companies, or government agencies (local or national). Such organisations 'never die'.

Registration of leases

One possibly confusing feature of the English system of land registration is that it extends not just to fees simple ('freeholds') but also to leases for longer than 21 years. Basically, as the law **now** stands:

(a) if a new lease is created which is to last more than 21 years, that lease must be registered;

(b) if an existing long lease is 'assigned' (i.e. transferred from one person to another) the title to the lease must be registered if the lease has more than 21 years still unexpired.

You should carefully note that if the above rules are satisfied, the lease must be registered even if the fee simple out of which the lease is derived is not registered! (The rules relating to registration of leases were simplified by the Land Registration Act 1986, and there is no need to worry about the old pre-1986 rules.)

Voluntary registrations

Prior to 1990, provided the land was situated **within** a compulsory area, it was always possible for somebody with an unregistered title to register that title voluntarily, thus not waiting for the next time the land was sold. With the whole country now a 'compulsory area', this general right to register voluntarily now extends throughout England and Wales.

You may perhaps be surprised to learn that prior to 1990 it was not uncommon for registered titles to be found in non-compulsory areas. This was (usually) the result of voluntary registration of new housing estates, such registrations being encouraged by the Land Registry.

In 1973 my parents and I jointly bought a bungalow in Hitchin (North Hertfordshire). The title was registered, and had been since 1958, when the bungalow (and its neighbours) was first built. North Hertfordshire did not become an area of compulsory registration of title until November 1985.

Transactions with a registered title

Once a title has been registered, all subsequent transactions with that title must be registered. When registered land is sold a 'land transfer' is executed by the parties. However, ownership of the land does not pass until that transfer is registered.

2.6 Real Property and Personal Property

Most foreign legal systems divide property (and rights in property) into two types: moveable property and immoveable property. The distinction is a perfectly logical one. All land (including buildings) is immoveable; all other property is moveable. Unfortunately, English law (and other legal systems such as Australian law and Jamaican law which are derived from English law) draws a less logical distinction. English law distinguishes between real property and personal property.

2.6.1 REAL PROPERTY

All property rights relating to land (fees simple, mortgages, easements, profits, etc.) are real property, **except leases**.

2.6.2 PERSONAL PROPERTY

This concept includes:

(a) rights in all types of property except land (so things as diverse as goods and chattels, money, stocks and shares, patents, and copyrights are all personal property);

and

(b) leases.

It will be immediately apparent that the big anomaly is leases. The reason for the anomaly is purely historical. In the Middle Ages a lease was regarded as a purely contractual right enforceable only against the landlord, not as a property right against the land itself.

Happily, the distinction between real property and personal property became much less important after 1925. Prior to 1926, if someone died intestate (without making a will) there was one set of rules governing the succession to his real property, and another different set of rules governing the succession to his personal property. After 1925, if someone dies intestate, the same rules of succession apply to both types of property.

There is one situation where the distinction between real property and personal property remains of some significance. This is where a legal document such as a will or trust is drawn up using the phrases 'real property' and 'personal property'. In interpreting the will or other document, these phrases must be given their technical legal meaning.

Suppose that Charley Proper makes his own will, without getting any form of legal advice. The will reads: 'I leave my real property to my dear wife Florinda and my personal property to my son David.'

Charley was quite wealthy, and his assets included a 99-year lease over 'Greenroof', the former matrimonial home. Who will inherit the lease?

His son would inherit that lease, though that was probably not what Charley really intended.

2.7 Conclusion

We have just discussed the distinction between real and personal property, a distinction which fortunately is not of great significance today. But other matters dealt with in this chapter are of vital importance. As we shall see in later chapters (especially **Chapter 10**) the results of cases with apparently similar facts may well be different depending upon whether the land in dispute is registered or unregistered title.

Trusts of land is also a vitally important topic. Although strict settlements are (fortunately) largely things of the past, trusts for sale are very common. For reasons which will not become apparent until we reach **Chapters 14 to 16**, there are literally millions in existence in England and Wales. Indeed, many readers of this book are (probably without knowing it) trustees of a trust for sale.

CHAPTER THREE
TENURES

3.1 Objectives

By the end of this chapter you should:

■ be able to explain the concept of tenures;

■ appreciate why it is of limited significance today.

3.2 Introduction

In medieval times, there were two legal concepts of fundamental importance to English land law. These concepts were 'tenures' and 'estates'. Where a person lawfully occupied a piece of land, he held that land under a tenure for the duration of an estate. (We will be considering estates in **Chapter 4**.)

Originally there were many different types of tenure. Where a person occupied land his **tenure** indicated the type of **conditions** upon which he held his land. His estate indicated **the length of time** for which he held his land.

3.3 Feudal Tenures

What I am about to say may remind you of school history lessons! We have already referred to the fact that in strict legal theory somebody who 'owns' a piece of land in fact holds a fee simple estate off the Crown under 'freehold tenure'. In the days of the feudal system (approx 1066–1300) there were lots of different tenures. As you may know, after the Norman Conquest the king and other feudal lords granted land in **fee simple** to their supporters in return for the supporters rendering various types of services to the King or the other feudal lords. A man's tenure indicated the kind of services he had to perform. For example if a man held land under a 'military tenure', he had to supply troops for the army. If he held under 'socage' tenure, he had to help farm his lord's land. If he held in 'frankalmoigne' tenure, he had to pray for the salvation of his lord's soul!

Happily for England, the system of holding land in return for rendering physical services began to die out as early as the thirteenth century. By a statute called 'Quia Emptores' passed as early as 1290 (and still in force), Parliament banned further 'subinfeudation', i.e. a fee simple can no longer be granted in return for the grantee rendering services.

Existing obligations on fee simple owners to perform services continued after 1290, but these obligations gradually disappeared as a result of a mixture of economic and historical factors. Many tenures also just disappeared, but some were abolished by Act of Parliament. In particular the Tenures Abolition Act 1660 (part of the agreed compromise which led to the restoration of Charles II) abolished military tenure. 'Copyhold' tenure (a form of tenure originally very important for small-scale farmers) was not abolished until 1925.

The result of all this is that today there is only one tenure left which has its origins in feudalism, namely freehold tenure. (Freehold tenure is actually the modern name for 'socage' tenure.) If somebody owns land, he (in technical terms) holds that land off the Crown under freehold tenure for a fee simple estate. Thankfully, though, he does not have to render any services to the Crown!

Old Joe Bloggs has owned 'Greytrees' for a very long time. You are trying to explain basic land law to him. He suddenly interjects, 'Does this all mean that I don't really own Greytrees, but the Queen does and that I am merely her tenant and I have to do a lot of work for her?'. How do you reassure Joe?

I think you will say something like this: 'You, Joe, are in the same position as every other landowner in England and Wales. You are technically a 'tenant' of Her Majesty, but you are not a lessee. You hold your land for a fee simple estate, a right to the land which goes on forever. You hold that fee simple estate under a "freehold" tenure. Once upon a time freehold tenure meant that a landowner had to work hard for his land, but nowadays the obligation to work for your land has disappeared.'

3.4 Leasehold Tenure

Leases did not exist under the feudal system of medieval times. The practice of granting land **for a fixed period** in return for a regular money payment (i.e. rent) only commenced about 1450.

Where there is a lease the **tenant** holds the land off his **landlord,** and (normally) the tenant must pay for holding the land. The position of a tenant holding a lease from his landlord for a rent has been regarded as analogous to a medieval fee simple owner holding his land off the king or other feudal lord in return for rendering services. (I am somewhat sceptical of this analogy, but I am very much outvoted!)

The practical result of drawing this (somewhat strained) analogy between leases and feudal tenures is that 'leasehold' is today regarded by both textbook writers and Parliament as a form of tenure. For example, legislation sometimes refers to 'land of any tenure'.

24

TENURES

3.5 Conclusion

The practical conclusion to be drawn from this short chapter is very simple. In modern land law there are just two tenures, freehold and leasehold.

CHAPTER FOUR

ESTATES

4.1 Objectives

By the end of this chapter you should:

■ be able to explain the concept of a fee simple estate, both in its pre-1926 form and in its post-1925 form;

■ be able to distinguish between a fee simple upon condition subsequent and a determinable fee simple;

■ be familiar with the (archaic) rules which govern the duration of a fee tail estate;

■ have a basic idea of the (anachronistic) rules governing the barring of entails;

■ be familiar with the various forms which can be taken by a life estate;

■ be able to distinguish between an estate in possession, an estate in remainder and an estate in reversion.

4.2 Introduction

We have already seen that in modern law the concept of **tenures** is of very limited significance. By contrast, the concept of **estates** remains of prime importance. If a person holds a piece of land, his 'estate' indicates the period of time over which he (and his successors) can continue to hold that land. Some of the basic rules regarding estates are easy to follow; but I must also warn you that there are also some complex and confusing anachronisms.

At common law there were four types of estates:

■ Fee simple

■ Fee tail   } estates of freehold

■ Life estate

■ Lease

The three 'estates of freehold' are far more ancient in origin than the leasehold estate, and they are discussed below.

4.3   Fee Simple

The fee simple estate in land has always been the most valuable and the most important of the estates. It has always been an 'estate of inheritance', i.e. an estate which can pass on from generation to generation. Indeed, a fee simple has always been capable of lasting indefinitely.

Since the very early days, the owner of a fee simple has been able to sell it. He has also been able, on his death, to leave the fee simple by his will to whomever he chooses, even though that might mean that his 'heir' (who would have inherited the land on intestacy) was disappointed.

The 1925 legislation made quite important changes to the nature of a fee simple, and you still need to know the pre-1926 nature of a fee simple, as well as the modern position.

4.3.1   FEES SIMPLE PRE-1926

Prior to 1926 the fee simple was dominated by the (old-fashioned) concept of the 'heir'. This dominance manifested itself in two ways.

In the first place, a fee simple estate continued indefinitely, subject only to the possibility of 'natural determination'. Natural determination occurred where the present owner of a fee simple died intestate without leaving any traceable **heir**. In the (rare) event of there being no traceable heir, there was an 'escheat'. The fee simple terminated and the Crown became entitled to the land.

Secondly, if you wanted to convey a fee simple to a human being you had to include the magic words 'and his heirs' in the conveyance. Thus to convey to John Smith a fee simple in Blackacre, the conveyance had to grant Blackacre 'To John Smith and his heirs'. If a conveyance said 'To John Smith' or 'To John Smith forever', John would get only a life estate. Prior to 1882, even saying 'to John Smith in fee simple' would not work to convey a fee simple.

This rule, that you had to add 'and his heirs' after the name of the grantee, looks even sillier when you remember that the heir of the owner of a fee simple had no guarantee that he would actually inherit the estate. In my example of a grant of Blackacre to John Smith, John is free to sell or give away his fee simple at any time, or he can leave it by his will to whomever he chooses.

4.3.1.1   Rules for identifying the heir

The following rules, which to us now may seem rather archaic, had to be applied if somebody died **intestate** owning a fee simple in land. As a general rule the closest blood relative of the deceased was his heir. If the deceased left children, the eldest son was the heir. If the deceased left no son, but daughters, the daughters jointly constituted the heir. If the deceased left neither children nor remoter descendants (grandchildren, etc.) then a collateral relative (such as a brother, an uncle or a cousin) could inherit the fee simple as heir.

You should not attempt to learn the detailed rules set out in some textbooks. Just remember the following points, which show the rather antique nature of the rules for identifying heirs:

(a)   The rules always preferred males over females.

(b)   Amongst males (only), the rules preferred the eldest over the others.

(c) The deceased's surviving spouse could never be heir, even if the deceased had only very remote blood relatives, or no blood relatives at all.

John died intestate in 1920. His main asset was a fee simple estate in Vastacres, worth £500,000. He left a widow with no financial resources of her own. He also left a sister aged 80, and two brothers aged 75 and 70. The brothers emigrated to Australia in 1900 and John never saw them again. Both became extremely prosperous. Who inherited the fee simple?

Applying the rules set out above, your answer should be as follows. The widow cannot be heir, males are preferred over females, and between males the eldest takes. Thus the 75-year-old brother inherits the fee simple to Vastacres.

4.3.2 FEES SIMPLE AFTER 1925

For purposes connected with fees simple (though not for certain other purposes) the old rules relating to heirs have been abandoned. The old concept of escheat has also been abolished.

As you may well remember from **Chapter 1**, a fee simple estate is now in principle eternal, and owning a fee simple is really no different from owning any other type of property. If a person dies intestate all his property passes to his **statutory next-of-kin**. The rules relating to next-of-kin give preference to surviving spouses, do not discriminate between the sexes, nor do they discriminate between elder and younger children. If someone dies intestate without statutory next-of-kin then all his property vests in the Crown as 'bona vacantia' (ownerless property).

With regard to conveying a fee simple after 1925, the law on this point has been brought into line with common sense. To convey a fee simple after 1925 to John Smith it is sufficient to say 'To John Smith': Law of Property Act 1925, s. 60.

4.3.3 MODIFIED FEES SIMPLE

So far, we have assumed that all fees simple are **absolute**, i.e. that in principle they go on for ever, subject to the (remote) possibility of the current owner dying intestate without any relatives capable of inheriting the estate. Now, in the late twentieth century, the overwhelming majority of fees simple are absolute. Unfortunately it is still just possible to come across 'modified fees simple'. No doubt you will quickly agree that modified fees should have been abolished in 1925. They are anachronisms, just like fees tail (see **4.4**).

A fee simple is modified if it may come to a premature end for some specified reason other than lack of people to inherit. Just to confuse matters further, there are two types of modified fee simple, the **determinable fee simple** and the **fee simple upon condition subsequent**.

4.3.3.1   Determinable fee simple

This can be defined as a fee simple which terminates automatically on the occurrence of a specified event which may never happen. For example:

(a)   To John Smith in fee simple until he marries Fanny Bloggs.

(b)   To the X charity in fee simple while my grave remains in good condition.

(c)   To Ann Green in fee simple during the time that she remains a faithful Protestant.

4.3.3.2   Fee simple upon condition subsequent

This can be defined as a fee simple where the grantee is given an apparently absolute fee simple, but a clause is then added to the effect that if a stated condition is broken, the estate shall be forfeit. For example:

(a)   To John Smith in fee simple provided that he never marries Fanny Bloggs.

(b)   To the X charity on condition that my grave remains in good condition.

(c)   To Ann Green in fee simple unless she forsakes the Protestant religion.

(d)   To David Brown in fee simple, but not if he marries a Roman Catholic.

What do you think was the motivation of the grantor in the two examples '(a)' in 4.3.3.1 and 4.3.3.2 above?

It is fairly obvious that the grantor (who is perhaps John's father) does not want John to marry Fanny. He is in effect saying to John, 'If you marry that wretch of a woman you lose your land!'.

4.3.3.3   'It's all a matter of words'

It is very easy to identify a modified fee simple, but it is not always so easy to tell whether it is a determinable fee or a fee on condition subsequent. It depends on the kind of wording used by the grantor. If he uses words of a **temporal** nature, such as 'until', 'during the time that', 'whilst' etc., then there is a determinable fee. If he uses words of a **conditional** nature, such as 'provided that', 'on condition that' or 'unless', it is a fee simple upon condition subsequent.

4.3.3.4   The differing rights of the grantor

With a determinable fee, the grantor retains a **possibility of reverter**. If the determining event takes place, the possibility of reverter automatically takes effect and revests an absolute fee simple in the grantor. Consider example (a) in **4.3.3.1**. If John marries Fanny then he loses the fee simple as soon as the marriage takes place. The grantor regains the fee simple without having to make any claim for it.

With a fee simple upon condition subsequent the grantor retains a **right of entry**. (The phrase 'right of entry' is really a euphemism for a 'right to forfeit'.) If the condition is broken the fee simple remains vested in the grantee until the grantor chooses to exercise the right of entry.

Consider example (a) in 4.3.3.2. If John marries Fanny, when (if at all) does he lose the land?

Now when the priest/registrar says 'I hereby pronounce you man and wife' John retains the fee simple until the grantor chooses to reclaim the land. (The grantor has got 12 years to get the fee simple back. He will, normally, get the fee simple back by repossessing the land. If the grantor allows twelve years to elapse without reclaiming the land, John can breathe again! He keeps the fee simple.)

4.3.3.5 Public policy

One reason why modified fees should be abolished is that they are out of line with modern ideas of freedom, particularly religious freedom. Amazingly, modified fees limiting freedom to marry and freedom of religion are valid. In 1975 the House of Lords unanimously **upheld** a condition subsequent which provided for forfeiture on the grantee becoming a Roman Catholic: (*Blathwayte* v *Lord Cawley* [1975] 3 All ER 625.)

Read the extracts from *Blathwayte* v *Lord Cawley* in *Cases and Materials* (4.1.1.1), and note their Lordships' reasons for upholding the condition subsequent.

(The Law Lords stressed the freedom of landowners to give away their land on whatever conditions they saw fit.)

On a few occasions (mainly in the nineteenth century) the courts have held a particular modified fee to infringe public policy. Notably, modified fees which discourage entry into the armed forces (e.g., to X provided he does not join the Navy) are ineffective. Apart from this point (and the religion point already mentioned) there is no need for you to remember the public policy rules. Modified fees are (thank goodness) virtually obsolete.

4.4   Fee Tail

The fee tail is a strange legal relic which has somehow survived into the late twentieth century. Fees tail were first recognised as an estate in land in 1285. Until the nineteenth century land (particularly the large country estate) was often subject to a fee tail. Very few fees tail exist today. They should have been abolished in 1925; they are totally out of place in the twentieth century. A fee tail cannot be bought or sold, or given away or left by will. (However, as we shall see at **4.4.2**, a fee tail can often be converted into a fee simple by the process of 'barring the entail'. This possibility should be ignored for the moment.)

A fee tail is an 'estate of inheritance', i.e. it can pass on from generation to generation within the same family. **It is an estate which lasts as long as the original grantee or any of his lineal descendants are still alive.** If all the descendants of the original grantee die out the fee tail will terminate. Consider the following example:

Whiteacre is granted to Brian in fee tail. His 'family tree' is as in **Figure 2**.

Figure 2   Example: Alfred's family tree

When an owner of a fee tail dies, the old rule regarding 'heirs' still has to be applied, **even after 1925**. Thus:

■ When Brian dies the fee tail passes to Eric.

■ When Eric dies the fee tail passes to Hugh.

■ When Hugh dies he is childless; the fee tail passes to Isabel.

■ When Isabel dies she is childless. The fee tail can pass to Frank or Gillian, if either is still alive.

What happens to the fee tail if Frank and Gillian both die childless?

The answer is that the fee tail is at an end, as Brian's descendants have now all died out. (Applying rules discussed at **4.6.2**, the right to the land will revert to the person who granted the fee tail.)

A fee tail cannot pass to the collateral relatives (e.g. brothers, sisters, cousins) of the **original grantee** (Brian in my example). This is a big difference between a fee tail and a (pre- or post-1925) fee simple. If, in my example, Brian had had a fee simple, that could pass to Charles, Daphne and their families. But the fee **tail** granted to Brian cannot pass to them.

4.4.1 THE INALIENABILITY OF FEES TAIL (AS SUCH)

As already mentioned, fees tail were popular from about 1300 to the late nineteenth century. They were employed by large country landowners (usually members of the aristocracy) anxious that the family lands should remain in the family from generation to generation.

Suppose Baron Blogtown owns Wideacres in fee simple. By his will, Baron Blogtown left Wideacres 'to my elder son Stephen in fee tail, remainder in fee simple to my younger son Keith'. Now it must be stressed that a fee tail is 'inalienable', i.e. it cannot be sold or given away, nor could it be left by will. Thus, in my example, Stephen is stuck with Wideacres for his lifetime. On Stephen's death the fee tail estate **must** pass to his heir, who is of course equally incapable of selling or giving away the fee tail. (And so on when the heir dies.)

A lot of fees tail were created in medieval times. That meant that a lot of land was 'frozen', as it were, to a particular family, and could not be bought and sold. This was not good for the prosperity of England. English lawyers found a solution to the problem when, in about 1450, they invented the process of 'barring an entail'.

4.4.2 BARRING AN ENTAIL IN POSSESSION

Anybody of full age who owns a fee tail estate in possession can 'bar' the entail. Prior to 1833, the barring of an entail was a complex and expensive process; since then it has been cheap and simple. All the fee tail owner (Stephen in my Wideacres example) has to do is to execute a document called a 'disentailing assurance'.

If a fee tail is 'barred' the following consequences ensue:

- the fee tail is converted into a fee simple;

- any fee simple existing in remainder or reversion to the fee tail being barred is destroyed.

Thus in my Wideacres example, Stephen will probably want to bar the entail. If he executes a disentailing assurance that will convert his unsaleable fee tail into a fee simple which he can dispose of in any way he chooses. Moreover, the disentailing assurance will also destroy Keith's fee simple in remainder.

You may be thinking, 'That's rough upon Keith. His rights are destroyed by Stephen signing a simple document. Does he get any compensation?'. The answer is a firm 'No!'. (If you were Keith, would you seriously expect that the land would ever come to you?)

4.4.3 BARRING A FEE TAIL BY WILL

As barring an entail is now so easy and cheap, almost everybody of full age who acquires a fee tail in possession will bar it immediately. That, of course, is the major reason why fees tail are almost extinct.

Suppose, however, that somebody acquires a fee tail, wishes to keep the land during his lifetime, but then wants to be free to leave the land to the person of his choice. Since 1925 a fee tail can be barred by will. All that is required is that the will specifically refers to the land subject to the fee tail.

Suppose in my Wideacres example Stephen wishes to keep the land until he dies, but he wants the land to then pass to his beloved daughter Florence rather than to his scoundrel eldest son Roger. If, when he died, his will simply read, 'I leave all my property to my daughter Florence,' that would not bar the entail. Roger would inherit the fee tail in Wideacres under the old rules about heirs. Moreover, Roger could then bar the entail!

If, on the other hand, Stephen's will had read, 'I leave all my property including Wideacres to my daughter Florence,' there is a specific reference to Wideacres, so the entail would be barred. Florence would get a fee simple in Wideadcres, and Roger would get nothing.

4.4.4   BARRING A FEE TAIL IN REMAINDER

Suppose land is granted, 'to Alice for life, remainder to Bertha in fee tail, remainder to Charlotte in fee simple'. Can Bertha bar the entail **before** Alice's death? This sounds like a very academic question, but if you look at some of the larger textbooks you will see that a lot of complex law has developed around the barring of fees tail in remainder. All these complications can be ignored.

All you need know is that to bar completely a fee tail in remainder, the owner of the fee tail must get the consent of the owner of the estate in possession. Thus, in my example, Bertha needs to get Alice's consent. If Bertha gets Alice's consent to the execution of a disentailing assurance Bertha will get a fee simple in remainder; Charlotte's rights will be destroyed.

4.4.5   FEES TAIL AND THE PROCESS OF SETTLEMENT AND RESETTLEMENT

Until about a hundred years ago it was common for a wealthy landowner, keen 'to keep the land in the family', to make a disposition (often referred to as a '**settlement**') along the lines of the following example:

David, the owner in fee simple of Broadacres, makes a 'settlement' granting Broadacres, 'To my son Edward for life, remainder in fee tail to Edward's first son to attain the age of twenty-one'. At the time of this grant, Edward did not yet have a son. The grant of property to an unborn person is however (subject to certain limits) permissible. In particular, because of **the rule against perpetuities** (about which you will learn when you study trusts law) you can usually grant property rights to the first unborn generation but not to later unborn generations.

One effect of this disposition is that Broadacres would be 'tied up' and unsaleable at least until **both** Edward was dead and his eldest son had attained the age of 21. At that point one might expect the eldest son (I will call him Frank) to bar the entail.

This, however, overlooks the fact that Frank would probably attain 21 during the lifetime of his father, Edward. Frank would now have a fee tail in remainder, which he could 'bar', but to do so he would need his father's consent. His father may not be too keen to give his son a completely free hand with Broadacres.

If matters followed their usual pattern Edward would be keen 'to keep the land in the family'. He would agree with his son that the entail should be barred, but on condition that a **resettlement** was immediately executed. (If Frank was not keen to make a resettlement, 'family pressures' would be brought to bear.)

The resettlement would read, 'To Edward for life, remainder to Frank for life, remainder in fee tail to Frank's first son to attain the age of twenty-one'. Thus Broadacres would be 'tied up' for another generation!

You can perhaps guess what would happen when Frank's eldest son (call him George) attained 21. Frank and George would bar the entail and execute a further resettlement! And in many wealthy land-owning families this sort of thing went on from generation to generation!

Nobody in their right mind would nowadays subject land to the processes just described. For a start, heavy capital taxation makes it unwise. Secondly, the Settled Land Acts (which we discuss later in this text) ensure that land cannot be 'tied up' and rendered unsaleable. The relevance of the settlement/resettlement process is that it explains developments in English law over the last 115 years or so.

In 1882, Parliament passed the first important Settled Land Act. This was designed to ensure that all settled land (such as Broadacres in my example) could be bought and sold freely. At the time, this was an enormous reform. Contemporary economists estimated that a large proportion of England and Wales (probably as high as 50 per cent by area!) was subject to settlements/resettlements.

In the years after 1882 the amount of settled land began to decline. In the early twentieth century, economic changes brought about by increased mechanisation and by the First World War accelerated that decline. Yet when Parliament enacted wholesale reforms of property law in 1925 it made the very short-sighted assumption that there would continue to be a lot of settled land.

Today there is very little settled land. Yet much of the 1925 reform is structured on the assumption that settled land is commonplace. This is one major reason why 'we need another 1925'.

4.5 Life Estates

While fees tail are exceedingly rare today, property rights which last 'for life' are still quite common. As you can probably guess, the essential feature of a life estate is that its duration is governed by the length of the life of a named person or persons. A life estate is bound to come to an end sooner or later!

Life estates can take various forms, e.g.,

(1) Property is granted 'To Jane Brown for life'.

This is the simplest and commonest form of life estate. Jane enjoys the property for her own lifetime. Her rights terminate on her death, and she will have nothing which she can pass on by her will. Other forms of life estate can be a little more complex, e.g.,

(2) Property is granted to 'Jane and John Brown for their lives', or

(3) Property is granted to 'Jane and John Brown for their joint lives'.

The second example lasts as long as **either** Jane or John is alive. The third example is not so good; it lasts only as long as they are **both** alive.

The form of life estate which people sometimes find difficult is the estate 'pur autre vie', e.g.,

(4)   Property is granted to 'Ann Green for the life of Karen White'. This means that the estate comes to an end when Karen dies, not when Ann dies. If Ann dies before Karen the estate continues until Karen dies, and the right to enjoy the property until Karen's death will pass to Ann's successors under her will. If there is no will it will pass according to the normal intestacy rules.

I should mention one other complication with life estates. Go back to my first example (1) above. Let us suppose that Jane sells (or gives) her life estate to Penny Pink. Penny acquires the right to enjoy the property for **Jane's** lifetime, not for her own. (Put another way, Penny acquires an 'estate pur autre vie' lasting for Jane's life.) If you stop and think for a moment, no doubt you will agree that this result is both logical and fair.

In 1985 Whiteacre was granted 'to Tom, Dick and Harriet for their joint lives'. Tom, Dick and Harriet have just executed a deed transferring to you their rights in Whiteacre. Tom is on his death-bed. Is it worth your moving into Whiteacre?

I think that you had better start praying for a miracle to restore Tom to full health! You have acquired an estate pur autres vies which will terminate when the **first** of Tom, Dick or Harriet dies.

4.6   Estates in Possession, Reversion and Remainder

In the preceding discussion we have often assumed one thing which is not always true. We have assumed that all estates are 'in possession'. In fact, while most estates are 'in possession', estates in reversion and in remainder can also exist.

4.6.1   ESTATE IN POSSESSION

This is almost self-explanatory. An estate in possession is one which confers on its owner an immediate right to occupy the relevant land.

4.6.2   ESTATE IN REVERSION

An estate in reversion arises where the owner of a greater estate (usually a fee simple) grants out of that estate a lesser estate. For example, Alfred owns fees simple in Blueacre, Greenacre, and Redacre. He grants Blueacre 'to Brian for life'. He grants Greenacre 'to Charles in tail'. He grants Redacre 'to David for 99 years'.

In each case, during the time that the life estate, fee tail and lease are in possession, Alfred retains an estate **in reversion**. When the life estate, fee tail and lease expire, the right to actual enjoyment of the land returns to Alfred. But what if, in the meantime, Alfred has died? An estate in reversion (also an estate in remainder) can be inherited just like any other property. So it will be Alfred's successors under the law of succession who will be able to claim possession of the land.

Two other points should be noted about reversions. First, sub-leases. Suppose David (in the example just considered) sub-leased Redacre to Edward for 50 years. David would also now have an estate in reversion. Secondly, unlike estates in remainder (see **4.6.3** below), an estate in reversion arises **by implication**. It arises whenever the owner of a greater estate creates a lesser estate but does not make express provision for what is to happen when the lesser estate expires.

4.6.3 ESTATES IN REMAINDER

An estate in remainder arises where the owner of a fee simple grants a life estate (or possibly a fee tail) and then in the same document grants a further estate to follow on after the termination of the life estate or fee tail. For example:

(a)   Frank owns the fee simple in Purpleacre. He grants Purpleacre 'to George for life, remainder to Henry in fee simple'. This means that on George's death the land will not revert to Frank. Rather it will pass on to Henry. If Henry died before George, the land would pass on to Henry's successors under the law of succession.

It is possible to have a series of 'remainders', one after another. For example:

(b)   Frank owns the fee simple estate in Mauveacre. He grants Mauveacre 'to Ian for life, remainder to John in fee tail, remainder to Keith in fee simple'. Notice that Keith (or more likely his successors) will have to wait for John's fee tail to expire before he/they can enjoy the land. They may be waiting a very long time!

(c)   Frank owns the fee simple estate in Orangeacre. He grants Orangeacre 'to Norma for life, remainder to Olivia for life, remainder to Philippa for life . . ., remainder to Wendy in fee simple'. This sort of thing is possible, but highly unlikely.

Note that one thing Frank cannot do is to grant land 'to Leonard in fee simple, remainder to Malcolm in fee simple'. Having granted the fee simple to Leonard, he has given all his rights away. Malcolm gets **nothing**.

SAQ 17

Frank owned Greenacre in fee simple. He executed a deed granting the land 'to Quentin for life, remainder to Richard in fee tail'. There are now three estates in Greenacre; what are they?

Applying the rules set out above, you should conclude that Quentin has a life estate in possession and Richard has a fee tail in remainder. But Frank also still has an estate, as he retains a fee simple in reversion.

4.7   Interests Under Trusts

For the purposes of **land law** you need only understand the general idea of interests under trusts. Details can wait until you study the law of trusts.

Equitable interests under a trust (of any type of property) may be in possession or in remainder. Suppose Peter owns 10,000 shares in ICI:

(a)   He transfers 6,000 of those shares 'to Tim and Tom as trustees, on trust for Quentin for life, remainder to Richard absolutely'. This means that during Quentin's lifetime he will get the (net) dividends from the shares. When Quentin dies, Richard (or if he is dead his successors) will have outright ownership of the shares.

(b)   He transfers the other 4,000 shares 'to the National Westminster Bank plc, on trust for Stephen for life, remainder to Thomas for life'. The obvious question is, 'What happens to the shares after both Stephen and Thomas are dead?'. The answer is that Peter retains an interest under **a resulting trust**. This resulting trust will take effect after the death of Stephen and Thomas, so that Peter (or his successors) will regain outright ownership of the shares.

(One other point about the above example: It is quite common nowadays to appoint as trustee a bank, or (say) accountants or solicitors. Why do you think this practice has become common?)

4.8   Conclusion

The cornerstone of English land law has been, for hundreds of years, the fee simple estate. The 1925 legislation changed (somewhat) the nature of the fee simple, but (as we shall see from ensuing chapters) the cornerstone status of that estate was enhanced.

Life estates (and also life interests under trusts) have been important for hundreds of years. Though they occur less frequently than in the past, no one doubts their continued utility to property law generally (not just land law). The same cannot be said regarding fees tail and modified fees simple.

In 1989, the Law Commission produced a report which contained proposals for reform of 'Trusts of Land'. This topic included settled land and a wide variety of related issues, including fees tail and modified fees.

Read in *Cases and Materials* **(4.4) the edited versions of paras 16.1 and 17.1 of the Law Commission report. Compare the Law Commission's views with my own views set out below.**

In my view the report (on this aspect of the law) is rather disappointing, as the proposals for law reform do not go far enough. In the autumn of 1989, *Trust Law and Practice* published an article by me which included the following passages:

> As every law student knows, land law is still cluttered up with strange devices such as fees tail, determinable fees and fees upon condition subsequent. The Commission does propose that no new entails should be created; any attempt to create an entail would in future result in a fee simple being transferred. This proposal does not, however, go far enough.

> In its working paper, the Commission proposed to convert all existing fees tail into fees simple, but this is another proposal which has disappeared (without any explanation) from the final report. The Commission should have stuck by its original proposal. Indeed it should have gone further. Modified fees should also be banned, and any existing ones converted into absolute fees simple. (Many modified fees where the 'modification' relates to marriage or religion must surely infringe the European Convention on Human Rights.)

4.9   End of Chapter Assessment Question

'As every law student knows, land law is cluttered up with strange devices such as fees tail, determinable fees and fees upon condition subsequent. The Law Commission [merely] proposes that no new entails should be created. This proposal does not, however, go far enough.' (Article in *Trust Law and Practice*.)

Critically examine this statement.

See *Cases and Materials* (4.6) for a specimen answer.

CHAPTER FIVE

LEGAL AND EQUITABLE RIGHTS IN LAND

5.1 Objectives

By the end of this chapter you should:

- appreciate that property rights in land fall into two classes, 'legal' and 'equitable';

- have firmly grasped that there are more **types** of equitable property right in land than there are **types** of legal property right;

- be able to explain how **legal** property rights are created;

- be able to explain the many various ways in which **equitable** property rights are created;

- be familiar with the concept of an 'estate contract', and the consequences which flow from the existence of an estate contract.

5.2 Introduction

The rules of modern English land law are derived from three sources, common law, equity, and (increasingly in the twentieth century) statute. All three sources are represented in this (lengthy) chapter, which is mainly concerned with how property rights in land are created. You will see that the common law contributed a (relatively) straightforward set of rules, while the contribution of equity is altogether much more complex. You will also see that a modern statute, the Law of Property (Miscellaneous Provisions) Act 1989, has also contributed to this area of law.

5.3 Legal and Equitable Property Rights

5.3.1 LEGAL PROPERTY RIGHTS

As you saw from reading **Chapter 1**, there is a wide range of property rights which can exist with respect to land. Most (but not all) of these property rights were recognised by the common law. Property rights recognised by the common law were (and still are) classified as either **legal estates** (e.g., fees simple or leases) or **legal interests** (e.g., easements, profits or rentcharges).

Prior to 1875, if somebody had a legal property right, he could protect that right by proceedings in either the common law courts or in the Court of Chancery. Suppose in 1840, Harold, owner in fee simple of Westacre, executed a deed granting Ian, owner in fee simple of neighbouring Eastacre, a right of way across Westacre to get to Eastacre. Ian has a **legal easement** over Westacre.

Suppose that in 1845 Kevin buys Westacre, and then blocks the right of way. Ian's **legal** property right binds everyone, not just Harold. Ian can sue Kevin in a common law court for the remedy of **damages**. He can also sue Kevin in the Court of Chancery for the equitable remedy of an **injunction** prohibiting the obstruction of the right of way.

5.3.2 EQUITABLE PROPERTY RIGHTS

From a very early stage in the history of the Court of Chancery, it became clear that it was possible to create property rights which **were not** recognised by the common law courts, but which **were** recognised and enforced by the Court of Chancery. These rights became known as **equitable interests**.

In **Chapter 2** we have already (briefly) considered the most important type of equitable interest, namely the right of a beneficiary under a trust. We have also seen that if the beneficiaries of a trust tried to enforce their rights in a common law court they were sent away disappointed (see **2.3.1**). If, however, they went to the Court of Chancery, their (**equitable**) property rights were enforced.

Another very important type of equitable interest in land, never recognised by the common law, is the restrictive covenant. (We mentioned restrictive covenants at **1.4.2**.) Suppose in the Westacre/Eastacre example just considered, Harold, in the deed granting the easement, had also promised not to build upon Westacre. When Kevin bought Westacre in 1845 he knew of this 'covenant'. He nevertheless started to build on Westacre.

If Ian sued Kevin in a common law court, what would be the result of the case?

His action would fail. The common law regarded the 'no buildings' promise as binding only on the **original** covenantor (Harold in the example). But if Ian sued Kevin in the Court of Chancery, he would win and obtain an injunction. The Court of Chancery regarded a restrictive covenant as an **equitable** property right over the **servient** land which, subject to certain limitations, was binding on subsequent purchasers of the land.

5.3.3 LEGAL AND EQUITABLE PROPERTY RIGHTS AFTER 1875

As you should already know from your studies of the development of the English legal system, common law and equity, have, ever since 1875, been administered by a unified court system. However, the 1875 court reform legislation did not abolish the distinction between legal property rights and equitable property rights. (Nor did the 1925 property reform legislation.) As we shall see (especially in **Chapter 6**), important consequences flow from whether property rights are 'legal' or 'equitable'.

5.4 Creation and Transfer of Legal Property Rights

The common law has always been keen on formalities. It was long ago laid down that to transfer an existing legal property right, or to create a new one, a **deed** was required. This rule has now been embodied in s. 52(1) of the Law of Property Act 1925. There are certain exceptions to this rule that a deed is required to create or transfer a legal estate or interest, but these exceptions can for present purposes be ignored.

5.4.1 FORMALITIES FOR A DEED: THE TRADITIONAL RULE

(Unfortunately, we must make a slight digression and discuss this issue).

The traditional rule is applicable to all deeds executed up to 30 July 1990.

The traditional rule has been that for a document to be a deed it must be signed, sealed, and delivered. A document is normally 'delivered' when it is handed over. As for sealing, special sealing wax used to be used, but in modern times almost everybody executing a deed 'sealed' it by attaching a small piece of adhesive red paper. Under the traditional rule there was no legal requirement for the signature(s) on the deed to be witnessed, though usually they were.

5.4.2 FORMALITIES FOR A DEED: THE MODERN RULE

The modern rule is applicable to all deeds executed on or after 31 July 1990.

Study the extracts from s. 1 of the Law of Property (Miscellaneous Provisions) Act 1989 set out in *Cases and Materials* (5.1.1). What is its effect with regard to deeds?

Section 1 was brought into force by the Lord Chancellor as from 31 July 1990. The effect of the provision is that as from that date to be a deed a document need not be sealed. The document must, however:

(a) be 'clear on its face that it is intended to be a deed'; and

(b) be validly executed.

For a deed to be 'validly executed' by a person it must;

(i) be signed;

(ii)   (a new requirement) that signature must be witnessed by **one** witness;

(iii)   the deed must be 'delivered'.

What ought to happen to the hallowed English phrase, 'signed, sealed and delivered'?

I hope you agree with me that amongst lawyers, it **ought** to fall into disuse. We **ought** now to use some sort of phrase such as 'signed as a deed, witnessed, and delivered'. But of course old habits die hard!

5.5   Creation of Equitable Interests in Land

While, as we have just seen, legal estates and legal interests can normally be created only if a deed is used, equitable interests in land can be created in a wide variety of different ways:

(a)   by express trust;

(b)   by a contract to convey or create a legal estate or interest;

(c)   by the granting of an estate or interest which is void at common law for want of the correct formalities;

(d)   by a grant of an estate or interest by a person who owns only an equitable interest;

(e)   by a grant of an interest which can exist only in equity;

(f)   by constructive trust or proprietary estoppel.

Before we look at these headings in more detail, there is one other potentially confusing point which we must consider carefully.

5.5.1   'EQUITY FOLLOWS THE LAW' AS TO TYPES OF PROPERTY RIGHT

Although you have probably been studying the law only for a brief period, you should have already realised that the system of rules known as equity was developed by the Lord Chancellors to correct some of the harsh injustices of the common law. We have already considered the concept of the trust (see **Chapter 2**). The rigid and inflexible common law refused to accept the trust as imposing legal duties on the trustees; but equity ruled otherwise and enforced trusts.

The maxim 'equity follows the law' simply means that equity **copied the various types of property right** recognised by the common law. Put another way, one can say that for every kind of legal estate or legal interest in land recognised by the common law there is an equivalent equitable interest capable of existing.

Thus, as legal fees simple can exist, so can equitable fees simple. As you can have legal leases, so also you can have equitable leases (a particularly important example, as we shall see). There are legal mortgages, and so there are also equitable mortgages. There can be legal easements and legal profits, so therefore there can be equitable easements and equitable profits. And so on. . . .

On the basis of what I have just said, you might conclude that the list of types of equitable property rights in land would be identical to the list of the types of legal property rights in land. This of course would be wrong, as there are (as I have already hinted) certain types of equitable interests which have no legal equivalents. These include:

(a) restrictive covenants;

(b) licences by estoppel (proprietary estoppel);

(c) constructive trusts;

(d) estate contracts.

It is because of the existence of restrictive covenants, constructive trusts, etc. that the list of types of equitable interest is longer than the list of types of legal estate and interest.

5.5.2 CREATION OF EQUITABLE INTERESTS IN LAND BY EXPRESS TRUST

Though express trusts of land are of enormous importance, there is only one point we need to note at this stage – s. 53(1)(b) of the Law of Property Act 1925.

ACTIVITY 8

Read s. 53(1)(b) in *Cases and Materials* (5.2.1). What is its effect in practice on the creation of an equitable interest by express trust?

The practical effect of this provision is that you cannot create an express trust of land simply by word of mouth. It can only be done by an **inter vivos** written document (which strictly speaking does not have to be a deed, though it is normal to use a deed) or by a will. (Remember that a will takes effect only on the death of the testator.)

5.5.3 CREATION OF EQUITABLE INTERESTS BY A CONTRACT TO CONVEY OR CREATE A LEGAL ESTATE OR INTEREST

Before we can discuss this heading it is necessary for us to engage in a very lengthy digression.

5.5.3.1 Contracts for the sale of estates or interests in land

As we saw in **Chapter 2**, if land is being bought or sold it is normal for the transaction to take place in two stages. There is first the 'contract stage', followed (normally a few weeks later) by the 'completion stage'. A deed is executed only at the completion stage, **so it is only at completion that the legal estate passes to the purchaser.**

This two-stage process is not obligatory, but it is normal when purchasing a fee simple. It is also usual to have the two stages when a lessee is taking a new long-term lease, or where an existing long lease is being sold. It is also possible (though unusual) to have the two stages where other property rights such as easements, profits or rentcharges are being created.

5.5.3.2 Formalities for contracts to sell estates or interests in land

As you have probably already learnt from your studies of the law of contract, in English law, **as a general rule**, no special formalities are required for a valid contract. Contracts to sell property rights in land are **the big exception** to this general rule.

Just to complicate matters, the law on formalities for land contracts has been changed recently. Contracts entered into before 27 September 1989 are governed by s. 40 of the Law of Property Act 1925 (a statutory provision which was first enacted in 1677). Contracts entered into on or after 27 September 1989 are governed by s. 2 of the Law of Property (Miscellaneous Provisions) Act 1989.

Law of Property Act 1925, s. 40

Study s. 40 in *Cases and Materials* (5.2.2.1). **What was its practical effect?**

(Unfortunately it is still necessary to know something about the pre-1989 law. I would stress, however, that what you are about to read is all you need to know about s. 40. When you look at s. 40 in *Cases and Materials* you may find the wording rather difficult; but it is the practical effect of the section which matters.)

The practical effect of s. 40 was that if a contract relating to land was to be enforceable and so create rights, one of the following three conditions had to be satisfied:

(a) The contract was in writing, signed by the person (usually the vendor) promising rights over his land, or by his agent.

(b) The contract was purely oral, but subsequently a document came into existence evidencing the contract. This 'note or memorandum' had to be signed by the person promising rights over his land, or by his agent.

(c) The contract was purely oral, but the person claiming rights under the contract (e.g., the purchaser or prospective tenant) did some act of 'part performance'. 'Part performance' meant some conduct which indicated the existence of a contract between the parties. For example, (in particular) if the contract envisaged transfer of possession of the land to (say) a tenant or even a purchaser, that tenant/purchaser taking possession of the land was considered an act of part performance: see *Steadman* v *Steadman* [1974] 2 All ER 977.

It should be stressed that a contract which did not comply with s. 40 was not void, but merely **unenforceable**. If, with respect to such a contract, conditions (b) or (c) above were **subsequently** fulfilled, the contract **became enforceable**. (There is a sharp contrast with s. 2 of the 1989 Act, which we will be discussing shortly.)

Suppose (pre-1989) Victor entered into a purely oral contract to sell Brownacre to Percy. At that stage the contract was unenforceable and Percy had no rights. But what if Victor subsequently signed a document recording the terms of the contract?

Surprising as it may seem, the contract became enforceable and Percy acquired rights. (See rule (b) above.)

Suppose, in the example we are currently considering, Victor never signed anything, but after the oral agreement allowed Percy to take possession of Brownacre. What then?

I hope you realised that the taking of possession was 'part performance' by Percy, and the contract became enforceable by virtue of that fact. (See rule (c) above.)

Law of Property (Miscellaneous Provisions) Act, s. 2

Section 2 of the 1989 Act came into force on 27 September 1989, over 10 months before the coming into effect of s. 1, which we have already discussed at **5.4.2**. Section 2 repeals s. 40 of the Law of Property Act 1925, and also abolishes the rules about part performance. All contracts for the sale of estates and interests in land must now be **in writing and signed by the parties**. Although s. 2 is to be found in *Cases and Materials* **(5.2.2.1)**, the first three subsections are so important that they are set out here.

(1)   A contract for the sale or other disposition of an interest in land can only be made in writing and only by incorporating all the terms which the parties have expressly agreed in one document or, where contracts are exchanged, in each.

(2)   The terms may be incorporated in a document either by being set out in it or by reference to some other document.

(3)   The document incorporating the terms or, where contracts are exchanged, one of the documents incorporating them (but not necessarily the same one) must be signed by or on behalf of each party to the contract.

Although few lawyers were sad at the repeal of the old s. 40, the new provision is a strict one which must be complied with carefully. The crucial point about the new provision is that the contract **itself** must be in writing and signed by the parties. Any contract which is oral, or in writing but not signed by **all** the parties is **void**, and there are no obligations on the parties. Moreover, subsequent events such as the creation of a document recording the 'contract' or acts of 'part performance' cannot validate the void contract. Lawyers brought up in the 'old school' find this hard medicine to swallow!

If the events set out in SAQ 20 and SAQ 21 were to occur today, would Percy be able to claim any rights under the agreement?

The answer is no. The purely oral contract between Victor and Percy is totally void, and nothing which happens subsequently can give Percy rights under the void agreement.

Fortunately s. 2 leaves one hallowed land law tradition untouched. You will notice that both s. 2(1) and (3) refer to 'where contracts are exchanged'. It has always been possible for parties to contract to sell property rights in land by them both signing a single document setting out the agreed terms of the sale. However, solicitors have, on the sale of a fee simple, traditionally preferred to use an alternative method. Two identical documents are prepared, each setting out **all** the expressly agreed terms of the contract. The vendor signs one copy; the purchaser signs the other. Agreement is signified by 'exchanging contracts', i.e. there is a swap. The purchaser gets the copy signed by the vendor and vice versa. Contracts in this form are valid under the new law, and solicitors have (since 1989) generally stuck to the traditional practice of 'exchanging contracts'.

We can now at last return to the discussion of how equitable interests are created.

5.5.3.3   Estate contracts

Once a contract for the sale of a fee simple has been made, equity regards the purchaser as owning an equitable interest known as an estate contract. This equitable interest is normally of only short duration, as it comes to an end 'on completion', i.e. when the legal estate is conveyed to the purchaser. Despite the short duration of estate contracts, the whole concept is important and we need to examine it in a little more depth.

I should first mention the reasoning which gave rise to the concept of an 'estate contract'. The Lord Chancellors developed the broad maxim, 'Equity looks on that as done which ought to be done'. Applying this maxim to contracts to sell land, the Chancellors reasoned that the purchaser should be regarded as having a right to the land once the contract had been signed **without having to wait for the conveyance of the legal estate**. Moreover, the Chancellors backed up this argument with a weapon. **Contracts for the sale of land, or rights in land, are always in principle enforceable by the decree of specific performance.**

'Specific performance' is a remedy which prior to 1875 was available only in the Court of Chancery, and is therefore even today referred to as an 'equitable remedy'. As its name perhaps implies, it is an order of the court that the contract actually be carried out.

For most types of contract, the remedy of specific performance is **not** available. Suppose I have contracted to purchase a ton of potatoes from Farmer Giles, and he fails to deliver. I can always get potatoes elsewhere, so for this breach of the contract the court would not grant specific performance. I would have to be content with the usual remedy for breach of contract, namely **damages.**

Suppose, by contrast, I contracted to buy a field, Highacre, from Giles. Now each piece of land is unique, a fact which equity recognised. If Giles refuses to convey Highacre to me, I cannot buy Highacre from anyone else. I may well be able to buy a field of similar dimensions and value, but that replacement field will inevitably be in a different location. I may well not want that location. I will therefore seek a decree of specific performance compelling Giles to convey Highacre to me. In principle the court (pre-1875 it would have been the Court of Chancery) will grant me that decree.

The consequences of an estate contract

It is often said that in the period between contract and completion the vendor is a 'trustee' for the purchaser. This is rather misleading. If the vendor were a 'trustee' in the usual sense of that word, the **purchaser** would become immediately entitled to enjoy all the benefits of the land. Yet between contract and completion the **vendor** retains the right to enjoy all benefits from the land. Thus he can occupy the land until completion.

What if the land which has been contracted to be sold is currently leased to a tenant. Who is entitled to the rent?

It is the vendor who is entitled to the rent up to the date the legal estate is conveyed to the purchaser, 'the date of completion'.

There are, however, two important consequences which **do** flow from creation of an estate contract:

(a) **The vendor must take good care of the property and consult the purchaser before taking any managerial decisions regarding the property.**

Between contract and completion the vendor cannot (unless the purchaser agrees) demolish, alter or reconstruct the property. Other important decisions about the property can be taken only with the agreement of the purchaser.

In *Abdullah* v *Shah* [1959] AC 124 the vendor owned a row of three shops. At the time the contract of sale for the shops was signed all three of them were leased to tenants. Between contract and completion one of the tenants (unexpectedly) terminated his tenancy. The vendor, **without asking the purchaser**, immediately relet the shop. The purchaser would have preferred the shop to have been left empty.

The Judicial Committee held that the vendor should have consulted the purchaser about the proposed reletting. In consequence the purchaser (who was willing to go through with the deal) was, as compensation, entitled to a reduction in the agreed price.

(b) **The risk of anything untoward happening to the property passes to the purchaser when the contract is signed.**

In this context, the 'estate contract' concept **usually** works to the purchaser's disadvantage. There are two kinds of 'disaster' which can befall a property between contract and completion. The first is actions taken by a public authority.

In *Hillingdon Estates* v *Stansfield Estates* [1952] 1 All ER 853 the local authority, after the contract was signed, slapped a compulsory purchase order on the property. The court held that the vendor was entitled to insist on completing the sale, even though the purchaser would then have to convey the land to the local authority. (The purchaser would of course get the compensation payable on compulsory purchase.)

In *Amalgamated Property Co. Ltd v John Walker Ltd* [1976] 3 All ER 509 the defendants (the well-known whisky firm) contracted to buy an old building which they planned to demolish and replace with modern offices. The local authority then 'listed' the building as one of special historical interest, thus effectively preventing the redevelopment. The court held that Walkers must nevertheless complete the purchase.

Unexpected action by a public authority can improve the value of a property.

SAQ 24

Suppose last week I contracted to purchase a petrol station. Today the local authority announces new traffic plans which will take more traffic past my petrol pumps! Can I insist that the vendor completes the deal?

The answer is of course yes, and at the original price, even though the land is more valuable than it was a week ago.

Destruction of the property

The second kind of 'disaster' which might occur is destruction of the property. The traditional position has been that, unless the parties agree otherwise, the purchaser of land must bear the risk of destruction once a contract of sale has been made. Suppose last week I contracted to buy a house. Yesterday the house was destroyed by fire (or hurricane or earthquake). I must still complete the deal at the agreed price even though I am now getting a bare site with perhaps some useless ruins on it!

The moral of this little tale is that a purchaser of a building (unless he intends to demolish) should insure the building immediately he agrees the contract to purchase.

One fairly recent change should however be noticed. In March 1990, the Law Society published brand new 'Standard Conditions of Sale'. It is intended that these Standard Conditions will be used by solicitors when drafting contracts to sell land, though **their use is not obligatory**. Clause 5 reads:

> 5.1.1 The seller will transfer the property in the same physical state as it was at the date of the contract (except for fair wear and tear) which means that the seller retains the risk until completion.
>
> 5.1.2 If at any time before completion the physical state of the property makes it unusable for its purpose at the date of the contract:
> (a) The buyer may rescind the contract, . . .

(The rest of Clause 5 does not really help the present discussion.)

Thus **provided the contract is drafted using the new Standard Conditions,** the traditional rule that risk of physical destruction passes to the purchaser on the contract of sale being made no longer applies. In practice, most contracts for sale of residential properties follow the new Standard Conditions, but contracts for sale of commercial properties often do not use the Standard Conditions.

5.5.3.4 A contract to create rights in land itself creates an equitable interest in the land

The preceding discussion has focused on contracts to **transfer** an **existing** fee simple estate in land. We must now consider the situation where an owner of a fee simple estate contracts to create out of that estate some property right such as a lease, mortgage, easement or profit.

In practice the problem is most likely to arise in the context of leases, because, as indicated earlier, where a long-term lease is to be created the transaction often proceeds in two stages. The parties sign a contract for the lease, followed by a formal deed a few weeks later. The leading case of *Walsh* v *Lonsdale* (1882) 21 Ch D 9 concerned a situation where the parties had made a **contract** for a seven-year lease, the tenant had gone into possession, but the parties had forgotten to execute the formal deed needed for a valid legal lease.

Read the extracts from *Walsh* v *Lonsdale* in *Cases and Materials* (5.2.2.3), taking care not to get bogged down in the detailed terms of the contract. Try and establish in your own mind the fundamental principle laid down in the case.

Some textbooks go into immense detail about *Walsh* v *Lonsdale*, but in my view that is rather unnecessary. The crucial issues were the effect (if any) of the contract, and the clause in that contract regarding the payment of rent. This clause (in effect) provided that under the lease the rent should be £X per year payable in advance, i.e. at beginning of each year.

Despite the absence of a deed granting a legal lease, the landlord demanded the rent in advance. The tenant claimed that as there was no deed, and therefore no proper lease, any rent should be payable in arrear. The Court of Appeal decided in the landlord's favour.

The court held that the contract created an **equitable lease** enforceable between the parties. Moreover, the terms of the contract formed the terms of the equitable lease, and therefore the landlord was entitled to have the rent paid in advance. In the circumstances of the case, it did not really matter that the parties had forgotten to execute the deed.

As a result of *Walsh* v *Lonsdale*, a contract for a lease creates an equitable lease. Similar reasoning can be applied to all other types of right in land. A contract for an easement will create an equitable easement. A contract for a profit will create an equitable profit.

What will a contract for a mortgage create?

You will undoubtedly have said that it will create an equitable mortgage. (But never lose sight of the fact that a contract relating to rights in land must now comply with s. 2 of the 1989 Act. I will return to this point at **5.5.4.1**.)

5.5.4   AN INFORMAL GRANT OF RIGHTS IN LAND IS TREATED AS A CONTRACT AND SO CREATES AN EQUITABLE INTEREST IN LAND

One thing may have struck you about the preceding discussion. There is **in logic** a difference between saying 'I promise to grant you this land' and 'I grant you this land'; between 'I promise to give you a lease' and 'I grant you this lease now'. Nevertheless, equity, with decisions such as *Walsh* v *Lonsdale* has blurred over this logical distinction. The following discussion contributes further to this blurring.

In *Parker* v *Taswell* (1858) 119 ER 230 the landlord and tenant signed a document which purported to **grant** a lease to the tenant. The document did not bear a seal, and therefore was not a deed. It therefore could not create a **legal** lease. (Remember that for legal property rights a deed is required.)

The Court of Chancery held that a purported **grant** of property rights in land which lacked the necessary formality (i.e. a deed) to create a legal estate should be deemed to be a **contract,** which could be enforced by a decree of specific performance. The court indeed awarded the plaintiff specific performance of the transaction deemed to be a contract.

Although this may not have been realised in 1858 (when *Parker* v *Taswell* was decided), the effect of that decision is that if a grantor purports to create property rights informally (i.e. other than by deed) the informal grant creates an equitable interest. Put simply:

informal grant = deemed contract = equitable interest

A fairly modern example of this reasoning is the House of Lords decision in *Mason* v *Clarke* [1955] AC 778 at 797 (Lord Horton's speech). SM Ltd granted a legal lease of a farm to Clarke. As is common in leases of agricultural holdings, the lease included a clause whereby the landlord retained the right to hunt and/or trap wild animals roaming over the leased land.

In 1950, the land in question (in common with much of the rest of England) was plagued by rabbits. In October 1950, SM Ltd granted to Mason (a specialist rabbit-catcher) the right for one year to catch all rabbits on the farm. This transaction was purely oral. Mason paid £100 for the right, and entered the land and set traps. Clarke interfered with the traps. The House of Lords gave judgment for Mason.

It was held that the oral grant of the right to catch rabbits should be deemed a contract; that entering the land and setting the traps should be considered to be part performance (see **5.5.3.2**, remembering that this is a pre-1989 case); and that therefore Mason had an equitable profit to catch rabbits for one year.

5.5.4.1 Limits on the principle that a contract or informal grant creates an equitable interest

There are two limitations to the broad principle that a contract or informal grant of rights creates an equitable interest. The first limitation is the formalities required for a **contract** to transfer or create rights in land. The rules applicable before and after 27 September 1989 are summarised below. For further details, turn back to **5.5.3.2**.

Position prior to 27 September 1989

For a contract or an informal grant (which, remember, is deemed to be a contract) to be enforceable and thus create an equitable interest, the contract/informal grant must be:

(a) in writing, or

(b) evidenced in writing, or

(c) oral, but with part performance.

In *Mason* v *Clarke* (above) the transaction was originally purely oral. If nothing more had happened, Mason would not have been able to claim an equitable interest. However, the crucial fact was Mason's entering the land and setting his traps. This constituted 'part performance' and therefore he could claim an equitable profit.

Position after 26 September 1989

Contracts to create or transfer interests in land are now governed by s. 2 of the Law of Property (Miscellaneous Provisions) Act 1989. It follows from this that for a contract or informal grant to create an equitable interest in land the contract or informal grant **must be in writing signed by both parties**. A contract or other transaction with land which is oral, or which is unsigned writing will be **void**. Moreover, subsequent events cannot validate the contract.

What if the facts of *Mason* v *Clarke* were to recur today. Would Mason acquire an equitable profit?

No he would not. The purely oral grant would be void, and Mason's entering and setting his traps would be a trespass.

ACTIVITY 11

Change the facts of *Mason* v *Clarke* so that even today an equitable profit would be created.

In re-writing the facts of the case, you should have concluded that the agreement between SM Ltd and Mason would have to be in writing, signed by both parties.

ACTIVITY 12

It would appear that as a result of s. 2 of the Law of Property (Miscellaneous Provisions) Act 1989, fewer equitable interests will arise by 'informal' grant. Consider why this is the case.

(See the conclusion to this chapter.)

The second limitation on the principle that contracts/informal grants create equitable interests is that **the right to treat a contract or an informal grant as creating an equitable interest depends on the availability of specific performance.** This second limitation is long standing, and fortunately unaffected by modern statute.

As we saw earlier in this chapter (at 5.5.3.3), all contracts (and transactions deemed to be contracts) for the transfer or creation of rights in land are in principle enforceable by the equitable remedy of specific performance. However, you may have already come across the maxim that 'All equitable remedies are discretionary', and also perhaps the quaintly worded maxim that 'He who comes to equity must come with clean hands'. It is not appropriate at this point to give you all the detailed ramifications of these two maxims. What matters now is their practical application in the context of the current discussion.

If somebody enters into a contract (or a transaction deemed to be a contract) to acquire rights in land, but he is then in **substantial** breach of his own obligations under that contract, he will be said to have 'unclean hands'. The court will consequently refuse to order specific performance of the contract. Moreover, because he is not entitled to the remedy of specific performance to compel completion of the transaction, the party with 'unclean hands' cannot claim that the contract or informal transaction has created an equitable interest in his favour.

The point is best illustrated by the case of *Coatsworth* v *Johnson* [1886–90] All ER Rep 547. Johnson entered into an agreement to lease a farm to Coatsworth for 21 years. The agreement contained a clause (even today to be found in agricultural leases) to farm 'in a good and husband-like manner', i.e. Coatsworth promised to farm efficiently and to take good care of the land.

Coatsworth took possession of the farm without a formal deed being executed. Within a few months of his taking possession he had allowed the condition of the land to deteriorate very badly. Johnson evicted Coatsworth from the farm.

Coatsworth sued for wrongful eviction, contending that the agreement created an equitable lease lasting 21 years. Now if Coatsworth had taken good care of the farm he would have undoubtedly won the case. However, his failure to take good care of the farm meant that (metaphorically) he had 'unclean hands'. If he had claimed specific performance of the agreement it would not have been granted because of his substantial breach of his side of the bargain. The Court of Appeal therefore held that as Coatsworth was not entitled to specific performance he could not contend that the agreement created an equitable lease. That in turn meant that Coatsworth had no right to be on the land, and so his action for wrongful eviction failed.

(It is worth noting that if Coatsworth had had a legal lease, he could not have been summarily booted off the land, however bad a farmer he had been!)

In 1992, Lenny and Terry signed a written contract (not a deed) under which Lenny agreed to lease a corner shop to Terry for 10 years. Lenny is a fundamentalist Christian, and the contract therefore included a clause that Terry must not open on Sundays. Since the changes in the Sunday trading laws Terry has opened on Sundays and has done a roaring trade. Can Lenny argue that, like the tenant in *Coatsworth v Johnson*, Terry has lost his right to claim that he has an equitable lease?

You will probably agree that the answer is not clear-cut. Terry will argue that in the light of the changes in the Sunday trading laws his breach of contract was **trivial**, and not such as to amount to 'unclean hands' depriving him of the right to specific performance, and therefore of his equitable lease. Lenny will argue that although Terry's conduct is no longer an offence, his activities still constitute, from Lenny's point of view, a **substantial** breach of contract.

5.5.5 GRANT OF AN ESTATE OR INTEREST BY A PERSON WHO OWNS ONLY AN EQUITABLE INTEREST

Somebody who owns only an equitable interest in land has no rights recognised by the common law. Therefore, if he executes a deed purporting to create a right derived from his equitable interest, that right is itself only equitable. A brief example should suffice.

Suppose Leonora owns the fee simple in Yellowacre. Last year she and Teresa sign a document which is not a deed, under which Leonora leases Yellowacre to Teresa for ten years. The lease will, under principles just discussed, be only an equitable lease. This year Teresa executes a **deed** under which she sub-leases Yellowacre for five years to Stephen. Although a deed has been used, this sub-lease will also only be equitable. At common law Teresa's lease does not exist, and of course it follows that she cannot create a legal right from something which does not exist!

5.5.6 GRANTS OF INTERESTS WHICH CAN EXIST ONLY IN EQUITY

Restrictive covenants and express trusts are usually created by using a formal **deed**. Yet, as has already been mentioned, restrictive covenants and interests under trusts are recognised only by equity.

5.5.7 CONSTRUCTIVE TRUSTS AND PROPRIETARY ESTOPPEL

These are (in terms of history) relatively new types of equitable interest. In **Chapter 1** we saw (in outline) how these interests arise. The thing particularly to note in the present context is that these interests normally arise as a result of the **conduct** of the parties, rather than as a result of some document (whether or not a deed).

5.6 Conclusion

We have seen that to create **legal** property rights in land a formal deed is required. **Equitable** property rights in land can (by contrast) arise in a number of different ways, even by conduct of the parties.

In the past many equitable interests arose as a result of contract (**5.5.3.3**) or 'informal grant' (**5.5.4**). But the limiting effect of s. 2 of the 1989 Act must be carefully noted. A contract or 'informal' grant, to be valid and therefore create an equitable interest, must now (slightly paradoxically) have a degree of formality! While a deed is not required, the transaction must be in writing and signed by both parties.

5.7 End of Chapter Assessment Question

(a) Norma owns the legal fee simple estate (unregistered title) in 'Ramsey House'. Two months ago she entered into a written agreement (not in the form of a deed) to let Ramsey House to Matthew for five years. The agreement specifically stated that the house should be used for residential purposes only.

Matthew has just been made redundant, and is now considering using Ramsey House for a business repairing bicycles. He has heard rumours that Norma is about to sell the house.

Advise Matthew, who is concerned that, as his lease is not in the form of a deed, he might be evicted by Norma.

And

(b) Last week, by a written contract, Teresa agreed to sell 'Taylor Cottage' to Henry, the sale to be completed in six weeks time.

Unfortunately yesterday, a bus racing one of its competitors to the next stop, crashed into Taylor Cottage causing considerable damage.

This morning Teresa demolished a small outhouse which stood at the bottom of the garden of Taylor Cottage.

Advise Henry, who wants either to rescind the contract or at least obtain a reduction in the previously agreed price.

See *Cases and Materials* **(5.4)** for a specimen answer.

CHAPTER SIX

DIFFERENCES IN VALIDITY BETWEEN LEGAL PROPERTY RIGHTS AND EQUITABLE PROPERTY RIGHTS

6.1 Objectives

By the end of this chapter you should be able to:

■ demonstrate why legal property rights are 'stronger' than equitable property rights;

■ appreciate that legal property rights are good against the whole world;

■ appreciate that, by contrast, equitable property rights are (traditionally) subject to the doctrine of notice;

■ explain the elements of the equitable doctrine of notice, especially constructive notice and imputed notice;

■ explain the maxim 'first in time, first in right', and the implications of that maxim for equitable property rights.

6.2 Introduction

In order to explain this topic in a comprehensible way, I have to make (for the moment) two very big assumptions which are not in fact true: (i) that all land remains **unregistered** title; (ii) that this area of law was unaffected by the reforms made in 1925.

I must also make a broad assertion which, just for the moment, may not seem to make much sense. This assertion underlies much of what is said in this chapter. I assert that from the point of view of somebody who owns a property right, it is better that the right should be legal rather than equitable. This is because **legal property rights are good against the whole world; equitable property rights are subject to the doctrine of notice**.

6.3 Legal and Equitable Property Rights: The Tale of High Chimneys

Before going any further, you must familiarise yourself with the facts of a story designed to illustrate most of the points which we will encounter in this chapter.

Imagine that last winter I purchased the fee simple in a large country house, High Chimneys, together with its quite extensive garden. I bought the house from Vanessa, a wealthy and elderly spinster. Before completing the purchase, I, my solicitor, and my surveyor made very careful enquiries regarding High Chimneys. There was a careful examination of the title deeds going back to a root of title in 1951, which was when Vanessa had bought the property. My surveyor and I made a very careful physical inspection of both the house and garden.

As a result of these careful enquiries I concluded that the land was not subject to any third party rights such as easements, profits, restrictive covenants, mortgages, etc. I therefore completed the purchase in March.

The last few months have been quite traumatic. First of all I had a visit from Norman, owner of neighbouring Low Stacks. He produced a deed dated 1910. By that deed the then owner of High Chimneys granted to the then owner of Low Stacks a right of way across the garden of High Chimneys. This right of way was expressly granted for the benefit of Low Stacks, and was to last in perpetuity. Norman explains that the right of way has not been used for five years (which is why my surveyor did not detect any sign of a worn path or track), but that now he intends to use it every day as a short cut to the nearest station.

Soon after Norman came Philip, owner of Smokey Farm, which adjoins the foot of my garden. He produced a deed dated 1920. By that deed the then owner of High Chimneys granted to the then owner of Smokey Farm a right to graze 15 sheep in the large garden. This right was expressly granted for the benefit of Smokey Farm, and was to last in perpetuity. Philip explains that he has not owned any sheep for about the last eight years, but now he has acquired some and intends to graze them in my garden. (I hope you have noted that Norman owns a **legal** easement, while Philip owns a **legal** profit.)

Lastly, George arrives. He explains that from 1949 to 1992 he was Vanessa's 'gentleman friend', but they have now split up. He further explains that he contributed a substantial amount of money both to the original purchase of High Chimneys and to its subsequent renovation. He therefore has a constructive trust interest in the property. That interest is **equitable.** George claims that his equitable interest in the land binds me. He is very anxious to claim against me because Vanessa has taken the whole price I paid to her and emigrated to Bolivia.

Do the rights of Norman, Philip and George bind me?

6.3.1 THE LEGAL PROPERTY RIGHTS OF NORMAN AND PHILIP

Here the position is very simple, and I am afraid that I am the loser. I am going to have to put up with Norman tramping across my land and with Philip's sheep. Each of these two rights is a **legal** property interest.

It is a fundamental principle that **legal** property rights are 'good against the whole world'. That means that, once a legal property right has been created with respect to a piece of land, that right binds everybody else who later acquires that land or other rights in that land.

Put another way, legal rights are in principle indestructible. I must particularly stress that I am stuck with Norman's easement and Philip's profit even though, at the time I bought High Chimneys, neither I nor my advisers knew or could have known of these rights. (Remember that we had all made careful enquiries. Incidentally, as my solicitor and surveyor exercised all due care, there is no possibility of my suing them for professional negligence.)

Suppose that John owned the legal fee simple in Blackfields. In 1993, John granted a legal lease of Blackfields to Kenneth for 20 years, but Kenneth has not as yet taken any steps to occupy Blackfields. John has now sold the fee simple in Blackfields to Leonard, who knew nothing of Kenneth's lease. Is Leonard bound by the lease?

Now it may well strike you that as a matter of simple moral justice Leonard should not be bound by Kenneth's lease. Leonard probably had no way of knowing that there was a lease, and Kenneth could not even be bothered to take possession of Blackfields. Yet the law is that Kenneth's lease does bind Leonard. It is a legal property right, and (like Norman's easement and Philip's profit) will bind everybody who later acquires the relevant land or rights in that land. It is no good Leonard saying, 'Kenneth was not in possession, so how could I know that there was a lease'.

6.3.2 THE EQUITABLE PROPERTY RIGHT OF GEORGE

Now here, for me, things are a lot more hopeful. Equitable rights are not totally indestructible. An equitable interest is good against the whole world **except** a bona fide purchaser for value of a legal estate or legal interest who took without notice of the equitable interest. Thus to be free of George's interest I must prove four things. I must prove that at the time I purchased High Chimneys:

(a) I acted 'bona fide', i.e. in good faith; and

(b) I was a purchaser for value; and

(c) I acquired a legal estate or legal interest; and

(d) I had no notice of George's equitable interest.

Before examining the four elements of the doctrine of notice listed above, I want us to recall a point made previously: 'From the point of view of somebody who owns a property right, it is better that the right should be legal rather than equitable.' Put slightly differently, legal property rights are stronger than equitable property rights.

Consider the story of High Chimneys from the points of view of Norman and Philip on the one hand, and George on the other. Norman and Philip can sleep soundly in their beds, while George's position may not be so comfortable. Why is that?

The crucial point for Norman and Philip is that they have **legal** interests (as had Kenneth in **SAQ 28**). They can therefore relax. They can rest assured that whatever happens to High Chimneys, and whoever buys High Chimneys their rights will still continue. They will continue even against me, who knew nothing of their rights. Their rights are (in effect) indestructible.

George's position is not quite so comfortable. His right will bind somebody who is given or inherits the land. It will bind somebody who buys the land **with notice** of George's interest. But it has one weakness. It will not bind a bona fide purchaser for value of a legal estate or interest who took without notice of George's interest. If I am such a purchaser then George's rights will not bind me. His only claim will be against Vanessa for cash compensation. It will be his tough luck that she has just emigrated to Bolivia!

6.4   The Elements of the Doctrine of Notice

All four elements set out at **6.3.2** must be proved by a purchaser (me in the High Chimneys story) if he is to take a piece of property free from an equitable interest affecting that property.

6.4.1   BONA FIDE

When talking about the doctrine of notice, lawyers usually use the Latin phrase **'bona fide'**. This simply means **'good faith'**. A person acts in good faith if he acts honestly and without any fraudulent intent. In disputes which arise involving the doctrine of notice, it is usually easy for a purchaser to establish that he has acted in good faith. (As we shall see at **6.4.4**, it may be much more difficult for him to prove that he is 'without notice'.)

6.4.2   PURCHASER FOR VALUE

If a person acquires a piece of land as a result of an inter vivos gift, or if he inherits it from somebody, he is clearly not a purchaser for value. He will always be bound by any equitable interests affecting the land.

What would be the result if in my High Chimneys story Vanessa had given me the property; or if she had died and left me the property by her will?

I hope you realised that in both cases I would always be bound by George's equitable interest. It would be no use my protesting that I had no 'notice' of George's interest. If you think about it, that is only fair. It would be wrong that he should lose his rights to somebody who has not had to do or pay anything for the property.

6.4.2.1 The meaning of 'value'

Suppose, in my High Chimneys story, I had paid a price for High Chimneys, but Vanessa was so anxious to get a quick sale that she sold it to me at a bargain price which did not represent the real value of the land. Would I be a purchaser for value? The answer is '**Yes**'. Suppose I had paid only a nominal price of £1 for High Chimneys. Would I be a purchaser for value? The answer (you may be perhaps surprised to learn) is 'Yes'!

In your studies of the law of contract you are probably already encountering the 'doctrine of consideration'.

Refer to your contract book, and quickly reread the chapter on what constitutes 'consideration'. It may help if you list the more important points.

In contract you learn that even the tiniest payment, or the most minimal 'detriment' may constitute consideration. As I hope you have guessed, anything which constitutes 'consideration' in the law of contract will be 'value' for the purposes of the law of property.

6.4.2.2 Marriage as 'value'

This may seem a rather obscure point, but it is of some significance to the historic development of property law. Until 1970, an engagement to marry was a legally enforceable contract. (You have probably heard of actions for breach of promise of marriage!) As a result of the Law Reform (Miscellaneous Provisions) Act 1970, engagements to marry are no longer legally enforceable. It follows that a promise to marry is no longer 'consideration'; nor is it 'value' for the purposes of the doctrine of notice.

Suppose Vanessa conveyed High Chimneys to me. In return, I did not pay a cash price, but I **promised** to marry her. She then disappeared to Bolivia before we could have a ceremony. I would not be a 'purchaser for value' of High Chimneys. Had the facts occurred before 1970 (say, in 1965), I would have been a purchaser for value.

Change the story in a slightly different way. Suppose Vanessa conveyed High Chimneys to me in March 1995 in return for my actually marrying her. Would I be a purchaser for value? (Put another way, is my actually marrying her consideration?)

The crucial point in answering this question is to realise that the actual act of marrying is a 'detriment' suffered by me. (I have given up the freedom of my single status.) It is 'consideration' and therefore it is 'value'; thus (on this version of the story) I am, even today, a purchaser for value!

6.4.3   PURCHASER OF A LEGAL ESTATE OR LEGAL INTEREST

This may strike you as a rather technical and arbitrary aspect of the doctrine of notice. Under this rule, a purchaser of an equitable interest cannot claim the benefit of the doctrine of notice. If you buy only an equitable interest in Blackacre, any existing equitable interest(s) in Blackacre is/are automatically binding on you.

Suppose in my High Chimneys example I did not buy the legal fee simple; instead I **entered into a contract** with Vanessa under which she agreed to lease me the property for 99 years. I paid her an agreed 'premium' (capital lump sum) of £100,000, and took possession. Vanessa then ran off to Bolivia without executing a deed in my favour. On these facts I have 'purchased' only an equitable lease. I will therefore be bound by George's equitable interest, even if I can establish that I had no notice of that interest.

Suppose (by contrast) that Vanessa did execute a deed leasing the property to me before she disappeared westwards. Now on this version of the story **I am a purchaser of a legal estate.** I therefore will not be bound by George's interest if I can prove the other elements of the doctrine of notice. (Note that this last illustration confirms the proposition that legal property rights are 'better' than equitable property rights.)

Another way of looking at the same point is that if there are two or more equitable interests affecting the same piece of land the rule is **'first in time, first in right'**. The first equitable interest to be created has the first claim, the second equitable interest has the second claim, and so on. Suppose that in 1993, Xerxes, the owner of Greenacre, granted an equitable lease for 10 years of Greenacre to Yorick. In 1994, while Yorick was absent from Greenacre because of a lengthy hospitalisation, Xerxes granted an equitable lease for 10 years of Greenacre to Zebedee.

Yorick has just come out of hospital, and we now have Yorick and Zebedee arguing as to who can occupy Greenacre. Yorick will win the argument. His equitable interest was created first, therefore he has first claim to the land. His right has **priority** over any later-created equitable interest(s).

Let us now add just one more twist to this Greenacre story. Suppose that in 1997 Yorick has no more use for Greenacre, so he assigns (i.e. transfers) his equitable lease to his friend Albert. Can Zebedee come along and say, 'I got my interest before Albert got his; I am first in time and should now be allowed to occupy Greenacre!'?

Zebedee's claim to occupy Greenacre will still fail. It is the order of **creation** of interests which matters, not the order of **acquisition**. Albert's interest was, of course, **created** before Zebedee's. It was **created** when, in 1993, it was granted to Yorick. It would be very strange if, when Yorick disposed of his equitable interest to Albert, that interest lost its priority.

In 1987, Harry acquired West House. In 1990, his lady-friend, Letitia, acquired a constructive trust interest in West House. (She paid substantial sums to renovate the house.) Harry has now left, and has just granted an equitable lease of West House to Martha for 10 years. Does Letitia's right bind Martha?

Would your answer be different if Martha's lease was a legal lease?

On the first version of the facts, we have two competing equitable interests with respect to the same piece of land. It follows that we must apply the 'first in time, first in right' rule. Letitia's right will have 'priority' and will bind Martha.

If, however, Martha's lease was a legal lease, she would be a purchaser of a legal estate. Thus, if she acted in good faith, gave value (e.g. agreed to pay rent) and was without notice of Letitia's right, Martha would not be bound by Letitia's interest.

6.4.4   WITHOUT NOTICE OF THE EQUITABLE INTEREST

In any dispute involving the equitable doctrine of notice, the most likely cause for arguments is the question of whether the purchaser has notice of the relevant equitable interests. In my High Chimneys story, the crucial question will be, 'Did I, Roger Sexton, at the time the fee simple estate in High Chimneys was conveyed to me, have notice of George's equitable interest?'.

As purchaser I will have the task of proving that I was without **any form** of notice of George's interest. Notice comes in three forms:

(a)   actual notice;

(b)   constructive notice;

(c)   imputed notice.

A purchaser has actual notice if, at the time of the purchase, he **actually knew** of the existence of the equitable interest.

A purchaser has constructive notice if, at the time of the purchase, he **ought to have known** of the existence of the equitable interest.

A purchaser has imputed notice if, at the time of the purchase, his agent (solicitor, surveyor etc.) knew or ought to have known of the existence of the equitable interest.

6.4.4.1 Actual notice

This is, of course, of considerable importance, but requires no further explanation.

6.4.4.2 Constructive notice

A purchaser has constructive notice of any equitable interest which **he would have discovered** had he made those enquiries which a reasonable purchaser would make.

Study s. 199(1) of the Law of Property Act 1925 in *Cases and Materials* (6.1.4.2), especially sub-paras (a) and (b). These sub-paragraphs are in effect a statutory restatement of the equitable doctrine of notice.

As you already know, when somebody buys a piece of land he needs to make all sorts of careful enquiries with respect to that land. Some of these enquiries may relate to the physical condition of the land (e.g., is it liable to subsidence or flooding?), but many of these enquiries relate (at least in part) to property law matters.

When buying a piece of land the wise purchaser always checks:

(a) whether the vendor has a good title to the land;

(b) whether there are any third party rights (legal or equitable) such as easements, profits or restrictive covenants affecting the land.

As you have probably already guessed the constructive notice rule in effect places a duty upon the purchaser to act wisely. The rule requires a purchaser to make those enquiries which a reasonable man, **with competent legal advice**, would make. (Rightly, in my view, the rule makes no concessions to 'do-it-yourself' conveyancers who buy land without taking legal advice.)

Legal interests, you will recall, always bind the purchaser, whether he discovers them or not. So a wise purchaser always looks very carefully for legal interests. Under the constructive notice rule he is expected to look just as carefully for equitable interests. In particular, there are two types of enquiry which every purchaser is expected to make:

(a) inspect the land; and
(b) investigate the vendor's title.

Inspect the land

When the wise purchaser inspects the land, some of the things he is on the look out for will relate to the physical condition of the land, e.g., is there evidence of subsidence? But the wise purchaser will also be on the alert for matters such as worn tracks or grazing sheep. Their presence might indicate the existence of easements or profits. He will also want to establish whether anybody other than the vendor is occupying the whole or part of the land. Such a person might have a lease (perhaps legal, perhaps equitable), or might claim a constructive trust interest in the land or possibly some other right in the land.

If anyone (other than the vendor) is in possession of the land or part of it, the 'rule' in *Hunt* v *Luck* applies. (The case is reported [1902] 1 Ch 428, but, contrary to what you might expect, a consideration of the details of the case is not a great deal of help.) Under this rule, the purchaser must look for person(s) in possession, and if he finds anybody he must ask that person what interest he claims in the land. If the purchaser fails to discover a person who is in possession, or fails to ask such a person whether he claims any interest in the land, he has not made adequate enquiries. The purchaser is deemed to have constructive notice of any equitable interest owned by that person.

Put another way, a purchaser has notice of any equitable interest owned by a person in possession (of whole or part of the land) unless enquiry is made of that person and he does not reveal his interest.

Suppose that in my High Chimneys example Harry was living in the house last winter (when I bought it). Harry is another 'gentleman friend' of Vanessa. He too made substantial contributions to the purchase and renovation of the property. He too therefore has an interest in High Chimneys under a constructive trust.

Suppose, further, that on my visit to High Chimneys I somehow failed to realise that Harry was there. Or perhaps I saw him, but I assumed that he was some kind of servant so I asked no questions. Either way, I have not made proper enquiries. I will have constructive notice of Harry's equitable interest.

Let us now suppose that I did see Harry, and I went up to him and said, 'Excuse me sir, do you claim any kind of right or lease over this house?'. If he tells me that he has made substantial contributions to the house, or words to that effect, I have actual notice of his interest. But if he replies, 'Mind your own business!', or something similar but perhaps even less polite, I have sufficiently pursued this line of enquiry. I will not have notice of Harry's interest.

SAQ 33

In 1990, Norma bought East House. In 1992, Oswald started to cohabit with her in East House. He acquired a constructive trust interest in East House by paying off the bulk of the mortgage on the house.

The relationship has now broken up, and Oswald is living alone in East House. This morning a couple of surveyors called wanting to inspect the house. Oswald told them to **** off!'. The surveyors left saying, 'We will be back tomorrow.'

Advise Oswald.

I hope you may have concluded that Oswald is a very lucky man, as he will get a second chance to tell the surveyors about his constructive trust interest. The surveyors are probably acting on behalf of a potential purchaser or mortgagee. Oswald should tell them of his interest, so that the purchaser/mortgagee will have notice of his interest. If, on the other hand, Oswald continues to be rude, then the purchaser/mortgagee will be able to say that he had made adequate enquiries and that he had no notice of Oswald's interest.

Investigate the title

As was explained in **Chapter 2**, a purchaser should always investigate the vendor's title. The deeds and other documents relating to the land must be inspected going back to the **root of title**, which is normally the most recent conveyance which is at least 15 years old, i.e. the purchaser should inspect the root of title and all **later** documents. There is no duty to inspect documents which are dated before the root of title. (These documents are said to be 'behind' the root of title.)

If a purchaser fails to inspect a document which he should have inspected, then he has constructive notice of the contents of that document. In particular, he has constructive notice of all equitable interests **created or revealed** by that document.

The primary purpose of a conveyance is to transfer legal ownership from the vendor to the purchaser. But conveyances often do more than that. A conveyance will often also **create** third party rights such as easements, profits and restrictive covenants. For example, let us suppose that Edwina owned two adjoining fields, Green Field and Yellow Field. She recently sold Green Field to Frank. As well as transferring ownership, the conveyance:

(a)   grants Frank a right of way (easement) over Yellow Field to get to Green Field;

(b)   contains a restrictive covenant entered into by Frank that he will use Green Field for agricultural purposes only.

Conveyances **creating** third party rights are commonplace. You may be more puzzled by the reference to conveyances **revealing** third party rights. The point is really a simple one: Where land is sold, that land may already be subject to third party rights such as easements or restrictive covenants. These may have been created some time ago, perhaps a hundred years or more. If land is sold subject to existing third party rights it is normal practice, though not absolutely obligatory, for the conveyance to mention ('recite') those existing rights.

Example of constructive notice through failure to investigate

The recent history of Purple House is as follows:

■   In 1950 Norma sold Purple House to Malcolm.

■   In 1967 Malcolm sold Purple House to Leonard.

■   In 1983 Leonard sold Purple House to Keith.

■   In 1995 Isobel purchased Purple House from Keith.

When Isobel bought the land, the correct root of title should have been the 1967 conveyance from Malcolm to Leonard. (It is the most recent document which is **at least** 15 years old.) Isobel should therefore have inspected both the 1967 and the 1983 conveyances. She (foolishly) inspected only the 1983 conveyance.

The 1967 conveyance, which Isobel did not inspect, revealed a restrictive covenant (not mentioned in the 1983 conveyance) in favour of a neighbouring property. That covenant, entered into as long ago as 1910, limited Purple House to residential purposes only.

Isobel, who intended to convert Purple House into offices, is bound by the restrictive covenant. She should have inspected the 1967 conveyance, and that would have revealed the 1910 covenant. She has constructive notice of that equitable interest.

Suppose, however, that the 1910 restrictive covenant was mentioned in the 1950 conveyance from Norma to Malcolm, but not in any later conveyances. Under the rule about 'root of title' Isobel does not have to investigate the 1950 conveyance. Therefore (whether or not she looked at the 1967 conveyance) she would not have constructive notice of the covenant.

SAQ 34

In 1922, Peter sold North House to Quentin. The 1922 conveyance contained a restrictive covenant under which Quentin promised to use the house for residential purposes only.

In 1984, Quentin sold North House to Richard.

Stephen is now buying North House from Richard. Will he have notice of the restrictive covenant?

Would your answer be different if the conveyance from Quentin to Richard took place in 1976?

On the basis that the sale from Quentin to Richard took place in 1984, there can be no doubt that Stephen would have notice of the restrictive covenant. The root of title, the most recent conveyance **at least 15 years old**, is that executed in 1922. If Stephen looked at the 1922 conveyance he would have actual notice. If he did not bother to look at the 1922 conveyance, he would have constructive notice.

If the conveyance from Quentin to Richard took place in 1976, then that conveyance would be the root of title. If that (1976) conveyance **recited** the (1922) restrictive covenant, then Stephen would still have notice of the restrictive covenant. But if the 1976 conveyance did not mention the restrictive covenant, then there would not be notice. The only mention of the covenant would be in a document 'behind the root of title', which Stephen has no duty to investigate.

6.4.4.3   Imputed notice

In most purchases of land, agents such as solicitors and/or surveyors are employed. The purchaser does not personally make the necessary enquiries. In view of this fact, a rule of 'imputed notice' is essential if the doctrine of notice is to operate fairly. If an agent, while acting for a particular purchaser with respect to a particular transaction, receives actual or constructive notice of an equitable interest, that notice is ascribed to the purchaser himself. This rule applies to all forms of agent, and is not just confined to solicitors and surveyors.

Suppose that in my example at **6.4.4.2**, of Isobel purchasing Purple House, Isobel had employed a solicitor, Bloggs, to investigate the title to the house. Bloggs did look at the

1967 conveyance, noticed the 1910 restrictive covenant, but omitted to tell Isobel. Isobel will have imputed actual notice of the covenant.

What if Bloggs looked only at the 1983 conveyance, and failed to look at the 1967 conveyance? In that case Isobel will have imputed constructive notice of the restrictive covenant.

In either of these two situations Isobel will be justifiably annoyed with Bloggs! She will be bound by the restrictive covenant. But she has one consolation. She can sue Bloggs for damages for professional negligence.

For a further example let us go back to one version of my High Chimneys story. In one version of the story (see **6.4.4.2**) Harry, a gentleman-friend of Vanessa with a constructive trust interest in the property, is living in the property at the time of my purchase.

Let us now suppose that I did not visit High Chimneys prior to the purchase but left inspection of the property to my surveyor, Muggins. When Muggins visited the property, Harry was out. Vanessa made no mention of Harry, but there were male clothes lying around in some of the rooms. Muggins never reported this fact to me, nor did he take up with Vanessa the presence of the male clothing. It appears that I would have imputed constructive notice of Harry's interest.

This last example is very loosely based on the case of *Kingsnorth Finance* v *Tizard* [1986] 2 All ER 54, which you should read in *Cases and Materials* (6.1.4.3), and then try to answer the following questions:

(a) Was Mrs Tizard living in the house?

(b) What additional enquiries should the surveyor have made?

(c) What additional investigations did the judge specifically say need not be made?

(I do not know whether the surveyor in that case was sued for professional negligence, but I would certainly be suing Muggins!)

6.5 Position of Successors in Title to a Purchaser Without Notice

If a purchaser of a legal estate to which an equitable interest was subject takes his estate free from the equitable interest because of the doctrine of notice, all persons who derive title from that purchaser take free from the equitable interest as well.

To explain this point I must go back to the original version of my High Chimneys story (see **6.3**, where George left in 1992). In my dispute with George I shall contend that I am a bona fide purchaser for value of a legal estate without notice of George's interest. George does not accept this, and sues me in a court case which is splashed all over the local papers. I win. I succeed in proving:

(a)   I was acting bona fide;

(b)   I was a purchaser for value;

(c)   that I purchased a legal estate;

(d)   that I was without notice of George's interest. (Remember that in the **original** version of my story both my agents and I made very careful enquiries which did not reveal even George's existence.)

Although I have won the case, I am sick of High Chimneys. I put it up for sale. Beatrice is the first prospective purchaser to visit the property. Luckily, she does not mind the sheep, nor does she mind Norman cutting across the garden. But suddenly she says, 'Is this not the house there was that big court case about? A fellow called George came along and claimed he had some sort of share in it. I read all about it in the *Maxwellshire Sun*'.

'Yes', I reply, 'but I won the case.'

'Congratulations', says Beatrice, 'but is there a risk that his claim will bind me? I seem to remember that you won because at the time you purchased you neither knew nor could have known of George's claim. **I do know** that George has a claim!'

Why has Beatrice no need to worry?

Beatrice need not worry, for the reason given in the first paragraph of this section: once an equitable interest is void against a purchaser for value without notice, it is void against everybody else who **derives title** from that purchaser. This is so even if (like Beatrice) a successor in title has actual knowledge of the equitable interest.

This is both logical and fair. It would be illogical if an invalid equitable interest could in effect revive against a later purchaser. Such a revival would also be grossly unfair to somebody in my position. I (personally) would not be bound by George's claim. But nobody would want to buy from me for fear that George would claim against them.

One final point. I have referred to 'persons who derive title' from the purchaser without notice. 'Persons who derive title' is not just confined to later purchasers. It extends to anyone whose rights are derived directly or indirectly from the original purchaser without notice. So if Beatrice does buy, all her successors are also protected from George's claim. If I decide not to sell, but to lease, or perhaps even to give away the property, the lessee or donee is not bound by George's claim.

6.6 Conclusion

Before you became a law student, you probably already knew that buying land (a house or any other type of land) was time-consuming. You now know one of the major reasons for the delays. It is essential that if you are buying land you make very careful enquiries regarding easements, profits, constructive trust interests, etc. Moreover, if you fail to discover a **legal** property right (e.g. a legal easement) you are stuck with it. You are bound by the right even though the most careful of enquiries would not have revealed its existence.

But if you fail to discover (say) a constructive trust interest, you may yet escape. You will not be bound by the interest if you are what old-fashioned lawyers sometimes call 'equity's darling', i.e. a bona fide purchaser for value of a legal estate or interest without notice of the equitable interest.

CHAPTER SEVEN

THE IMPACT OF THE 1925 LEGISLATION

7.1 Objectives

By the end of this chapter you should:

■ appreciate fully that the 1925 legislation reduced quite drastically the number of types of **legal** property right;

■ be able to explain the concepts 'fee simple absolute in possession' and 'term of years absolute';

■ be able to identify the various types of property interest in land which can still exist as **legal** interests;

■ appreciate that all 'estates' and interests which fall outside s. 1(1) and (2) of the Law of Property Act 1925 can now exist only as equitable interests;

■ in particular, appreciate that life 'estates', fees tail and fees simple in remainder can exist only as equitable interests.

7.2 Introduction

In the previous chapter we deliberately ignored changes made by the great reforming legislation of 1925. We must now start to consider these changes. Before going into matters of detail, it will help if I state, in general terms, what the 1925 legislators were trying to achieve in this field. They had two main objectives:

(a) to reduce the number of types of legal estates and legal interests;

(b) to reduce substantially the importance of the equitable doctrine of notice.

In this chapter we will be looking at how the first objective was achieved; the second objective will be considered in **Chapter 8**.

7.3 Legal Estates and Interests and the 1925 Legislation

7.3.1 THE NUMBER OF TYPES OF LEGAL ESTATES AND INTERESTS PRIOR TO 1925

Prior to 1925 there was a quite wide variety of types of right in land recognised by the common law. But (as explained in **Chapter 5**) there was an even wider variety of types of right recognised by equity. Expressed diagrammatically, you should think of two lists:

List of legal rights   List of equitable rights

(I hope that you have remembered that all types of property right recognised by the common law are also recognised by equity. But there are some types of right, e.g., restrictive covenants and estate contracts, which have never been recognised by the common law. That is why the list of equitable rights is longer.)

7.3.2   THE EFFECT OF THE 1925 LEGISLATION

List of legal rights   List of equitable rights

As a result of the 1925 reform, the length of the list of types of legal right is reduced. The list of types of equitable right remains the same length.

The 1925 legislators did not totally abolish any type of property right. (It might have been better had they done so!) Rather they (in effect) provided that certain types of right which previously were recognised by **both law and equity** are now recognised **by equity alone**. Property rights which were treated in this way include, e.g., fees tail, determinable fees, life estates, and fees simple in remainder. You may well be wondering why this was done.

It was hoped that, by limiting the number of types of legal right, land law would be simplified, and that conveyancing transactions (buying and selling land, leasing, etc.) would be made easier. It is debatable whether these ends have in fact been achieved.

7.3.3   LAW OF PROPERTY ACT 1925, SECTION 1

The Law of Property Act 1925 does not contain a long list of rights which used to exist at law but which can now only exist in equity. Instead, s. 1(1) and (2) set out those types of property right which are still capable of existing **at law** after 1925. Section 1(3) then provides: 'All other estates, interests and charges in or over land take effect as equitable interests.'

If a particular property right is one of the two 'estates' listed in s. 1(1), or falls into one of the five categories of legal interest listed in s. 1(2), then it can be a legal property right. But if it falls outside all seven headings then (applying s. 1(3)) it can only be an equitable interest.

SAQ 36

If you now look now at s. 1(1) and (2) in *Cases and Materials* (7.1) you will find no reference to fees tail. What follows from the fact that these subsections do not mention fees tail?

It follows that any fee tail existing after 1925 exists only as an equitable interest.

7.4   Legal Estates Existing After 1925

(Remember that an 'estate' is a right to enjoy possession of a piece of land for a period of time.)

By s. 1(1) of the Law of Property Act 1925 there are now only two legal estates:

(a)   fee simple absolute in possession;

(b)   term of years absolute.

7.4.1   Term of Years Absolute

ACTIVITY 16

Although you will probably not find it very enlightening, read the definition of 'term of years absolute' contained in s. 205(1)(xxvii) of the Law of Property Act 1925; s. 205(1)(xxvii) is set out in *Cases and Materials* (7.2.1).

The statutory phrase 'term of years absolute' is very misleading. Worse still, the phrase is given a very elaborate definition by s. 205(1)(xxvii) which many people (myself included) do not find very helpful. The matter can, however, be explained much more simply than is done in s. 205(1)(xxvii). To all intents and purposes 'term of years absolute' is synonymous with 'lease'! The concept of a lease is explained at **1.3.2**, and in particular that leases come in two forms, 'fixed term' and 'periodic tenancies'. It may prove useful to read that explanation again.

I can now go on to tell you that all forms of lease (including a fixed term for, say, just six months, or a weekly periodic tenancy) are technically 'terms of years absolute'. (I said the phrase was misleading!) The conclusion is thus very simple. All forms of lease (even very short ones) are still capable of existing as a legal estate.

7.4.2   FEE SIMPLE ABSOLUTE IN POSSESSION

You may recall from **Chapter 4** that fees simple, fees tail, and life estates were, at common law 'estates of freehold'. Leases were not.

The basic plan underlying s. 1(1)(a) of the 1925 Act and its concept 'fee simple absolute in possession' is easy to understand. It was that the only estate of freehold to be recognised by law is one which:

(a)   in principle goes on for ever; **and**

(b)   gives its owner an immediate right to enjoy the land.

'Absolute' (in this context) means going on for ever. 'In possession' means giving a right to immediate enjoyment. We must now consider the phrases in greater detail.

7.4.2.1   'In possession'

In **Chapter 4** we considered 'estates in possession, remainder and reversion' (see **4.6**). I then said that an estate in possession is one which confers on its owner an **immediate** right to occupy the relevant land. In the context of a general discussion on the nature of estates, that definition is, I insist, perfectly sound; but in the context of the present discussion we need to add a qualification to this definition. First, though, an example:

Suppose Roger owns a legal 'fee simple absolute in possession' in Blueacre. He leases Blueacre to Tamsin for six months at £5 per week rent. In a literal sense, Roger will not be 'in possession' of Blueacre for the next six months; Tamsin will be. Nevertheless it would be very strange if, having had a legal estate in Blueacre, Roger should lose it, only to regain it after just six months. Moreover, if this were correct, nobody would seem to 'own' Blueacre during the six months of the lease.

The answer to this puzzle is tucked away in s. 205(1)(xix) of the Law of Property Act 1925. This states that for the purposes of the 1925 Act, '"Possession" includes receipt of rents and profits or the right to receive the same, if any; . . .'

Now you may find this wording strange and archaic. What it really means is that a right to receive rent with respect to a piece of land (even a nominal rent or one which is not in fact collected) is deemed to be possession of that land. A slightly different way of putting it is to say that the right to receive rent from a piece of land is 'constructive possession' of that land. It follows that a fee simple **in reversion to a lease** counts as 'in possession' for the purposes of s. 1(1) of the Act. So in my Blueacre example Roger retains a legal fee simple estate during the six months of the lease.

SAQ 37

Leonora owns the legal fee simple absolute in possession with respect to Greenacre. She executes a deed leasing Greenacre to Tamsin for 10 years. Almost immediately Tamsin executes a deed sub-leasing Greenacre to Susan for five years. How many legal estates now exist with respect to Greenacre?

There are three. Leonora, despite what has happened to Greenacre, retains her legal fee simple absolute in possession. Tamsin and Susan **both** own terms of years absolute.

One other complication. You may well recall from **4.6.2** that a fee simple can exist in reversion, not just to a lease, but also to a life estate or fee tail. Now when somebody grants a life estate or fee tail, in practice he does so gratuitously. Unlike when he grants a lease, he does not charge a rent. A fee simple in reversion to a life estate or fee tail is therefore not, even under the wide statutory definition, 'in possession' and can exist only as an equitable interest. (Who owns the **legal** fee simple to the land in this situation will emerge later in **7.6**.)

7.4.2.2 'Absolute'

The original plan in 1925 was that **all** modified fees simple should merely be equitable interests. Unfortunately two exceptions have been made to this principle.

Statutory determinable fees simple

In **4.3.3.1**, when discussing determinable fees simple, I gave illustrations: 'To John Smith in fee simple until he marries Fanny Bloggs'; 'To Ann Green in fee simple during the time that she remains a faithful Protestant'. Such determinable fees **are not absolute.** After 1925, a determinable fee simple granted to a human being must be an equitable interest.

The complication is not with determinable fees of the kind we have just considered. Rather it is with those fees simple which are made determinable by statute. In the first half of the nineteenth century, a lot of land was taken by way of compulsory purchase for railways and canals. To soften the blow for the expropriated landowners the relevant legislation (usually the Lands Clauses Acts) provided that should a railway or canal close down, the land taken should revert to its original owner or his heirs.

The facts of a case which you learn about in constitutional law illustrate this point. In *Pickin* v *British Railways* [1974] AC 765, land had in effect been granted 'to the Bristol and Exeter Railway in fee simple until the Clevedon to Yatton railway is abandoned'. The railway in this case (and in countless other similar situations) obtained a statutory determinable fee simple.

In 1925, Parliament was well aware of these special fees simple, and decided that they should not be downgraded to equitable interests. Section 7(1) of the Law of Property Act 1925 therefore provides:

> A fee simple which, by virtue of the Lands Clauses Acts, the School Sites Acts, or any similar statute, is liable to be divested, is for the purposes of this Act a fee simple absolute, and remains liable to be divested as if this Act had not been passed . . .

As a result of this provision, a statutory determinable fee simple remains a legal estate.

School Sites Acts

You will notice that the School Sites Acts are also mentioned in s. 7(1). These Acts were passed in the nineteenth century. They were designed to encourage (but **not compel**) wealthy landowners to donate land for schools, village halls, etc. The School Sites Acts provided for the land to revert from the trustees of the school to the original grantor or his heirs should the school close.

As you may have guessed, problems have arisen in the late twentieth century where a school has closed, but it is difficult to trace the original grantor's heirs, the grantor having died a long time ago. The problem was considered in two modern cases (*Re Clayton's Deed* [1980] Ch 99 and *Re Rowhook Mission Hall* [1985] Ch 62) which came to conflicting solutions. The problem has now been solved by the Reverter of Sites Act 1987.

You need not worry about the cases or the 1987 Act, except to note that the cases **agreed** on one point. A fee simple liable to be divested under the School Sites Act or similar legislation is a special type of determinable fee simple and, unlike determinable fees generally, it continues to exist as a legal estate after 1925.

Fees simple subject to a right of entry

'Right of entry' is a rather misleading phrase we have already come across and will encounter again at **7.5.5**. It is not a right simply to go on somebody else's land. It is much more drastic than that. It is a right for a grantor of land to forfeit the grant and reclaim the land should the grantee break some condition.

Rights of entry (i.e. forfeiture) are commonplace in leases; leases usually provide that the landlord can terminate the lease prematurely if the tenant breaks the terms of the lease. In contrast, rights of entry attached to the conveyance of a fee simple are fortunately relatively rare. 'Fortunately', because clearly for an owner to lose a fee simple back to the original grantor is a disaster. In practice there are two possible situations where a right of entry attached to a fee simple may be encountered:

(a) Where there is a fee simple upon condition subsequent. (Refer back to the discussion in **4.3.3.2** and examples such as 'to John Smith in fee simple provided he never marries Fanny Bloggs'.)

(b) Where land has been conveyed in return for a rentcharge, and a right of entry for non-payment of that rentcharge has been imposed.

Situation (b) takes a little bit of explaining. In about 1900 a rather strange way of selling land enjoyed a period of popularity in and around Manchester. Land was sold not for a capital price (say £200, a tidy sum in those days), but in return for a rentcharge.

Rentcharges were discussed at **1.4.5**, and I suggest that you refer back for a moment to remind yourself of what a rentcharge is. We have already looked at an illustration drawn from the (fairly modern) **Bristol** practice. We will now consider an example of the old **Manchester** practice.

In 1905, Tatlock sold the fee simple in Raineyacre to Sharples in return for a rentcharge of £12 per annum. (This figure is realistic.) As a result of this transaction **three** property rights existed:

(a) a **fee simple** estate in Raineyacre vested in Sharples;

(b) a **rentcharge** for £12 per year charged on Raineyacre, payable to Tatlock;

(c) a '**right of entry**' (i.e. forfeiture) in favour of Tatlock which he could exercise if the rentcharge was not paid.

It was the inclusion of this 'right of entry' in the old Manchester transactions (rights of entry were not normally included in the more modern Bristol transactions) which caused a problem when the 1925 legislation was enacted.

January 1926 — Panic in Manchester

It is clear that the 1925 legislators originally intended that fees simple upon condition subsequent should, like non-statutory determinable fees simple, in future exist only as equitable interests. But they totally overlooked fees simple subject to a right of entry for non-payment of a rentcharge. As a result of this oversight, there was in early 1926 worry and confusion amongst solicitors and landowners in the Manchester area. It appeared that any person who owned a fee simple subject to **a right of entry** for non-payment of a rentcharge no longer had an **absolute** fee simple. They therefore no longer owned a legal estate but only an equitable interest.

To meet this problem, the Law of Property Amendment Act 1926 hastily added a further clause to s. 7(1) of the Law of Property Act 1925: 'a fee simple subject to a legal or equitable right of entry or re-entry is for the purposes of this Act a fee simple absolute'. This provision was made retrospective to 1 January 1926. It ensured that a fee simple subject to a right of entry for non-payment of a rentcharge can still exist as a legal estate. But this provision also has one (probably unintended) side effect.

As we have already seen, a fee simple upon condition subsequent is (by its nature) also a fee simple subject to a right of entry. Thus it appears that, contrary to the original 1925 plan, a fee simple upon condition subsequent is 'absolute' for the purposes of the 1925 Act and can therefore still exist as a legal estate.

Janet owns the legal fee simple absolute in possession in Broadacre. She executes a deed conveying Broadacre, 'To my daughter Karen in fee simple on condition that she does not marry a professional footballer'. Has Karen acquired a legal estate?

Karen has of course only a fee simple (in possession) upon condition subsequent. The original intention in 1925 was that such a modified fee should be an equitable interest only. But as Karen's fee simple also fits the description 'a fee simple subject to a right of entry', it is caught by the 1926 amendment and will be a legal estate.

7.5 Legal Interests Existing After 1925

As already indicated, under s. 1(2) of the Law of Property Act 1925, there are five categories of legal interests. The categories are lettered (a) to (e). In the case of categories (a), (b) and (d) (see **7.5.1**, **7.5.2** and **7.5.4**), the actual wording of the legislation leaves something to be desired.

7.5.1 (a) EASEMENTS AND PROFITS

This category covers any easement or profit, provided its duration is equivalent to a fee simple absolute in possession or a term of years absolute. Thus rights such as private rights of way (an easement) and grazing rights (a profit) are normally going to be legal interests. However, carefully note the requirement regarding duration. If, for example, I granted my neighbour Charley a right 'for the rest of his life' to cross my land to get to his own house, Charley would have an easement for life. That right, even if granted by deed, could exist only as an equitable interest.

7.5.2 (b) RENTCHARGES

A rentcharge which in its duration is either 'perpetual' or for 'a term of years absolute' (i.e. lasts for a fixed period) is capable of being a legal interest. Again note the duration requirement. At one time rentcharges granted for the life of the recipient of the payments were quite common. If any such rights survive today, they **must** be equitable interests.

As we saw in **1.4.5**, the Rentcharges Act 1977 prohibits (subject to exceptions) the creation of new rentcharges. It also provides that existing perpetual rentcharges can endure for only another 60 years (i.e. they will all expire in the year 2037). The 1977 Act, while it ensures the gradual decline in number of rentcharges, does not affect the question whether a particular rentcharge is a legal interest or an equitable interest only.

7.5.3 (c) 'A CHARGE BY WAY OF LEGAL MORTGAGE'

The 'charge by way of legal mortgage' is the standard modern form of 'legal mortgage'. There must be literally several million of this type of legal interest in existence today.

7.5.4 (d) ALL INTERESTS IN LAND WHICH ARISE BY OPERATION OF STATUTE

In this text we have so far assumed that all rights against a piece of land are created by action of the relevant parties. This is not entirely correct. Some rights arise against a piece of land by operation of an Act of Parliament. The owner of the rights will in practice be some form of government department.

In modern law, there are two (very contrasting) rights arising by statute which are sufficiently important for them to be mentioned as part of a land law course.

7.5.4.1 The charge for inheritance tax

When a person dies owning a lot of property, the Revenue will claim what is often still loosely referred to as 'death duties'. With a very wealthy person, the bill for 'death duties' is substantial. 'Death duties' has, however, never been the official name for this tax. Prior to 1971 it was estate duty. From 1971 to 1984 it was capital transfer tax. Since 1984 it has been inheritance tax.

The important point for our purposes is that where inheritance tax is payable with respect to a piece of real property, that tax becomes a 'charge' on the land in favour of the Inland Revenue. (The same used to be true of estate duty and capital transfer tax.) The Revenue has (in effect) a legal interest in the land.

7.5.4.2 The legal aid charge

Where a legally aided litigant 'recovers or preserves' land, the costs of the litigation (in so far as they are not recovered from the other side) become a charge on the land in favour of the Legal Aid Fund. This rule is particularly important where former spouses or cohabitees have been litigating about who owns their former home. The winner may find that she or he gets the house, but encumbered by a substantial charge (in effect a legal interest rather akin to a mortgage) in favour of the Legal Aid Fund.

7.5.5 (e) RIGHTS OF ENTRY

Section 1(2)(e) of the 1925 Act covers 'Rights of entry exercisable over or in respect of a legal term of years absolute, or annexed, for any purpose, to a legal rentcharge'.

As explained earlier, 'right of entry' is synonymous with 'right to forfeit'. The practical effect of s. 1(2)(e) is that:

(a) a landlord's right to forfeit a lease if the tenant breaks the terms of the lease;

(b) a rentcharge owner's right (if any) to reclaim the land if the money is not paid,
     can both be legal interests.

In the example given in SAQ 38, Janet will retain a right of entry exercisable *for breach of a condition subsequent*. Is that right legal or equitable?

A right of entry for breach of a condition subsequent is not within s. 1(2)(e), nor of course is it within any other paragraph of s. 1(1) and (2). Therefore such a right of entry can **only be an equitable interest**, even though the fee simple upon condition subsequent can still (thanks to the 1926 amendment) be a legal estate.

Which of the following can exist as legal property rights after 1925?

(a)   An easement to last for 10 years.

(b)   A profit to last for the life-time of the grantee.

(c)   A determinable fee simple, 'To John in fee simple until he marries Fanny'.

(d)   A restrictive covenant.

(e)   A weekly periodic tenancy.

Only (a) and (e) come within s. 1(1) or (2), and they (alone) **can** be legal property rights. Right (a) comes within s. 1(2)(a); contrast (b), which does not come within the same paragraph, as it lasts for a lifetime, not for a 'term of years'. Right (e) **can** be a legal property right because (paradoxically) it is a 'term of years absolute' within s. 1(1)(b).

7.6   Equitable Interests after 1925

The first point to remember is that if a property right falls within one of the seven headings in s. 1(1) and (2) of the Law of Property Act 1925, it **can** be a legal right; it does **not** follow that it **must** be a legal right. In particular remember that at **5.4** it was stressed that to create or convey legal property rights a deed is required. Thus let us suppose that Len owns Blue Field. He and Tom sign a document which is not a deed, under which Len leases Blue Field to Tom for 10 years. They have created a 'term of years absolute' within the meaning of s. 1(1)(b), but the transaction is, of course, only an equitable lease as it is not in the form of a deed.

7.6.1 THE STATUS OF FEES TAIL, FEES SIMPLE IN REMAINDER, DETERMINABLE FEES, LIFE ESTATES

Fees tail, fees simple in remainder, determinable fees, and life estates can now exist only as equitable interests. Any legal fees tail, legal life estates etc. existing on 1 January 1926 were automatically downgraded to equitable interests.

Suppose that in 1900, land had been granted by deed, 'To Alfred for life, remainder to Brian in fee tail, remainder to Charles in fee simple'. Until 1925, Alfred, Brian and Charles would each have a legal estate in the land. The legal ownership of the land was said to be divided up into 'temporal slices'. One legal estate followed on after another. Since 1925 it has been impossible to divide up the legal **freehold** ownership of land into 'temporal slices'. **For every piece of land in the country there must now be just one legal freehold estate, a fee simple absolute in possession.**

Suppose that today Blackacre is granted by deed, 'To Alfred for life, remainder to Brian in fee tail, remainder to Charles in fee simple'. This will be a 'strict settlement'. (Refer back to **2.4.1.**) The life interest of Alfred, and the interests of Brian and Charles, will be equitable interests only.

As we also saw at **2.4.1**, the strict settlement is a form of trust peculiar to land. As you may have been able to guess, the legal fee simple absolute in possession in Blackacre will therefore be held by a trustee or trustees in trust for Alfred, Brian and Charles.

Now comes the surprising point. Thinking back to **Chapter 2**, and/or just applying some common sense, you may be thinking that the legal fee simple estate in Blackacre must (after 1925) be vested in independent trustees (for the sake of argument, let us call them Tim and Tam). You would be wrong to think this.

As a result of the **Settled Land Act 1925**, where, as in our Blackacre example, there is a 'strict settlement' of land, the trustee(s) of the legal fee simple estate will not normally be independent people such as Tim and Tam. Rather the '**life tenant in possession**' will be the sole trustee. Thus in our Blackacre example, Alfred (remember he has a life interest in possession) will hold the legal estate on trust for himself, Brian and Charles. Do not panic if this seems very strange. Particularly, remember that in **Chapter 2** it was said that strict settlements were a legal anomaly, and that they are rare today.

Vastacres has been granted to Leonard for life, remainder to Malcolm in fee tail, remainder to Norma in fee simple.

   (a)   **Are the rights expressly granted to Leonard, Malcolm and Norma legal or equitable?**

(b)   Who will own the legal 'fee simple absolute in possession' to Vastacres?

The right expressly granted to Leonard is an equitable life interest in possession, while Malcolm has an equitable fee tail in remainder, and Norma has an equitable fee simple in remainder. Leonard will also own the legal 'fee simple absolute in possession', holding it in trust for himself, Malcolm and Norma.

7.7   Conclusion

In this chapter we have examined the seven categories of property right which can still exist as legal property rights after the quite fundamental changes made by the 1925 property legislation. No property rights were abolished by s. 1 of the Law of Property Act 1925, but some rights were 'downgraded' (as it were) so that they could exist only as equitable interests. Prominent among those 'downgraded' are rights the duration of which is measured by the life or lives of person(s), including life estates, an easement or profit for life, and even a rentcharge to last for the life of a person.

This downgrading meant that when the new legislation came into force (1 January 1926) there was an immediate increase in the absolute **number** of equitable property rights. This increase led to other consequences which we examine in the next chapter.

CHAPTER EIGHT

STATUS OF EQUITABLE INTERESTS AFTER 1925

8.1 Objectives

By the end of this chapter you should:

■ appreciate why and how the 1925 property legislation reduced the importance of the equitable doctrine of notice;

■ be able to explain how the system of land **charges** registration operates;

■ be able to list those important property rights which are registrable as land charges;

■ be able to explain the concept of overreaching, and how it operates;

■ be able to list those equitable interests which are still subject to the equitable doctrine of notice.

8.2 Introduction

As I hinted at the end of **Chapter 7**, the effect of s. 1 of the Law of Property Act 1925 in statistical terms was that, at the stroke of midnight on 1 January 1926, the number of **legal** rights in land decreased sharply, and the number of equitable interests increased sharply. Now, as the number of equitable interests dramatically increased, you might be thinking that the equitable doctrine of notice (discussed at **6.4**) became post-1925 even more important than it was prior to the great reforms. For reasons which will now be explained, this is a wrong conclusion.

8.2.1 THE DESIRE TO REDUCE THE IMPORTANCE OF THE DOCTRINE OF NOTICE

As I noted at **7.2**, the 1925 legislators actually aimed to **reduce** the importance of the doctrine of notice. This policy aim is easy to understand. If somebody owns an equitable interest he can never be 100 per cent sure that his rights will remain enforceable against the land. There is always the risk that a purchaser of the land will come along who is a bona fide purchaser for value of a legal estate without notice of the equitable interest.

Prior to 1926 almost all equitable interests were subject to the doctrine of notice. Since 1925 only a minority are subject to the doctrine. The 1925 legislation divides equitable interests which exist with respect to land which is **unregistered title** into three groups:

(a) equitable interests registrable as land charges;

(b) equitable interests which are 'overreachable';

(c) equitable interests which are neither registrable as Land Charges nor overreachable, and are therefore still subject to the doctrine of notice.

8.3 Registration of Land Charges

As we shall shortly see, a wide variety of equitable interests are registrable as land charges. A person who owns an equitable interest which is registrable as a land charge is well-advised to register it. Why?

(a) If the interest is registered then s. 198(1) of the Law of Property Act 1925 provides that the registration shall constitute actual notice to the whole world of the equitable interest. Thus if you register your right as a land charge, you can be sure that it will be binding on a purchaser.

(b) If an interest is registrable as a land charge, but it is not registered, then by the Land Charges Acts 1925 and 1972, the interest is void against a purchaser for value, (whatever the state of that purchaser's knowledge).

Read the statutory provisions set out in *Cases and Materials* (8.1), and study the important case of *Hollington Brothers* v *Rhodes* [1951] 2 All ER 578 (also at 8.1).

This case is a dramatic illustration of the second principle. H 'leased' some offices to R for seven years by a document which was not a deed. R therefore acquired only an equitable lease. An equitable lease is (since 1925) **registrable as a land charge** (see 8.3.3.1). R took possession of the premises, but omitted to register his lease as a land charge.

The equitable lease was valid against H, but H then sold its estate in reversion to D. This sale was expressly 'subject to and with the benefit of such tenancies as may affect the premises'. There can be no doubt that D had 'notice' of R's equitable lease. Nevertheless D was not bound by it. The court emphasised that where an equitable interest is registrable as a land charge, **the doctrine of notice is irrelevant**.

The moral of this case (and the case of *Midland Bank* v *Green* discussed at 8.3.5.1) is clear. If you have an equitable interest which is registrable as a land charge, register it! If you do not, you will lose your rights if the land is sold. You will lose your rights even if the purchaser knew of your interest and/or could see you were occupying the land.

In 1991, Lenny granted an equitable lease of his house 'Broomtrees' to Tommy for 10 years. Tommy lives in the house. The house is unregistered title. Recently Lenny sold the fee simple in the house to Percy. Percy knew of the equitable lease, because both Lenny and Tommy told him about it. Is Percy bound by Tommy's equitable lease?

Percy will be bound by Tommy's equitable lease **only if** Tommy had registered it as a land charge. If Tommy has not so registered, then his equitable lease will be void against a purchaser such as Percy. It is irrelevant that Percy knew of Tommy's lease.

8.3.1 THE OPERATION OF THE LAND CHARGES REGISTER

Before examining this topic, remember that the Land Charges Register is relevant only where the **title** to land is **unregistered**. The Land Charges Register must not be confused with the Register of Title. As more and more titles are registered, the Land Charges Register will become less and less important.

The decline in importance of the Land Charges Register is very welcome, as it operates in a rather strange way. A person who owns a registrable interest registers it not against the land, but against the **name** of the owner (at the time the interest was created) of the legal estate out of which the interest is derived.

The Land Charges Register is basically an immensely long list of names of landowners. It used to be a gigantic card-index system, kept at Kidbrooke in south-east London (one name, one card!). For a long time critics predicted that the register would grow so large that it would become unmanageable. By the early 1970s, so many entries had been made that the crisis point seemed to be upon us. The situation was saved (in 1974) by transferring the Land Charges Register on to a computer kept at Plymouth. One of the clear defects in the 1925 property legislation was (largely) solved, not by legislation but by a technology unheard of in 1925!

I said a moment ago that an owner of a registrable interest must register against the name of the owner of the legal estate out of which the interest is derived. To be more accurate, registration must be against the name **as shown in the title deeds.** Suppose I own Pinkacre, and someone wishes to register a land charge against me. The conveyance of Pinkacre to me names me as 'Rodger Norman Sexton'. Registration must be against 'Rodger Norman Sexton', even though on my birth certificate and in every day life I am 'Roger' without the 'd'.

Suppose, however, that you want to register a land charge, but you do not have access to the relevant title deed(s) to see how the name has been written. What do you do then? The answer (strange as it sounds) is that you register against all possible alternative versions of the name. (This quite often happens with 'Class F' rights of occupation charges, discussed below at **8.3.3.3.**)

Wendy comes into your office in a flood of tears. She explains that her husband of nearly 50 years has just left her. She is still in the matrimonial home, which her husband bought in his sole name in 1949. The house is unregistered title. She is frightened that her husband will sell the house and she will be out on the street. She tells you, 'He usually called himself Stuart Pearse, but I am not sure that is the correct spelling. On the marriage certificate it says "Stewart Pierce".'

In this situation every good lawyer will 'drop everything' and immediately register a land charge. But what do you do about the names problem?

I would register against **six** versions; the two versions of the husbands' first name multiplied by the three possible spellings of the surname (remember 'Pearce' is very common).

8.3.2 SEARCHES OF THE LAND CHARGES REGISTER

As a result of s. 198 of the Law of Property Act 1925, all interests which have been correctly registered are automatically binding upon a purchaser. You should therefore have already realised that when a purchaser is buying land which is unregistered title, one enquiry he always should make is a 'search' of the Land Charges Register. He needs to know what (relevant) entries there are on the register.

The computerisation of the Land Charges Register does not alter the fact that when a purchaser is buying unregistered land he 'searches' by supplying the Land Charges Registry with a list of the names of the past owners of the land, if possible going back to 1925. For reasons already indicated, those names should be supplied as they have been spelt in the relevant deeds.

Read in *Cases and Materials* (8.1.1) *Diligent Finance* v *Alleyne* (1972) 23 P & CR 346 and *Oak Co-operative B.S.* v *Blackburn* [1968] Ch 730 to appreciate just how awkward and cumbersome this system of registration against names can be!

8.3.3   EQUITABLE INTERESTS REGISTRABLE AS LAND CHARGES

The Land Charges Act 1925 (now replaced by the Land Charges Act 1972) introduced a system of classes of land charge. For our purposes these classes are discussed below in order of importance, rather than alphabetical order.

8.3.3.1   Class C(iv): Estate contract

'Estate contract' I defined at **5.5.3.3** as the equitable interest which a purchaser of land acquires in the (usually fairly brief) period which elapses between the contract for sale and its completion by conveyance of the legal estate. This may be called the traditional definition. The definition of 'estate contract' contained in the Land Charges Act 1972 (see s. 2(4)(iv)) is far wider than the traditional definition. In consequence, quite a wide variety of rights are registrable under the general heading 'estate contract':

(a)   Any contract to create or convey a legal estate.

(b)   Equitable leases arising under contracts or informal grants (hence the need to register the lease in *Hollington* v *Rhodes*: see **Activity 17** above).

(c)   Options.

(d)   Rights of pre-emption (i.e. first refusal).

8.3.3.2   Class D(ii): Restrictive covenants

Any restrictive covenant entered into after 1925 (except one contained in a lease) is registrable as a land charge. Restrictive covenants entered into before 1926 (of which there is a tremendous number) are not registrable as land charges. They remain subject to the doctrine of notice.

Pippa recently purchased Snooty House. Snooty House was unregistered title. When Pippa investigated title, the root of title was a conveyance dated 1975. That conveyance revealed a large number of restrictive covenants affecting Snooty House. Some were imposed on the house in 1910; others were imposed in 1940. When Pippa had a search made of the Land Charges Register, the official search certificate revealed no restrictive covenants. Is Pippa bound:

(a)   by the 1940 covenants?

(b)   by the 1910 covenants?

Provided she searched against the correct name(s) she will not be bound by the 1940 covenants, even though she knew about them. She will be bound by the 1910 covenants. The doctrine of notice applies to these 'old' covenants, and Pippa had notice of them because they were recited in the root of title.

8.3.3.3   Class F: Spousal rights of occupation

Where one spouse has the legal title to the matrimonial home in his or her sole name, the other spouse **automatically** has a statutory right of occupation with respect to the home. This right of occupation is registrable as a land charge.

The 'Class F' right is **in addition** to any right under a constructive trust which the spouse who does not have the legal title **may** have by virtue of having contributed substantially to the cost of acquisition of the matrimonial home. Confusingly, a constructive trust interest is an equitable interest which is still subject to the doctrine of notice!

8.3.3.4   Class C(iii): General equitable charge

'General equitable charge' can be defined as an equitable charge for money where the owner of the charge does not take possession of the title deeds to the legal estate affected by the charge. You may not find that particularly meaningful. What really matters is that there are two significant equitable interests covered by this concept:

(a)   An equitable mortgage where the mortgagee does not take the title deeds to the property mortgaged;

(b)   An 'unpaid vendor's lien'.

(An unpaid vendor's lien arises where a vendor of land conveys the land to a purchaser, but allows the purchaser to delay paying part or the whole of the price. It is a kind of equitable interest in the land which exists in favour of the vendor until he is paid in full.)

8.3.3.5   Class D(iii): Equitable easements and profits

This class of land charge is relatively rare as most easements and profits are legal interests, and like legal interests generally they bind purchasers whatever the circumstances.

Equitable easements and equitable profits are registrable under Class D(iii) if created after 1925. (Equitable easements and equitable profits created pre-1926 are not registrable as land charges. They are still subject to the doctrine of notice.)

8.3.3.6   Class C(ii): A 'limited owner's charge'

This form of equitable interest is relatively rare nowadays. It arises in favour of a person who has only a life interest in a piece of land, but he pays off out of his own pocket a financial incumbrance burdening the fee simple, such as a mortgage, or a charge for inheritance tax or the taxes now replaced by inheritance tax.

8.3.3.7   Class E: Annuities

This class is totally obsolete, and we need not bother with it.

8.3.4   LEGAL INTERESTS REGISTRABLE AS LAND CHARGES

We now come to an annoying anomaly in the law, actually the result of the 1925 reforms. The vast majority of property rights registrable as land charges are equitable interests which otherwise would have been subject to the doctrine of notice. Rather strangely, a few legal interests are also registrable as land charges.

To put the matter bluntly, the rights we are about to consider are **called** 'legal interests', as they fall within s. 1 of the Law of Property Act 1925. But ironically, as they are registrable as land charges, they are deprived of the all-important characteristic of legal interests, which is that they bind purchasers of the land whatever the circumstances. If an interest of one of the types discussed below is not registered as a land charge, it will be void against a purchaser in the usual way. It will even be void against a purchaser who actually knew of the unregistered interest. (Cf. *Hollington Brothers* v *Rhodes*).

8.3.4.1   Class C(i): Puisne mortgage

('Puisne' is pronounced 'puny'.) A puisne mortgage is a legal mortgage where the mortgagee does not take possession of the title deeds.

Where land is mortgaged, the mortgagee (i.e. the lender) normally takes possession of the title deeds relating to the land mortgaged. However, as you may already know, a piece of land may be mortgaged more than once, so that there are (simultaneously) two or more mortgages with respect to the same piece of land. Where this is the case, the first mortgagee (i.e. the lender whose mortgage was created first) will in practice have taken the deeds to the land. The later mortgagees (second, third, etc.) will therefore not be able to take any deeds.

This in turn means that if a second or later mortgage is a legal mortgage, it will be a 'puisne' mortgage and registrable as a Class C(i) land charge. (If a second or later mortgage is an equitable mortgage, it will constitute a general equitable charge registrable as a Class C(iii) land charge: see **8.3.3.4**.)

If these points regarding mortgages have left you somewhat baffled, do not worry unduly. We will return to them when we study the law of mortgages in **Chapter 32**.

8.3.4.2   Class D(i): Charge for inheritance tax

This charge was mentioned at **7.5.4.1** when discussing types of legal interest. The inheritance tax (in earlier days the capital transfer tax or estate duty) which may be payable with respect to a piece of real property is a charge on that real property. It is a legal interest, **but it is registrable as a land charge, Class D(i)**. The charge can arise only in favour of the Inland Revenue, and the taxpayer (the person who has inherited the land) is permitted to pay off the tax by annual instalments over 10 years.

Strangely, it is the practice of the Revenue to register a Class D(i) charge only in exceptional cases where it anticipates having difficulty getting its money.

Harold recently died. He owned, *inter alia*, Hugeacres (unregistered title), worth about £10 million. His will appointed the National Westminster Bank to be his sole executor, and it (as it is entitled to) has put Hugeacres up for sale. Your wealthy friend Leonard is thinking of buying, but in conversation he asks, 'Hugeacres must be subject to a whopping bill for inheritance tax. If I bought Hugeacres, could the taxman claim the money from me?'. Advise Leonard.

Although the inheritance tax is a 'legal' interest against Hugeacres, it is registrable as a land charge. It would bind a purchaser such as Leonard only if the Revenue registered its claim on the computer at Plymouth. The Revenue would be confident of getting its money from National Westminster Bank, so it would not bother to register.

8.3.4.3   Classes A and B: Certain types of right created by Act of Parliament

We need not bother with the details of these charges, which are nowadays mostly unimportant. There is, however, one very important type of Class B charge – the 'legal aid charge' – which was discussed briefly at **7.5.4.2**. This arises in favour of the Legal Aid Fund for the costs of litigation involving a legally aided person in which a piece of land is 'recovered or preserved' for that person.

It is the policy of the Legal Aid Board (and was the policy of the Law Society which used to administer legal aid) to register all Class B charges arising in its favour.

8.3.5   CONSEQUENCES OF FAILURE TO REGISTER A LAND CHARGE

I have been saying that an unregistered land charge is void against a purchaser for value of the land. This is something of an oversimplification. The exact consequences of failure to register a land charge depend on the type of charge involved.

8.3.5.1   Failure to register an estate contract, restrictive covenant, inheritance tax charge, or equitable easement/profit

A failure to register as a land charge one of these types of interest will mean that it is void against a purchaser for money or money's worth of a legal estate or legal interest. It must, however, be stressed that the interest will still be valid against the original grantor, donees from him, and people who inherit the land from him.

The case of *Midland Bank* v *Green* [1981] 1 All ER 583 defined what was meant by a purchaser for 'money or money's worth'. In that case a father owned a farm. He granted his son an option to purchase the farm at any time in the next 10 years. The son should have registered the option as an estate contract, but omitted to do so.

Father and son later fell out. In order to spite the son, the father sold the farm (worth about £40,000) to his wife for just £500. The wife, of course, knew all about the option. Was she bound by it? The Court of Appeal, presided over by Lord Denning, found that the wife was bound by the option. That court said that 'money or money's worth' meant a fair price, which £500 clearly was not.

To the great relief of property lawyers, that decision was overturned by the House of Lords. The House of Lords held that 'money or money's worth' was synonymous with the traditional concept of 'value', except that marriage does not count as money or money's worth. Thus the wife was not bound by the option.

Would the wife have been bound if she had paid just £1 or some other nominal consideration?

The answer is, of course, 'No'. As we saw at **6.4.2.1**, even a nominal consideration constitutes 'value'.

8.3.5.2 Failure to register other land charges

Midland Bank v *Green* demonstrates what may be described as a 'tough' rule; tough, that is, on people who forget to register land charges such as estate contracts and restrictive covenants. An even tougher rule applies where there is a failure to register land charges of a type not mentioned in the previous heading. The charges subject to the even tougher rule include Class F rights of occupation and general equitable charges, as well as less important matters such as limited owner's charges.

This even tougher rule is that failure to register makes the interest in question void against a purchaser for value of any estate or interest in the land, **legal or equitable.** A particular point should be made about the Class F rights of occupation. In statistical terms, the number of Class F rights has been in decline ever since they were first invented in 1967. This is because nowadays almost all married couples buy their matrimonial homes in their joint names. However, there are still some marriages where the legal title to the home is in the husband's sole name. This is particularly true of marriages contracted in the 1940s and 1950s. In these cases the wife has 'Class F' rights.

In practice, however, the wife probably has not registered her right. Class F rights are usually registered only when the marriage gets into difficulties and the wife goes to see a solicitor. The solicitor will immediately (while the wife is still in the office) register the Class F charge, but it may be too late. The husband may have already sold, leased or mortgaged the home, or contracted to do so.

8.3.6 OTHER REGISTERS ASSOCIATED WITH THE LAND CHARGES REGISTER

There are four specialised registers (one of them now obsolete, but the other three of some significance) which are closely associated with the Land Charges Register. These registers used to be incorporated into the card-index system at Kidbrooke, and are now on the computer at Plymouth.

8.3.6.1 The Register of Pending Actions

If any court proceedings are brought which in any way relate to a piece of land, those proceedings should be registered as a 'pending action' (whether or not any proprietary rights are being claimed). This ensures that the outcome of the proceedings will bind any purchaser of the land.

You need not worry about the detailed law relating to 'pending actions', except that you do need to have a basic understanding of one point. This point involves another instance where land law and family law overlap. Where divorce proceedings are commenced, it is common for the less wealthy spouse (usually but not necessarily the wife) to claim a **property adjustment order** under ss. 23 to 25 of the Matrimonial Causes Act 1973. The divorce courts are given by these sections virtually unlimited powers to, in effect, redistribute property (of all kinds) belonging to one or other, or both of the spouses. *Inter alia*, the court can order:

(a) property to be transferred from one spouse to the other;

(b) property solely owned by one spouse to be shared between the spouses;

(c) property jointly owned by the spouses to be transferred into the name of one spouse;

(d) property jointly owned by the spouses to be sold and the proceeds divided as the court sees fit.

If an application for a property adjustment order does, or even may possibly, relate to a piece of land (the ex-matrimonial home or any other land), it should be registered as a pending action. In practice, in divorce proceedings where the legal title to the home is in the husband's name, the wife usually seeks a property adjustment order with respect to that home. This claim is **in addition to:**

(a)   her Class F rights under the Matrimonial Homes Act 1983, which (anyway) cease on decree absolute of divorce;

(b)   any constructive trust interest she may have by virtue of having made a substantial contribution to the cost of the matrimonial home.

The issue of property adjustment orders will crop up again in later chapters of this text. So read the case of *Perez-Adamson* v *Perez-Rivas* [1987] 3 All ER 20 in *Cases and Materials* (8.1.4.1). Note:

(a)   **that the outcome of the case illustrates the wisdom of the (ex-) wife registering a pending action; and**

(b)   **the important point made in the first paragraph of the brief judgment of Nicholls LJ.**

8.3.6.2   The Register of Writs and Orders Affecting Land

Any judgment or court order which affects a piece of land should be placed in this register. Though there are others, two kinds of order are commonly found in this register:

(a)   **An order charging land with a judgment debt.** A judgment debt arises where a court has awarded damages, but they have not been paid. Suppose you have successfully sued Charley Farnsbarn for damages for (say) breach of contract, and the court has awarded you £60,000 damages. He still refuses to pay, so you wish to enforce your judgment by 'execution' on Farnsbarn's property. Suppose Farnsbarn's most valuable asset is Highacre, worth £100,000. You should get a charging order against Highacre, and register it in the register of writs and orders. If Farnsbarn still does not pay the £60,000, you can force a sale of Highacre, and get your money out of the proceeds.

(b)   **A receiving order in bankruptcy.** (When somebody goes bankrupt all his property is vested, by court order, in his 'trustee in bankruptcy'.)

8.3.6.3   Register of Deeds of Arrangement

A few hundred such deeds (at most) are entered into every year. If somebody cannot pay all of his debts, we say that he is 'insolvent'. Normally, somebody who is insolvent goes bankrupt. If, however, an insolvent person has a limited number of creditors, all of whom are willing to accept payment of only a percentage of their debts, a 'deed of arrangement' is a simpler way out. The costs and stigma of bankruptcy are avoided.

A deed of arrangement usually transfers most/all of the insolvent person's assets to a trustee who holds the property for the benefit of the creditors.

8.3.6.4 The Register of Annuities

This is now totally obsolete.

8.3.7 SEARCHES OF THE LAND CHARGES REGISTER – THE IMPORTANCE OF THE OFFICIAL SEARCH CERTIFICATE

The usual method for a solicitor to request a search is by post, but it is also possible to telephone, telex, or call in at Plymouth personally. Though telephoned or telexed replies are given, you should always wait to receive the official search certificate through the post. (Searches requested by post take only a few days. During the crisis period at the beginning of the 1970s delays of six weeks were not unknown.)

8.3.7.1 The official search certificate is conclusive in favour of an intending purchaser

Provided the purchaser has searched against the correct names, if by some accident a correctly registered charge has been omitted from the search certificate, the purchaser will take free from the omitted charge. The registry's error will (in effect) destroy the rights of the owner of the charge. Such errors are, fortunately, extremely rare, and it appears that the registry would pay compensation to the owner of the charge which they had accidentally destroyed.

8.3.7.2 The official certificate 'priority period'

When buying land, a purchaser needs in practice to search the register a few days before completing the purchase. The priority period rule gives the purchaser protection against charges which are registered in the period between search and completion. A purchaser is not bound by a charge registered between search and completion provided:

(a) the purchase is completed within 15 working days from the date of the search certificate; **and**

(b) the charge registered in the intervening period was not registered in pursuance of a 'priority notice'.

Priority notices

It would appear that not much use is made in practice of this legal device. A priority notice can be used by someone who contemplates a land charge being created in his favour in the near future, and he wishes to ensure that his charge has priority over and is binding upon other transactions which happen to the relevant land.

For example, Xerxes is selling Greenacre to Yorick. It is envisaged that the conveyance will grant to Xerxes an option to repurchase Greenacre. Xerxes knows that Yorick intends to mortgage Greenacre to Zebedee to secure funds for the purchase price. Xerxes wishes to ensure his option binds Zebedee. He therefore enters a priority notice.

For the priority notice device to work:

(a) there must be an interval of at least 15 working days between the entry of the priority notice and the creation of the land charge; **and**

(b) the charge must be created and registered within 30 working days of the entry of the priority notice.

If these conditions are satisfied then registration of the charge is deemed to have taken place at the moment the charge was created.

Working days

Any day when the registry is open counts as a working day. Thus 15 working days is normally approximately three weeks, as the registry is open Monday to Fridays, excepting Bank and statutory holidays. There will usually be **three working days** between Christmas and New Year.

8.4   Overreachable Equitable Interests

Those equitable interests which are 'overreachable' fall into two related categories:

(a)   Interests under a strict settlement;

(b)   Interests under a trust for sale.

You may remember from **Chapter 2** that strict settlements and trusts for sale are two of the three possible forms of trust of land capable of existing after 1925 (see **2.4**). The 'beneficiaries' who acquire equitable interests under such trusts have usually not paid for them; they probably have to thank the generosity of the settlor. Having been given rights in the land, they should not have too much of a sense of grievance if they find that those rights are converted from being rights in land to rights in something else.

8.4.1   THE ESSENCE OF OVERREACHING

The essence of overreaching is that if the land is sold the rights of the beneficiaries of a strict settlement or trust for sale cannot bind the purchaser. Provided the purchase price is paid to the correct persons, the purchaser, irrespective of whether he had notice of the beneficiaries' rights, will take the land free from those rights.

The rights of the beneficiaries are not totally lost, however. These rights are transferred to the purchase price. This money will form a trust fund which must be invested. The beneficiaries will now have equitable interests in the trust fund.

8.4.2   OVERREACHING WHERE THERE IS A STRICT SETTLEMENT

In **7.6** I gave you an example where land was granted, 'To Alfred for life, remainder to Brian in fee tail, remainder to Charles in fee simple'. I also explained (the possibly surprising point) that under the Settled Land Act 1925, Alfred ('the life tenant in possession') is trustee of the legal estate in the land for himself and the other beneficiaries. Now we meet another possibly surprising point arising from the Settled Land Act 1925. By virtue of his status as 'life tenant', Alfred can sell the land, and the rights of Brian, Charles (and Alfred) **will be overreached**.

There is one condition, which may at this stage strike you as slightly odd. To achieve overreaching, the purchaser must pay the purchase price not to Alfred (who might squander the money) **but to independent people**, called 'trustees of the settlement for the purposes of the Settled Land Act'.

These 'SLA trustees' (who will have been appointed by the settlor in case there is a sale) must invest the proceeds of sale. In effect, a trust fund is created with those proceeds, **and the fund is regarded as representing the land**. During his life, Alfred, instead of enjoying the benefits from the land, will get the income from the trust fund. On Alfred's death, Brian will be entitled to the income from the fund. If, however, Brian bars the entail, he will have a 'fee simple' in the fund! He can then claim the fund from the SLA trustees, and the trust will be at an end.

If the entail granted to Brian is not barred and expires because Brian's descendants die out, Charles (or his successors if Charles is dead) will be entitled to the 'fee simple' in the fund. The fund will be claimed from the SLA trustees, and the trust will be at an end.

In 1985, 'Widetrees' (a very attractive Nottinghamshire farm) was made the subject of a strict settlement. The land was granted 'to Timothy for life, remainder to Winifred for life, remainder to Yorick in fee simple'. Last month Timothy sold Widetrees to Philip. Philip paid the purchase price to Tam and Tom, who were the 'trustees for the purposes of the Settled Land Act'. Timothy died last week.

Winifred and Yorick feel hard done by: 'We have been defrauded of our land,' they complain.

What would you say in answer to their complaint?

You would first remind them that they were **given** their interests under the settlement, perhaps citing the old proverb, 'Don't look a gift-horse in the mouth'. Then you would stress that the law expressly allowed Timothy to sell the land, **but did not allow him to keep the proceeds.** Tam and Tom must now invest the proceeds and pay the income from the investments to Winifred. When Winifred dies, Yorick will become outright owner of the investments.

8.4.3 OVERREACHING WHERE THERE IS A TRUST FOR SALE

At **2.4.2** we had a basic explanation of the trust for sale. We also considered an example: Greenacres is conveyed by X to Tim and Tom as Trustees with a direction that they must sell the property and invest the proceeds; the investments are to be held in trust for X's children.

Where there is a trust for sale the process of overreaching is very simple to follow. When the trustees actually decide to sell, the purchase price is paid to the trustees themselves. The only condition is that there must be at least two trustees. In the example just given, any purchaser will get the land free from the rights of X's children provided they pay the money to Tim and Tom. Tim and Tom then invest that money and hold the fund for the benefit of X's children. What could be simpler!

8.4.4 OVERREACHING ON A SALE BY PERSONAL REPRESENTATIVES

This is a point where land law and succession law overlap, and it need be dealt with only briefly. As I explained in **2.5.2.1**, where a person dies his affairs are wound up by personal representatives, who will be either executors or administrators. Almost all deceased persons leave some debts (even if it's only the gas and electricity bills). Moreover, if the deceased was wealthy, there may be a huge taxation bill to pay. The personal representatives of the deceased have a completely free hand to sell whatever assets of the deceased they like so that they can pay the debts and/or taxes.

If the personal representatives sell any land owned by the deceased, the purchaser will always get a good title. The rights of people left property by the will are always overreached. Moreover, a purchaser from personal representatives is under no duty to check whether a sale is really necessary.

Suppose George (a fairly wealthy widower) has just died. His will appoints Eddie and Edwina to be his executors. He leaves his large house, 'High Manor', to his son Alfred. The 'residue' (i.e. the rest) of his property he leaves to be divided equally between his three daughters, Betty, Cath, and Diana.

Eddie and Edwina need to sell something in order to pay debts/taxes. The 'residue' consists almost entirely of shares in small family private companies. Such shares are not easy to sell. They therefore sell High Manor. Alfred cannot object to the sale. He will however, be able to claim compensation (the value of High Manor) out of the residue.

Suppose, however, that the residue consists of shares in large public limited companies ('PLCs') quoted on the stock exchange. Such shares are very easy to sell. Eddie and Edwina still choose to sell High Manor. They are perfectly within their powers to do so. The purchaser (who, remember, need not check whether a sale is necessary) will get a good title and Alfred will still have to claim compensation out of the residue.

8.4.5   OVERREACHING ON A SALE BY A MORTGAGEE OF MORTGAGED LAND

This point can be left until we deal with the law of mortgages in **Chapter 30**.

8.5   Equitable Interests Still Subject to the Doctrine of Notice

Quite a few such interests remain, indeed rather more than was anticipated by the 1925 legislators:

(a)   An equitable fee simple under a bare trust.

(b)   An equitable mortgage where the mortgagee does take the title deeds. (We will come back to this one later.)

(c)   A restrictive covenant created before 1926.

(d)   A restrictive covenant contained in a lease.

(e)   An equitable easement or equitable profit created before 1926.

(f)   A right of entry for breach of a condition subsequent.

(g)   A licence by estoppel (proprietary estoppel).

(h)   A right under a constructive trust.

8.6   Conclusion

In this chapter we have seen that, in an endeavour to reduce the importance of the equitable doctrine of notice, the 1925 legislators decreed that several important equitable interests should be registrable as land charges, and that other interests (especially interests under a trust of land) should be overreachable. But the doctrine of notice **was not abolished.**

As we have just seen, there are quite a few rights still subject to the doctrine. It is particularly worth noting that (statistically) there are still a lot of 'old' (pre-1926) restrictive covenants in existence. However, it is the explosion of rights in the last two categories just listed ((g) and (h)) which (more than anything) accounts for the continued importance of the doctrine of notice. Indeed, constructive trust interests occur so frequently that they can be described as 'commonplace'. I should add, though, that rights under a constructive trust can sometimes be overreached. How this can come about will have to wait until we consider the law of co-ownership (see **16.4**).

8.7   End of Chapter Assessment Question

In 1960 Ruth purchased the fee simple in Grand Villa, a large country house with two acres of grounds. The title was unregistered in an area which did not become an area of compulsory registration until 1988. Grand Villa was conveyed to Ruth in her sole name.

Four weeks ago William purchased Grand Villa from Ruth. Since the execution of the conveyance, the following matters have come to light.

(a)   Martin, Ruth's husband, has returned from an extended business trip to Malaysia, and is alarmed to discover that Ruth has sold Grand Villa to William. Martin claims that, since in 1980 he paid £200,000 for a total reconstruction of Grand Villa, he has 'rights' which bind William.

(b)   David has arrived at Grand Villa and has produced a document (not in the form of a deed) which Ruth and David signed six months ago. The document is a lease for fifteen years of part of the grounds of Grand Villa.

(c)   Harry, owner of neighbouring Blackview, has arrived at Grand Villa and produced a deed executed some time in the 1920s. (The exact date is difficult to read.) This deed was executed by the then owner of Grand Villa, and contains a restrictive covenant in favour of the owners of Blackview to the effect that Grand Villa is to be used for residential purposes only. William plans to convert Grand Villa into a conference centre.

Advise William as to whether any of these matters will affect him.

See *Cases and Materials* (8.3) for a specimen answer.

CHAPTER NINE

REGISTRATION OF TITLE – THE BASIC PRINCIPLES

9.1 Objectives

By the end of this chapter you should:

■ be able to explain the circumstances in which the title to a fee simple estate must be registered;

■ be able to explain the circumstances in which the title to a leasehold estate must be registered;

■ appreciate what happens when there is a first registration of an estate;

■ be able to distinguish between the various 'grades of title' granted by the Land Registry;

■ be familiar with the form which the 'land certificate' takes.

9.2 Introduction

The discussion in **Chapters 6, 7 and 8** focused exclusively on the legal principles which relate to land which is unregistered title. In view of the fact that the whole country is now an area of compulsory registration this may seem a rather artificial approach. However, you should always remember two things. First, there is still a lot of land which is unregistered title. Secondly, in order to understand the principles of registered land, some understanding of the principles governing unregistered land is essential. Unless there is further radical reform in English land law, I cannot see it ever being possible for land law teachers to ignore the principles governing unregistered title.

In this chapter we will be dealing with the basic principles which govern the substantive registration of **estates** in land. The position of 'third party rights' (restrictive covenants, easements, etc.) existing against a registered estate will be discussed in **Chapter 10.**

9.3 Categories of Rights in Registered Land

With registered land, the division of property rights into legal rights and equitable rights is (while not irrelevant) of less importance than with unregistered land. For most purposes rights in registered land divide into four categories:

(a) **Estates and interests capable of substantive registration**: fees simple; leases over 21 years.

(b) **Overriding interests**: for example, legal leases not exceeding 21 years; legal easements; legal or equitable profits. These interests bind the registered proprietor and any purchaser from him irrespective of:

      (i)   whether they are entered on the register in any way;

      (ii)   whether the proprietor knew or ought to have known of them.

(Cf. **legal interests** in unregistered land.)

(c) **Minor interests**: for example, restrictive covenants; estate contracts. These interests bind the purchaser of a registered title only if they are 'protected' in some way by an entry on the **register of title**. (Rather confusingly, overreachable equitable interests are also classified as 'minor' interests. They are, as with unregistered title, overreached provided the purchase price is paid to the correct trustees.)

(d) **Mortgage by registered charge**: the standard form of registered land mortgage.

9.4   Circumstances in Which Registration is Compulsory

Though we touched on this in **Chapter 2**, it would be a good idea if we recapped, and added one or two new points.

9.4.1   COMPULSORY REGISTRATION IN A COMPULSORY AREA

The estate transferred (or created) must be registered if there has been:

(a)   a conveyance on sale of a fee simple;

(b)   a grant of a lease for more than 21 years, even if the estate in reversion is not registered;

(c)   an assignment of a lease with more than 21 years unexpired, even if the estate in reversion is not registered.

SAQ 48

In what circumstances will you encounter an unregistered freehold title in areas which have been 'compulsory registration' for many years?

You will meet such a title whenever an unregistered freehold has not been **sold** since the date on which the relevant area became compulsory.

9.4.2   COMPULSORY REGISTRATION IN NON-COMPULSORY AREAS

Though this somewhat paradoxical concept is now past history as the whole of England and Wales is now a 'compulsory area', it should be mentioned briefly. A fee simple or lease had to be registered, even though it was situated in a non-compulsory area:

(a)   on the exercise by a council tenant of the 'right to buy' under the Housing Act 1985;

(b)   on the granting of a lease for 21 years or more where the estate in reversion was registered.

9.5   Voluntary Registration

Prior to 1966, voluntary registration was possible at any time, whatever the circumstances and wherever the land was situated. After 1966, voluntary registration was still permitted without restriction in **compulsory** areas.

In **non-compulsory** areas the Land Registration Act 1966 and rules made under that Act limited voluntary registration to:

(a)   exceptional situations such as lost title deeds;

(b)   developments where a large area of land was being sold off in at least 20 units. (This used to apply only to housing estates, but in 1982 the rule was extended to all developments.)

With the whole country being now a compulsory area, we are in effect back to the pre-1966 position.

9.6   Register of Estates not Register of Plots

Most foreign systems of land registration (e.g., the much-admired German and Swedish systems) work on the basis that for each plot of land there will be just one file kept at the registry. That file will show who owns the plot of land, all leases of the plot, and all third party rights affecting the plot.

The English system is not as efficient. There are very good geographical 'index maps', but each **estate** in a plot of land (except leases for not more than 21 years which cannot be registered) has a separate file.

Suppose Leonard owns the fee simple in Blue House, situated in central London. He grants a lease of Blue House to Teresa for 100 years. Teresa sub-leases Blue House to Susan for 50 years. How many files will there be in relation to Blue House?

Each of the three estates must be registered separately, and therefore there will be three files.

Another curiosity of the English system of land registration is that one (quite commonly) encounters a situation where a lease is registered, but the fee simple out of which it is derived is not.

How could this situation arise?

This situation would arise where the landlord acquired his fee simple **before** the relevant area became compulsory, but granted a lease for more than 21 years **after** the area became compulsory. (It could also arise where the landlord acquired his fee simple before the relevant area became compulsory, granted a long lease **before** the date set for compulsory registration, and then that lease is assigned with more than 21 years unexpired **after** the area became compulsory.)

9.7   Procedure Where a Sale or Lease Gives Rise to First Registration

The transaction goes through basically as an unregistered transaction, but with additional stages at the end:

(a)   The purchaser investigates the title deeds, inspects the land and searches the Land Charges Register.

(b)   The legal title passes on the execution of the conveyance.

(c)   The purchaser must apply for first registration within two months of the execution of the conveyance.

(d)   If he fails to do so, the legal title revests in the vendor on trust for the purchaser.

(e)   The purchaser can then apply for late registration, but he may have to pay a late fee.

9.7.1   APPLICATIONS FOR FIRST REGISTRATION

Failure to register within two months is (unfortunately) not that unusual. The sanctions for failure to register within the two months are weak, and may strike you as slightly strange.

As I have just stated, the legal title revests in the vendor on trust for the purchaser. Yet the vendor has almost certainly moved away, and has no idea of his trustee status! Equally, when the purchaser does belatedly register, the legal title revests in the purchaser without the vendor ever knowing (or needing to know) that he has lost his trustee status!

The only real sanction against late registrations is that the registry **may** charge a late fee. It seems that it very rarely does so in practice.

ACTIVITY 20

Dumphouse is unregistered title. Joe Gormless now purchases Dumphouse. Joe does his own conveyancing. Dumphouse is conveyed to Joe, but he omits to register his title. Consider when (and by whom) the error is likely to be discovered.

There are I think three possibilities. First, when Joe comes to sell Dumphouse, the new purchaser's solicitor will discover the error. Secondly, if Joe wants to mortgage Dumphouse, the potential lender will investigate Joe's title and discover the error. Thirdly, when Joe dies, his personal representatives will probably discover the error.

On an application for first registration, the purchaser produces all the title deeds to the registry. The Land Registry then conducts its own (very thorough) investigation of title. It decides what grade of title to grant (see **9.8**). When in the course of its investigations it discovers (in the deeds or on the Land Charges Register) 'minor interests' such as restrictive covenants, it enters the appropriate notices on the register. ('Notices' will be explained in **Chapter 10**.)

On first and later registrations the registry issues a **land certificate** to the **registered proprietor**.

9.7.2 PROCEDURE ON TRANSFER OF A REGISTERED TITLE

(a) The vendor proves his title by reference to the register. Note that the purchaser will still have to check whether there are any overriding interests, as these bind him even though they are not usually mentioned on the register.

(b) The vendor executes a document known as a **land transfer**. This must be a deed. It is, for the purposes of the 1925 property legislation, a 'conveyance'. However, unlike a conveyance of unregistered land, a land transfer does not vest the legal title in the purchaser.

(c) The purchaser applies for registration, producing the land transfer and the land certificate. (There is no time limit within which the application must be made.) The changing of the files at the registry passes the legal title, though the change in legal ownership is retrospective to the date when application for registration was made. A new land certificate is issued to the new registered proprietor.

9.8 Grades of Title

9.8.1 FREEHOLDS

Once the registry has investigated the title of an applicant for first registration, it can grant to him as registered proprietor one of three grades of title. In almost all cases an

absolute grade is granted. However, in a significant minority of cases (about 1 per cent of all titles) only a **possessory** grade is granted. A **qualified** grade is also possible, but they are extremely rare.

9.8.1.1   Absolute title

This is the grade of title which is granted where the applicant's title is sound, i.e. the title deeds are in order and it appears that nobody else could possibly claim the land. Where an absolute title is granted, the government (through the agency of the land registry) is in effect saying to the registered proprietor (and anybody who wants to buy the land from him) 'We guarantee that you own this land'.

Nevertheless, a fee simple registered with absolute title is subject to:

(a)   overriding interests;

(b)   minor interests protected by entry on the register;

(c)   if the registered proprietor is a trustee, equitable interests under the trust of which he has notice.

9.8.1.2   Possessory title

This is the grade of title which is granted where the applicant for registration's claim to ownership is debatable. It particularly occurs where the title deeds he can produce are inadequate, or if he cannot produce any at all. The applicant may even admit that the land was not originally his, but claim that he now has a title by virtue of 'adverse possession'. (As we saw in **2.5.2.1** when discussing investigation of title, the adverse possession rule means that if somebody has been in control of a piece of land for 12 years, all rival claims are normally automatically destroyed by lapse of time.)

When it is first granted, a possessory title is of only limited comfort to the registered proprietor. The Registry is merely accepting that the proprietor is currently in control of the land; it does not guarantee that he is owner. Any rival claimant to the land whose rights have not been time-barred under the adverse possession rule can still reclaim the land.

The great value of a possessory title is in the long term. If somebody is registered with a possessory title to a piece of land and remains in undisputed possession of that land for 12 years after registration, his title will normally be upgraded to 'absolute'. He then (just like any other proprietor with an absolute title) will have a clear guarantee that he is undisputed owner of the land.

9.8.1.3   Qualified title

This grade of title is extremely rare. It is granted where there is some minor question mark over an otherwise sound claim to ownership.

A qualified title is in effect 'absolute but for such-and-such'. A qualified title is the same as absolute, apart from a specified exception against which the proprietor is not guaranteed. This exception (qualification) can be either:

(a)   with respect to claims arising before a certain date; or

(b)   with respect to claims arising under a specified instrument.

For example, if a document of title was only partly legible, the Registry might qualify a grant of title, saying that the proprietor is not protected from claims arising under the partially legible document.

(The paucity of qualified titles may perhaps be explained by the Land Registry's policy on technical defects. If there is an application for registration of a title, but there is some technical defect in the documents, e.g., documents going back 13 but not 15 years, the registry usually deliberately ignores the technical defect and grants an absolute title.)

9.8.2 LEASEHOLDS

There are four grades of title which may be granted to a lease: absolute, 'good leasehold', qualified, and possessory. **Possessory leasehold** is granted where the landlord's reversion to the lease is registered with a possessory title. **Qualified leasehold** is virtually unknown. That leaves absolute leasehold and good leasehold, both of which are common, though the percentage of 'good leasehold' should gradually decline.

9.8.2.1 Good leasehold

The existence of the good leasehold grade of title is really an unfortunate by-product of an outdated common law rule which ought to be abolished. That rule is that when a tenant takes a lease (even a very long lease) he is not entitled to examine the landlord's title deeds; neither is he entitled to insist that the deeds be produced to third parties such as the Land Registry. In effect, the tenant must take a chance that the landlord owns the land!

Where a lease for more than 21 years is granted out of a reversion which is not registered, the lease must be registered. Normally it can only be registered with good leasehold title, as neither the Registry nor the tenant will have access to the landlord's title deeds. The granting of a good leasehold title guarantees that the lease is valid and that the tenant is owner of that lease, **but only on the assumption** that the lessor's title to the reversion is sound. If it turns out that the landlord was leasing out land which was not his, there is no come-back against the Registry!

9.8.2.2 Absolute leasehold

This is an out-and-out guarantee that the lease is valid and that the tenant is owner of the lease. It is in practice granted where either:

(a) the landlord's reversion is already registered with absolute title; or

(b) (rare in practice) the tenant has been able to persuade the landlord to produce his title deeds to the registry. (This may happen if the tenant is some large organisation which has made it clear that it will take a lease of the property only if it has access to the title deeds.)

I said at 9.8.2 that 'the percentage of good leasehold should gradually decline'. Why is this so?

Good leasehold is designed for the (currently quite common) situation where the lease is registered but the freehold from which it is derived is not registered. As more and more freeholds are registered, there will be proportionately **fewer** registered leases created out of unregistered freeholds. (See also point (a) below under the heading 'Upgrading of Title'.)

9.8.3 UPGRADING OF TITLE

This area of law has been simplified by the Land Registration Act 1986. (We need not worry about the pre-1986 rules.) In appropriate cases the registered proprietor may apply for an upgrading of his title; but the registrar can (and often does) act without waiting for an application.

Of the four situations listed below, (a) and (b) occur frequently, while (c) and (d) are (in the nature of things) rare.

The registrar may upgrade a title in the following cases:

(a) A good leasehold may be upgraded to absolute if the registrar 'is satisfied as to the title to the freehold and the title to any intermediate leasehold'. In practice, where a registered lease has been created out of an unregistered fee simple, and that fee simple is **later** registered with an absolute title, the lease will be immediately upgraded from good leasehold to absolute.

(b) A possessory freehold may be upgraded to absolute if the title has been registered for 12 years, or the registrar is for some other reason satisfied that the proprietor's title is sound. As indicated at **9.8.1.2**, if a possessory title has been registered without challenge for 12 years, it will be upgraded to absolute more or less automatically.

(c) A possessory leasehold may be upgraded to good leasehold if the title has been registered for 12 years.

(d) A qualified title may be upgraded to absolute (or good leasehold) if the registrar is now satisfied that the title is sound.

9.9 The Form of the Register

Study the specimen land certificate in *Cases and Materials* (9.4), noting carefully the various divisions within the document.

The current form of the Land Register is a file for each title (estate) registered. The file consists of at least four pages. The file is divided into three parts, called:

(a) The Property Register;

(b) The Proprietorship Register;

(c) The Charges Register.

The use of the word 'Register' is in this context very unfortunate. When I first came across it as a student I was totally confused! I thought there were **three** files for each **title** registered! But in fact there is only one file, divided into three **parts**, which I will call the Property Part, the Proprietorship Part, and the Charges Part.

9.9.1 THE PROPERTY PART

In this part of the Land Register there is a verbal description of the land, and a reference to the 'file plan'. The boundaries shown on this file plan are normally only 'general', i.e. approximate. (Another feature of English land registration strange to foreign eyes is that our system does not fix the exact boundaries of each plot. The Land Registry like to boast that their plans are **in fact** accurate to within a few inches. No doubt they usually are, but in *Lee* v *Barrey* [1957] Ch 251, there was a discrepancy of eight feet between the plan and the actual boundary on the ground!)

The property part indicates the estate registered, and in the case of a lease the duration of the lease. In the case of a lease created out of a registered reversion, it will contain a reference to the 'title' (i.e. file) number of that reversion.

If the land is 'dominant' with respect to any easements or restrictive covenants (i.e. benefited by such rights), the existence of such rights may be 'noted' in this section, but unfortunately this 'noting' is not mandatory. (Why 'unfortunately' will become apparent when we deal with the law of restrictive covenants.)

9.9.2 THE PROPRIETORSHIP PART

This part of the Land Register states the grade of title. It gives the name and address of the registered proprietor(s) and it indicates the cautions, inhibitions, and restrictions affecting the right to deal with the land. (We consider these concepts in **Chapter 10.**)

9.9.3 THE CHARGES PART

This part of the Land Register contains 'notices' of minor interests such as restrictive covenants. It contains a note of any mortgage by registered charge created out of the estate registered and a note of any other registered estate (i.e. a lease) created out of the estate registered.

9.10 The Land Certificate

This is a copy of the relevant register file, which is issued whenever an estate is first registered or is subsequently transferred to a new owner. In principle it is issued to the registered proprietor, but if the estate is mortgaged by registered charge the land certificate is kept at the Registry. (In practice, as a result of the rule which operates when the land is mortgaged, an enormous number of certificates are kept at the Registry.)

The land certificate is not 'a title deed' or a 'document of title'. As a new certificate is created only when the estate in question is transferred, it may not accurately reflect the current state of the register. A purchaser should therefore never rely on the certificate, but should always search the register.

The land certificate is nevertheless an important document. It must be produced to the Registry (if not already there):

(a) on an application to transfer the title;

(b) on an application to enter a notice or restriction. (This latter point is of considerable significance, as we shall see at **10.4.2**.)

9.11 Conclusion

In this chapter we have discussed the rules governing which estates must be registered, what grades of title can be granted, and the form of the register and the land certificate. These rules may be rather dull and mechanical, but they are extremely important. Perhaps the most crucial point is that to talk of 'registered **land**' is, strictly speaking, inaccurate. A piece of land (i.e. the physical area upon which you can walk) is never registered. It is the 'estate(s)' in that land which is or are capable of registration.

CHAPTER TEN

OVERRIDING INTERESTS AND MINOR INTERESTS

10.1 Objectives

By the end of this chapter you should:

■ be familiar with the important concept of 'overriding interests';

■ be able to explain the significance of Land Registration Act 1925, s. 70(1)(g), and the complexities surrounding this very special overriding interest;

■ appreciate that 'minor interests' have a major role to play in registered land;

■ be familiar with the concepts 'notices', 'cautions' and 'restrictions', and be able to distinguish between them.

10.2 Introduction

In the previous chapter we saw that fees simple and leases for more than 21 years are capable of substantive registration. What, then, is the position of leases for not more than 21 years, and third party rights such as easements, profits, restrictive covenants and constructive trust interests?

Leaving aside mortgages of a registered estate (a topic we consider in **Chapter 33**), all third party rights against a registered estate are either **overriding** interests or **minor** interests. If a third party right against a registered estate is 'overriding' then it automatically binds all purchasers of that estate. (This is roughly comparable to a legal interest against an unregistered title.) If a third party right is not overriding then it will be a minor interest, and it will be binding on purchasers of the estate only if protected by some kind of entry on the register. (This is roughly comparable to a registrable land charge.)

10.3 Overriding Interests

It is extremely important to know whether a third party right (such as an easement) is overriding or minor. The types of overriding interest are listed in s. 70(1) of the Land Registration Act 1925. Many of these types of overriding interest are unimportant, and here we will concentrate on the important ones. Section 70(1) consists of a number of lettered paragraphs, considered in greater detail below.

10.3.1 '(a) . . . PROFITS À PRENDRE, . . . AND EASEMENTS NOT BEING EQUITABLE EASEMENTS REQUIRED TO BE PROTECTED BY NOTICE ON THE REGISTER'

The wording of s. 70(1)(a) is somewhat archaic, but certain consequences are clear:

(i)   A legal profit is an overriding interest.

(i)   An equitable profit is also an overriding interest. (Contrast unregistered land, where an equitable profit is registrable as a land charge.)

(iii)   A legal easement is an overriding interest.

That leaves equitable easements. Now on the wording of paragraph (a) you are probably thinking, as everybody used to think, that equitable easements are not overriding interests but minor interests, and that to be binding upon a purchaser they need to be protected by an entry on the register. However, in *Celsteel Ltd* v *Alton House Holdings Ltd* [1985] 2 All ER 562, Scott J, by some very strained logic, managed to hold that an equitable easement was also an overriding interest within s. 70(1)(a). To put it mildly, this decision appears to be wrong.

You have a client who owns an *equitable* easement against a registered fee simple. Do you take the position, 'Great! My client has got an overriding interest applying the *Celsteel* case – no need to put an entry on the register!?'

You would be well advised to play safe and assume that the *Celsteel* case is wrong. You should assume your client has only a minor interest, and protect it by an entry of a 'notice' or a 'caution'.

10.3.2 '(f) . . . RIGHTS ACQUIRED OR IN THE COURSE OF BEING ACQUIRED UNDER THE LIMITATION ACTS'

Exactly how the law of adverse possession applies to registered land will be explained in **Chapter 21**.

10.3.3 '(i) RIGHTS UNDER LOCAL LAND CHARGES . . .'

Local land charges have not been mentioned before, as they are a matter peripheral to a study of pure land law. Each District Council in England and Wales keeps a register of local land charges, and the system of local charges operates irrespective of whether title to the land is registered or unregistered. Thus, when buying land, the wise purchaser always 'does a local search'.

What sort of matters are local land charges? Basically they cover 'public law' rights such as the special charge which sometimes exists for the making up of a road; the 'listing' of a building as of historic interest; tree preservation orders, and many other matters connected with town and country planning.

10.3.4 '(k) LEASES GRANTED FOR A TERM NOT EXCEEDING TWENTY-ONE YEARS'

This is an enormously important category of overriding interest, and there are a number of points which must be noted carefully.

First, the Land Registration Act 1925, s. 70(1)(k) must not in any circumstances be confused with s. 70(1)(g) of the Act, which we will be considering next! (Depending on the circumstances a lease may come within both paragraphs, one but not the other, or neither!)

Secondly, it is clear that paragraph **(k)** is confined to legal leases. An equitable lease can **never** be overriding within s. 70(1)(k) (though, as we shall see, it may well come within s. 70(1)(g)).

Thirdly, and perhaps most importantly, a legal lease for not more than 21 years (and that includes periodic tenancies) is automatically an overriding interest within s. 70(1)(k). This is so even if the tenant is **currently not occupying** the property. It is also so even if the tenant refuses to tell enquirers what his rights are with respect to the land.

Lastly, a rather obscure point. Prior to the Land Registration Act 1986, a legal lease where the landlord charged a premium (i.e. a capital lump sum) for the granting of the lease was excluded from s. 70(1)(k). The 1986 Act removed this anomalous exception.

10.3.5 SECTION 70(1)(g) A VERY DIFFERENT AND IMPORTANT OVERRIDING INTEREST

The Land Registration Act 1925, s. 70(1)(g) sets out the following overriding interest:

> The rights of every person in actual occupation of the land or in receipt of the rents and profits thereof, save where enquiry is made of such person and the rights are not disclosed.

Even 20 years ago, the extreme importance of this provision was not fully realised by many lawyers. Indeed, some did not really see its significance until the decision of the House of Lords in *Williams and Glyn's Bank* v *Boland* [1980] 2 All ER 408. Before we consider *Boland's* case, the following story illustrates the impact of s. 70(1)(g):

A tale of two fields

Letitia owned in fee simple two adjoining fields, Upper Field and Redwood Field. Because she acquired Upper Field a long time ago and Redwood Field only recently, Upper Field is **unregistered** title, while Redwood Field is **registered** title.

Last year Letitia met Terri. They signed an agreement under which Letitia agreed to lease both fields to Terri for 10 years. Terri took possession of both fields, and has remained in possession ever since. However, as the agreement was not in the form of a deed, Terri has only an equitable lease of the two fields. Moreover, Terri has not taken any legal advice, and therefore she has not taken any steps to register her equitable lease as a land charge.

Letitia has now sold both fields to Rachel for £30,000. Rachel knew that Terri was occupying the fields, but did not ask Terri what right(s) she (Terri) claimed over the fields. Rachel now wants to evict Terri as quickly as possible.

Does Terri's equitable lease bind Rachel?

Your answer to this question may have required some thought. The answer is both 'No' and 'Yes'. The answer with respect to Upper Field is 'No'. Terri should have registered her equitable lease as a land charge. As she did not, it will be void against a purchaser for money or money's worth. It will be void even against a purchaser who knew of her equitable lease. (Remember *Hollington* v *Rhodes* and *Midland Bank* v *Green* at **8.3**.)

The answer with respect to Redwood Field is 'Yes'. Terri was (and still is) in 'actual occupation' of that field. Rachel never asked her what her rights were. Thus she has an overriding interest within s. 70(1)(g).

If Terri had not been occupying Redwood Field, her equitable lease would have been only a 'minor interest' which would have needed protection by an entry on the register of title. But as she was occupying the field, s. 70(1)(g) promotes her interest into an overriding interest. If, however, Rachel had, before buying Redwood Field, made enquiries of Terri, and Terri had replied, 'Go to B . . . !', Terri's rudeness would deprive her of her overriding interest.

10.3.6 *WILLIAMS AND GLYN'S BANK* V *BOLAND* [1980] 2 ALL ER 408

The material facts of this case are very simple. Mr Boland ('H') bought a house, registered title, in his sole name. His wife ('W') made substantial contributions to the cost of acquisition, and therefore acquired a constructive trust interest in the house.

While H and W were living happily together in the house, H decided to borrow some more money. Without telling his wife, he borrowed it from the bank. He granted the bank a mortgage by registered charge. The bank did not bother to send an employee to the house, and certainly did not ask W any questions.

H defaulted on repaying the loan, and the bank wished to enforce its mortgage by taking possession of the house and selling. Was W's interest binding on the bank? If it was, the bank was effectively prevented from enforcing its security.

To almost audible groans from all the big banks (*Boland* was very much a test case) the House of Lords unanimously found that W's constructive trust interest was an overriding interest by virtue of s. 70(1)(g) of the Land Registration Act 1925 and was therefore binding on the bank.

Their Lordships, in a judgment given by Lord Wilberforce, clarified a number of points about s. 70(1)(g) and related matters. The first two points should be noted in particular, as they may come as a bit of a surprise:

(i) Their Lordships pointed out (what land lawyers already knew) that the equitable doctrine of notice had no application to registered land.

(ii) It therefore followed that, as 'the rule in *Hunt* v *Luck*' (see **6.4.4.2**) is part of the equitable doctrine of notice, s. 70(1)(g) is not 'the rule in *Hunt* v *Luck*'. Section 70(1)(g) is a rule for registered land akin to (but not necessarily identical with) *Hunt* v *Luck*.

(iii) The word 'rights' in s. 70(1)(g) should be construed to cover every proprietary interest in land. Every type of property right in land can be an overriding interest provided there is actual occupation at the relevant time by its owner. The only exception is the 'rights of occupation' conferred on a spouse who does not own the matrimonial home by the Matrimonial Homes Acts. The Matrimonial Homes Act 1983, s. 2(8)(b) expressly excludes 'rights of occupation' from the scope of s. 70(1)(g).

(iv) As 'rights' in s. 70(1)(g) includes all proprietary rights (except those under the Matrimonial Homes Act), the word 'rights' includes an equitable interest arising by way of constructive trust where Y has contributed substantially to the cost of acquisition of property the legal title to which is registered in X's name. Thus, although Mrs. Boland's rights of occupation under the Matrimonial Homes Act 1983 could not be overriding, her **entirely separate** constructive trust interest could be overriding within s. 70(1)(g).

(v) The words 'actual occupation' must be construed literally.

(vi) Consequently, if a registered proprietor is occupying the property but members of his family (or even strangers) are living there too, these members of the family or strangers **are 'in actual occupation'**. Their Lordships rejected the argument that where the registered proprietor is in actual occupation, nobody else can be.

(vii) Their Lordships very strongly disapproved *Caunce* v *Caunce* [1969] 1 All ER 722. The material facts of that case were identical to those in *Boland*, except that the title to the house was unregistered. The judge held that, for the purposes of the rule in *Hunt* v *Luck*, W was not in occupation of the home and that therefore the mortgagee did not have constructive notice of her equitable interest. *Caunce* has never been formally overruled, but everybody (particularly legal advisers to purchasers and mortgagees) acts on the assumption that it is wrong.

10.3.7 *ABBEY NATIONAL BUILDING SOCIETY* v *CANN* **[1990] 1 All ER 1085**

This fairly recent House of Lords case further clarified s. 70(1)(g). The essential facts of the case are as follows. George Cann purchased a maisonette in his sole name. His mother (who lived with him) made a substantial contribution to the cost of acquisition and thus was entitled to a constructive trust interest.

At about 11.45 a.m. on 13 August ('the date of completion') furniture removers acting on behalf of Mrs Cann started laying carpets and bringing in her furniture. (She was on holiday in the Netherlands.) At 12.20 p.m. the same day, a land transfer was executed in favour of George. As is normal in these situations, he immediately executed a mortgage in favour of the building society. The society were of course lending a substantial proportion of the purchase price, and were taking the mortage as security for the loan.

Both the land transfer and the mortgage were registered on 13 September ('the date of registration'), by which time Mrs Cann was living in the maisonette with her son. (A delay of one month before registration is by no means excessive.)

As you have probably guessed, George defaulted in repaying the loan. Mrs Cann then claimed that her constructive trust interest was an overriding interest under s. 70(1)(g) binding on the building society.

The principal issue which their Lordships had to decide was, on what date a person must be in 'actual occupation' to have an overriding interest under s. 70(1)(g) binding upon a purchaser/mortgagee. Was it the date of completion of the sale/mortage, or was it the (inevitably later) date of registration? Their Lordships held in favour of the 'date of completion'; on the facts of the case, 12.20 p.m. on 13 August.

Was Mrs Cann in occupation at that time (after all, men were fitting her carpets and bringing in her furniture)? Their Lordships found that this activity did not amount to 'actual occupation'.

10.3.8   THE MEANING OF ACTUAL OCCUPATION

Lord Oliver, who delivered the only speech in *Abbey National* v *Cann*, elaborated on the issue of what constitutes 'actual occupation':

> It is, perhaps, dangerous to suggest any test for what is essentially a question of fact, for occupation is a concept which may have different connotations according to the nature and purpose of the property which is claimed to be occupied. It does not necessarily, I think, involve the personal presence of the person claiming to occupy. A caretaker or the representative of a company can occupy, I should have thought, on behalf of his employer. On the other hand, it does in my judgment, involve some degree of permanence and continuity which would rule out mere fleeting presence.

10.3.9   *STRAND SECURITIES* v *CASWELL* [1965] 1 All ER 820

This relatively old case highlights how quirkish s. 70(1)(g) can become. Caswell took a 39-year lease of a London flat. As the lease was for over 21 years, it should have been registered. Caswell did not register the lease. The practical effect of this failure to register the lease was that it took effect only as an equitable lease. The reversion was sold to Strand, who would be bound by Caswell's lease only if it was an overriding interest within s. 70(1)(g).

Caswell did not personally live in the flat, but did drop in for the night from time-to-time when he was in London. The permanent occupant of the flat was his step-daughter. He let her live there **rent-free**, as her marriage had broken down.

The Court of Appeal held that Caswell was not in actual occupation and therefore he had no overriding interest within s. 70(1)(g). Later cases, especially *Abbey Nationa* v *Cann*, underline the correctness of this conclusion. Two startling points should however be noticed:

(i)   If Caswell had charged his step-daughter a rent (even a nominal rent) he would have been 'in receipt of rents' and therefore would have had an overriding interest under s. 70(1)(g).

(ii)   Alternatively, if he had employed her as his caretaker, he would (as *Cann* confirms) have been **through her agency** 'in actual occupation' and therefore have an overriding interest under s. 70(1)(g).

SAQ 54

Leonard was the registered (freehold) owner of two houses, Alpha House and Beta House. He granted an *equitable* lease of both houses to Tony. Tony was going abroad, so he sublet Alpha House to Susan and arranged for his friend Charley to live in Beta House as caretaker. Leonard has just sold both houses to Rowena. Is Rowena bound by Tony's equitable lease?

Applying the principles discussed above, Rowena will be bound by the equitable lease with respect to both houses, unless she asked **Tony** what rights he claimed and he refused to reveal his lease. With respect to Alpha House, Tony's equitable lease is overriding within s. 70(1)(g) because he will be 'in receipt of rents . . .'. With respect to Beta House, Tony's lease is overriding because **he** is 'in actual occupation' through the agency of Charley.

10.3.10   *WEBB* v *POLLMOUNT* [1966] 1 All ER 481

This case is perhaps the most surprising of all the s. 70(1)(g) cases. It is, however, undoubtedly correct. It is the clearest illustration of the proposition that 'Every type of property right in land can be an overriding interest provided there is actual occupation at the relevant time by its owner'.

L granted to Webb a legal lease to last for seven years. This lease was overriding under s. 70(1)(k) (see **10.3.4**). The lease also granted to Webb an option to purchase the fee simple reversion. Options to purchase land are normally 'minor interests', and therefore should be protected by entering a notice or caution on the register. No notice or caution was entered to protect Webb's option. The fee simple was sold to Pollmount Ltd, who claimed that the option was not binding on it. Section 70(1)(g) came to Webb's rescue. He was actually occupying the leased property at the time of the sale, therefore his **option** was an overriding interest within s. 70(1)(g).

Webb was of course occupying the property by virtue of his **lease**, but that was held not to matter. 'Rights of a person in actual occupation' is not to be confined to the right by virtue of which that person occupies the land. Section 70(1)(g) makes overriding all his property rights in the land!

10.4   Minor Interests

Minor interests are all proprietary interests in registered land which are not:

(1)   capable of substantive registration; or

(2)   overriding interests, or

(3)   mortgages by registered charge.

Rights which are **normally** minor interests include:

(i)   estate contracts, restrictive covenants, unpaid vendor's liens, equitable easements (assuming the decision in *Celsteel* is wrong, see **10.3.1**), and rights of occupation under the Matrimonial Homes Acts;

(ii)   overreachable interests arising under a strict settlement or trust for sale.

It should be remembered, though, that with the exception of 'rights of occupation' under the Matrimonial Homes Act, all minor interests are capable of being promoted to 'overriding' by operation of s. 70(1)(g) of the 1925 Act if the owner of the interest is in actual occupation (see **10.3.5**).

This is even true of overreachable equitable interests arising under a strict settlement or trust for sale. However, if an owner of an overreachable equitable interest is in actual occupation of the land, his rights can still be overreached provided the purchase price is paid by the purchaser **to the correct trustees**. The House of Lords so decided in *City of London Building Society* v *Flegg* [1987] 3 All ER 435. If you do not follow this point yet, do not worry. I shall deal with *Flegg's* case when we consider the law of co-ownership. (See **16.4.2**.)

10.4.1   PROTECTION OF MINOR INTERESTS

As I have already said several times, the owner of a minor interest should always protect it by entry on the register. By s. 20(1) of the Land Registration Act 1925, a purchaser for valuable consideration of a registered title takes free from minor interests which have not been properly protected. This will be so, even if he knew of the unprotected minor interest. (Compare this point with. the House of Lords decision in the unregistered land case of *Midland Bank* v *Green*, see **8.3.5.1**.)

However, the decision in *Lyus* v *Prowsa Developments* [1982] 1 WLR 1044 in effect creates a slight exception to the above principle. There a land transfer was executed, expressly subject to a minor interest which had not been protected by entry on the register. The purchaser was held to be bound by the minor interest, **because it had expressly undertaken to give effect to the unprotected minor interest.** Though 'justice may have been done', the case is questionable. It makes a very odd contrast with the unregistered land case of *Hollington Brothers* v *Rhodes* (see **8.3**).

According to most textbooks there are four ways of protecting minor interests: notices, cautions, restrictions, and inhibitions. However, inhibitions seem to be used only in emergency situations largely unconnected with minor interests. Restrictions are used only in certain specialised situations. Thus a minor interest is usually protected either by a notice or by a caution.

10.4.2   NOTICE

From the point of view of the owner of a minor interest, the entry of a notice is the best method of protecting that minor interest. Entry of a notice automatically ensures that the minor interest is binding on a purchaser. Once a notice has been entered, the owner of a minor interest can sleep easy in his bed, confident that his rights cannot be destroyed. (Compare this point with the registration of a land charge in unregistered land, discussed at **8.3**.)

There is, however, one significant limitation which has been put upon the entry of notices on to the register. To enter a notice, the land certificate for the estate affected must be produced to the Registry. This in practical terms means that to enter a notice consent of the registered proprietor is required (even if the certificate is already at the Registry). Thus notices can be used only where the registered proprietor accepts that the minor interest is valid and binding upon the land. (I should add that proprietors often do agree to the entry of notices.)

There is one exception to the rule that the relevant land certificate is needed to enter a notice. Section 2(8)(a) of the Matrimonial Homes Act 1983 provides that 'rights of occupation' under the Act are to be protected by entry of a notice without any need to produce the land certificate to the Registry. (Rights of occupation cannot now be protected by the lodging of a caution.)

10.4.3 CAUTION

A caution is lodged without the production of the relevant land certificate to the Registry. Thus a caution is used when the owner of a minor interest cannot get the proprietor's agreement to a notice being placed on the register. (Indeed, the proprietor may be disputing the very existence of the minor interest. This happens quite regularly with estate contracts and options.)

In strict legal terms, the lodging of a caution gives (as we shall see in a moment) the owner of the minor interest only rather limited protection. In practical terms, however, the lodging of a caution against an estate is likely to put off all but foolhardy purchasers.

As a matter of law the lodging of a caution merely entitles the person lodging it (the cautioner) to 14 actual days' warning from the Registry of any transaction presented for registration which relates to the relevant land. If the cautioner wants to ensure that his proprietary interest is binding on the prospective purchaser, he must act quickly once he receives the warning from the Registry. He must object to the transaction within 14 days. If he does not object within the 14 days the Registry must allow the transaction to go through unhindered. **Any interest of the cautioner is then void against the purchaser**.

If the cautioner does object, the Registrar, subject to appeal to the court, must decide whether the cautioner has a valid proprietary interest in the property. If he decides that the cautioner has a valid claim, then he will either ban the proposed transaction, or permit it to go through subject to a **notice** which he imposes protecting the interest in question.

If the Registrar decides that the cautioner has no claim against the land, the caution is of course deleted and the transaction goes ahead unimpeded. The limited legal protection of cautions is demonstrated by the following case.

10.4.3.1 *Clark v Chief Land Registrar* [1993] 2 All ER 936; [1994] 4 All ER 96 CA

The Jarvises, the owners of Spinners Corner, owed the Clarks money under a judgment debt. The Clarks, in an effort to enforce their judgment, obtained a charging order against Spinners Corner. This gave them an interest in Spinners Corner similar to that of an equitable mortgagee. They perfectly correctly protected their interest by lodging a caution.

The Jarvises then executed a legal mortgage of Spinners Corner to Jones. When Jones presented his mortgage for registration as a mortgage by registered charge, the Land Registry made a mistake. (Fortunately such mistakes are very rare.) It omitted to send a warning of the proposed transaction to the Clarks. Thus the Clarks did not object to Jones registering his mortgage by registered charge.

The Court of Appeal, affirming Ferris J, held

(a) That Jones was not bound by the Clarks' charging order (even though Jones presumably knew of the caution). (Put another way, Jones's mortgage had 'priority' over the Clarks' charge.)

but

(b) The Clarks were entitled to claim compensation from the Land Registry, whose negligence had effectively destroyed their rights.

ACTIVITY 22

Read the extracts from the judgments of Ferris J and Nourse LJ in *Cases and Materials* (10.2.2). In reading the case, notice carefully a number of points:

(a) **The Clarks got the result they wanted. They 'won' and were awarded their costs.**

(b) **The Land Registry was contending that the mere lodging of a caution did make the Clarks' charging order binding on the mortgagee, and that the Registry's error in not warning the Clarks of the mortgage lodged for registration did not deprive the Clarks of their priority over the mortgagee.**

(c) **This contention of the Registry was in direct conflict with the leading textbook on registered land, edited (in different editions) by five former Chief Land Registrars.**

We are left wondering why the current Chief Land Registrar rejected the views of his predecessors!

(I suspect the Registry was desparate to save money.)

10.4.3.2 The warning off procedure

Cautions are often used where a person claims some sort of interest in a piece of registered land, but that claim is disputed by the registered proprietor. Disputes over estate contracts (has there been a valid contract to sell or has there not?) are particularly prevalent.

If a caution is lodged with respect to X's land, the presence of the caution on the register is usually enough to put off prospective purchasers. (It is rare for somebody to apply for a transaction to be registered while there is a caution lodged with respect to the land.) From the point of view of X, the presence of the caution is going to make his land extremely difficult to sell. X will therefore usually invoke the 'warning off' procedure before he puts the land on the market.

Under the warning off procedure the registered proprietor in effect challenges the cautioner to prove the validity of his claim to an interest in the land. The cautioner has 14 actual days in which to respond to the challenge, and if there is no response the caution is 'warned off', i.e. deleted. (In practice, there is often no response to the challenge.)

If there is a response from the cautioner, then the Registrar (subject to appeal to the court) must decide whether the cautioner has a valid claim. If he decides there is a valid claim he will impose a notice. If he decides that there is no valid claim he will delete the caution.

SAQ 55

What do you do if you are lodging a caution, but are intending to go away on business or holiday for (say) three months to somewhere a long way away (e.g., Bolivia)?

When I ask this question in oral tutorials, usually some students say, 'Don't go'. This is unnecessary advice. When lodging a caution you obviously have to give an address to which 'warning notices' should be sent. If you are likely to be away from home a lot, give the address of your solicitors.

10.4.4 RESTRICTION

A restriction is entered on the register where there is some special limit on the registered proprietor's freedom to dispose of the land. For example, a few 'corporate persons' (a corporate person is an artificial entity such as a limited company or local authority) do not have complete freedom to dispose of their land. If such a 'person' is a registered proprietor, an appropriate restriction should be entered.

The important point for the purposes of this text is that a restriction should be used where registered land is subject to a strict settlement or trust for sale. (The equitable interests under such trusts are technically minor interests, but they are overreachable as with unregistered land. Refer back to 8.4.)

(a) Where land is subject to a strict settlement, the life tenant is owner of the fee simple and is therefore the registered proprietor. A restriction should be entered indicating that 'capital money' (e.g., in particular the purchase price when the land is sold) must be paid not to the registered proprietor but to the trustees of the settlement for the purposes of the Settled Land Act.

(b) Where land is held under a trust for sale, the trustee(s) are of course the registered proprietors. A restriction should be entered, however, requiring there to be at least two trustees for a valid disposition. (The significance of this point will emerge in **Chapters 15** and **16**.)

One possible problem is that a restriction can be entered only if the land certificate is produced to the Registry. Thus (as is generally the case with notices), a restriction can be entered only with the consent of the registered proprietor(s). Usually such consent is forthcoming. But if consent were not forthcoming the beneficiaries of the settlement or trust could protect themselves only by lodging a caution. (In an emergency they could perhaps ask the Registrar to impose an inhibition.)

10.4.5 INHIBITION

An inhibition is a drastic measure which can be entered only by order of the court or the Registrar. The inhibition in effect imposes a total freeze on the land. It prevents all transactions with the land, either for an indefinite period or for a fixed period.

Inhibitions appear to be fairly rare, and seem only to be used in emergency situations. Examples given in the textbooks are:

(a) where a Land Certificate has been lost;

(b) a 'bankruptcy inhibition' where a receiving order in bankruptcy is made against the registered proprietor.

10.5 Searches of the Register

The tradition of English land registration (to be contrasted with foreign systems) has until recently been one of privacy. The Registry was not open to the public, and to inspect a particular registered title you needed the permission of the registered proprietor. However, a person who had contracted to buy a registered title was automatically entitled to receive permission to inspect the register.

The Land Registration Act 1988 came into force in December 1990, and this allows any person to inspect any registered title on payment of an appropriate fee. Nevertheless, the wise purchaser will still (as before) ask the Registry to make an official search.

In practice, a purchase of registered land is not completed on the day of the official search, but only after a few days have elapsed. Once an official search certificate is issued the purchaser has a priority period of 30 working days (which cannot nowadays be extended). Provided the purchaser lodges the land transfer for registration within this priority period, he is not bound by entries (notices, cautions, etc.) made on the register in the intervening period.

10.6 Conclusion

When you read the introduction to this chapter, you may well have thought, 'This is going to be easy. I learn the list of overriding interests; every right not on that list is a minor interest which you enter on the register much as you enter a land charge on the computer at Plymouth if the title to the land is unregistered.'

I hope that you now see that matters are not nearly as straightforward as that. Two sources of complexity particularly should be stressed. Section 70(1)(g) of the Land Registration Act 1925 has created enormous problems (three House of Lords cases since 1980!), while the distinction between notices and cautions is far from straightforward. We recently witnessed the Land Registry, in *Clark* v *Chief Land Registrar*, (seemingly) trying to reduce the differences between notices and cautions.

I would also like to recount two matters which have occurred during my teaching career which I think illustrate the need for reform of this area of law. A few years ago there was an enormous public clamour regarding the cost of conveyancing. During that period I was at a meeting addressed by a Member of Parliament who obviously thought that anybody (not just legally qualified people) could easily undertake transactions with registered land: 'What is the big difficulty? Everything you need to know is on the register.' 'What about overriding interests?' somebody asked.

ACTIVITY 23

Think for a moment about what the MP's answer might have been.

As the questioner (a fellow land law teacher) expected, the MP was unable to give an answer. He did not understand the question! Now in my view, what our MP friend should be advocating is that this country should abolish all overriding interests and go over to German-style land registration.

Some years ago, I had in my land law classes a very good student of Austrian extraction. She already had an Austrian law degree. Now Austrian law is heavily influenced by German law; in particular Austria has adopted the German system of land registration. Under this system **all** property rights with respect to a piece of land must to be valid be entered in the land register (*Grundbuch*). My Austrian student found the whole idea of overriding interests (but particularly s. 70(1)(g) and *Boland*) absolutely ridiculous: 'In Austria, every schoolchild knows that if you claim a right in land you must enter it on the *Grundbuch*.'

I would abolish overriding interests, making all third party rights minor interests. Then we would be at least approaching the position which already exists in some countries within the European Union, where it is actually true that, 'Everything you need to know is on the register'.

10.7   End of Chapter Assessment Question

George is currently setting himself up as a farmer. In the last month he has acquired the following property rights.

(a)   A freehold title to Broad Field acquired from Harry. The title is unregistered, and Harry was only able to produce one title deed, the conveyance to him when he bought the land ten years ago.

(b)   The grant of a new lease for 30 years over Wide Field.

(c)   The grant of a new lease over Low Field for 18 years.

(d)   The grant of a profit to graze 100 sheep on East Moor. The profit is to last for George's lifetime.

(e)   An agreement for a right of way across West Meadow to get to Broad Field.

Advise George as to:

(i)   which of these property rights will acquire substantive registration;

(ii)   the effects of such registration;

(iii)   the consequences of failure to register a title which should have been registered;

(iv)   whether any of the rights which are not capable of substantive registration should be protected by an entry on the Register of Title or on the Land Charges Register.

See *Cases and Materials* (10.3) for a specimen answer.

CHAPTER ELEVEN

SETTLEMENTS OF LAND

11.1   Objectives

By the end of this chapter you should:

■   be familiar with the concepts strict settlement and trust for sale, and be able to explain the basic differences between the two concepts;

■   be familiar with the various situations where the Settled Land Act 1925 applies;

■   be able to explain the problems caused by accidental strict settlements;

■   be familiar with the concept 'life tenant' as defined by the Settled Land Act;

■   be familiar with the concept 'trustees for the purposes of the Settled Land Act';

■   be able to explain the complex documentation required for strict settlements.

11.2   Introduction

A settlement can be (roughly) defined as any disposition of any property which creates a succession of interests in that property (e.g., a grant of property to A for life, remainder to B in fee simple).

Settlements can be created at any time, though traditionally the most frequent occasions for a settlement have been:

(a)   on marriage;

(b)   on death, by will;

(c)   on a child of the settlor attaining his majority.

There are two types of settlement of land:

(i)   strict settlement;

(ii)   trust for sale.

I hope that you have already spotted that these two forms of settlement of land are also the two major forms of trust of land. Indeed, nowadays the concepts of 'settlement' and 'express trust' are almost synonymous. In this chapter we will consider the basic characteristics of the two forms of trust, and then go on to consider in some detail the complex law which still governs strict settlements.

11.3   The Traditional Strict Settlement

With such a transaction, the settlor envisages that the land will be retained and enjoyed as such by successive beneficiaries. He wants the land to be **kept**, not to be sold. Pre-1926 a strict settlement could be created in two ways:

(a)   by a succession of legal estates, e.g., 'to X for life, remainder to Y in fee tail, remainder to Z in fee simple', **or**

(b)   (rare but possible) by a succession of equitable interests, e.g., 'to T1 and T2 as trustees in trust for X for life, remainder to Y in tail, remainder to Z in fee simple'. (You should note that this is not a trust for sale as the trustees are not placed under any **duty** to sell.)

Since 1925, all strict settlements must involve a succession of equitable interests and **must** involve a trust. (This is a consequence, of course, of s. 1 of the Law of Property Act 1925, which we considered in **Chapter 7**.) However, as we saw at **7.6**, the law requires that the legal title to the land be held not by independent trustees but by the life tenant, acting as a trustee for himself and the other beneficiaries.

11.3.1   IS THE STRICT SETTLEMENT A LEGAL ANOMALY WHICH SHOULD BE SCRAPPED?

Virtually every teacher of and writer on land law wants to abolish strict settlements. In 1989, the Law Commission added its voice to the chorus.

When Parliament first reformed some aspects of Land Law in 1881–82 there was an enormous amount of land in England and Wales subject to strict settlements. Some estimates go as high as 50 per cent of the total area of the country. Typical 'settled land' was the large country estate. Probably most large country estates were subject to a strict settlement. However, the idea of an individual house being subject to a strict settlement would have been regarded as absurd by our Victorian forebears.

When Parliament passed the massive 1925 reforms, the amount of settled land was already in decline, and the social upheaval caused by the First World War accelerated that decline. Yet Parliament assumed that large amounts of settled land would still continue to exist. It also assumed that the typical settled land would still be the large country estate. These assumptions help to explain a number of features of the Settled Land Act 1925 which now strike us as outmoded:

First, it helps to explain the decision to make the life tenant trustee of the legal title. The 1925 legislators thought, 'It is the life tenant who is going to live on the land, cultivate it, etc. He therefore should own the land. Ownership should **not** be given to independent trustees.'

Secondly, it helps to explain the extremely cumbersome rules regarding the documents necessary to set up and operate a strict settlement.

Thirdly, it helps to explain the elaborate rules governing the life tenant's powers of disposition over the settled land.

Read Sch. 3 to the Settled Land Act 1925, set out in *Cases and Materials* (11.2). Schedule 3 deals with the various 'improvements' which a life tenant is authorised to carry out to the settled land. There is certainly no need to learn this schedule. There are two points, though, that you should note. First, this schedule is a fascinating piece of social history. Secondly, this schedule was clearly designed for a large estate of perhaps thousands of acres. It seems ill-suited to the small suburban house in Muswell Hill (North London) involved in the case of *Ungurian* v *Lesnoff* [1990] Ch 206. Yet the house (for reasons we will come to) was held to be settled land!

11.3.2 THE CONTINUED NEED TO STUDY SETTLED LAND

A colleague once said in a meeting, 'We have no business teaching settled land. Strict settlements are nowadays never deliberately created; they only arise by accident' (e.g., as in *Ungurian* v *Lesnoff*).

His second sentence is (substantially) correct. Where a lawyer creates for a client a trust of land, he never uses the strict settlement; he always uses the trust for sale. (This is even true of large country estates.) However, I obviously do think there is a continuing need to teach settled land. Why?

First, as another colleague puts it, 'We need to teach students about strict settlements so that in their professional careers they know **not to create the damned things!**'

Secondly, much of the 1925 legislation was enacted on the assumption that settled land would continue to be a common phenomenon. Without a knowledge of the law of settled land, much of the 1925 legislation does not fully make sense.

Thirdly, the powers of disposition which are given to life tenants (discussed in **Chapter 12**) are of continuing enormous importance, because the same powers (which in modern conditions are somewhat defective) are also given to trustees for sale.

Fourthly, a few of the old-fashioned traditional 'large country estate' strict settlements still do exist.

Fifthly, though this is not a point we can explore in this text, the continued existence of settled land as a legal concept causes complications in the law of succession, especially regarding grants of probate.

Lastly, strict settlements which arise 'by accident' are not infrequent and cause enormous headaches. Although lawyers have on occasion been responsible for an accidental strict settlement (e.g., in the case of *Binions* v *Evans* [1972] Ch 359 which will be mentioned again later), the usual cause of accidental settlements is lay people undertaking transactions with land without proper legal advice. There are at least three possible reasons for accidental settlements:

(a)   There are people who make their own wills in terms such as, 'I leave my house to my dear wife Flo for her life, and after her death the house shall go to my son Jack'.

(b)   There are people who enter into inter vivos transactions which produce the result that somebody has the right to occupy a house or other land, but only for their lifetime. The recent case of *Ungurian* v *Lesnoff* [1990] Ch 206, is an illustration.

(c) A strict settlement automatically arises if there is an attempt to convey land to somebody who is not of full age.

In each of these situations the property involved is unlikely to be very big, probably a typically English semi-detached house. As a result of the accidental strict settlement the extremely cumbersome machinery of the Settled Land Act, designed for the large country estate, has to be applied to a poor little suburban semi!

11.4   Introduction to Trusts for Sale

Although this chapter is primarily concerned with strict settlements, we do need, before we go any further, to consider certain aspects of trusts for sale.

Refer back to the example I gave of a trust for sale at 2.4.2. You should note that Tim and Tom are told that they (in theory) must sell Greenacre. What would be the position if by the terms of the trust Tim and Tom were merely permitted to sell, but were under no obligation to do so?

The vital identifying feature of a trust for sale is that land is conveyed to trustees who are, by the document(s) setting up the trust, placed under a **duty** to sell the land. If land is conveyed to trustees who are given merely a **power** to sell the land, then a (highly irregular) strict settlement has been created. I say 'highly irregular' because (as we have already seen) where land is subject to a strict settlement the 'life tenant' should own the legal title and have the power to sell the land. Steps will have to be taken to regularise the situation.

11.4.1   THE EQUITABLE DOCTRINE OF CONVERSION

This is another archaic rule which should have been abolished in 1925, but has been allowed to linger on. Where a trust for sale is set up, the maxim 'Equity looks on that as done which ought to be done' is applied to the trust to produce what to modern minds is a rather strange result.

As I mentioned at **2.4.2**, the trustees of a modern trust for sale invariably have a **power to postpone sale**. You will probably not be surprised to learn that in modern conditions this power to delay sale is often exercised. However, under the doctrine of conversion (an application of the maxim 'Equity looks on that as done which ought to be done') the trustees of a trust for sale are deemed to have sold the legal estate the moment the trust is set up. It therefore follows that the interests of the beneficiaries of a trust for sale of land are **personal** property not **real** property, whether or not the land is sold immediately.

We saw at **2.6.2** the distinction between real property and personal property is far less important than it was pre-1925. But it remains significant if a legal document uses terms such as 'real property' and 'personal property'. If a document uses the phrase 'personal property', that phrase will **include** equitable interests under a trust for sale of land.

SAQ 56

In a case which arose shortly after 1925, a solicitor was the owner of an absolute (fee simple) interest under a trust for sale of a piece of freehold land, i.e. he was a beneficiary of the trust for sale. He made his own will, which in effect said, 'I leave my real estate to X and my personal property to Y'. Who received the interest under the trust for sale?

The answer is that Y was held entitled to the interest under the trust for sale.

11.4.2   DOCUMENTS EMPLOYED IN CREATING A TRUST FOR SALE

Simple trusts for sale with only a limited number of beneficiaries are nowadays still created by just one document. That one document conveys the land to the trustees, places them under a duty to sell and sets out the equitable interests. A trust for sale of land created by only one document is perfectly valid. (The reason for stressing this point will emerge later.)

Where an elaborate trust for sale is being created it has long been the practice to use two documents:

(a)   **a conveyance** to the trustees for sale of the legal estate, specifically stating their duty to sell, but not stating the equitable interests;

(b)   **a trust instrument** setting out the equitable interests of the beneficiaries.

A purchaser is entitled to see only the conveyance, and has no right (and certainly is **under no duty**) to inspect the trust instrument. This two document arrangement is said to create a 'curtain' and the trust instrument is said to be 'behind the curtain'.

Why should people want to create this 'curtain'? First, it makes things easier for a purchaser who, instead of wading through a long document, has to look only at a (relatively short) conveyance. Secondly, it maintains privacy. Remember that trusts are often created to benefit various members of the same family. The 'curtain' prevents a purchaser from seeing family secrets as to who owns what equitable interests. (The purchaser might just be a reporter from a tabloid newspaper!)

Where a trust for sale is created by will there should always be two documents. The will acts as the trust instrument. The **assent** from the deceased's personal representatives to the trustees for sale takes the place of the conveyance on trust for sale. (Refer back to 2.5.2.1 for what is meant by an 'assent'.)

Where a trust for sale exists with respect to registered land, the trustees are registered as proprietors, with a suitable restriction entered against them. (See the discussion on restrictions at 10.4.2.3.) The equitable interests under a trust for sale **never** appear on the register. They must be set out in a separate trust instrument kept by the trustees.

11.5   Introduction to the Settled Land Acts

(For the purposes of **this preliminary discussion**, 'life tenant' can be defined as the person who is entitled to the life estate or life interest in possession over the relevant land. As we shall see later, the Settled Land Act 1925 gives an (artificially) wider definition.)

Prior to 1882, the existence of a strict settlement over a piece of land had the following drawbacks:

(a)   The land was virtually unsaleable. The life tenant could sell only his life estate. He could not sell a fee simple in possession, the only type of estate which normally interests purchasers.

(b)   The life tenant could not grant leases binding upon his successors under the settlement.

(c)   The land could not be mortgaged to pay for improvements.

In the 1870s English agriculture suffered a severe depression, largely the result of North American imports. In economic terms it clearly made sense for poorer quality agricultural land to be developed for industry or housing. But much of that land was settled land. The life tenant could not sell to builders or industrialists, neither could he mortgage the land to raise finance so that he personally could carry out developments or other improvements such as land drainage.

The Settled Land Act 1882 was passed as a response to this crisis. It was a promoted by a Conservative, Lord Cairns, during a Liberal administration. It gave the life tenant power to sell the fee simple in the land, to mortgage the fee simple to pay for improvements, and to grant leases over the settled land binding on his successors.

Bearing in mind the enormous amount of settled land which existed in 1882, the Act was nothing short of revolutionary. It also (in one respect) rather defied logic. It gave to the life tenant the power to sell or mortgage a fee simple in possession which he did not own!

The Settled Land Act 1925 continued (and expanded) the policy of giving the life tenant wide powers of disposition over the settled land. But the 1925 Act added a new policy rule to which I have already referred. Where land is subject to a strict settlement, the legal fee simple absolute in possession is vested in the life tenant as trustee for himself and the other beneficiaries. Thus if there is a strict settlement 'To X for life, remainder to Y in fee tail, remainder to Z in fee simple', X holds the legal fee simple estate in trust for himself, Y and Z. If X decides to sell (or mortgage) the fee simple, he will (unlike under the 1882–1925 law) be conveying an estate **he does own**.

Generally speaking, it is now impossible to have a strict settlement where the legal estate is vested in separate trustees. Instead the life tenant is a 'trustee'. (He must not, however, be confused with the people designated 'trustees of the settlement for the purposes of the Settled Land Act'.)

This mandatory rule that the life tenant **must** be trustee of the legal title makes strict settlements very anomalous when compared with other trusts, e.g., trusts for sale, trusts of stocks and shares, etc. It also is a significant exception to the general policy of the 1925 legislation, to make property rights in land as similar as possible to property rights in moveable property.

Where a strict settlement was in existence on 1 January 1926 (and there were still plenty of strict settlements in those days) a strange thing happened on the stroke of midnight.

A legal fee simple absolute in possession was automatically vested in the life tenant to hold in trust for himself and the other beneficiaries. (Whether any life tenants jumped in the fountains in Trafalgar Square to celebrate their new status is not recorded!)

11.5.1 SETTLED LAND DEFINED

The Settled Land Act 1925, s. 1, contains an extremely lengthy definition of 'settled land'. The basic format of s.1 is that land, **provided it is not held on trust for sale**, is settled land if it falls into any one of seven categories. Only categories (a) and (e) are of real significance today:

(a) Where a disposition has created a series of equitable interests in the land, e.g., 'to X for life, remainder to Y in fee simple'; or 'to A for life'. (Remember that in this second example the grantor will have an equitable fee simple in reversion.)

(b) Where the land is subject to a fee tail.

(c) Where land is subject to a fee simple upon condition subsequent.

(d) Where land is subject to a determinable fee simple.

(e) Where a disposition grants a fee simple or a term of years absolute to a minor.

(f) Where a disposition creates a 'springing interest' in land. A 'springing interest' in land is one which takes effect only if a condition **precedent** is fulfilled, e.g., 'To John Smith in fee simple if he attains the age of 30'; 'To Mary Brown in fee simple if she qualifies as a solicitor'.

(g) This category, land subject to family charges, (s. 1(1)(v) of the 1925 Act) is so unimportant in modern land law that there is no point in trying to explain it.

I hope you have noticed from this list of categories that the statutory definition of 'settled land' is wider than the traditional idea of a 'strict settlement'. Traditional strict settlements fall into category (a). Note particularly category (e), which, as already indicated, is still of real relevance today.

The explanation for the wide definition (and particularly category (e)) is that the 1925 legislators wished at all costs to avoid having situations where a piece of land is unsaleable. By bringing situations such as category (e) within the definition, they ensured that all land is capable of being sold.

11.5.2 ACCIDENTAL SETTLEMENTS – CONVEYING LAND SUBJECT TO A RIGHT TO RESIDE

Read the extracts from *Binions* v *Evans* and *Ungurian* v *Lesnoff* in *Cases and Materials* (11.3.2). With respect to *Binions* v *Evans* it should be appreciated that the views of Lord Denning as to the applicable law are generally considered to be incorrect. The views of Megaw and Stephenson LJJ are to be preferred. With respect to *Ungurian* v *Lesnoff*, the judge's finding that Lesnoff had acquired a life interest (rather than a constructive

128

SETTLEMENTS OF LAND

trust share) is perhaps a little surprising. But, given the finding that there was a life interest, the rest of the judgment follows logically from that finding.

In *Binions* v *Evans* [1972] 2 All ER 70 the trustees of the Tredegar Estate owned a cottage in which there resided rent-free Mrs Evans, the widow of an employee of the Estate. The trustees sold the cottage to Binions, expressly on the condition that Mrs Evans should be allowed to live there for the rest of her life. Binions paid a reduced price because of this condition.

Binions nevertheless tried to evict Mrs Evans; he claimed that she had no proprietary interest in the land. Not surprisingly Binions found no sympathy in the Court of Appeal. The majority of the Court of Appeal (Megaw and John Stephenson LJJ) found that the conveyance to Binions created a life interest in favour of Mrs Evans. Therefore the land was 'settled land' within the meaning of the 1925 Act, with Mrs Evans as life tenant.

The majority view in *Binions* v *Evans* was applied in the fairly recent case of *Ungurian* v *Lesnoff* [1990] Ch 206. This case concerned a cohabiting couple who eventually split up. Mr Ungurian bought a house in Muswell Hill (North London). Ms Lesnoff moved in, and spent an enormous amount of time, energy and money renovating the house. The judge **found as a fact** that this money was spent on the understanding that Lesnoff should be able to occupy the house **for the rest of her life**. He therefore held that Lesnoff had a life interest in the house (rather than a constructive trust share in the house), and that meant the house was settled land. Lesnoff was life tenant. The judge even ordered that a vesting deed (the function of this document is explained at **11.8.1**) should be executed in her favour.

11.5.3 ACCIDENTAL SETTLEMENT BY HOME-MADE WILL

It is thought that reasoning similar to that employed by the majority in *Binions* v *Evans* would apply in the following type of situation. John Knowall, who thinks all solicitors charge extortionate fees, drafts his own will. He leaves his house 'To my dear son Edward, but on condition that he allows my beloved wife Hilda to occupy the house for the rest of her life'. It appears that here we have a strict settlement.

Who will be the life tenant?

In effect the land has been given to Hilda for life, remainder to Edward in fee simple, therefore Hilda will be the life tenant, and she will hold the legal estate in trust for herself and Edward.

11.5.4   CONVEYANCES OR LEASES TO MINORS

A minor (i.e. a person under 18 years old, formerly 21) cannot own a legal estate in land. Any attempt to grant a minor a legal estate is not, however, totally void. The minor will acquire an equitable interest equivalent to the legal estate intended to be granted. Thus if Fred Idiot conveys the fee simple in Blackacre to his son George, aged 15, George acquires only an equitable fee simple. The legal fee simple remains with Fred. That is straightforward enough.

What is more difficult is that the Settled Land Act 1925 provides that where there is an attempt to grant a minor a legal estate, the land shall be settled land (category (e) at **11.5.1**). Why did Parliament make this apparently strange provision?

The answer is that Parliament was anxious to ensure that land 'belonging to a minor' should be saleable. Making such land settled land 'solves' (in a fashion) the problem. As we shall see at **11.6**, the legal estate will be vested in 'statutory owners', who will have the power to sell the land.

11.6   Who is the Life Tenant under the Settled Land Act?

If you were able to ask a pre-1925 lawyer how he would define 'life tenant', he would say something like, 'A life tenant is a person with a life estate in possession in a piece of land'.

We have already seen that the modern concept of 'settled land' under the Settled Land Act 1925 is wider than the traditional concept of a strict settlement. We have also seen that it is the general policy of the 1925 Act that the legal title to settled land should be vested in the 'life tenant'. It necessarily follows that the definition of 'life tenant' in the 1925 Act (ss. 19 and 20) is wider than the traditional definition. The 'life tenant' is the person for the time being beneficially entitled in possession under the settlement. All the following, **if in possession,** count as 'life tenants' for the purposes of the Act.

(a)   The owner of a life interest/estate.

(b)   The owner of an estate/interest pur autre vie.

(c)   The owner of a fee tail.

(d)   The owner of a fee simple upon condition subsequent.

(e)   The owner of a determinable fee.

(f)   Any person currently entitled to the income from the settled land. For example, a legal estate is purportedly conveyed to trustees T1 and T2 on trust to pay the income of the land to X for life, remainder to Y for life, etc. In this situation the settlor has attempted to make independent trustees the 'bosses' of the settled land. He cannot do this, and X will be the life tenant. X will hold the legal title.

The life tenant is said to be the 'boss' of the settled land for three reasons:

(1)   The life tenant holds the legal title to the land, not independent trustees.

(2)   The life tenant can sell, lease or make various other dispositions with the land. Normally he does not need the consent of 'the trustees for the purposes of the Settled Land Act'. (SLA Trustees).

(3)   The SLA trustees have various miscellaneous functions to perform, but they normally do not own, manage, or otherwise deal with the land itself.

11.6.1   EXCEPTIONS TO THE RULE THAT THE LIFE TENANT IS BOSS

Just to confuse matters, however, there are two situations where the SLA trustees **are** the 'bosses' of the settled land, and they **do** have the ownership of the legal title and the power to sell, lease etc. the land. Their 'boss role' is, however, likely to be temporary.

(a)   **Position where there is no life tenant**. This could occur in rare situations, e.g., where there is a 'springing interest'. (Refer back to category (f) in the definition of settled land at **11.5.1**.) Suppose Whiteacre is granted 'To John Smith in fee simple if he attains the age of 30.' Pending John attaining the age of 30 there is no life tenant. What happens to Whiteacre in the meantime? The answer is that the SLA trustees own the legal title in the meantime.

To be accurate, the rule is that where there is no life tenant the legal title to the land is vested in a 'statutory owner'. However, the SLA trustees are automatically the 'statutory owner'! (A settlor could appoint some person(s) other than the SLA trustees to be 'statutory owner', but this is highly unlikely.)

(b)   **Position where the life tenant is a minor**. A situation where the Life Tenant is 'under age' could arise in two types of case:

(i)   Where there is a traditional strict settlement in the form 'to X for life, remainder to Y, etc.', but at the time the settlement is created X is under age.

(ii)   The 'category (e)' situation already referred to in **11.5.1**, where there is an attempt to grant a legal estate to a minor.

In both these situations the legal title (and the management of the land) will be vested in a 'statutory owner'. In practice the SLA trustees always fill this role.

11.7   Who are the Trustees of the Settlement for the Purposes of the Settled Land Act?

You will find that the Settled Land Act 1925 (especially s. 30), and the larger textbooks, set out extremely elaborate rules as to who should be the SLA trustees. These rules are frankly virtually irrelevant to modern conditions. What I say below is all you need to know.

11.7.1   DELIBERATELY CREATED STRICT SETTLEMENTS

Ever since 1882, where a strict settlement has been deliberately created by a settlor who has sound legal advice, the settlement has always expressly appointed 'trustees for the purposes of the Settled Land Act'. With these settlements there is no further problem.

11.7.2   ACCIDENTALLY CREATED STRICT SETTLEMENTS

Of course, virtually all strict settlements created today arise by accident, and with accidental settlements no SLA trustees have been expressly appointed. A strict settlement without SLA trustees is (unfortunately) still valid. SLA trustees will have to be found somewhere.

If the accidental settlement has arisen under a will, there is no real problem; the deceased's personal representatives (executors or administrators) are automatically the SLA trustees. If, however, the accidental settlement has arisen inter vivos (i.e. not by will) then usually there is a major problem. Normally, application will have to be made to the court for it to appoint SLA trustees. The delay and expense of going to court can be avoided only in those cases (rare in practice) where it is possible to rely on the ancient principle of equity known as 'the rule in *Saunders v Vautier*'.

11.7.3   THE RULE IN *SAUNDERS* v *VAUTIER* (1841) 4 Beav 115

To discuss **the rule in *Saunders* v *Vautier*** here is something of a digression, but since it must be mentioned sometime, it might as well be now. This rule is that if the beneficiaries of a trust (of any type of property) are all of full age and in unanimous agreement, they can (in effect) dictate what is to be done with the trust property.

Suppose Tim and Tam are the trustees of a trust fund invested in stocks and shares. They hold the fund in trust for A for life, remainder to B absolutely. A and B are of full age. A would like to get his hands on some capital. B would also like some capital, but does not want to wait until A dies. They therefore agree to end the trust, and split the fund (say) 50–50. A and B have the right to do so under *Saunders* v *Vautier*.

Suppose, however, that A and B are happy with their existing equitable interests under the trust, but do not like Tim and Tam as trustees. They would prefer Tom and Terri. A and B can invoke *Saunders* v *Vautier* and sack Tim and Tam and appoint Tom and Terri in their place. And it will be no good Tim and Tam protesting, 'We have done a great job as trustees – it's wrong that they should get rid of us'.

Returning to settled land, the point is, of course, that if an accidental settlement arises inter vivos but there are no SLA trustees at all, the need for a court application (inevitably expensive) is avoided if:

(a)   all beneficiaries are of full age, **and**
(b)   they can all agree as to who they want as SLA trustees.

11.7.4   APPOINTMENT OF LATER SLA TRUSTEES

Once the initial SLA trustees have been appointed under the rules discussed above, new appointments can usually be made by the trustees themselves. (Trustees generally, not just SLA trustees, are 'self-perpetuating'. We shall be returning to this point later, at the end of **Chapter 13**.)

11.8   Documents Necessary Where Land is Settled Land

We now come to what is often reckoned to be the most complex part of the law of settled land. The complexities regarding documents for settled land stem from two major mistakes made by the 1925 legislators:

(a)   As has already been stressed on a number of occasions, the 1925 legislators insisted that the legal title to settled land should be vested, not in independent trustees, but in the life tenant.

(b)   The 1925 legislators insisted that every piece of settled land should be equipped with a 'curtain'. To understand what is meant by 'curtain', refer back to **11.4.2** and to what was said about, 'Documents employed in creating a trust for sale'.

Where somebody creates a trust for sale, he in effect has a choice whether to use one document to set up the trust, or two. If he chooses to use two documents, there will be a conveyance to the trustees for sale, and a separate trust instrument. The advantages of this two document 'curtain' arrangement are, first, that it makes things simpler for a purchaser and, secondly, it maintains privacy for the beneficiaries as a purchaser does not see who owns what equitable interests under the trust.

Under the 1925 legislation this two document curtain is optional for trusts for sale, but compulsory where land is settled land. Whenever it is intended to create a strict settlement, the settlor should execute:

(a) a vesting deed; **and**

(b) a trust instrument.

11.8.1 THE VESTING DEED

This document should contain all the matters which a potential purchaser of the settled land needs to know:

(a) a description identifying the land settled;

(b) a provision vesting the legal estate in the life tenant (or, where appropriate, the 'statutory owner');

(c) the names of the trustees for the purposes of the Settled Land Act;

(d) details of any powers of disposition additional to those conferred by the Settled Land Act.

11.8.2 THE TRUST INSTRUMENT

The trust instrument should contain details of all the equitable interests created by the settlement. A purchaser of (unregistered) settled land should inspect the vesting deed, but normally has no right to inspect the trust instrument. Thus a 'curtain' is created. A purchaser will obviously know who the life tenant is, but he will not know (and certainly has no need to know) who are the other beneficiaries under the settlement.

11.8.3 STRICT SETTLEMENTS CREATED BY WILL

Where a will creates a strict settlement (e.g., 'I leave my house to my dear wife Wendy for her life and then to my beloved daughter Flora') matters should proceed as follows:

(a) The deceased's executors should (as normal) get a grant of probate with respect to the will.

(b) The executors should (as normal) pay off debts and taxes.

(c) The executors should then execute a **vesting assent** in favour of the life tenant (Wendy in the example just given). A vesting assent (though technically not a deed) contains the same particulars as a vesting deed.

The deceased's will acts as the trust instrument. Any purchaser of the land should, when investigating title, check the grant of probate and the vesting assent, but need not examine the detailed provisions of the will.

11.8.4 SETTLED LAND WHICH IS REGISTERED TITLE

A vesting deed or vesting assent should be executed in favour of the life tenant (or statutory owner), who should then apply to become registered proprietor. As explained at **10.4.4**, a 'restriction' is entered indicating that 'capital money' must be paid to named trustees for the purposes of the Settled Land Act. The register does not contain details of the equitable interests under the settlement. These are still set out in a separate trust instrument, which a purchaser has no right to see.

11.8.5 PRE-1926 SETTLEMENTS EXISTING ON 1 JANUARY 1926

The next point is worth mentioning simply because it shows how obsessed Parliament was in 1925 with the notion, 'Every strict settlement should have both a vesting deed and a trust instrument'. As has already been mentioned, where a strict settlement existed on 1 January 1926, a legal fee simple absolute in possession was automatically transferred to the life tenant without anybody having to do anything. However, the trustees for the purposes of the Settled Land Act were required, as soon as possible, to execute a vesting deed in favour of the life tenant. This document simply recorded the vesting of a legal estate which had already happened by operation of law. But until it was executed, the land could not be sold! (The old settlement document became the trust instrument.)

11.8.6 INTER VIVOS SETTLEMENTS CREATED BY ONE DOCUMENT AFTER 1925

Let us suppose that Freda Chump executes a single deed which grants Blueacre 'to my boyfriend Donald for life, remainder to our son George in fee simple'. Now it would have been much simpler if Parliament had said that all strict settlements created by only one document should be totally void. Instead, Parliament provided:

(a) the single document operates as a trust instrument creating the equitable interests intended;

(b) the legal estate to the land remains vested in the settlor;

(c) until a vesting deed is executed the land is 'paralysed', i.e. nobody can sell or make any other disposition with the land. (Settled Land Act 1925, s. 13).

Thus in my Freda Chump example, Freda still has the legal title to Blueacre, although she holds it in trust for Donald and George. But until a vesting deed is executed, the land cannot be sold.

Now you may well be thinking, 'Freda should put things right by belatedly executing a vesting deed transferring the legal title from her to Donald, the life tenant'. This is logical, but wrong! Where a settlement is created by one document a belated vesting deed should be executed, but **not** by the settlor. It should be executed by the trustees for the purposes of the Settled Land Act in favour of the life tenant. This vesting deed takes the legal estate from the settlor and transfers it to the life tenant. (You should note that the SLA trustees are transferring a legal estate which they do not, in any sense, own!) So in my Freda Chump example the SLA trustees (**not Freda**) should execute a vesting deed in Donald's favour.

Now I hope that you have already spotted another difficulty. Freda almost certainly executed her settlement without legal advice, and almost certainly has not appointed any SLA trustees. If Donald and George are both of full age, they can by acting together appoint the SLA trustees (see the discussion of *Saunders* v *Vautier*, at **11.7.3**); but if, **as is very likely**, George is under 18, in that case there will be no alternative to an expensive application to the court for it to appoint the SLA trustees.

SAQ 58

In 1992, Tom Brainless executed a single deed which simply said, 'I grant my farm Bluefields to Carol for life, remainder to David for life, remainder to Edward in fee simple. I appoint Terri and Tammy to be trustees for the purposes of the Settled Land Act'. Assuming that all the parties involved are of full age, what will need to be done (and by whom) to ensure that Carol has the legal title to Bluefields?

Tom may be Brainless, but (unlike Freda Chump) he has helped matters by appointing SLA trustees. Those trustees must execute a vesting deed in favour of Carol. This deed will take the legal estate from Tom and grant it to Carol.

11.8.7 SITUATIONS WHERE THE TRUST INSTRUMENT IS NOT 'BEHIND THE CURTAIN'

We now come to what is probably the silliest point of all. The whole idea of the compulsory two document 'curtain' arrangement is to ensure that purchasers of settled land inspect only the vesting deed, and do not have to look at the trust instrument. There are, however, two situations where a purchaser of settled land is both entitled and obliged to look at the trust instrument to check that the particulars contained in the vesting deed are correct. These are:

(a)   All settlements created before 1926.

(b)   A settlement created after 1925 by one document only where the vesting deed has been added later by the SLA trustees (my Freda Chump example).

SAQ 59

How many strict settlements do you think exist today where there is an effective curtain (i.e. the purchaser needs only to inspect the vesting deed)?

Probably very few! Lawyers advise their clients against creating strict settlements. The few strict settlements which do exist are usually accidents created by people like Freda Chump, people who do not realise that there should be two documents!

There are also a few 'old' strict settlements around created in the early part of this century. If that settlement is pre-1926 it will have had a 'vesting deed' executed, but the original settlement (now the trust instrument) will not be 'behind the curtain'.

11.8.8   DOCUMENTS WHERE THERE IS A CHANGE OF LIFE TENANT

This is another area where the complications are caused by Parliament's insistence that the life tenant should be the 'boss' of settled land, not independent trustees. Suppose that Middleacre has been settled 'to Anthea for life, remainder to Betty for life, remainder to Charles in fee simple'. Tim and Tam have been appointed trustees for the purposes of the SLA. While Anthea is still alive, she will hold Middleacre as life tenant in trust for herself, Betty and Charles. When Anthea dies, Betty will become life tenant, and hold Middleacre in trust for herself and Charles.

The problem is the documentation necessary to effect the transition which will happen when Anthea dies. Where a life tenant dies (but the land remains settled land) then, unlike the rest of his or her property, the legal estate in the settled land does not vest in his or her **ordinary** personal representatives. Instead it vests in the SLA trustees as '**special personal representatives**'. The 'special PRs' then transfer the legal estate to the new life tenant by a new vesting assent.

I will forgive you if you are puzzled by the last three sentences. I will try and explain them by reference to the Anthea/Betty/Charles example. Let us suppose that Anthea has just died. In addition to being life tenant of Middleacre, she was also outright owner in fee simple of Northacre and also owned a lot of personal property. Anthea, by her will, appointed Eddie and Ernie to be her executors, and left all her property to her husband Horace.

Now Eddie and Ernie will obtain probate of Anthea's will in the usual way, but that grant of probate will not extend to the settled land, Middleacre. Eddie and Ernie will (in the usual way) gather together all Anthea's property (except Middleacre) and pay any debts, taxes, etc. They will then transfer all the property to Horace. With respect to Northacre they will sign an (ordinary) assent in his favour.

With respect to Middleacre things are very different. Tim and Tam get a special grant of probate limited to the settled land. They then execute a **vesting assent** in favour of Betty.

If Anthea had died intestate, letters of administration would be issued with respect to all her property, but excluding Middleacre. Tim and Tam would get a special grant of letters of administration limited to the settled land. They would then execute a **vesting assent** in favour of Betty.

SAQ 60

Suppose in the example in SAQ 58 a vesting deed has been executed in Carol's favour but she has now died. David and Edward are both still alive. Carol's will appoints Ena and Ezekial to be her executors, and leaves all her property to Frank. Do Ena and Ezekial have any role to play with respect to Bluefields farm?

On this scenario, the answer will be 'No'. The land remains settled land. Terri and Tammy will obtain a special grant of probate confined to Bluefields, and will execute a vesting assent in David's favour.

11.8.9   TERMINATION OF SETTLEMENTS

In effect a piece of land ceases to be settled land if a person of full age becomes entitled **in equity** to a fee simple absolute in possession. Whether that person holds the legal estate is irrelevant.

11.8.9.1   Where the legal estate at the time the settlement ends is vested in a statutory owner

As we have seen, a minor cannot own a legal estate in land. Suppose that in my Middleacre example at **11.8.8**, Anthea and Betty are both dead, but Charles is still under 18. The land will continue to be settled land until Charles's eighteenth birthday. Tim and Tam will hold the legal title to the land as 'statutory owner'. On Charles attaining his majority the land will immediately cease to be settled land. Tim and Tam (who have ceased to have any other functions to perform) must convey the legal estate to Charles by **ordinary conveyance**. (A vesting deed must not be used as that would suggest that the settlement is still continuing.)

11.8.9.2   Where the legal estate was vested in a life tenant, and the settlement ends on that life tenant's death

This would be the case if, in my Middleacre example at **11.8.8**, Charles is over 18 at the time of Betty's death. What happens in this situation is extremely strange – the most farcical aspect of a generally farcical law. The key to understanding what happens is to remember that Charles becomes entitled (in equity) to Middleacre the moment Betty dies. At that moment the land ceases to be settled land. **At that moment** the SLA trustees (Tim and Tam) cease to have any functions.

Let us suppose that, in addition to being life tenant of Middleacre, Betty was also outright owner in fee simple of Southacre and also owned a lot of personal property. By her will she appointed Edna and Elspeth to be her executors, and left all her property to her husband Keith.

Edna and Elspeth obtain a grant of probate, but that grant extends to include the **ex**-settled land, Middleacre. You may have been thinking from what I said earlier that Tim and Tam would get a special grant of probate confined to Middleacre. But this is impossible. 'Special probate' is possible only for settled land, and Middleacre ceases to be settled land **the moment Betty dies!**

Thus Betty's 'ordinary' executors take temporary charge of Middleacre. However, while they will pass all the rest of Betty's property to Keith (with respect to Southacre they will execute an (ordinary) assent in his favour), they must pass Middleacre to Charles. They will execute an (ordinary) assent in his favour.

Suppose in the example in SAQ 58 a vesting deed has been executed in Carol's favour but she has now died. David died before Carol, while Edward is still alive. Carol's will appoints Ena and Ezekial to be her executors, and leaves all her property to Frank. Do Ena and Ezekial have any role to play with respect to Bluefields farm?

There is of course a crucial difference between **SAQ 61** and **SAQ 60**. If David dies before Carol, Edward becomes entitled, **on Carol's death**, to an equitable fee simple absolute in possession. The strict settlement ends immediately on Carol's death, and from that moment Terri and Tammy cease to have any functions.

Ena and Ezekial will obtain an ordinary grant of probate, and that grant of probate will extend to Bluefields farm. However Edward, not Frank, will be entitled to Bluefields. So Ena and Ezekial will transfer the legal estate in Bluefields to Edward using an **ordinary assent**.

11.9 Conclusion

Having struggled through this inevitably very long chapter, I hope you see why one of my colleagues says, 'We need to teach students about strict settlements so that in their professional careers they know not to create the damned things'.

If you go into legal practice as a conveyancer, you are unlikely to come across settled land very often. But if you do encounter settled land, you will be in for a testing time. Identifying the life tenant and the trustees for the purposes of the Settled Land Act is (normally) going to be relatively easy. But working out which are the correct documents to use (and even who should sign them) is often a difficult problem. And if you get it wrong, you might face a claim for professional negligence.

CHAPTER TWELVE

THE STATUTORY POWERS OF THE LIFE TENANT

12.1 Objectives

By the end of this chapter you should:

■ be able to explain the various statutory powers of disposition granted to life tenants by the Settled Land Act 1925;

■ be able to criticise the (sometimes out-of-date) restrictions placed on those powers;

■ be conversant with the various (statutory and common law) safeguards which exist to prevent a life tenant abusing his position.

12.2 Introduction

This chapter forms a natural link between the preceding chapter on strict settlements and the ensuing chapter on trusts for sale. Much of what I said in **Chapter 11** is (arguably) of limited practical significance, as strict settlements are fortunately relatively rare. By contrast, the discussion of life tenants' powers of disposition is undoubtedly of substantial practical significance, as these powers (**with their defects**) also apply to trustees for sale. Trusts for sale are very common!

12.3 Life Tenant's Statutory Powers of Disposition: General

The thinking in 1925 was **not** to give the life tenant totally unrestricted powers over the settled land. Rather it was to give him only those powers which a 'reasonable landowner' would want. Unfortunately, in the light of changed economic conditions, some of these powers are today inadequate. For example, a life tenant can usually only grant leases for a maximum period of 50 years. In modern economic conditions, with 99-year leases commonplace, this 50-year maximum is too short.

As we shall see later in more detail, a settlor creating a strict settlement cannot cut down the life tenant's powers. The 1925 Act in effect spells out the **minimum** powers which he is to have. A settlor can, however, expand the powers of disposition (e.g., permit leases for any length of time). A well-advised settlor should do this. But then well-advised settlors do not create strict settlements!

12.3.1 THE CONSEQUENCES OF A LIFE TENANT EXCEEDING HIS STATUTORY POWERS

Section 18 of the 1925 Act provides that a disposition by a life tenant in excess of his powers (e.g., a lease for residential purposes for more than 50 years) is void as to the legal estate, and binds only the life tenant's equitable interest. The most likely victim of this rule is somebody who took a longer-than-50-years lease of settled land without realising that the land was settled land. The hapless lessee in this situation will discover the truth only on the death of the life tenant who granted the lease. (Remember, as we saw in **Chapter 9**, a lessee cannot normally inspect his landlord's title deeds.)

12.3.2 THE DUTY TO OBTAIN THE BEST CONSIDERATION

The statutory powers of the life tenant are subject to a general rule that he must obtain the best consideration (price, rent, etc.) reasonably obtainable. One should, however, stress s. 110(1) of the Settled Land Act 1925. This provides that a purchaser in good faith dealing with a life tenant is presumed to have given the best consideration reasonably obtainable.

Suppose Bloggs is life tenant of Widetrees. He sells Widetrees to Percy for £400,000. Percy almost immediately resells Widetrees to Stephen for £600,000. The other beneficiaries under the settlement may well be upset at what has happened. But unless Percy acted in bad faith, their only remedy would be to claim compensation from Bloggs.

It would not be bad faith for Percy, on seeing an advert, 'For sale, Widetrees. £400,000' to think, 'That's a tremendous bargain, I will buy'. It would be bad faith if Bloggs told Percy, 'Widetrees is worth a lot more than £400,000 but I am selling cheap to spite the other beneficiaries under the settlement'.

12.3.3 PAYMENT OF CAPITAL MONEY TO THE TRUSTEES FOR THE PURPOSES OF THE SETTLED LAND ACT

One last preliminary point before we examine the statutory powers. It is a point we first met at **8.4.2**. To ensure overreaching, any purchaser or other person dealing with a life tenant must pay any 'capital money' arising on the transaction (price on sale, premium on grant of a long lease, money raised by a mortgage, etc.) to the SLA trustees.

12.4 The Statutory Powers

12.4.1 POWER OF SALE

Under s. 37 of the Settled Land Act 1925, the life tenant may sell whole **or part** of the settled land. Obviously this is the most important power, but no further comment is needed.

(Note that all the SAQs in this chapter involve the same strict settlement.)

The enormous Bigpots Estate is subject to a strict settlement. The Duke of Plaza Toro is life tenant. His son Luiz is entitled to the (equitable) fee simple in remainder to take effect in possession on his father's death. Tito and Tonio are the trustees for the purposes of the SLA.

The Duke has just sold an outlying field to a friendly neighbouring farmer, Giorgio. The price was £8,000 pounds, a figure which Luiz considers to be 'far too cheap'. Can Luiz claim:

(a)   that his equitable interest binds Giorgio; or

(b)   (if his claim against Giorgio fails) compensation from his father?

To succeed under claim (a), Luiz would have to show that either

(i)   Giorgio paid the price to the Duke rather than to the SLA trustees, Tito and Tonio; or

(ii)   Giorgio acted in bad faith. This would be the case if he and the Duke colluded together to agree a low price which they knew did not represent the true value of the land.

If claim (a) fails, then Luiz would still succeed in a claim for compensation against his father if Luiz could show that his father failed in his duty to get the best price reasonably obtainable.

12.4.2   POWER OF EXCHANGE

You may be asking, why would somebody want to exchange one piece of land for another? Actually, swaps of land are quite common in rural areas; farmers may want to straighten out a boundary, or even swap whole fields to make their farms more manageable.

Under s. 38 of the 1925 Act, a life tenant can exchange all or part of the settled land for land owned by a third party. If the land acquired is worth more than the land given up, 'capital money' already in the hands of the SLA trustees may be used to balance up. (If necessary, the settled land can be mortgaged in order to raise the balancing payment.) If the imbalance is the other way, a balancing payment must be paid to the SLA trustees as capital money.

12.4.3   POWER OF LEASING

Some textbooks give a lot of detail on this issue; there is no need to get bogged down in those details.

Sections 41 to 48 provide that a life tenant may lease all or part of the settled land, subject to restrictions on the length of the lease. All leases except those which qualify as 'building', 'mining', or 'forestry' are subject to a (maximum) limit of 50 years. In particular leases for residential or commercial purposes (shops, offices, etc.) are subject to this unrealistically short limit, unless they qualify as 'building' leases. Agricultural leases are also subject to the 50-year limit.

A 'building lease' may be granted by a life tenant for up to 999 years (sic). A building lease is one where the lessee agrees **to construct or reconstruct** buildings on the land. Thus, for example, it would be permissible for a life tenant to grant a lease for 500 years to a property company which undertakes to build a block of flats and/or offices on the land.

A 'forestry lease' may also be granted for up to 999 years. Such a lease is obviously one granted for the purposes of growing trees. However, it can be granted only to the Forestry Commission or the Ministry of Agriculture under the Forestry Act 1967.

A 'mining lease' may be granted for up to 100 years. A mining lease is one under which the tenant has the right to extract minerals from the land. 'Minerals' is very widely defined and covers such things as sand, gravel, clay and quarrystone.

Where a life tenant grants a lease, the rent must be the best reasonably obtainable in the circumstances existing at the time of the grant of the lease. Sometimes landlords charge a 'premium' for the grant of a long lease. A life tenant is permitted to charge a 'premium' for the grant of a lease, but this premium will be capital money payable to the SLA trustees. By contrast, the rent from a lease is income belonging to the life tenant.

With mining and forestry leases the rent may vary with the mineral extracted/wood cut, etc. With mining leases the life tenant is not allowed to keep all the rent as income; a proportion of the rent must be paid to the trustees as capital. The exact rules are discussed at **12.7.3**.

There are a number of empty cottages on Bigpots Estate. Bloggs Ltd are offering to take a long lease (perhaps as long as 100 years) of one of the cottages for the purposes of offices. They would want to pay a large premium for the grant of the lease, but with a low rent to compensate. Is such a lease within the Duke's powers?

Unless the lease is drafted as a 'building lease' (which would be the case if Bloggs Ltd undertook to 'reconstruct' the cottage) a lease for 100 years would not be possible. The maximum of 50 years would apply. Granting a lease at a premium is allowed, but the premium is 'capital money' which must be paid to the SLA trustees.

12.4.4   POWER TO MORTGAGE THE SETTLED LAND

A life tenant may not mortgage the land for his own private purposes. So he cannot mortgage the land to raise finance for, say, his own personal business enterprise. He can mortgage the land only for the following purposes (all these purposes benefit the land rather than just the life tenant):

(a)   In order to discharge an existing mortgage or encumbrance (e.g. a charge for inheritance tax) on the land.

(b)   To pay for authorised improvements (see **12.4.5**).

(c)   To provide a balancing payment on exchange of land (see **12.4.2**).

Money raised by mortgage is 'capital money'. The mortgagee must therefore pay it not to the life tenant but to the SLA trustees.

12.4.5   USE OF CAPITAL MONEY TO PAY FOR 'AUTHORISED' IMPROVEMENTS

(As with the power to grant leases, some textbooks go into unnecessary detail.)

Capital money in the hands of the SLA trustees may (at the demand of the life tenant) be used to pay for improvements authorised by sch. 3 of the Settled Land Act 1925, provided:

(a)   a certificate is provided by an engineer or surveyor certifying that the improvements have been carried out properly, and specifying the amount properly payable; **or**

(b)   the court orders payment out of capital money.

The money paid out for the cost of improvements may be money raised by mortgaging the settled land (see **12.4.4**), or money raised by earlier transactions (e.g. sale of part of the land).

Schedule 3 of the 1925 Act is a wonderful piece of social history, but obsolete by the standards of the late twentieth century. The idea behind sch. 3 is that in certain circumstances the life tenant must use **income** from the settled land to repay to the SLA trustees **capital** expended on improvements. Schedule 3 is divided into three parts:

Part I   For example, drainage and irrigation works; building cottages for agricultural labourers. If the improvement falls within Part I, the life tenant cannot be required to repay out of income the capital expended.

Part II   For example, houses for managerial staff; offices. If the improvement falls within Part II, the SLA trustees have a discretion to order repayment out of income. Repayment must be by half-yearly instalments. The SLA trustees also have a discretion as to the number of instalments (except that they must not exceed 50), but no discretion to order partial repayment.

Part III   For example, heating and lighting in buildings; agricultural machinery. The SLA trustees must order the repayment of the capital, by half-yearly instalments not exceeding 50.

The idea of the 1925 legislators was to put in Part I those improvements which were considered permanent in nature; in Part II those which were semi-permanent; in Part III those which were transitory. In the light of modern conditions, some of the choices made in 1925 look very strange.

SAQ 64

Suppose the Duke of Plaza Toro wants to mortgage Bigpots Estate to raise cash:

(a) so that he can buy shares in a company bidding for private railway franchises;

(b) so that work can be carried out to protect low-lying fields from flooding.

Would such a mortgage be within his statutory powers?

As to (a), the answer is, of course, no; this transaction would be for private purposes unconnected with the land or the settlement.

As to (b), this is of course an authorised improvement and so mortgaging Bigpots for this purpose is allowed. But note:

(i) the money raised will be paid (initially) to the SLA trustees, not to the Duke;

(ii) (unless a court order is obtained) the trustees will not be able to pay the contractors carrying out the flood defence work until a certificate is obtained from a surveyor or engineer that the job has been done;

(iii) this improvement will fall within Part I of Sch. 3, and therefore the Duke cannot be compelled to reimburse the money expended out of the income from the Bigpots estate.

12.4.6   POWER TO GRANT OPTIONS

ACTIVITY 27

Refer back to what I said about options at 1.4.10, noting in particular the terms upon which the option over Purple House was granted.

The power to grant options contained in s. 51 of the Settled Land Act 1925 is in modern conditions **virtually useless**. Under s. 51, an option may be granted over the whole or part of the settled land. The option must:

(a) be exercisable within a period not exceeding 10 years; and

(b) fix the price payable on the exercise of the option. This price must be the best
reasonably obtainable in the light of circumstances existing at the time of the grant
of the option.

Surprisingly, the life tenant need not demand a consideration for the grant of the option,
but any consideration which is charged is 'capital money' payable to the SLA trustees.

**Referring back to what I said about options at 1.4.10, consider why the life tenant's
statutory power to grant options is virtually useless.**

In these days of often highly volatile land prices, no sane person grants an option (save
perhaps a very short-term one) where the price to be paid on exercise of the option is
fixed by the option agreement itself. Rather, as in my Purple House example, there is
provision for the price to be fixed by an arbitrator selected by the president of the RICS
or some other reputable body.

12.4.7 POWER TO EFFECT ANY TRANSACTION WITH THE COURT'S CONSENT

The life tenant may go beyond his statutory powers provided he obtains the consent of
the court. So with the prior consent of the court a life tenant can grant an option with
the price to be fixed by an arbitrator. Or he can grant a residential lease to last for 99
years. But applications to court cost money!

12.4.8 POWER TO DIRECT INVESTMENT ETC. OF CAPITAL MONEY

Here we have another illustration of the 'life tenant is boss' philosophy of the 1925 Act.
With all trusts **other than those governed by the Settled Land Act**, it is the trustees who
decide how trust funds are to be invested and the beneficiaries cannot (normally)
interfere in such decisions. With SLA trusts, all 'capital money' is paid to the SLA
trustees, yet it is the life tenant who can instruct the SLA trustees as to the use of the
money. Only if he makes no decision do the SLA trustees decide.

Capital money may be used:

(a) to buy investments authorised by the Trustee Investment Act 1961 (e.g., certain
types of stocks and shares; government and local authority bonds);

(b) to buy fees simple, or leases with at least 60 years to run (this new land purchased
will become settled land, and a vesting deed transferring the land to the life tenant
will have to be executed);

(c) to pay for improvements;

(d) to discharge mortgages or other encumbrances (e.g. the charge for inheritance tax)
upon the settled land.

Tito and Tonio hold £500,000 'capital money' as a result of earlier sales of small parts of Bigpots. This money is currently invested in shares in a range of plcs, and is bringing in a good income. The Duke asks them to sell the shares and spend the £500,000 on Smallacres, a local farm which has just come onto the market. The SLA trustees would prefer to retain the existing investments, so must they comply with this demand?

In principle, the answer is 'Yes', they must. But if £500,000 was an excessive price for Smallacres, the trustees could presumably argue that the Duke is in breach of his duty to get the best consideration reasonably obtainable on any transaction.

12.5   Invalidation of All Restrictions on a Life Tenant's Powers

The approach of the Settled Land Act 1925, as I have said several times, is that 'the life tenant is boss of the settled land'. Section 106 re-emphasises that this 'boss' role is sacrosanct. Any attempt to remove or restrict the powers of the life tenant is void, as are attempts to discourage the life tenant from exercising his powers.

Section 106 covers (*inter alia*) determinable life interests, conditions subsequent, consent clauses and residence clauses. All such provisions are invalid in so far as they prevent or discourage the exercise of the statutory powers. Thus:

(a)   If Redacres is granted to 'John for life or until he sells the land', s. 106 requires the deletion of the last six words. John will get a perfectly normal life interest.

(b)   If Pinkacres is granted to 'Jean for life provided that she does not dispose of the land', the last nine words will be deleted. Jean will get a perfectly normal life interest.

(c)   If Whiteacres is granted to 'Ken for life, but he shall only dispose of the land if he gets the consent of the SLA trustees', Ken can sell without getting anybody's consent.

Suppose, however, that there is a **residence clause**. Green Mansion is granted to 'Fred for life until he ceases to reside in Green Mansion'. Such a clause is invalid only in so far as it discourages the exercise of the statutory powers. Thus:

(a)   If Fred ceases to reside in the Mansion as a result of his exercising any of his statutory powers his life interest will continue. (If he has sold the land his life interest will be overreached in the usual way and will transfer to the purchase price paid to the trustees.)

(b)   If, however, Fred leaves simply because he prefers to live elsewhere, then he does lose his life interest.

SAQ 66

Suppose that Bigpots estate was granted to the Duke 'for life provided he continues to reside on the estate'. Imagine it is January. The Duke's Rolls-Royce pulls into your office car-park laden with skis, toboggans, etc. The Duke tells you: 'The Duchess is having dreadful problems with her breathing, so we are going to move to the Swiss health resort of Davos. But I cannot afford to lose my rights under the settlement of Bigpots.' Advise the Duke.

The Duke should of course sell (or lease) the whole of Bigpots, so that he cannot possibly reside there. He will then avoid forfeiting his interest, as s. 106 will protect him from the condition subsequent. But selling (leasing) a large estate cannot be done overnight, so until that is achieved, Davos cannot become his home. It must remain just a nice place for him to spend his holidays.

12.6 Safeguards Against the Life Tenant Abusing His Position

There are certain safeguards against the life tenant abusing his 'boss' role, but I have always felt that these safeguards are rather inadequate.

12.6.1 THE 'TRUSTEE' ROLE OF THE LIFE TENANT

Textbooks usually say that a life tenant is a 'trustee' not only of the legal estate, but also of his statutory powers. Apart from the duty to get the best consideration reasonably obtainable, this 'safeguard' does not amount to much.

It is true that in deciding upon dispositions the life tenant is supposed to consider how other beneficiaries would be affected, e.g., would they be disappointed if the land were sold? But a life tenant is under no duty even to consult other beneficiaries about proposed dispositions, let alone get their consent.

12.6.2 NOTICE TO THE SLA TRUSTEES

Under s. 101(1), the life tenant must give one month's notice to the SLA trustees, and to their solicitor if known, of his intention to exercise his statutory powers. This safeguard is of limited value for the following reasons:

(a) A 'general notice' suffices, except for the power to mortgage. (By a 'general notice' I mean something like 'I hereby give notice that I intend from time to time to exercise all or any of my powers under the Settled Land Act'.)

(b) If the SLA trustees hear of a proposed transaction which appears undesirable, they may intervene (if necessary seek an injunction) but they are under no duty to do so. Suppose that the SLA trustees hear that the life tenant is proposing to sell for £200,000. The trustees know that the land is worth £300,000. They **may** seek an injunction to prevent this sale at an undervalue. But if they cannot be bothered to go to the court and the sale goes ahead, the beneficiaries who have lost out from the deal cannot sue the SLA trustees for breach of trust. Put another way, SLA trustees are **not** under the duty, imposed on all other types of trustee, to ensure that when trust property is sold, the property is sold for the best price reasonably obtainable.

(c) Lack of notice to the SLA trustees does not invalidate a disposition in favour of a purchaser in good faith.

12.6.3 DISPOSITIONS OF THE PRINCIPAL MANSION HOUSE

The 'principal mansion house' is the main residence on the settled land. However, a house only counts as a 'principal mansion house' if together with its 'pleasure grounds or park' it occupies at least 25 acres (sic). We are thus thinking in terms of a 'stately home' set in formal gardens laid out by some landscape gardener such as 'Capability Brown'. (There cannot be many principal mansion houses left today!)

Where there is a principal mansion house, the law provides a small exception to s. 106 of the Settled Land Act. A disposition of the principal mansion house requires the consent of the SLA trustees **or** the court if either:

(a) the settlement is pre-1926 and does not provide to the contrary; or

(b) the settlement is post-1925 and specifically requires the consent of the SLA trustees or the court.

The Bigpots Estate settlement was made in 1950. The Duke now wants to lease the Great Hall, the largest house on the estate, to the National Union of Law Lecturers ('NULL') for 40 years. (NULL wants the Hall for a conference centre.) Tito and Tonio (the SLA trustees) are opposed to the lease. Advise them.

A lease for 40 years is (in principle) within the life tenant's powers. But remember that the Duke is under a duty to get the best consideration reasonably obtainable. So if the proposed rent and/or premium is inadequate, the trustees could **on that ground** seek an injunction preventing the granting of the lease (see **12.6.2**).

The trustees' **consent** to the lease will be required only if:

(a) the Great Hall is a principal mansion house, **and**

(b) the settlement includes an express clause requiring the consent of the trustees to dispositions affecting the principal mansion house.

But remember that the Great Hall will be a principal mansion house only if, together with its 'pleasure grounds or park', it occupies at least 25 acres. Even if the Great Hall falls within this restrictive definition and the settlement contains an appropriate consent clause, the Duke might still by-pass the Trustees by getting the consent of the court.

12.7   The Doctrine of Waste

Here we have an ancient common law doctrine of rather limited significance in modern conditions. '**Waste**' can be defined as any action which changes the nature of a piece of land in any way. A life tenant's liability for waste depends on the type of waste alleged, and on the terms of the settlement.

12.7.1 AMELIORATING WASTE

This is where the change in the nature of the land actually improves its value, e.g., the life tenant builds upon land which was previously only poor quality agricultural land. It has been clear, at least since 1882, that a life tenant is free to improve the settled land, even if the other beneficiaries object.

12.7.2 PERMISSIVE WASTE

This is where the change in the nature of the land is brought about by the inaction of the life tenant, e.g (in particular), he allows buildings to fall into disrepair, or allows farm land to become flooded. A life tenant is not liable for permissive waste, unless the settlement expressly provides that he shall be under a duty to keep the property in good condition.

In old-fashioned strict settlements it was unusual for the life tenant to be placed under a duty to repair buildings. This is to be contrasted with tenants under long-term leases, who usually are placed under a duty to keep the property in good repair.

12.7.3 VOLUNTARY WASTE

Voluntary waste is any positive action by the life tenant which reduces the value of the settled land, e.g. (in particular), the cutting of timber and the extraction of minerals. At common law a life tenant is prima facie 'impeachable for waste', i.e. he cannot commit voluntary waste. Prior to the Settled Land Act 1882, that might well have meant that valuable minerals under the settled land could not be extracted.

Quite a few traditional strict settlements did, however, include a clause that the life tenancy was granted 'without impeachment for waste'. A life tenant 'unimpeachable for waste' was thus able to carry on mining or forestry operations and keep all the profits for himself. These common law rules have now been modified by the 1925 Act.

12.7.3.1 Cutting timber

A life tenant 'impeachable for waste' can always grant a forestry lease, but if he wishes to cut timber himself he must comply with s. 66 of the 1925 Act. Under this provision he must:

(a) get the consent of the SLA trustees or the court; **and**

(b) pay three-quarters of the net proceeds to the trustees as capital money.

12.7.3.2 Mining

A life tenant 'impeachable for waste' cannot personally extract minerals from the land, but he can grant mining leases. Three-quarters of the rent must be paid to the SLA trustees as capital money.

A life tenant 'unimpeachable for waste' may personally extract minerals, and keep all the proceeds, or he may grant mining leases. If he grants a mining lease he keeps only three-quarters of the rent; the other quarter goes to the SLA trustees as capital money.

12.7.4 EQUITABLE WASTE

In the eighteenth and nineteenth centuries there seem to have been a number of life tenants who, having been granted their life estates 'without impeachment for waste', thought that they were totally free to destroy the property and leave just a worthless ruin for the other beneficiaries to 'enjoy'. In the earliest case (*Vane* v *Lord Barnard* (1716) 2 Vern 738 the life tenant started to pull down the ancestral (Norman) castle. In another case, a Capability Brown formal garden was destroyed.

Ever since 1716 the courts have consistently held that a life tenant 'unimpeachable for waste' is nevertheless liable for 'equitable waste'. Equitable waste can be defined as acts of wanton destruction which reduce the value of the land without bringing any benefit to the life tenant.

The Duke of Plaza Toro was granted his life estate 'without impeachment for waste'. Small Grange is a pleasant country house on a quiet corner of Bigpots. It was built by a distinguished architect, but it is not a 'listed building'. The Duke considers it to be a 'hideous monstrosity', and wants to demolish it. Advise Luiz (remember he is entitled to the fee simple in remainder), who wants the building preserved.

Luiz should seek an injunction against his father, alleging that the demolition would be 'wanton destruction' and therefore equitable waste. But he should act quickly. In *Vane* v *Lord Barnard*, a son obtained an injunction against his life tenant father. But by the time the injunction was served on the father the demolition had largely been completed.

12.8   Conclusion

As mentioned at the beginning of the preceding chapter, most law **teachers** want to scrap strict settlements. That would mean scrapping most of the Settled Land Act 1925. The 'life tenant is boss' philosophy of that act, the source of many of the difficulties discussed in the previous chapter, is also the cause of most of the problems discussed in the present chapter. On the one hand, Parliament has fought shy of giving the life tenant the same powers of disposition as an absolute owner. On the other hand, the safeguards against the life tenant abusing his powers are generally considered to be inadequate.

The law discussed in this chapter is both complex and out-of-date for modern economic requirements. Moreover, it must always be remembered that these complex but anachronistic rules apply not just to life tenants of strict settlements (of which there are now only a few) but also to trustees of trusts for sale (of which there are very many). The need for reform is urgent.

CHAPTER THIRTEEN

TRUSTS FOR SALE OF LAND

13.1 Objectives

By the end of this chapter you should:

■ be familiar with the basic definition of a trust for sale;

■ be able to explain the paradoxical concept of a trust for sale subject to consents;

■ be able to explain the quite varied powers of trustees for sale;

■ be familiar with the basic rules for the appointment, retirement and removal of trustees.

13.2 Introduction

As I have been hinting in the last few chapters, and as we shall now see in this and the ensuing chapters, the trust for sale concept is of fundamental importance to modern English land law. The basic idea of a trust for sale is easy enough: land is conveyed to trustees subject to a duty to sell that land and invest the proceeds for the benefit of the beneficiaries. Yet the basic concept is hedged round with all sorts of complications. Nowadays trustees for sale can (and very often do) exercise their power to postpone the sale. When they postpone sale, the obvious question arises, 'What is done with the land in the meanwhile?'. As we shall see in this chapter, the answer to this question is not entirely straightforward.

We shall also see that, unlike where there is a strict settlement, with a trust for sale 'the trustees are boss'. But that can lead to complications, particularly if there is friction between beneficiaries and trustees.

13.3 Trusts for Sale Defined

Trusts for sale of land are (thankfully) outside the scope of the Settled Land Act 1925 and are instead governed by ss. 23 to 33 of the Law of Property Act 1925. Section 205(1)(xix) of that Act rather unhelpfully defines a trust for sale as an 'immediate binding trust for sale'. (That is rather like defining a spade as 'a spade with a handle and a blade'.) If a trust of land is not an 'immediate binding trust for sale' then (unless it is a bare trust, i.e. a trust with just one adult beneficiary) it must be a strict settlement governed by the Settled Land Act.

There are a number of difficult situations where it is not at first sight clear whether a disposition creates a strict settlement or a trust for sale:

(a) Suppose a trust is created where the trustees are given merely the **power** to sell the land, but are under no **duty** to do so. This will be a strict settlement, though ironically it will be the life tenant who has power to sell the land.

(b) Land is conveyed to trustees 'on trust to retain or sell'. The Law of Property Act 1925, s. 25(4) provides that such a disposition shall be construed as a trust for sale.

(c) Land is conveyed to trustees on trust for sale, but subject to a clause that the consent of a named person(s) be obtained to the sale. (The named person will probably, but not necessarily, be a beneficiary under the trust.) For example, land is conveyed 'to Tim and Tam on trust for sale for X for life, remainder to Y. The sale shall take place only if W and X agree to it'. This sort of arrangement definitely **is** a trust for sale, even though Tim and Tam can carry out their 'duty' to sell only if W and X agree. I will forgive you if you find this point extremely surprising.

(d) A house is conveyed to trustees for sale, but subject to a direction that they permit the beneficiary with the current life interest to live in the house as long as he or she wishes. In *Re Herklot's Will Trusts* [1964] 2 All ER 66, such a disposition was treated as a valid trust for sale, the sale to be subject to the consent of the beneficiary.

Read *Re Herklot* in *Cases and Materials* (13.1), and keep the outcome of that case firmly in mind when reading the next few pages.

Everybody accepts that the will in *Re Herklot* was itself badly drafted. However, it was the inspiration for a form of will which is nowadays quite common.

Suppose you have a client making his will. He wishes to ensure that his widow can live in his house until her death, and on her death he wishes the house to be sold and the proceeds split between his children. He should create a trust for sale, with the equitable interests to W for life, remainder to the children in equal shares. The trust for sale should include clauses:

(i)   making any sale subject to W's consent;

(ii) empowering the trustees to permit W to live in the house pending sale.

Other dispositions which may cause problems are as follows:

(e) A trust is created on the following lines. Blackacre is conveyed 'to Tim and Tam as trustees for sale, the sale to be subject to the consent of X'. The equitable interests under the trust read 'to W for life, remainder to X if the land is unsold at W's death, otherwise remainder to Y'.

Imagine you are X. If you agree to Blackacre being sold you lose your interest under the trust. So you are not going to agree! **If the trust is valid**, then the settlor creating the trust has in effect made it impossible to sell Blackacre. In *Re Inns* [1947] Ch 576, a judge was faced with a will creating a trust like that currently under discussion. The actual dispute was, however, on another point. The judge **assumed** the trust was valid. I think that that was wrong. The trust should have been declared void. To uphold such a trust would go against the policy of the 1925 legislation of ensuring that all land can be bought and sold without too much difficulty.

(f)   A trust for sale is created to take effect only on some future date. For example, land is conveyed to Tim and Tam as trustees, in trust for Z and to sell the land when Z attains the age of 25 (Z is, say, aged 15). In this case the trust for sale is not 'immediate'. Therefore, pending Z attaining 25, there is a strict settlement governed by the Settled Land Act 1925.

A more likely example of a future trust for sale is where land is granted to W for life, remainder to Tim and Tom as trustees for sale in trust for X and Y in equal shares. The land will be settled land during W's lifetime, and become subject to a trust for sale on her death.

If you are thinking, 'A situation where land is first settled land and then later held on a trust for sale is going to be awfully complicated,' then you are right. Legal advisers should at all costs avoid such a situation.

13.4   Trusts for Sale Subject to Consents

As you can see from examples (c), (d) and (e) at **13.3**, the whole question of 'trusts for sale subject to consents' is not an easy one. Such trusts are anomalous and should perhaps be prohibited. However, you should remember:

(i)   that, except in the situation discussed in example (d), trusts for sale subject to consent are uncommon;

(ii)   that with most trusts for sale (whether or not there is a consent clause) the duty to sell is purely theoretical. The trustees usually exercise their 'power' to postpone sale; sale is often postponed for many years.

In principle, where there is a clause in a trust for sale requiring the consent of named person(s) to a sale, a sale without the requisite consent(s) is void. Suppose land is conveyed to Tim and Tom as trustees for sale, the sale to take place only with the consent of A, B, C, D, E, F, G, H, I, J, K, L, M, N, O, P, Q, R, S, T, U, V, W, X, Y and Z. You may be thinking, 'Very clever, it will be impossible to get the agreement of all 26 "consenters". The person creating this trust has effectively ensured that the land cannot be sold'.

The person who created this trust reckoned without s. 26(1) of the Law of Property Act 1925. This provides that, in favour of a purchaser, where the consent of more than two people is required for a sale by trustees for sale, the consent of **any two** will suffice. Thus, in our rather absurd example with 26 'consenters', the agreement of only two out of A to Z is necessary for a valid sale. By listing a lot of 'consenters' the person creating the trust has (ironically) made it easier to sell the land than if he had listed just two!

I should also mention s. 26(2). This provides that if a 'consenter' is under 18, then in favour of a purchaser his consent is not required.

Tom owns a large house. He has a wife, Wendy, and a son, Simon. Tom is in poor health, and wishes to make a will under which Wendy would have the right to occupy the house for the rest of her lifetime, but without any power to sell or lease the house. On Wendy's death the house would pass to Simon absolutely.

Why should Tom be advised to create, not a strict settlement, but a trust for sale, and what sort of provisions should that trust contain?

There are two reasons why Tom should not create a strict settlement. First, we would not want his family to get entangled in the highly complex law discussed in the preceding two chapters. Secondly, if a strict settlement were created, Wendy would be life tenant, and she would have a power to sell the house which could not be taken away. (Remember s. 106 of the Settled Land Act 1925 at **12.5**.)

Tom should appoint as trustees for sale people who are sympathetic to his wishes. He should also include clauses:

(a)   requiring that any sale be with the consent of **both** Wendy and Simon;

(b)   requiring the trustees to permit Wendy to live in the house pending sale.

13.5   Powers of Trustees for Sale

13.5.1   MANAGEMENT OF THE LAND WHERE THE SALE IS POSTPONED

If the sale is postponed the trustees carry on the day-to-day management of the land. The net income is paid to the beneficiary(ies) who would be entitled to the income from the proceeds if the land were already sold. Where the trust property includes a dwelling house it is perfectly possible for a beneficiary to be allowed the income 'in kind' by being permitted to reside on the property.

Suppose a large farm, Broadacres, is conveyed to T1 and T2, 'on trust to sell Broadacres and hold the proceeds in trust for X for life, remainder to Y and Z in equal shares'. The trustees decide to postpone sale. They should personally (or through agents) cultivate the farm, and pay the net profits from the farm to X. (That is obviously fair. Why should X be prejudiced by the decision to postpone sale?) If there is an empty house on the farm, they can permit X to live there.

13.5.2   DISPOSITIONS OTHER THAN SALE

By s. 28 of the Law of Property Act 1925, trustees for sale of land have all the powers of disposition, etc. which the Settled Land Act grants to life tenants.

What would be another sensible alternative for the trustees in our Broadacres example to adopt if they decide to postpone sale? (It might be particularly appropriate if the trustees had no experience of farming.)

They could lease the farm to a tenant-farmer for a period not exceeding 50 years.

You may recall that I indicated at **12.3** that some of the life tenant's powers granted by the Settled Land Act 1925 are inadequate in modern conditions. It is these same inadequate powers which are given to trustees for sale. In view of the large numbers of trusts for sale in existence today, the problem is potentially very serious.

Most trusts for sale overcome the problem in a very simple way. When the trust is created the lawyer drafting the trust includes a clause giving to the trustees the same powers of disposition as would be enjoyed by an outright owner. Thus the trustees can lease the land for any period considered appropriate, and they can grant options where the price is to be fixed by an arbitrator.

13.5.3 CONSENTS TO DISPOSITIONS OTHER THAN SALE

If the trustees' duty to sell is subject to consent(s), the same consent(s) must also be obtained to any exercise of the powers of disposition 'borrowed' from the Settled Land Act. I must grudgingly admit that this is logical. Suppose in my Broadacres example at **13.5.1** there is a clause in the trust requiring X's consent to a sale. It would be strange if the trustees could lease the land for a long period without X's consent.

13.5.4 DELEGATION OF MANAGEMENT AND LEASING POWERS

Where a trust is governed by the Settled Land Act 1925, 'the life tenant is boss'. With all other trusts, including trusts for sale of land, the trustees are boss. Section 29 of the Law of Property Act 1925 is a fairly small exception to this 'trustees are boss' rule. (In the law of trusts you learn about the principle that 'trustees must not delegate their trust'. I must therefore stress that s. 29 of the 1925 Act is an exception to that general principle.)

Under s. 29, if trustees for sale of land postpone sale they may delegate certain of their powers to the person(s) currently entitled to the income from the land. These powers are:

(a) day-to-day management of the land;

(b) leasing of the property.

Any delegation under s. 29 must be in writing, and can be revoked at any time. While a delegation remains in force the beneficiary (X in my example) must exercise the delegated powers with proper care in the interests of all the beneficiaries of the trust. If the beneficiary fails in this duty it is he, **not the trustees**, who is liable for any losses sustained.

SAQ 71

In my Broadacres example, if the trustees decide to postpone sale, what therefore is yet another course of action open to them?

They can delegate management of the land (and/or leasing powers) to X.

SAQ 72

What if X has no experience of farming, and the trustees are worried that 'he might make a mess of things'? Can the trustees still delegate their leasing/management powers?

The answer is 'Yes.' Moreover, the trustees can 'sleep easy' in the knowledge that they cannot be liable for any losses caused by X, and that they can (if need be) revoke the delegation at any time.

13.5.5 POWERS OF INVESTMENT OF TRUSTEES FOR SALE

As you will learn more fully when you study the law of trusts, trustees of a trust where the **original** trust property is **not** land but personal property, such as money, stocks, shares, and debentures etc., can as a general rule invest only in investments authorised by the Trustee Investment Act 1961. Such trustees cannot invest in the purchase of land.

Trustees for sale of **land** are luckier. They have the same powers of investment as SLA trustees. Consequently they can invest proceeds of sale in purchasing freeholds or leases with 60 or more years to run; or they can invest in investments authorised by the Trustee Investment Act 1961. If 'new' land is purchased by the trustees, this 'new' land will itself automatically be held on trust for sale.

There is, however, one problem. If trustees for sale of land sell all the land they hold, it appears that they cease to be 'trustees for sale of land'. They therefore cannot invest in the purchase of 'new' land!

There are many trusts for sale in existence today where the trust property consists of just one house. If the trustees sell that house, they have no **statutory** power to buy a replacement.

Good solicitors, when drafting trusts for sale, know how to overcome this difficulty. What do they do?

You may have realised that the way to overcome this difficulty is for solicitors to include in the document creating the trust for sale an express power authorising the trustees to invest proceeds of sale in the purchase of 'new' land even if they have sold all the original land.

Think what you would do if you had a trust for sale where the trust property consists of just one house (and its garden), the trustees want to sell that house and buy a replacement, but the solicitors who created the trust (not your firm) did not include the express power referred to in the answer to SAQ 73.

I hope the bracketed 'and its garden' gave you a clue. What you do is sell the first house, **except for a tiny corner of the garden**. The trustees (who are still trustees for sale of land because they retain the tiny corner) then buy the replacement house. Finally the trustees convey the tiny corner (for a nominal consideration) to the purchaser of the first house.

13.6   Involvement of Beneficiaries in the Trust for Sale

Although with a trust for sale 'the trustees are boss', the beneficiaries do, in some situations, have a say in what is to be done with the land. I have already mentioned the possibility of the trustees delegating certain powers under s. 29 (see **13.5.4**). There are other points which I should also mention.

13.6.1   DUTY TO CONSULT BENEFICIARIES

Section 26(3) of the Law of Property Act 1925 is a very complex looking provision, but in reality it is not as important as you might at first think:

> Trustees for sale shall as far as practicable consult the persons of full age for the time being beneficially entitled to the rents and profits pending sale, and shall, so far as is

consistent with the general interest of the trust, give effect to the wishes of such persons, or in the case of dispute, of the majority (according to the value of their combined interests) of such persons, but a purchaser shall not be concerned to see that the provisions of this sub-section have been complied with.

Why is this provision not quite as important as you might think? First, it applies only to certain trusts for sale. In particular, it applies only to a deliberately created trust for sale if the trust **expressly provides** that there **shall** be a duty to consult. Thus in our Broadacres example at **13.5.1**, the trustees would be under a duty to consult X (the current beneficiary) only if there was a clause in the trust document saying that there should be a duty to consult.

(As we shall see in **Chapter 15**, a trust for sale is imposed by statute upon co-owners of land. The s. 26(3) duty to consult also applies to such **imposed** trusts for sale.)

Secondly, where the s. 26(3) duty does apply, it is only a duty to **consult**; it is not a duty to **obey**. The trustees do not have to give effect to the wishes of the beneficiary(ies) if they (the trustees) consider those wishes to be contrary to 'the general interest of the trust'.

Which rule, which we encountered in Chapter 11 and is about to be mentioned again, is in sharp contrast to that in s. 26(3)?

The rule in *Saunders* v *Vautier*, which does allow the beneficiaries, **if unanimous**, to dictate the fate of the trust property.

Thirdly, transactions by trustees made without consulting beneficiaries will always be valid.

13.6.2   SECTION 30 OF THE LAW OF PROPERTY ACT 1925

Now this provision is of very great significance:

If the trustees for sale refuse to sell or to exercise any of the powers conferred by either of the last two sections, or any requisite consent cannot be obtained, any person interested may apply to the court for a vesting or other order for giving effect to the proposed transaction or for an order directing the trustees for sale to give effect thereto, and the court may make such order as it thinks fit.

This provision may be invoked where:

(a)   the trustees are refusing to sell despite the wishes of a beneficiary;

(b)   the trustees are in disagreement over whether to sell the land, or in disagreement over some other proposed transaction (e.g., a lease) which is within their powers;

(c)   the trustees are refusing to carry out some other disposition within their powers though that disposition is desired by one of the beneficiaries;

(d)   the trustees are refusing to exercise their power under s. 29 of the Act to delegate their leasing/management powers;

(e)   a proposed sale/transaction cannot take place because a requisite consent(s) cannot be obtained.

The court has a broad discretion whether or not to make the order sought, considering the wishes and interests of the various beneficiaries. Section 30 has given rise to quite a lot of case law; but almost all the cases also involve the law of co-ownership. We will therefore delay considering these cases until **Chapter 16**.

13.6.3   THE RULE IN *SAUNDERS* v *VAUTIER* AND TRUSTS FOR SALE

We examined this important rule at **11.7.3**. Where all possible beneficiaries of a trust for sale (or any other kind of trust) are identifiable, of full age, and in **unanimous agreement**, they can dictate to the trustees what is to happen to the trust property. They can insist that the land be sold; they can insist that the land be retained, etc; they can even insist on the replacement of the existing trustees (**however satisfactory**) with trustees of their own choice.

13.7   Appointment, Retirement and Removal of Trustees

You will need to know more about these topics when studying the law of trusts. What follows are certain basic principles you need to know for the purposes of a study of land law.

13.7.1   THE ORIGINAL TRUSTEES

The general rule is that the settlor appoints the original trustees by the document(s) setting up the trust. A person appointed at the outset can 'disclaim' the trust, i.e. refuse to act. (You should note that, **unless the trust instrument provides otherwise**, trustees are not allowed to charge for their services, though they may claim the expenses of running the trust out of trust income.)

With a trust of land, there is a **maximum** of four trustees. As we shall see in **Chapters 15 and 16**, this rule is important. If a document purports to appoint more than four trustees, the first four named are the trustees.

Suppose a deed conveys Greenacre to Alfred, Bernard, Charles, David, and Eric on trust for sale (all are of full age). Eric will not be a trustee. Suppose that Bernard dies shortly after the trust is set up. Alfred, Charles and David continue as trustees, but Eric **does not become a trustee**. As we shall see, Alfred, Charles and David can now appoint a colleague, **who can be anybody they wish**. There is no obligation on them to appoint Eric.

A minor cannot be appointed to be a trustee, though an attempt to do so will not invalidate the trust. Suppose a trust instrument appointed Angela, Betty, and Cathy to be trustees, but Betty was only 17. Angela and Cathy will be the trustees. Betty **would not become a trustee** on her attaining 18. As you may have guessed, Angela and Cathy can appoint up to two colleagues, who can be **whoever they wish**. There is no obligation on them to appoint Betty when she attains her eighteenth birthday.

A settlor creates a trust for sale of land, with George, Harriet, Isobel, John, Karen, Leonard, and Marina as trustees. Five of these people are over 40 years old, but Harriet and Karen are both aged only 16. Who will be the trustees?

The first four named of full age. They will be George, Isobel, John, and Leonard. Moreover, those four will still be the trustees when Harriet and Karen attain 18.

13.7.2   APPOINTING FRESH TRUSTEES TO AN EXISTING TRUST

There are basically four rules:

(a) New appointments may be made by the person(s) nominated by the trust instrument as having the power to appoint new trustees. It is, however, relatively rare for a trust to make provision for appointments by an 'outsider'. Such a provision is sometimes found in charitable trusts, or in pension fund trusts.

(b) If there is no provision for appointment by an outsider(s), or the outsider(s) refuses to act, the existing trustee(s) appoints new trustee(s). In practice this rule that existing trustees appoint new trustees is the rule which operates in the vast majority of cases. It is particularly important to realise that this rule operates even where (for whatever reason) there is currently only one trustee. That one trustee can appoint up to three colleagues.

(c) Suppose all the trustees of a trust die. The rule then is that the personal representatives (executors or administrators) of **the last trustee to die** are automatically temporary trustees of the trust and have the power to appoint permanent trustees. It is perfectly permissible, indeed it is quite common, for the personal representatives to appoint themselves permanent trustees.

(d) The court may have to appoint trustees, though this will in practice happen only in cases of special difficulty, e.g., where all the trustees are incapacitated by mental illness.

13.7.3   WHEN MAY NEW APPOINTMENTS BE MADE?

13.7.3.1   Additional trustees

These may be appointed at any time provided the number of trustees is not increased above the maximum of four.

13.7.3.2   Replacement of trustees

A new trustee may be appointed to replace an existing trustee if the existing trustee:

(a) remains outside the United Kingdom for more than 12 months continuously;

(b) desires to retire from the trust;

(c)   becomes unfit to act (due to bankruptcy, criminal conviction, etc.);

(d)   becomes incapable of acting by reason of lunacy, old age, infirmity, or some other reason;

(e)   is removed under a power contained in the trust instrument.

(A trustee who is retiring may participate in the appointment of a replacement trustee.)

13.7.4   REMOVAL OF TRUSTEES

Trustees may be removed if they fall within categories (a), (c), (d), and (e) in **13.7.3.2**. They may also be removed:

(i)   by the court.

(ii) where the beneficiaries, all being of full age and in agreement, desire the removal of a trustee. (This is merely one application of the rule in *Saunders* v *Vautier*. Under that rule, if all the beneficiaries of a trust are of full age and unanimous in their wishes, they can sack the trustees, put an end to the trust, etc.)

As we shall see more clearly in **Chapters 15** and **16**, there are situations where a trustee is also a beneficiary under the trust. Indeed, as we shall see, where there is co-ownership it is quite normal for a person to have dual roles as both trustee and beneficiary. The point to understand **now** is that if somebody is both trustee and beneficiary and he sells or gives away his equitable interest, he nevertheless remains a trustee of the legal title. The disposal of his equitable interest is not to be treated as a resignation or retirement from the trust, nor is it as such grounds for removing him from the trusteeship.

13.7.5   RETIREMENT OF TRUSTEES

A trustee may retire:

(a)   if another trustee is appointed in his place;

(b)   if after his retirement there will be at least two persons continuing as trustees;

(c)   by employing an express power to retire granted by the trust instrument;

(d)   by getting the unanimous consent of all the beneficiaries;

(e)   by getting the court's consent.

13.7.6   METHOD OF APPOINTMENT OF TRUSTEES

An appointment of a new trustee must be in writing; in practice it is normally made by deed in order to take advantage of s. 40(1) of the Trustee Act 1925. If the deed contains a declaration that the trust property shall vest in the new trustee(s), it conveys the legal title in the trust property from the existing trustees to the persons who will be the trustees after the appointment. For example, suppose A, B, and C are the existing trustees, and they appoint D to replace C who is retiring from the trust. The declaration conveys the legal title from A, B, and C to A, B, and D.

ACTIVITY 31

What I have just said rather assumes that any land involved is unregistered title. What do you think happens if (as is increasingly likely) new trustees are appointed to a trust where the land involved is registered title?

The trustees prior to the new appointment(s) are the registered proprietors until the deed of appointment is presented to the Land Registry. The necessary change(s) are then made to the register. The (new) trustees will be issued with a new land certificate.

13.8 Unanimity of Trustees

13.8.1 THE GENERAL RULE

It is a general rule of the law of trusts that trustees can act only if there is unanimous agreement. Thus if there are four trustees of a trust for sale of land, and the land is to be sold, **all four** must sign both the contract and the conveyance. Please remember this point, particularly when answering examination questions.

SAQ 76

If there are three trustees of a trust for sale, and the land is to be sold, how many trustees must sign both the contract and the conveyance?

The answer is of course three. Why am I labouring this point that **all** the trustees must sign? Because every year I read exam answers which either expressly state or assume that where there are three or four trustees, the signatures of any two will suffice to make a transaction valid.

13.8.2 EXCEPTIONS TO THE UNANIMITY RULE

(a) If the trust instrument provides for decisions to be taken by a majority. (Such a provision is today not uncommon.)

(b) If land is held subject to a charitable trust. In the case of such a trust the law permits there to be more than four trustees. But it also provides that decisions may be taken by majority of the trustees of the charity.

13.9 Conclusion

In the last few pages of this chapter we have been dealing with certain rules which are common to all types of trust (e.g., trusts of stocks and shares); these rules are not confined to trusts for sale of land.

This serves to underline a very important point. The trust for sale of land is merely one species of a very large family of 'animals' all of which are classified as 'trusts'. Remember that, as was said in **Chapter 2**, 'any type of property can be subjected to a trust'.

Land is, however, a very different type of asset from, say shares or debentures. It cannot be moved, but it can be put to all sorts of uses and made subject to a wide range of transactions. It therefore necessarily follows that trustees **of land** need wide powers of disposition and management which will be irrelevant to trusts of abstract assets such as shares or debentures.

As you may have gathered from hints in this chapter (especially the comment on s. 30 of the Law of Property Act 1925 at **13.6.2**), we are by no means finished with trusts for sale. The trust for sale has a crucial role to play in the post-1925 law of co-ownership. That role will be considered in **Chapters 15** and **16**.

13.10   End of Chapter Assessment Question

You are consulted by Sarah in connection with the making of her will. Sarah owns two properties: a large family house, 'The Gables', which she has recently inherited from her husband Thomas; and a country cottage.

Sarah lives at The Gables with her elder sister Jane. Soon after Thomas's death Sarah asked Jane to live with her because of Sarah's ill health. Jane has little money of her own and is rather inexperienced about financial matters.

Sarah tells you that she wishes Jane to be able to live at The Gables for as long as she wishes, and that on Jane's death or on Jane's ceasing to reside at The Gables, for the property to pass to Thomas's godson, James, who has always shown a great interest in the property. However Sarah is particularly anxious that Jane should not be able to use The Gables in order to raise any finance for herself.

With regard to the cottage, Sarah wants a close friend, Amy, to live there if she wishes and that after Amy's death the proceeds of sale are to be divided equally between Sarah's cousin's children. Sarah adds that the cottage is situated rather remotely and so if Amy wishes she should be allowed to sell the cottage and buy another property which is more suitable for her.

Advise Sarah.

See *Cases and Materials* **(13.7)** for a specimen answer.

CHAPTER FOURTEEN

CO-OWNERSHIP OF LAND – THE BASIC CONCEPTS

14.1 Objectives

By the end of this chapter you should:

■ be able to explain the crucial concepts of 'joint tenancy' and 'tenancy in common', **and the differences between them;**

■ appreciate the problem which existed at the beginning of this century caused by tenancies in common existing with respect to a legal estate;

■ appreciate why the 1925 legislators chose to impose a trust for sale upon all co-owners;

■ have very firmly in your mind that a tenancy in common cannot now exist with respect to a legal estate;

■ be able to apply the rules which determine whether co-owners are joint tenants or tenants in common of their equitable interests under the trust for sale.

14.2 Introduction

The law of co-ownership is a topic which directly affects the private lives of many of the readers of this Text. Most married (and unmarried) couples co-own the fee simple of the house in which they live. Alternatively, they co-own a fixed-term lease or periodic tenancy of the house or flat in which they are living. I should, however, stress that co-ownership is not confined to domestic/family situations. For example, (in particular) business partners may well be co-owners of the premises from which they conduct their business.

This chapter (the first of three on co-ownership) will focus on certain basic principles. It has two main themes. The first is that there are **two (very distinct) forms** of co-ownership in modern English property law. The second is the way Parliament, in 1925, endeavoured to solve problems which existed at that time in relation to co-ownership.

14.3 Unity of Possession – the Cornerstone of Co-ownership

Co-ownership exists with respect to a piece of land only if 'unity of possession' between two or more people exists with respect to that piece of land. There is unity of possession if two or more people have concurrent rights to enjoy the **whole** of the relevant piece of land. For example, Jack and Jill Smith own Dream House. Like all normal (married or unmarried) couples they each have rights to possess and enjoy the whole of the house. There is unity of possession and therefore co-ownership.

Contrast Dream House with Hollowtree Field. Farmers Dan and Giles 'own' Hollowtree Field. To the ordinary passer-by it appears to be a perfectly normal field. However there is an imaginary line running north-south across the field. Dan and Giles know where this boundary line is. Everything to the east of that line belongs exclusively to Dan, and Giles has no rights. Everything to the west belongs to Giles, and Dan has no rights. Is there co-ownership in this situation? Of course not. There is no unity of possession and therefore no co-ownership. There are two separate individual ownerships.

14.4   The Four Forms of Co-ownership Recognised by the Common Law

There are theoretically four forms of co-ownership, but two of those forms are obsolete:

■ **Tenancy by entirities**   Completely obsolete as no new ones can be created after 1882 (sic).

■ **Co-parcenary**   So rare today that we can safely ignore the concept. It arises where under the pre-1926 rules of inheritance to real property two or more females constituted the joint heir.

■ **Joint tenancy**   Extremely common today; it is the usual (but not obligatory) form of co-ownership where the co-owners are members of the same 'family'.

■ **Tenancy in common**   Common today. It is usual (but not obligatory) where the co-owners are in a business relationship. Occasionally found within a 'family'.

We need to discuss only 'joint tenancy' and 'tenancy in common'. (Note that in this context the words 'tenant' and 'tenancy' are used in their older, **broader**, sense. In that older sense the word 'tenant' connotes anybody who holds an Estate in land, whether a fee simple, fee tail, life estate or lease.)

14.5   Joint Tenancy

Joint tenancy, at least in modern circumstances, is the simpler of the two forms of co-ownership. Its crucial distinguishing feature is the right of survivorship.

14.5.1   RIGHT OF SURVIVORSHIP

On the death of a joint tenant his interest does not pass under the law of succession, but rather passes to the surviving joint tenant(s).

Suppose Alf, Ben, and Chris are joint tenants of Green Field in fee simple. Alf dies. His will leaves 'all my property to my sister Diana'. Diana acquires no interest in Green Field. Ben and Chris are now joint tenants of Green Field. This would even be true if Alf's will had said, 'I leave all my property including my interest in Green Field to Diana'.

Suppose that Ben now dies intestate, with his widow Elspeth as his sole 'statutory next-of-kin'. Elspeth acquires no interest in Green Field. Chris will be the sole outright owner in fee simple of Green Field. (When he dies normal succession laws will apply.) To put the matter crudely, there is a sort of 'survival of the fittest'. Where there is a joint tenancy, the joint tenant who lives longest gets outright ownership!

This survivorship rule is the main reason why husband and wife co-owners (and other co-owners who are in a close family-type relationship) usually choose to be joint tenants rather than tenants in common. They genuinely wish the land to go to whoever lives longest.

The survivorship rule also explains why people who are **trustees** of property (whether land or any other type of property) are always joint tenants of that property. There are no complications when a trustee dies. The legal title to the trust property automatically passes to the remaining trustee(s).

Humphrey and Wendy Smith are joint tenants of Bugthorpe Manor, worth about £300,000. Humphrey is killed in a hunting accident. He dies intestate. His assets (apart from Bugthorpe Manor) are worth £120,000. He leaves two children, Jack and Jill. On intestacy a surviving spouse is always entitled to the first £125,000 of the deceased's assets. Above that figure, and the children get a share.

Do the children inherit anything on their father's death intestate?

The children inherit nothing, and that would be true even if Bugthorpe Manor were worth not £300,000 but (say) £3,000,000. In working out who gets the deceased's assets on a death intestate, the fact that the deceased was a joint tenant of a (possibly valuable) piece of property must be totally ignored. Thus Wendy is entitled to the £120,000 'other' assets left by her husband.

14.5.2   THE 'FOUR UNITIES'

Wherever there is a joint tenancy, it necessarily follows that 'the four unities' exist between the co-owners:

■   **Unity of possession.**

■   **Unity of interest.**

■   **Unity of title.**

■   **Unity of time.**

'Unity of possession' I have already explained (see **14.3**), and it is of course an essential prerequisite of all forms of co-ownership. (Cf. my Dan and Giles, owners of Green Field, example.) For co-owners to be joint tenants, the unities of interest, title and time must also be present. If any of these three unities is absent, the co-owners will be tenants in common.

14.5.2.1   Unity of interest

For there to be unity of interest, each co-owner must have absolutely identical rights over the land in question. This sub-divides into two separate points:

- **Each co-owner must have the same estate**   It is of course possible for two or more people to be joint tenants of (say) a 10-year lease. What is not possible is a joint tenancy between (say) somebody with a 10-year lease and somebody with a 20-year lease.

- **Each co-owner must have an equal right to enjoy the land**   Where there is a tenancy in common it is possible for the co-owners to have unequal shares. But where there is a joint tenancy, each joint tenant must have an equal interest in the land.

Suppose Len, Mike, Norman, and Ossie are joint tenants in fee simple of Blue Field. They lease Blue Field to Terri. Each of the four joint landlords is entitled to 25 per cent of the rent. (Note that it is technically **wrong** to talk of joint tenants having **'shares'** in land. One should rather talk of joint tenants having **'interests'** or **'rights'**.)

14.5.2.2   Unity of title

This means that each joint tenant must have acquired his interest from the same document or transaction. (As we shall see later when talking about 'severance' (see **Chapter 15**), it is possible to have a situation where there is co-ownership but the co-owners have acquired their rights under different transactions. Such co-owners must necessarily be tenants in common.)

14.5.2.3   Unity of time

For there to be a joint tenancy, the rights of each joint tenant must 'vest in interest' at the same time. Put in more every-day language, the rights of each joint tenant must commence at the same moment.

It is relatively rare to come across situations where the rights of co-owners commence at different times. But sometimes land is left by will (or granted by deed) in terms such as 'to the children of X as each attains 21'. Now (unless all the children are twins/triplets/quads etc.) each child will attain 21 on a different date. There will be no unity of time. The children will therefore be tenants in common.

What if land were granted 'to the children of X when the youngest attains 21'. Could the children in this example be joint tenants?

There would be unity of time, and the children therefore could be joint tenants.

14.6   Tenancy in Common

14.6.1   THE CONCEPT OF UNDIVIDED SHARES

Where a tenancy in common exists, the co-owners are said to own the property in 'undivided shares'. Each co-owner is regarded as having a distinct share in the property.

The use of the adjective 'undivided' emphasises that there is unity of possession. The land in question has not been physically divided up between the owners.

When a tenant in common dies there is no right of survivorship. His share passes under the normal law of succession. Let us suppose that Alf, Ben and Chris, the same people mentioned at **14.5.1** as being joint tenants of Green Field, are also tenants in common in equal shares of Yellow Field. When Alf dies his one-third share in Yellow Field passes according to the terms of his will to his sister Diana. When Ben dies intestate his one-third share passes under the normal rules of intestacy to his widow Elspeth.

Humphrey and Wendy Smith are tenants in common in equal shares of Bugthorpe Manor, worth about £300,000. Humphrey is killed in a hunting accident. He dies intestate. His assets (apart from Bugthorpe Manor) are worth £120,000. He leaves two children, Jack and Jill. On intestacy a surviving spouse is always entitled to the first £125,000 of the deceased's assets. Above that figure, and the children get a share.

Do the children inherit anything on their father's death intestate?

This time, the answer is 'Yes'. On his death, Humphrey's assets are worth £270,000, his half share in Bugthorpe Manor plus his 'other' assets. Wendy will be entitled (outright) to the first £125,000. The remaining £145,000 is split between her and the two children employing a rather complex formula the details of which we need not consider.

14.6.2 UNEQUAL TENANCIES IN COMMON

As has already been stressed, unity of possession is an essential feature of a tenancy in common. The other three 'unities' (interest, title and time, see **14.5.2**) **may** be present in a tenancy in common, **but are not essential**.

It is particularly important to note that there can be a tenancy in common in **unequal** shares. Suppose Len, Mike, Norman and Ossie are tenants in common of Red Field, Len with a one-third share, Mike and Norman with a quarter share each, and Ossie with one-sixth. They must share the benefits of the field in the appropriate proportions.

Suppose the four men lease Red Field to Toni at £1,200 per annum rent. How should the rent be divided between them?

The rent should be divided £400 to Len, £300 each to Mike and Norman, and £200 to Ossie.

14.6.3   THE PROBLEMS WITH TENANCIES IN COMMON IN THE EARLY-TWENTIETH CENTURY

At the beginning of this century **joint tenancies** were far less common than they are today. The idea (so prevalent today) of members of a family buying a home as joint tenants was almost unknown. On the other hand, there were a lot of tenancies in common, probably far more than exist today. At the turn of this century, if a family 'owned' a farm, or a small business such as a shop, then usually the individual members of the family owned the land as tenants in common.

Nowadays, if a family 'owns' a farm or business premises, one usually finds (on closer examination) that the farm, shop or whatever is owned by a limited company bearing some title such as 'Bloggs Brothers **Limited**'. Bloggs Brothers Limited is in law **one person**, therefore the land is not co-owned. The individual brothers will be shareholders **in the company**. They will also probably be directors of the company, though that is not essential. (There is no legal limit on the maximum number of directors a company can have.)

Reverting to talking about co-ownership of land, you may have already noticed a practical conclusion to be drawn from my 'Alf, Ben and Chris' examples at **14.5.1** and **14.6.1**. Where there is a joint tenancy, the number of joint tenants will gradually decline by a process of natural wastage until the last survivor emerges as sole owner. Where there is a tenancy in common the fact that the shares of each co-owner pass according to the law of succession means that the number of co-owners is unlikely to decline, and the co-ownership is unlikely to come to an end.

I am at last getting to the problem which existed in the first part of this century. Suppose that in 1900 four brothers, Alan, Brian, Charles and David, were tenants in common in equal shares of the fee simple in Streamfield Farm. In 1901, Giles, a neighbouring farmer, offered to buy a field which is inconveniently remote from the rest of Streamfield. The brothers accepted the offer and conveyed the field to Giles. For the conveyance to be valid all four brothers had to sign, as all four had a share in the legal fee simple in the field. (Getting four signatures on a document is not that difficult, particularly if the four people live in close proximity. But let us continue the story of Streamfield Farm.)

In 1905 Alan died. His will said 'My share in Streamfield is to be divided in equal shares between my three children'. In 1910 Brian died. His will said 'My share in Streamfield is to be divided in equal shares between my four children'. In 1915 Charles died. His will said 'My share in Streamfield is to be divided in equal shares between my five children'. In 1920 David died. His will said 'My share in Streamfield is to be divided in equal shares between my six children'.

Thus in the early 1920s no fewer than 18 people were tenants in common of Streamfield Farm. This sort of situation was not uncommon. A whole host of people would be tenants in common of a piece of land. Some might have an extremely small share.

In 1921 Giles offered to buy the rest of Streamfield Field at a price which all 14 tenants in common still in Britain thought was irresistible. The problem was the four who were abroad. Eleanor, Alan's daughter, had married and gone to Australia; Frank, one of Brian's sons, was a sheep farmer in New Zealand; George, one of Charles's sons, was a 'Mountie' in (remote) north-west Canada; Harriet, one of David's children, had gone exploring in the Amazon jungle.

For a valid conveyance of the legal fee simple in Streamfield Farm, all 18 would have had to have signed. Some of the signatures could not be obtained. Reluctantly, Giles had to withdraw his offer. Effectively, Streamfield Farm was unsaleable.

Stories like the one of Streamfield Farm were commonplace in 1925. Remember that 1925 was in an era of large families and the far-flung British Empire. Passenger planes and telecommunications were in their infancy. Parliament therefore decided that a drastic remedy was needed to solve the problem caused by tenancies in common. This remedy also affected joint tenancies.

14.7   The Reform of Co-Ownership in 1925 – The Main Objective

Parliament was desperate to ameliorate the problem illustrated by our Streamfield Farm story at **14.6.3**. It thus passed reforms (to be found in ss. 34–36 of the Law of Property Act 1925) which ensured that where land is co-owned a maximum of four signatures is required on any conveyance or other transaction affecting that land.

14.7.1   DRASTIC TREATMENT FOR TENANCIES IN COMMON

It would clearly have been impossible to abolish completely tenancies in common. Parliament did, however, enact the Law of Property Act 1925, s. 34.

Read ss. 34 and 35 in *Cases and Materials* (14.3). Try and summarise the effect of these provisions.

The actual wording of these provisions may strike you as obscure or even intimidating. But Parliament is **in effect** saying, 'A tenancy in common can no longer exist with respect to a legal fee simple or other legal property rights. A tenancy in common can still exist with respect to an equitable interest'.

Does this mean that land cannot be 'owned' by tenants in common? No – land can still be 'owned' by tenants in common. Section 34(2) of the 1925 Act is, however, crucial. This provision in effect lays down that where an estate or interest in land is conveyed to co-owners as tenants in common, a 'statutory' trust for sale is **imposed** upon those co-owners. An example should explain how s. 34(2) operates.

Suppose that in 1990 the fee simple in Highfields Farm was conveyed 'to Keith, Leonard, Michael and Norman as tenants in common in equal shares'. This conveyance would have the following consequences:

(a)   Highfields Farm is subject to a trust for sale.

(b)   (Provided they were of full age at the time of the conveyance) Keith, Leonard, Michael, and Norman are the trustees of the trust for sale.

(c)   (Like all other trustees) they hold the legal fee simple in Highfields Farm as **joint tenants**.

(d) Keith, Leonard, Michael and Norman are also the beneficiaries of the trust for sale. Each has a quarter share of the equitable interest under the trust as **tenants in common**. While the land remains unsold, each is entitled to a quarter of any income derived from the land. ('Income' includes profits from personal cultivation or rent from tenants.) When the land is sold, each will be entitled to a quarter of the proceeds of sale.

(e) (Like trustees for sale generally) Keith, Leonard, Michael and Norman have the power to postpone the sale of land.

(f) (In practical terms perhaps the most important point) the four 'trustees' will almost certainly not want to sell the land immediately. They will therefore exercise their power to postpone sale. Indeed, the four men may not know that there is a trust for sale! If that is the case, they will be subconsciously exercising the power to postpone.

14.7.2 WHY IMPOSE TRUSTS FOR SALE ON TENANTS IN COMMON?

Take our Highfields Farm example a little further. Let us suppose that Keith died in 1992. His will read, 'all my property I give to my four daughters Olive, Penny, Quennie, and Rose in equal shares'. The ownership position regarding the farm is as follows:

■ **The legal estate**   This, of course, was held by the four men as trustees and as joint tenants. When Keith died there was a survivorship in the usual way. Thus Leonard, Malcolm, and Norman are now trustees of the legal title.

■ **The equitable interests under the trust for sale**   Leonard, Malcolm, Norman, Olive, Penny, Quennie and Rose are now all beneficiaries under the trust. The three men each have a quarter share. The four women each have a one-sixteenth share.

Suppose that Stephen is now keen to buy Highfields Farm, and is willing to pay an attractive price. He should make his offer to the three trustees. If the trustees do decide to sell, **they alone need sign the contract and conveyance**. When the sale takes place the rights of all seven beneficiaries will be overreached.

ACTIVITY 33

Just pause for a moment, think about this Highfields farm example, and consider why the imposition of the trust for sale on the tenants in common was a wise change in the law.

I hope you can now see the advantage gained by imposing the trust for sale upon the tenancy in common. The usual rule limiting the number of trustees of land to four applies; thus the number of owners of the legal title is strictly limited. Moreover it is the trustees who decide on whether the land should be sold, leased, etc. The 'overreaching' device ensures that the trustees' decisions bind the non-trustee beneficiaries.

The usual rules for the appointment, retirement and removal of trustees (discussed at **13.7**) apply to imposed trusts for sale. Thus, if in my Highfields Farm example Leonard,

Michael, and Norman **wish** to appoint **one** additional trustee they **may** do so. Moreover they can choose anybody. They are not obliged to pick from Olive, Penny, Quennie, and Rose.

(The usual rule that where there is a sale by trustees for sale **a minimum of two trustees** is required to effect an overreaching also normally applies to imposed trusts for sale. However, as we shall see at **16.4.1**, there is a significant exception to this 'minimum of two' rule. Under this exception a sale by a sole trustee will in certain circumstances be valid.)

(I must also again stress that if there are three trustees for sale of a piece of land, **all three** must sign conveyances and other transactions with the land. If there are four trustees for sale, **all four** must sign conveyances and other transactions with the land.)

14.7.3 WHAT IF THERE ARE MORE THAN FOUR TENANTS IN COMMON TO START WITH?

Suppose land is conveyed 'to A, B, C, D, E, F and G as tenants in common'. You may have already noticed that s. 34(2) of the 1925 Act provides an answer to this problem. There is a somewhat arbitrary rule that the first four people (of full age) named in the conveyance will be the trustees for sale.

Suppose that in my example C is only 17 at the date of the conveyance. A, B, D, and E will be the original trustees. They will of course remain the trustees when C attains 18. If (say) B dies, A, D and E will continue as trustees. They **may** appoint a fourth trustee. If they do, they can appoint anybody. They are not obliged to pick C, F or G.

In 1975 the fee simple in 'Faracres' was conveyed 'to Anthea, Betty, Camilla, Devina, Emily and Florence as tenants in common'. Camilla was then aged only 16, but the other five women were of full age. You are now buying Faracres. All six 'owners' are still alive. For a valid sale, which of them should sign the conveyance?

Anthea, Betty, Devina and Emily should sign the conveyance.

14.8 Joint Tenancies in the Early-Twentieth Century

Because of the convenience of the survivorship rule, trustees of property (land or any other property) have always been made joint tenants of the legal title to the property. Prior to 1925, joint tenancies of land were quite common. However, where such a joint tenancy existed with respect to a piece of land it usually transpired that the joint tenants held the land not for their own benefit but as trustees for other people.

In the early part of this century **beneficial joint tenancies**, i.e. joint tenants holding land for their own personal enjoyment rather than as trustees, were relatively rare. This is in very marked contrast to the position today. There must be now several million 'beneficial' joint tenancies. Most (but not all) of these joint tenancies will exist where husband and wife jointly own the matrimonial home.

14.8.1 IMPOSITION OF TRUSTS FOR SALE ON BENEFICIAL JOINT TENANTS

In 1925, Parliament (at a time when beneficial joint tenancies were rare) decided to impose a trust for sale on beneficial joint tenants. (See the Law of Property Act, s. 36(1)). As with Tenancies in Common the joint tenants are themselves the trustees for sale. In the unusual event of there being more than four joint tenants, the first four named in the conveyance (of full age) will be the trustees.

Suppose John and Jane Smith decide to buy the fee simple in Dreamhouse as joint tenants, a kind of transaction which today is extremely commonplace. The fee simple in Dreamhouse is conveyed 'to John and Jane Smith as beneficial joint tenants'. A trust for sale is imposed upon John and Jane and the ownership position regarding Dreamhouse is as follows.

- ■ **The legal estate**   This is vested in John and Jane as joint tenants and as trustees for sale.

- ■ **The equitable interests under the trust for sale**   John and Jane are of course also joint tenants of the equitable interest under the trust for sale.

Consider whether John and Jane Smith are likely to realise that they are trustees for sale.

The truth of the matter is that John and Jane (and countless people like them) do not know that a trust for sale has been thrust upon them. Moreover, there can be no doubt that John and Jane (and countless people like them) will (subconsciously) exercise 'the power to postpone sale' and enjoy the benefits of the trust by living in the house.

14.8.2 WHY IMPOSE A TRUST FOR SALE ON JOINT TENANTS?

I hope you have already been asking yourself this question. After all, we have already seen that, because of the survivorship rule, it is a natural characteristic of a joint tenancy that the number of joint tenants gradually dwindles to one. Moreover, although joint tenancies are far more common today than they were in 1925, modern joint tenancies usually start with only two joint tenants.

The answer to the question lies in the fact that Parliament in 1925 had to take into account the possibility of 'severance' of a joint tenancy. Every joint tenant has the right to 'sever' the joint tenancy. If a joint tenant does this, he converts his interest as joint tenant into a share as tenant in common. That share becomes subject to the normal law of succession.

Prior to 1925 a joint tenant could sever his right in the legal estate. Since 1925 this has not been possible. Since 1925 any severance affects only the equitable interest under the trust for sale. It is not necessary at this stage to explain how a severance is achieved (nowadays, as we shall see in the next chapter, it is easy to achieve). What I do need to give is an example of the effects of severance.

Let us suppose that in 1990 three close friends, Rachel, Sally, and Tanya, decided to buy Easthouse. The fee simple in Easthouse was conveyed to them as joint tenants. They consciously chose to be joint tenants as they wished the survivorship rule to operate. The result of the 1990 conveyance was that there was a trust for sale, but with the three women as both trustees of the legal title and joint tenants of the equitable interest under the trust.

Now suppose that in 1994 Tanya quarrelled with Rachel and Sally. She consequently severed the joint tenancy. The position as to ownership of Easthouse would now be as follows:

■ **Legal estate**   There would be no change. The three women would remain trustees and joint tenants of the legal fee simple estate in Easthouse.

■ **Equitable interests under the trust for sale**   Tanya now has a one-third share as tenant in common. The other two-thirds (note this carefully) are owned by Rachel and Sally as joint tenants.

Suppose now that Tanya has just died. Her will leaves all her property 'to be divided in equal shares between my gentlemen friends Unwin, Victor, Willy, Xerxes and Yorick'. The position as to ownership of Easthouse is now as follows:

■ **Legal estate** By virtue of survivorship, Rachel and Sally are the only trustees of the legal title.

■ **Equitable interests under the trust for sale** Rachel and Sally are still joint tenants of two-thirds. Each of the five men has a one-fifteenth share as Tenant in Common.

I hope you realise that this Easthouse example has now reached a position rather similar to my Highfields Farm example at **14.7.2**. The number of co-owners of Easthouse has grown, but the legal estate is vested in the two surviving women as trustees for sale.

You want to buy Easthouse. To whom do you make the offer?

You make the offer to Rachel and Sally only. As trustees for sale they can sell (or lease etc.) Easthouse, and the rights of all seven beneficiaries will be overreached.

14.9   The Modern Conveyancing Practice to Create an Express Trust for Sale

All modern property lawyers have been brought up knowing that wherever there is co-ownership of land there must be a trust for sale. They know that there is no escaping the effects of ss. 34–36 of the Law of Property Act. This has brought about a change in conveyancing practices.

Where land is conveyed to co-owners it is nowadays good conveyancing practice (followed by most but not all solicitors) to create an **express** trust for sale. The co-owners will be made the trustees (except in those cases, very rare nowadays, where there are more than four). The 'express declaration of trust' will make it clear whether the equitable interests under the trust are held as joint tenants or as tenants in common. If the co-owners are tenants in common the size of the shares is spelt out.

The express declaration of trust is usually contained in the conveyance or (if the land is already registered title) in the land transfer. Unfortunately, details of the express declaration of trust are not recorded on the register of title. The solicitor acting for the co-owners should therefore keep a copy of the conveyance or transfer.

By employing an express declaration of trust solicitors avoid the problems which we are about to discuss in the next section of this chapter. Moreover the practice of having an express declaration of trust has been endorsed by the Court of Appeal in two fairly modern cases which deserve to be better known.

In *Walker* v *Hall* (1984) 5 FLR 126, the Court of Appeal expressed the view that it might well be professional negligence for a solicitor acting for co-owners to fail to draw up an express declaration of trust. In *Goodman* v *Gallant* [1986] 1 All ER 311, the Court of Appeal held that if there is an express trust for sale declaring the co-owners to be joint tenants in equity, any severance must produce a tenancy in common **in equal shares.**

Read the extracts from *Walker* v *Hall* and *Goodman* v *Gallant* in *Cases and Materials* (14.4). After you have read 14.10, consider why it might be professional negligence for a solicitor acting for co-owners to fail to draw up an express declaration of trust.

14.10   Co-owners – Joint Tenancy or Tenancy in Common?

First, an elementary point rather overlooked by some textbooks. The rules which I am about to discuss **apply only where there is no express declaration of a trust for sale.** Where there is an express trust for sale, that trust for sale is conclusive as to whether the co-owners are joint tenants or tenants in common. Furthermore, where the beneficiaries hold their equitable interests as tenants in common, the express declaration is conclusive as to the size of their shares. (*Re Pavlou* [1993] 3 All ER 995, which conflicts with these principles, must be regarded as wrongly decided.)

With a co-ownership where there is **no** express declaration of trust (nowadays very much the minority of cases) the following rules apply. There is an initial presumption that the co-owners are joint tenants.

This presumption in favour of joint tenancy can be **rebutted** in favour of a tenancy in common in the following situations.

(a)   (Rather obviously) where the conveyance (or will) expressly describes the co-owners as tenants in common.

(b)   Where the conveyance (or will) uses 'words of severance', e.g., 'I convey Blackacre to A, B and C in equal shares', 'I grant Blackacre to be divided between my sons

Tom, Dick, and Harry'. Any words in a conveyance (or will) which indicate that the co-owners are to have distinct shares in the property, albeit those shares are geographically undivided, are 'words of severance'.

As you may have guessed, this rule about 'words of severance' is nowadays important only where lay people draft their own conveyances or wills. I should also add that you must not confuse 'words of severance' with the concept 'severance of a joint tenancy' which we shall be considering in the next chapter.

(c)   Where either unity of time, unity of title, or unity of interest is absent. (This of course follows from the very nature of joint tenancies and tenancies in common.)

(d)   Where the co-owners contribute to the purchase price in unequal shares. For example, Yorick and Zebedee buy Purple House for £60,000. Purple House is conveyed to Yorick and Zebedee. There is **no** express declaration of a trust for sale. Yorick contributed £45,000; Zebedee £15,000. Yorick and Zebedee will be tenants in common of the equitable interest under the trust for sale. Their shares will be proportionate to their contributions. Thus Yorick will have a three-quarters share and Zebedee will have a one-quarter share.

The example just given is a simple one, but rather unrealistic as Yorick and Zebedee paid 'cash down'. Consider now Andrea and Bobby. They decided to cohabit rather than get married. They bought 'Lovenest' (what I call a 'quasi-matrimonial home') for £100,000, of which £80,000 was borrowed from Bloggs Bank. They granted a mortgage to the Bank to secure the loan. The house was conveyed to them in their joint names **but there was no express declaration of a trust for sale**. Andrea paid the initial £20,000 deposit out of her savings, and she also paid some of the instalments. Bobby paid the rest of the instalments. They did not keep a detailed record as to who paid what. The relationship has now broken down.

In this kind of situation (which is quite frequent and was similar to the situation in *Walker* v *Hall*) calculating the size of Andrea's and Bobby's shares as tenants in common will be very difficult; I would say more-or-less guesswork! However, if there had been an express declaration of trust, arguments as to who contributed what **would not have arisen**. As I keep on repeating, if there is an express declaration of a trust for sale that declaration is conclusive as to the co-owners' equitable interests.

(e)   Where the property is acquired for use by a business partnership. For example, Alf, Bert and Charles buy High Tower for £300,000 to use as the office for their accountancy practice. They each contribute £100,000. High Tower is conveyed to them, **but there is no express declaration of a trust for sale**. (To save money, they do their own conveyancing.) Alf, Bert, and Charles will be tenants in common of the equitable interest under the trust for sale imposed by the Law of Property Act 1925, s. 34. Each will have a one-third share.

The reason behind this 'business partners are tenants in common' rule is as follows. Equity always considered that the very hit and miss 'survival of the fittest' survivorship rule which applies to joint tenancies is inappropriate in a commercial context. A businessman would (in most cases at least) want his interest in land held for use in the business to pass under his will. There is nothing, of course, to stop business partners making themselves joint tenants. Since 1925 they do so by creating an express trust for sale with the partners as **joint tenants** of the equitable interests under the trust.

(f)   Where there is a 'joint mortgage'. Of the six rules under which a tenancy in common can arise, this rule is perhaps the least important, but perhaps the most difficult to understand. A joint mortgage can arise if there are joint **lenders**. A joint mortgage has the following features.

- (i)   There is (normally) just one borrower.
- (ii)   There are two or more lenders who pool the money they are willing to lend.
- (iii) They lend the pooled money as one loan.
- (iv)   The borrower grants the lenders a **single** mortgage.
- (v)   The lenders are co-owners **of the mortgage**.
- (vi)   (Since 1925) the lenders hold their title **to the mortgage** on trust for sale for themselves as tenants in common.

When in practice might there be a joint mortgage? Suppose Greg owns Broadacres, worth something over £1,000,000. He wants to borrow £1,000,000, and is offering Broadacres as security. He approaches Alex's Bank, which says, 'Sorry we would like to lend the full sum but we have only £500,000 available'. He approaches Clive's Bank, which gives a very similar reply. A joint mortgage will satisfy everyone. The two banks pool their respective half millions. Greg gets a single loan for £1,000,000 and grants a joint mortgage to the two banks.

Greenacre is conveyed to Anne and Bertha. There is an express declaration of a trust for sale for themselves as joint tenants in equity. The price was £90,000. Anne contributed £60,000; Bertha contributed £30,000. Anne dies. Her will leaves all her property to Charles. Does Charles inherit any interest in Greenacre?

The answer is of course, 'No'. The express declaration of trust stating that Anne and Bertha are joint tenants in equity is conclusive. Thus when Anne dies, her equitable interest in Greenacre passes by survivorship to Bertha.

Alf, Barry and Charles (all of full age) have just bought High Farm for £120,000. Alf contributed £60,000, Barry £40,000 and Charles £20,000. The land has been conveyed to them, but there has been no express declaration of a trust for sale. What is the end result?

In these circumstances all three men are trustees for sale of the legal estate. But their equitable interests under the trust will be that Alf owns a half, Barry owns a third and Charles a sixth.

14.11   Conclusion

At the beginning of this chapter we discussed the basic characteristics of joint tenancies and tenancies in common. This involved our considering very long-standing common law-derived rules. At the end of this chapter the rules for determining whether co-owners are joint tenants or tenants in common were considered. Many of these rules are also of some antiquity.

The central part of this chapter was therefore something of a contrast. There we dealt with one of the fundamental changes made by the 1925 property legislation, namely the imposition on co-owners of a trust for sale. This cured one major problem thrown up by the common law – that of multiplicity of co-owners. But, as we shall see more clearly when we reach **Chapter 16**, the mandatory trust for sale brings with it its own crop of problems.

CHAPTER FIFTEEN

SEVERANCE OF JOINT TENANCIES

15.1 Objectives

By the end of this chapter you should:

■ be able to explain the effects of severance of a joint tenancy;

■ be thoroughly familiar with the various methods by which a joint tenancy can be severed;

■ have a basic understanding of property adjustment orders under ss. 23-25 of the Matrimonial Causes Act 1973.

15.2 Introduction

As you are probably already aware, there has been (as the twentieth century progressed) an enormous growth in the number of joint tenancies. Most (but not all) exist between married couples.

The great attraction of a joint tenancy for married (and unmarried) couples is the automatic right of survivorship which operates on the death of one of the co-owners. But this advantage of a joint tenancy may disappear if the joint tenants fall out with each other. It is thus fortunate that the law provides for severance of joint tenancies, i.e. a process whereby a joint tenancy is converted into a tenancy in common.

15.3 Severance of a Legal Joint Tenancy Impossible

Since 1925, a legal joint tenancy cannot be severed. Any severance affects only the equitable interests under the trust for sale.

Suppose that Blackacre has been conveyed to A, B, and C as joint tenants on trust for sale for themselves as joint tenants. Later A severs the joint tenancy by sending a written notice of severance to B and C. (We will consider details of this method of severance at **15.4.5.1.**) The position will now be:

■ **Legal title** This will be still vested in A, B and C as joint tenants and as trustees for sale.

■ **Equitable interest** A will have a one-third share as tenant in common; B and C will have the other two-thirds share as (between themselves) joint tenants.

Suppose that C dies. What is the position now?

The legal title is vested in A and B as joint tenants and as trustees for sale.
The equitable interests will be that A has a one-third share as tenant in common while B has a two-thirds share as tenant in common.

15.4 Methods of Severance

Under the post-1925 law, severance can be achieved in a variety of different ways.

15.4.1 TOTAL ALIENATION

If a joint tenant sells (or gives away inter vivos) his equitable interest, that effects a severance.

Suppose Blackacre was conveyed to Debbie, Ena, Felicity and Gillian as joint tenants on express trust for sale for themselves as joint tenants. Later, Gillian sells her interest in Blackacre to Henry. The position now is as follows:

■ **Legal title** This is unchanged. The four women remain joint tenants and trustees of the legal title. The fact that Gillian has sold her equitable interest does not mean that she has resigned as a trustee.

■ **Equitable interest** Henry has a quarter share as tenant in common. The other three-quarters are held by Debbie, Ena, and Felicity as (between themselves) joint tenants.

Let us now suppose that Felicity, Gillian and Henry all die. Henry's will leaves 'all my property to my old pal Keith'. What is the position now?

■ **Legal title** By virtue of survivorship, Debbie and Ena are the trustees. (Though there is no need for them to do so, they may appoint one or two additional trustees. Do you remember the discussion at **13.7**?)

- **Equitable interest** Keith has a one-quarter share as tenant in common. The other three-quarters belongs to Debbie and Ena as (between themselves) joint tenants.

15.4.2 BANKRUPTCY

If a joint tenant goes bankrupt, his equitable interest vests in his trustee in bankruptcy, to be held for the benefit of all his creditors. This compulsory transfer automatically severs the joint tenancy.

In modern conditions this is a short but not unimportant point. Suppose Harry and Winny Brown are joint tenants of Highroofs. Harry goes bankrupt. The position will now be:

- **Legal title** This will still be held by Harry and Winny.

- **Equitable interest** Winny and Harry's trustee in bankruptcy will be tenants in common in equal shares.

15.4.3 PARTIAL ALIENATION

A partial alienation would occur where a joint tenant mortgaged or leased his interest. If a joint tenant wished to sever the joint tenancy without his fellow joint tenant(s) knowing, he could do so by mortgaging his interest to a friend to secure a loan of a nominal amount (say £5)!

15.4.4 CONTRACT TO ALIENATE

If a joint tenant contracts to sell, lease, or mortgage his interest that will effect a severance.

15.4.5 WRITTEN NOTICE AND INFORMAL SEVERANCE UNDER THE LAW OF PROPERTY ACT 1925

These two forms of severance depend upon the rather opaque wording of the second paragraph of s. 36(2) of the Law of Property Act 1925.

> . . . where a legal estate . . . is vested in joint tenants beneficially, and any tenant desires to sever the joint tenancy in equity, he shall give to the other joint tenants a notice in writing of such desire

> or do such other acts or things as would, in the case of personal estate, have been effectual to sever the tenancy in equity, . . .

Study s. 36 of the 1925 Act, as set out in *Cases and Materials* (15.1.5). Then study the 'simplified version' of the second paragraph of s. 36(2) set out above. You need to understand that s. 36(2) contains *two* ways of severing a joint tenancy.

You will see that (to help clarify matters) in the simplified version a lot of words have been missed out and the paragraph has been split into two parts. The first part relates to severance by written notice; the second part relates to informal severance.

15.4.5.1 Severance by written notice

The basic idea is tolerably clear. A joint tenant can sever by sending a written notice to each of the other joint tenants saying, 'I am severing our joint tenancy' (or words to that effect). The notice of severance can be handed to the intended recipient. It is inadvisable to send the notice by ordinary post, as that may lead to disputes as to whether the notice has been received or not.

If the notice is sent through the post, registered post or recorded delivery should be used and the letter addressed to the recipient's residence or (where appropriate) place of business. This will take advantage of s. 196(4) of the Law of Property Act 1925. Under that provision a notice sent by recorded delivery or registered post to the correct address will be deemed to have been received by the addressee unless it is returned through the post office undelivered.

The case of *Re 88 Berkeley Road* [1971] 1 All ER 254 dramatically demonstrates the impact of s. 196(4). Two unmarried ladies, Miss Eldridge and Miss Goodwin, were joint tenants of their home, 88 Berkeley Road. Eldridge (who was 'a generation younger') announced that she was getting married. Goodwin consulted solicitors, who advised her to sever the joint tenancy. The solicitors drafted a notice of severance, and this was sent **recorded delivery** to Eldridge at her 'residence', 88 Berkeley Road.

When the postman called, Eldridge had already gone to work. Goodwin signed for the letter! Goodwin died soon afterwards. In the ensuing court case, Eldridge swore that she had never seen the letter. Had there been an effective severance of the joint tenancy? The judge held that there had been a severance. The letter had not been 'returned undelivered'.

15.4.5.2 What sort of wording is required in a notice of severance?

In the last 25 years there have been a number of cases where events have followed the following pattern:

(a) Two people (usually but not always husband and wife) buy a house as joint tenants.

(b) The relationship breaks down.

(c) One of the two makes a statement, writes a letter, or commences divorce proceedings or another form of litigation.

(d) Before matters can be resolved, one of the parties suddenly dies.

(e) There is litigation as to whether event (c) above has brought about a severance. The surviving partner is of course arguing (as Eldridge argued in *Re 88 Berkeley Road*) that there has been no severance. The personal representatives of the deceased argue that there has been a severance.

In my opinion the Court of Appeal has in two modern decisions laid clear rules for resolving these cases. The cases are *Burgess* v *Rawnsley* (discussed at **15.4.6**) and *Harris* v *Goddard*.

In *Harris* v *Goddard* [1983] 3 All ER 242 the Court of Appeal ruled that any written statement by a joint tenant either expressly indicating or implying that he wishes **immediately** to end the joint tenancy relationship will sever that joint tenancy, provided the statement is received (or is deemed to have been received under s. 196(4)).

The Court of Appeal in *Harris* v *Goddard* expressly approved the decision in *Re Draper's Conveyance* [1967] 3 All ER 853, where a wife applied under s. 30 of the Law of Property Act 1925 for an order for sale of the jointly owned matrimonial home. This application was held to have severed the joint tenancy. By demanding that the property be sold and the proceeds of sale split, the wife demonstrated that she wished an immediate end to the joint tenancy arrangement.

15.4.5.3 Property adjustment orders under ss. 23–25 of the Matrimonial Causes Act 1973

Before explaining *Harris* v *Goddard* I have to make a digression into elementary family law. You most certainly do not need to know the details of ss. 23–25 of the Matrimonial Causes Act 1973, but you do need to get the basic idea of a property adjustment order.

Where a marriage breaks down the divorce court has very wide powers over **all** property owned by the spouses. *Inter alia*, the divorce court can order:

(a) that the husband transfers property he owns to his wife, and/or vice versa;

(b) that one spouse transfers property he or she owns into joint ownership;

(c) that co-owned property be transferred into the sole ownership of one or other spouse;

(d) that an existing co-ownership of the matrimonial home be continued, but that the terms of the trust for sale should be altered;

(e) that co-owned property should be sold.

15.4.5.4 *Harris* v *Goddard*

Read *Harris* v *Goddard* in *Cases and Materials* (15.1.5.1). **The husband was killed in a car crash while divorce proceedings were pending. So who was arguing that there had been no severance of the joint tenancy over the matrimonial home?**

The wife was arguing that there was no severance.

In *Harris* v *Goddard*, husband and wife were joint tenants of the matrimonial home. The marriage broke down, and the wife petitioned for divorce. The petition included an application for a property adjustment order under s. 24 of the Matrimonial Causes Act 1973. The application was (as is quite usual) in very general terms:

That such order may be made by way of transfer of property and/or settlement of property and/or variation of settlement in respect of the former matrimonial home... as may be just.

(By 'variation of settlement' is meant, in this context, varying the terms of the existing trust for sale.)

This application was held not to have severed the joint tenancy. For a document sent by one joint tenant to amount to a severance it must show an intention to end **immediately** the joint tenancy arrangement. The application for an order of sale made in *Re Draper* satisfied that test, but the application in *Harris* v *Goddard* itself did not.

15.4.6 INFORMAL SEVERANCE

The gist of the last part of s. 36(2) of the Law of Property Act 1925 (see **15.4.5**) is that a joint tenant can sever by doing 'such other acts or things as would, in the case of personal estate, have been effectual to sever the tenancy in equity'.

Prior to 1926 it was possible to sever a joint tenancy in **personal** but not **real** property by informal conduct. The intention behind the last part of s. 36(2) was to extend the pre-1926 rules regarding informal severance by conduct to real property.

Unfortunately, the 1925 legislators rather overlooked the fact that the pre-1926 rules regarding informal severance were far from clear cut. Even today some textbooks go into great depth regarding certain nineteenth-century 'informal severance' cases in an effort to establish the rules for informal severance. This is totally unnecessary. The job has been done for us by Sir John Pennycuick in *Burgess* v *Rawnsley* [1975] 3 All ER 142.

ACTIVITY 38

Read *Burgess* v *Rawnsley* in *Cases and Materials* (15.1.6). Bear in mind that Lord Denning's judgment gives a graphic account of the facts, but his views as to the applicable law are incorrect. For the correct law, study Sir John Pennycuick's judgment noting his numbered propositions.

In *Burgess* v *Rawnsley* Mr Honick (a widower) and Mrs Rawnsley (a widow) met at a scripture rally in Trafalgar Square. They became close friends. They bought as joint tenants the fee simple to the house in Waltham Cross of which Honick had hitherto been a lessee. They later fell out. It was orally agreed that Honick should buy out Mrs Rawnsley's interest for £750 (sic). Before matters could finally be resolved, Honick died.

The Court of Appeal held that the oral agreement (though not an enforceable contract) was sufficient to sever the joint tenancy. After analysing the older cases Sir John Pennycuick concluded that there were three forms of informal severance:

(a) An oral agreement that the joint tenancy should be severed.

(b) An oral agreement that one joint tenant should buy the other out.

(c) '[A]cts of the parties, including, it seems to me, negotiations which, although not otherwise resulting in any agreement, indicate a common intention that the joint tenancy should be regarded as severed.'

15.5 Matters Which Are Not a Severance

15.5.1 UNILATERAL ORAL STATEMENTS

Lord Denning in *Burgess* v *Rawnsley* took the view that even a unilateral oral statement by one joint tenant to the other(s) could amount to a severance. This view is not shared by any other judge (ancient or modern) and is clearly wrong.

I have always considered the view taken by Lord Denning in *Burgess* v *Rawnsley* as hopelessly impractical. Why? (There are two reasons.)

Firstly, if Lord Denning were correct, then angry unilateral statements made in haste during a family quarrel would be effective to sever the joint tenancy. Secondly, there would be problems proving what exactly had been said in the heat of argument.

15.5.2 SUBSEQUENT USE OF PROPERTY FOR BUSINESS PURPOSES

In *Barton* v *Morris* [1985] 2 All ER 1032 a farm was conveyed to two cohabitees on express trust for themselves as joint tenants in equity. 'The property was run as a guest house and small farm on a partnership basis and Miss Barton kept partnership accounts which showed the farm as a partnership asset.'

This use of the property for the purposes of a partnership was held not to sever the joint tenancy.

15.5.3 'SEVERANCE BY WILL'

I should just remind you that you cannot sever a joint tenancy by will.

15.6 Conclusion

It is obviously extremely important for you to understand fully the various ways in which a joint tenancy can be severed. Some of these methods (e.g. written notice) are the result of the deliberate actions of the parties. Others (e.g in particular severance by bankruptcy) come about automatically, irrespective of any intention.

It is also very important to remember that certain matters **do not** constitute severance. The principle recognised in *Barton* v *Morris*, that **subsequent** business use of premises does not sever an expressly created joint tenancy, should always be kept very firmly in mind.

CHAPTER SIXTEEN

THE PROBLEMS WHEN CO-OWNERS FALL OUT

16.1 Objectives

By the end of this chapter you should:

■ appreciate fully the problems which arise where a tenancy in common exists because there is a constructive trust interest;

■ be familiar with how the courts apply s. 30 of the Law of Property Act 1925 in the co-ownership context;

■ appreciate the controversies over whether rights of co-owners are interests in land or interests in money;

■ appreciate the (limited) significance of the Law of Property (Joint Tenants) Act 1964.

16.2 Introduction

By imposing a trust for sale upon all co-owners, Parliament (in 1925) solved the problem of the saleability of land belonging to a multiplicity of co-owners. But this 'solution' to the problems set out at **14.7** has brought with it a whole crop of new difficulties. These difficulties relate to the exact legal nature of the rights of co-owners (e.g., does a co-owner have the right personally to occupy the land?) and as to what happens if co-owners disagree regarding the fate of the property.

The issues discussed in this chapter are of fundamental importance to late twentieth-century England and Wales. I say this because the **amount** of co-ownership has shown enormous growth since 1925. This growth is due not just to an increase in number of expressly agreed co-ownerships but also to the growth in tenancies in common arising because someone has acquired a constructive trust 'share' in a piece of land.

16.3 The Effect of Imposing a Trust for Sale upon Co-owners

Before I launch into perhaps the biggest problem created by the decision made in 1925 to impose a trust for sale upon all co-owners, I need to remind you of two points:

(a) A 'co-ownership trust for sale', like any other trust for sale, is subject to the 'maximum of four' limit on the number of trustees.

(b) While a co-ownership trust for sale can validly **exist** with only one trustee, a disposition (sale, lease, mortgage etc.) requires two trustees if it is to 'overreach' the rights of non-trustee co-owners. (As we shall see in a moment, there is however an important exception to this 'minimum of two' rule.)

16.4   Tenancy in Common Arising Because There is a Constructive Trust

(This is the heading I prefer, but some people prefer the heading, 'The problem of the undisclosed trust for sale.')

Refer back to **1.4.7** and the example of 'Chenu', Alfred and Bertha. You will recall that Alfred owns the legal fee simple estate in Chenu. However, Bertha (who may or may not be his wife) acquired an '(equitable) share in the property under a constructive trust'. You will also recall that Bertha acquired her **share** by paying £30,000 cash down towards a price of £90,000. She would equally have acquired a **share** (under a constructive trust) if she had made substantial contributions to mortgage instalments, or had made a substantial contribution to the improvement of Chenu.

Consider what my next point is going to be.

As Bertha acquires a **share** in Chenu, she and Alfred become tenants in common! Consequently, as a result of ss. 34–36 of the Law of Property Act 1925, there will be a trust for sale. Alfred will be a trustee for sale, in trust for himself and Bertha. This trust for sale will be irregular in two respects:

(a)   there will be only one trustee;

(b)   the people involved (Alfred, Bertha and later potential purchasers or mortgagees of Chenu) will probably not realise that a trust for sale exists. (Hence the phrase, 'undisclosed trust for sale'.) They will, therefore, probably not realise that a second trustee should be appointed before any disposition takes place.

You will not be surprised to learn that this problem of an irregular ('undisclosed') trust for sale is a frequent occurrence in contemporary legal practice. It arises frequently simply because cases of 'a constructive trust share' arise frequently.

16.4.1   DISPOSITIONS BY A SINGLE TRUSTEE

It will help your understanding if we continue to develop the 'Chenu' example.

Suppose Albert sells, leases or mortgages 'Chenu' acting entirely on his own. Put in more technical language, he makes a disposition without appointing a second trustee. Will Bertha's interest be overreached despite the absence of a second trustee? Or (and this is the only alternative) will it be binding upon the purchaser? ('Purchaser' in this context includes a mortgagee or lessee.)

16.4.1.1   Unregistered title

First, I should stress that where the relevant land is unregistered title, a constructive trust share is **not registrable as a land charge**. It is now well established that where a disposition is made by a sole trustee such as Alfred, the doctrine of notice must be applied. This was the approach taken, e.g., in *Kingsnorth Finance* v *Tizard* [1986] 2 All ER 54. This case was referred to at **6.4.4.3**.

If a purchaser from Alfred had notice (actual, constructive or imputed) of Bertha's interest (call it a 'share' if you like), he will be bound by Bertha's interest. Bertha's interest will not bind a purchaser only if that purchaser is a bona fide purchaser for value of a legal estate without notice of Bertha's interest.

In *Caunce* v *Caunce* [1969] 1 All ER 722 H had sole ownership of the matrimonial home. However, W paid a substantial part of the purchase price, and therefore had a constructive trust 'share'. Thus H held the legal title on trust for sale for H and W.

While they were happily living together in the home, H decided to borrow some money from Lloyds Bank. Lloyds lent the money, and H mortgaged the home to the bank to secure the loan. H never told W about the mortgage. **Lloyds neither visited the house nor made any enquiries of W.**

ACTIVITY 41

Consider how a court would decide this case today.

The court would reason in the following way:

(a)   The doctrine of notice must be applied.

(b)   Lloyds (or rather a representative acting for Lloyds) should have visited the house.

(c)   Lloyds' representative should have seen W living in the home.

(d)   The representative should have therefore asked her whether she claimed any interest in the home.

(e)   As Lloyds made no such enquiries, they have constructive notice of the wife's interest ('share') applying 'the rule in *Hunt* v *Luck*' and are therefore bound by it.

Amazingly, back in the dark ages of 1969 the judge (Stamp J) decided otherwise. He laid down a special exception to the *Hunt* v *Luck* rule. A purchaser (mortgagee or lessee) need not make enquiries of persons occupying the land if the vendor (mortgagor, lessor) is himself in possession. He thus held that Lloyds were a 'purchaser without notice' and were not bound by the wife's interest. In practical terms that meant that W could not stop Lloyds enforcing the mortgage and selling the home over her head.

It is now clear that the decision in *Caunce* to create an exception to *Hunt v Luck* was totally wrong. (See my earlier comments at **10.3.6**.)

SAQ 86

Charley is owner in fee simple of Superhouse (unregistered title). His cohabitee, Dinah, has contributed substantially to the cost of acquisition, and has therefore acquired a share under a constructive trust. The relationship has now broken down, and Dinah is contemplating the possibility of leaving. However, she wants to be sure that her interest will bind a purchaser of Superhouse. Advise Dinah.

First of all, I hope you realised that **there is no land charge** which Dinah can register. Rather, her constructive trust interest is subject to the equitable doctrine of notice. However, provided she stays put in Superhouse **and** reveals her interest to anybody who asks whether she has a share in the home, the rule in *Hunt v Luck* will (normally) protect her. If Dinah follows this advice, a purchaser from Albert will have notice of her equitable interest and be bound by it. (I should, however, add that I am temporarily ignoring the effect of the decision of the House of Lords in *City of London Building Society v Flegg*, which I will be discussing at **16.4.2**.)

16.4.1.2   Registered title

Reverting to my 'Chenu' example, if the house is registered title then the decision of the House of Lords in *Williams and Glyn's Bank v Boland* will apply. (I have already discussed this case at **10.3.6**, and you should re-read that discussion.)

It follows from *Boland* that if Chenu is registered title, Bertha, provided she is in 'actual occupation' of Chenu at the relevant time, will have an overriding interest within s.70(1)(g) of the Land Registration Act 1925 unless enquiry is made of her and she fails to reveal her interest.

The owner of a constructive trust interest/share in a registered title who is not 'in actual occupation' (e.g. Bertha has gone to live with another man) will have a minor interest. This minor interest can be protected by lodging a caution.

In *Elias v Mitchell* [1972] 2 All ER 153 two business partners had fallen out. One was the sole registered proprietor of their business premises, but both had 'shares' (as tenants in common) in the premises. The partner who was not the registered proprietor had left those premises. His interest was held to be a minor interest which could be protected by lodging a caution. (There can be no doubt that this decision can be applied to 'domestic' situations such as my Chenu example.)

SAQ 87

Charley is owner in fee simple of Superhouse (registered title). His cohabitee, Dinah, has contributed substantially to the cost of acquisition, and has therefore acquired a share under a constructive trust. The relationship has now broken down, and Dinah is contemplating the possibility of leaving. However, she wants to be sure that her interest will bind a purchaser of Superhouse. Advise Dinah.

Provided she stays put in Superhouse **and** reveals her interest to anybody who asks whether she has a share in the home, Dinah's interest will be an overriding interest under s. 70(1)(g) and a purchaser from Albert will be bound by it.

If Dinah moves out her position is better than that in **SAQ 86**. She should (like the partner in *Elias* v *Mitchell*) protect her minor interest by lodging a caution. (I should again add that I am temporarily ignoring the effect of the decision of the House of Lords in *City of London Building Society* v *Flegg*, which I will be discussing at **16.4.2**.)

16.4.2 WHAT IF ALFRED DID APPOINT A SECOND TRUSTEE?

Suppose that in our Chenu example Alfred does realise that there is a co-ownership, and that therefore he is a lone trustee for sale. If he wants to make a disposition (sale, lease or mortgage) Alfred can appoint a friend as co-trustee. The appointment of a second trustee changes the position dramatically:

(a) If the title to Chenu is **unregistered**, Bertha's interest will be overreached in the usual way.

(b) If the title to Chenu is **registered**, a disposition by two trustees will similarly overreach Bertha's interest, notwithstanding the operation of s. 70(1)(g) or the lodging of a caution. This is because it is an inherent characteristic of Bertha's interest (remember it is an interest under a trust for sale) that it can be overreached by a disposition made by two trustees.

The propositions I have just given are what almost everybody thought the law to be before the litigation in *City of London Building Society* v *Flegg*. They are also the law as it stands today. The erroneous decision of the Court of Appeal in *Flegg* briefly threw everything into confusion. Happily, the House of Lords came to a decision in line with the general pre-*Flegg* understanding of the law.

16.4.2.1 *City of London Building Society* v *Flegg* [1986] 3 All ER 989

Mr and Mrs Flegg both contributed to the purchase of a house; the title to the house was registered in the names of their daughter and son-in-law (the Maxwell-Browns). The Fleggs, as a consequence of their contributions, each had an interest as a tenant in common under a resulting trust. All four lived in the house, and were therefore in 'actual occupation'. The house was **subsequently** mortgaged to the building society.

The building society successfully argued (in the House of Lords) that the mortgage, being executed by **two** trustees, overreached the rights of Mr and Mrs Flegg. They could thus sell the house over the heads of the Fleggs.

16.4.2.2   The erroneous rulings of the Court of Appeal

The Court of Appeal had held that the mortgage did not overreach the rights of Mr and Mrs Flegg. It ruled:

(a)   That the decision in *Boland* meant that the Fleggs each had an overriding interest under the Land Registration Act 1925, s. 70(1)(g) which could not be overreached even by a disposition made by two or more trustees.

(b)   (Whether the land was registered or unregistered title) that Mr and Mrs Flegg were protected by s. 14 of the Law of Property Act 1925, which reads:

> This Part of this Act shall not prejudicially affect the interest of any person in possession or in actual occupation of land to which he may be entitled in right of such possession or occupation.

The generally held view of this provision is that it merely preserves the rule in *Hunt* v *Luck* (subject to the provisions of the Land Charges Act.) Yet the Court of Appeal held that it meant that the rights of tenants in common in occupation could not be overreached.

A, B, C, and D are the trustees for sale of a very large house. It is the residence of A, B, C, D, E, F, G, H, I, J, K, L, M, N, O, P, Q, R, S, T, U, V, W, X, Y and Z. All of them contributed to the purchase price. If the decision of the Court of Appeal in *Flegg* had been upheld, how many signatures would have been required on any conveyance of the house?

The answer is, of course, twenty-six!

16.4.2.3   The House of Lords Decision in *Flegg*

Read the extracts from *Flegg* set out in *Cases and Materials* (16.1.2), noting in particular the views of Lords Templeman and Oliver on the effects of imposing a trust for sale on co-owners.

The House of Lords in *Flegg* unanimously overruled the Court of Appeal on both issues raised in the case:

(a)   The ruling in *Boland* that a non-trustee co-owner had an overriding interest if he or she was in actual occupation did not mean that such an interest could not be overreached by a disposition made by **two** (or more) trustees. It was an inherent characteristic of an interest under a trust for sale that it could be overreached by a disposition made by two trustees.

(b)   The Law of Property Act 1925, s. 14 did not mean that the rights of co-owners in occupation could not be overreached.

Charley is owner in fee simple of Superhouse. His cohabitee, Dinah, has contributed substantially to the cost of acquisition, and has therefore acquired a share under a constructive trust. The relationship has now broken down, and Dinah is contemplating the possibility of leaving. However she wants to be sure that her interest will bind a purchaser of Superhouse. Charley has just appointed his friend Edward to be a second trustee of Superhouse. Advise Dinah.

First, I hope you realised that with this question, it makes no difference whether Superhouse is registered or unregistered title. Secondly, and this is the crucial point, as a result of *Flegg* there is **nothing** Dinah can do to be sure that her interest will bind a purchaser of Superhouse. Any sale (lease or mortgage) of Superhouse by the two trustees Charley and Edward will automatically overreach Dinah's interest.

16.5   Section 30 and the Co-Ownership Trust for Sale

We referred to s. 30 of the Law of Property Act 1925 at **13.6.2**. This provision (which of course applies to all trusts for sale) is of prime importance where co-owners disagree as to the fate of their property. Almost all reported cases under s. 30 have involved co-owners who have fallen out with each other.

Some older cases (e.g., *Jones* v *Challenger*) involve a marriage which has broken down. These cases still give us guidance as to how s. 30 should operate. However, I should immediately stress that disputes between divorcing couples are nowadays not settled under s. 30. They are usually resolved by employing ss. 23–25 of the Matrimonial Causes Act 1973, the 'property adjustment provisions' (see **15.4.5.1**). These provisions are not available when a cohabitation breaks down.

16.5.1 FACTORS CONSIDERED WHEN EXERCISING THE DISCRETION UNDER SECTION 30

The court, in exercising its discretion under s. 30, will consider:

(a) the purposes for which the property has been acquired and whether those purposes can still be continued (see particularly *Re Buchanan-Wollaston*, discussed below);

(b) the wishes of the majority (by value) of the co-owners. Unfortunately this is not much help where there are two co-owners each with equal rights!

16.5.2 SOLUTIONS THE COURT MAY ADOPT

On an application under s. 30 in a co-ownership case, it now appears that there are four alternative possible solutions.

16.5.2.1 Refuse a sale

Re Buchanan-Wollaston [1939] 2 All ER 302

Read the extracts from this case in *Cases and Materials* (16.2.1.1) noting why an order for sale was refused.

In this case there was a piece of open ground at Lowestoft in Suffolk separating four houses from the sea. This land was for sale, and the owners of the four houses clubbed together to buy it as tenants in common. They were anxious to preserve their view of the sea.

One of the four subsequently sold his house and moved away. He then applied to the court for an order that the open ground should be sold and the proceeds divided. He argued that as the land was held on trust for sale, it followed that if any of the four asked for a sale, a sale must take place.

This argument was firmly rejected by the Court of Appeal. Where land was bought for a specific purpose and that purpose could still be fulfilled, the courts should normally refuse to order a sale.

This decision was sensational back in 1939. Nowadays it appears as plain common sense. The Court of Appeal recognised (as most later courts have recognised) that the imposition of a trust for sale on co-owners is pure 'legal machinery' and it should not affect co-owners' substantive rights.

Re Evers [1980] 3 All ER 399

The facts of this case are very different, but involve the same principle as in *Buchanan-Wollaston*. A cohabiting couple bought a house as joint tenants, in order to house themselves and the three children for whom they had responsibility. The relationship broke up, and the man left. The other four members of the family continued to live in the house.

The Court of Appeal refused the man's application for an order of sale. The greater part of the purpose of acquiring the house (housing the family of five) could still be fulfilled. The court did, however, indicate that if or when circumstances changed (e.g., the children grew up and left home) a renewed application by the man would probably receive a sympathetic hearing.

16.5.2.2 Refuse a sale but charge a co-owner in possession rent

This solution does not seem to have been adopted very often, but was in the case of *Dennis* v *McDonald* [1981] 2 All ER 632, [1982] 1 All ER 590. A cohabiting couple bought a house as tenants in common in equal shares. They eventually had five children. The relationship broke up because of the man's violence. The woman left home, but had care of the two youngest children only. The three older children continued to live with their father in the house.

The Court of Appeal refused to order the sale of the house, but ordered the man to pay a 'rent' to the woman. This was fixed (logically enough) at **half** a 'fair rent' for the premises.

The facts of *Dennis* v *McDonald* are rather special, but I personally cannot see why this 'rent solution' should not be adopted in other types of case. I think it should be at least considered in any case where:

(a) it is socially undesirable to order the property sold; or

(b) it is unfair that the applicant should be excluded from all benefit from the property.

It could be used, e.g., where the co-owned property houses a flourishing business which might have to close if a sale were ordered. It seems, however, that if a court is looking for a compromise solution, it is more likely to adopt the solution set out at **16.5.2.4**.

16.5.2.3 Order a sale

This solution is the one normally adopted where the purposes for which the property was acquired have clearly failed. For example, the property was acquired for use in a business, and that business has failed.

In *Jones* v *Challenger* [1960] 1 All ER 785 the husband and wife bought their matrimonial home as joint tenants. The marriage broke down and the wife went to live with another man. The husband was left alone in the house. Despite protests from the husband that the wife's adultery was being 'rewarded' the Court of Appeal ruled that the purpose of acquisition of the house had failed and a sale should be ordered.

On a rather different point, I am sure that a court would normally also order a sale if there were a large number of co-owners and a clear majority **by value** wanted a sale.

16.5.2.4 Order a sale but suspend the order for a short period

The possibility of making an order in this form was expressly recognised by the Court of Appeal in *Jones* v *Challenger*. The court can suspend the order of sale for a few months so as to give a co-owner wishing to retain the property a chance to buy the other(s) out. He will of course have to pay the appropriate fraction of a fair value of the property.

ACTIVITY 44

If co-owners fall out, what is a sensible compromise solution which can be achieved without litigation?

The parties agree that the co-owner(s) wanting to keep the property buy out the co-owner(s) who 'want the cash'. (Arrangements will of course have to be made for the property to be valued.)

16.6   The Modern Position of Husband and Wife Co-owners on a Marriage Break-up

The next few paragraphs arguably represent something of a digression into family law. I would stress that what follows is all you need to know for the purposes of a land law course. There is no need to learn the detailed 'property adjustment' rules in ss. 23–25 of the Matrimonial Causes Act 1973.

Where husband and wife are co-owners of **any property** (usually it will be the matrimonial home) and the marriage has broken down, one spouse could still (in theory) invoke s. 30 of the Law of Property Act 1925. Alternatively a spouse could (in theory) still invoke a special procedure available only for inter-spousal property disputes laid down in s. 17 of the Married Women's Property Act 1882.

Neither under s. 30 of the 1925 Act nor under s. 17 of the 1882 Act do the courts have any power to **vary** the property rights of the spouses. However, as I explained at **15.4.5.3**, the divorce court does have nowadays very wide powers (under ss. 23–25 of the Matrimonial Causes Act 1973) to make property adjustment orders.

The co-owned property of divorcing couples is nowadays invariably dealt with under ss. 23–25 of the 1973 Act. If a divorcing spouse tried to invoke s. 30 (or even s. 17 of the 1882 Act), the court should refuse the application and order that the matter be dealt with by the divorce court under the 1973 provisions: see *Williams J.* v *Williams M.* [1977] 1 All ER 28.

Under ss. 23–25, the divorce court is particularly careful where young children are still living in the ex-matrimonial home (Usually, of course, a parent is there with them.) In such cases the divorce court is unlikely to order an immediate sale of the home. Rather, the normal practice is to **refuse** an order for immediate sale of the home and to make some kind of order which will ensure that the children can continue to live in the home until they have grown up: see *Mesher* v *Mesher* [1980] 1 All ER 126 (a case actually decided in 1973). Orders designed to protect children in this way are sometimes referred to as '*Mesher* orders'.

It is instructive to study the story behind the case of *Thompson* v *Thompson* [1985] 2 All ER 243. The order of the divorce court, made in 1981, directed that the ex-husband and the ex-wife, who remained the trustees for sale, should postpone sale of the home 'until the youngest child of the family . . . reaches the age of 17 years or finishes further education, whichever is later, or further order'.

The ex-wife continued to live in the home with the two children, the youngest of whom was (in 1985) aged 11. The ex-wife wanted to move from the home; ironically the ex-husband would not agree. She sought and obtained an order of sale, which was granted under s. 24A of the Matrimonial Causes Act 1973.

ACTIVITY 45

Look at the orders made in the cases of *Allen* v *Allen* [1974] 3 All ER 385 and *Harvey* v *Harvey* [1982] 1 All ER 693. These orders are set out in *Cases and Materials* (16.3). *Thompson, Allen* and *Harvey* (and many other cases) are, looked at from a land law point of view, quite striking for a number of reasons. Why do you think that is?

(a) The court continues as trustees (or, as in *Allen* appoints as trustees) two people who are estranged from each other.

(b) The court inserts into the trust for sale provisions (such as that in *Thompson*) designed to ensure that the land will not be sold.

(c) These modern divorce cases demonstrate the highly artificial nature of the trust for sale which the 1925 legislation forced upon all co-owners.

(It is also worth realising that solutions such as those adopted in *Allen* and *Harvey* are often reached by divorcing couples **by negotiation**, without the need for the divorce court to **impose** an order. However, one unfortunate side effect of the Child Support Act 1992 is that it discourages divorcing spouses from settling their differences on the basis that the spouse with care of the children gets **possession** of the former matrimonial home.)

16.7 Rights of Co-Owners in Equity – Are They Interests in Land?

In **Chapter 11, 11.4.1,** I referred to the 'archaic' equitable doctrine of conversion. Under that doctrine, the interests of beneficiaries under a trust for sale are personal property not real property.

Because of the fact that whenever there is a co-ownership there is a trust for sale, it follows that the equitable rights of the co-owners are inevitably subject to the equitable doctrine of conversion. Applying this doctrine, the equitable interests of co-owners are technically interests in money (personal property) not in land (real property). Thus in *Re Kempthorne* [1930] 1 Ch 268, the testator owned a half share in land as tenant in common. He died in 1927. His will was in terms such as 'I leave my real estate to X and my personal estate to Y'. His share as a tenant in common went to Y. I don't think that was what Mr Kempthorne (who had been a solicitor!) intended.

16.7.1   THE MODERN POSITION – THE RIGHTS OF CO-OWNERS ARE INTERESTS IN LAND

Since the decision of the Court of Appeal in *Bull v Bull* [1955] 1 All ER 253, it gradually has been accepted that a co-owner's equitable interest is not just an 'interest in money'. It is now accepted that (at least for most purposes) the equitable interest of a co-owner is a right in the land itself. The House of Lords in *Williams and Glyn's Bank v Boland* (see **10.3.6**) upheld the correctness of this approach. In effect, while the doctrine of conversion has not been abolished, modern judges normally do not apply it to equitable interests under a co-ownership trust for sale.

One vital consequence of this modern approach is that if (as in *Bull* and *Boland*) property is acquired by co-owners for personal occupation, then all co-owners have a right to possess the land irrespective of whether or not they are trustees. (See also *Jones A. v Jones F.* [1977] 2 All ER 231.)

In *Bull v Bull* [1955] 1 All ER 253 Bull 'the son' bought a house. His mother paid a substantial part of the purchase price. She thus acquired an equitable interest in the house. It followed that the son held the house on trust for sale for himself and his mother as tenants in common. The son later got married, and sadly the mother fell out with her daughter-in-law. The son sided with his wife, and told his mother to leave. When she refused he sued to evict her, contending that she was a trespasser. He argued that she had no interest in the land itself, but only an interest 'in money'. The Court of Appeal, led by Denning LJ (as he then was), found that notwithstanding the imposition of a trust for sale by the 1925 legislation, the mother had a right to live in the home.

This decision was regarded as very radical back in 1955. Nowadays it is trite law. It is now accepted that where property is acquired by co-owners for personal occupation, then all co-owners have a right to possess the land irrespective of whether or not they are trustees of the legal title. The law has been brought into line with common sense.

Digressing slightly, Lord Denning's judgment in *Bull* was far-sighted in one other respect. In carefully considered *obiter dicta* he realised that if the son appointed a second trustee, any sale by the son and his co-trustee would overreach the mother's interest. *Vis-à-vis* a purchaser she would then be a trespasser and eviction proceedings against her would undoubtedly succeed. In the light of later developments, especially the decision of the House of Lords in *Flegg* (see **16.4.2**), this is clearly correct.

However, as Lord Denning also pointed out in *Bull*, a potential purchaser from the son and his co-trustee might be unwilling to buy, once it was realised that the mother was determined to stay put. (Would you buy or lease a house where you knew that before you could move in you would have to take eviction proceedings against a recalcitrant trespasser?) The son (or anyone else in a similar position) would therefore probably have to apply under s. 30 of the Law of Property Act 1925 to resolve the situation before he put the house on the market.

Charley is owner in fee simple of Superhouse. His cohabitee, Dinah, has contributed substantially to the cost of acquisition, and has therefore acquired a share under a constructive trust. The relationship has now broken down, and Dinah is contemplating the possibility of leaving. Charley has just appointed his friend Edward to be a second trustee of Superhouse, and therefore we have already advised Dinah (SAQ 89) that her equitable interest will never be binding on a purchaser from Charley and Edward. Is there any further advice we can give to Dinah?

We should advise Dinah to try to put purchasers off when they come round to look at the house by:

(a) pointing out all the defects, e.g., 'There are an awful lot of burglaries round here' or 'The house has a terrible damp problem';

(b) making it clear that if they buy (lease) Superhouse, they will acquire the problem of evicting a scorned cohabitee.

(Dinah should however be warned that Charley and Edward might try to resolve the situation by taking proceedings under s. 30 of the 1925 Act. Unless young children are involved, the court would almost certainly order Dinah out of the house so that a sale could take place with vacant possession.)

16.7.2 RIGHTS OF CO-OWNERS ARE INTERESTS IN LAND FOR PURPOSES OF CONTRACT FORMALITIES

(First refer back briefly to **Chapter 5**, at **5.5.3**.)

Almost simultaneous to *Bull* v *Bull*, a different division of the Court of Appeal (not including Lord Denning) decided *Cooper* v *Critchley* [1955] Ch 431 (see especially p. 438). The court held that the equitable interest of a tenant in common is an interest in land for the purposes of s. 40(1) of the Law of Property Act 1925. Thus a contract to sell such an interest had to be in writing or evidenced in writing. The correctness of this view seems to be confirmed by *Williams & Glyn's Bank* v *Boland*.

Section 40 has, of course now been repealed and replaced by s. 2 of the Law of Property (Miscellaneous Provisions) Act 1989. Under s. 2(6) of the 1989 Act, an 'interest in land' is defined to include **an interest in the proceeds of sale of land**. Thus an interest of a tenant in common is definitely an interest in land for the purposes of s. 2 of the 1989 Act.

16.7.3 CASES WHERE THE DOCTRINE OF CONVERSION HAS BEEN APPLIED TO CO-OWNERS

Re Kempthorne [1930] 1 Ch 268
For the facts of this case, see **16.7**. This decision is probably still correct, but only for the proposition that for the purposes of interpreting wills and other legal documents, an interest as tenant in common is personal property.

Barclay v *Barclay* [1970] 2 All ER 676

This case, where the facts are in sharp contrast to *Bull*, must surely still be correct. A testator left a bungalow on trust for sale for five beneficiaries in equal shares. As it happened, one of the beneficiaries was living in the bungalow at the time of the testator's death. The Court of Appeal held that this beneficiary had no right to occupy the property. The deceased's executors could evict the beneficiary.

The crucial fact (distinguishing *Barclay* from *Bull*) was that it was undoubtedly the testator's **true** intention that the property should be sold as soon as possible and the proceeds divided. He had not envisaged the bungalow as being a home for any of the beneficiaries.

Cedar Holdings v *Green* [1979] 3 All ER 117

This decision of the Court of Appeal must surely be wrong. In this case H and W owned the matrimonial home as joint tenants. The marriage broke up. H and X went to Cedar asking for a loan. X (H's new lady-friend) made out that she was H's wife. H and X executed a deed mortgaging the home to Cedar Holdings. This mortgage was of course fraudulent and void as to the legal estate. Cedar Holdings, however, argued that s. 63 of the Law of Property Act 1925 should be applied.

The gist of s. 63 is that where a person executes a 'conveyance' of Blackacre then that conveyance affects whatever 'estate or interest' that person has in Blackacre. Thus, e.g., if Bloggs has a 99-year lease over Whiteacre, and executes a deed purporting to convey the **fee simple** in Whiteacre to Muggs, Muggs acquires the 99-year lease.

Consider what the Court of Appeal should have decided.

What the Court of Appeal **should** have held in *Cedar Holdings* v *Green* was that the deed executed by H was effective to mortgage his equitable interest in the house to Cedar. (The joint tenancy would have thereby been severed.)

What the Court of Appeal **actually** decided was that the rights of H under the trust for sale were not an 'interest in land' for the purposes of s. 63. Cedar thus had no security whatsoever. (This case was heavily criticised in *Boland*, but was not overruled.)

16.8 Law of Property (Joint Tenants) Act 1964

(This Act applies only to unregistered titles, and is thus of declining importance.)

Where two or more people are joint tenants at law and in equity, the joint tenancy of course comes to an end the moment there is only one joint tenant left, i.e. on the death of the penultimate joint tenant. It follows that the moment there is only one owner, the trust for sale also ends. The sole survivor can deal with the land as an absolute owner, and does not have to appoint another trustee to effect a sale, lease, etc.

Prior to 1964 there was, however, a practical difficulty if a last surviving joint tenant wanted to sell the land without appointing a second trustee. A purchaser from a last-surviving joint tenant might well ask, 'How do I know that the joint tenancy has not been severed?'. (If there has been a severance there will be a tenancy in common, and the trust for sale will still continue and a second trustee is needed for a sale.)

Just think for a moment. It is now easy to sever a joint tenancy. Indeed, it can be done without the knowledge of fellow joint tenants. Consequently it is impossible for the 'last survivor' to prove objectively that there has been no severance and that the trust for sale is at an end.

Prior to 1964, purchasers therefore insisted that the last survivor appointed a co-trustee before selling the property. This was a source of annoyance to solicitors and their clients, and the 1964 Act was designed to end the annoyance.

Under the 1964 Act a purchaser from the last-surviving joint tenant can assume that there has been no severance unless either:

(a) a memorandum of severance has been endorsed upon the conveyance to the joint tenants; or

(b) a bankruptcy petition or receiving order has been registered as a pending action.

Thus, unless one or other of the above conditions is fulfilled, a conveyance by a last surviving joint tenant acting on his or her own will convey a good title to a purchaser.

It should be noted that a 'memorandum of severance' is not another way of severing a joint tenancy: rather it is something which can be endorsed on the conveyance to 'tell the world' that a severance has already taken place.

16.9 Co-ownership of Registered Land

The co-owners are registered as joint proprietors, but as the register does not indicate any trusts affecting registered titles, the register will not indicate whether the co-owners are joint tenants or tenants in common; if the latter it will not indicate the size of the shares. Thus (as mentioned at **14.9**) a solicitor acting for co-owners should retain in his files a document expressly declaring the **equitable interests** of the co-owners.

There is, however, one further point which should be noted. When applying to register co-proprietors, the applicants' solicitor has to indicate, in answer to a question on the application form, whether a last-surviving co-proprietor can or cannot give a valid receipt for capital money arising upon a disposition. The answer 'can' will be given if the co-proprietors are joint tenants in equity. The answer 'cannot' will be given if the co-proprietors are tenants in common in equity, or if they are trustees for sale for other beneficiaries. If the answer is 'cannot', then a restriction will be entered in the proprietor-ship register in the following terms:

No disposition by a sole proprietor of the land (not being a trust corporation) under which capital money arises is to be registered except under an order of the registrar or of the Court.

If co-proprietors are registered without such a restriction being entered, that conclusively indicates that at least originally they were joint tenants in equity: *Re Gorman* [1990] 1 WLR 616. It is safe for a purchaser to deal with a last survivor if there is no such restriction, even if he suspects that there has been a severance.

A joint tenant who severs an equitable joint tenancy in a piece of registered land should insist on the insertion of a restriction. He must, however, arrange for the production of the land certificate to the registry.

SAQ 91

What should a joint tenant do if he cannot arrange for the production of the land certificate, because the co-owners have fallen out and it is the other co-owner(s) who have the certificate?

He should lodge a caution.

16.10   Conclusion

The 70 years which have elapsed since the compulsory imposition of a trust for sale on co-owners have seen both an enormous increase in the amount of co-ownership and the realisation that the 1925 legislators in solving one problem (multiplicity of co-owners) created several others.

Parliament's contribution to the solution of the problems has been minimal – the rather technical Law of Property (Joint Tenants) Act 1964, which despite its grandiose title tackles just one minor problem which is anyway confined to unregistered land.

In contrast, the judiciary have (usually) worked very hard to sort things out. The senior judiciary have brought an enormous amount of common sense into this socially very important area of law. As long ago as 1939, the Court of Appeal (*Re Buchanan-Wollaston*) refused to be blinded by the existence of the trust for sale imposed on all co-owners. They saw that the compulsory trust for sale is merely legal machinery which should not affect the substantive rights of the parties.

Subsequent generations of judges (with the unfortunate exception of the judges who heard *Cedar Holdings* v *Green*) have adhered to this commonsense approach. The House of Lords decision in *Flegg* is not an exception. In that case the Law Lords insisted that the trust for sale overreaching machinery must be allowed to operate as Parliament had intended. But, as our **SAQ 88** example (see **16.4.2**) is designed to demonstrate, the House of Lords decision avoids potentially absurd results.

Moreover, in *Flegg* (and *Boland*) the Law Lords unanimously endorsed an elementary commonsense proposition which Lord Denning had propounded back in 1955. When in *Bull* v *Bull* that highly innovative judge proclaimed that all co-owners, whether trustees or not, had a right to occupy the land, some land law experts were aghast. Nowadays *Bull* is very trite law.

In this area of law, common sense has (usually) triumphed over legal technicality. But the triumph will be complete only when the House of Lords consigns *Cedar Holdings* v *Green* to the rubbish dump.

16.11   End of Chapter Assessment Question

In 1987 four friends, Steven, Julia, Mark and Tracey, purchased a cottage called 'The Retreat' for the purpose of a holiday home. The conveyance to them contained no express declaration of a trust for sale. Title to The Retreat was unregistered. The purchase money was provided equally and at the time of the purchase Tracey was only 17 years of age.

In January 1994 Julia became short of cash and therefore obtained a bank loan which was secured on her interest in The Retreat.

Some months later Steven also found himself in financial difficulties. However his solution to the problem was to create frequent arguments with the others in which he would demand that they 'buy him out'. These outbursts were ignored by the others and Steven eventually stopped using The Retreat.

In October 1994 Steven and Julia were killed in a car accident. By their wills Steven left all his property to his mother Violet, and Julia left all her property to her sister, Karen.

Mark is keen to sell The Retreat and has just found a purchaser who wants an early completion. Tracey vehemently opposes the proposed sale as since the deaths of Steven and Julia she has been living at The Retreat permanently. Violet is in agreement with Mark, but Karen is uncertain.

Advise Mark as to:

(a)   exactly who owns The Retreat and in what proportions;

(b)   his prospects of forcing a sale.

See *Cases and Materials* (16.8) for a specimen answer.

CHAPTER SEVENTEEN

LEASES – THE BASIC REQUIREMENTS

17.1 Objectives

By the end of this chapter you should:

■ be able to list the basic requirements for a valid lease;

■ be fully conversant with the rules governing the duration of fixed-term leases and periodic tenancies;

■ appreciate the importance of the distinction between a lease and a licence;

■ be able to explain how the law determines whether a transaction is a lease or a licence;

■ be familiar with and be able to distinguish between the formalities required for the creation of (i) legal and (ii) equitable leases;

■ appreciate how periodic tenancies may arise by operation of law.

17.2 Introduction

As is obvious if you visit any law library, whole textbooks have been written on the law of leases, or 'landlord and tenant law' as it is often called. In this text (designed for a land law course where only three or four weeks are spent studying leases) we have space to consider only basic principles. It should therefore in particular be stressed that the following legislation is outside the scope of this text.

■ **The Rent Acts** These Acts (the history of which goes back to the First World War) grant special security to and control the rents of most residential tenants whose leases were granted before the Housing Act 1988.

■ **Housing Act 1988** This controversial Act removes **new** residential leases from the scope of the Rent Acts.

■ **Agricultural Holdings Acts** and the **Agricultural Tenancies Act 1995** which replaces those Acts The Agricultural Holdings Acts gave special protection to tenant farmers. The 1995 Act removes most of that special statutory protection.

■ **Landlord and Tenant Act 1954, Part II** This legislation grants special protection to lessees of business premises (e.g., shops, offices and factories). In particular when the lease of a business tenant (e.g., a shopkeeper) runs out, he can usually insist that the lease be renewed.

■ **Leasehold Reform Act 1967 and later similar legislation**   This legislation allows long lessees of certain types of houses compulsorily to purchase the freehold reversions of their houses from **private** landlords.

■ **Leasehold Reform, Housing and Urban Development Act 1993**   This statute (*inter alia*) gives the lessees of long leases living in certain types of flats the right compulsorily to purchase the freehold reversion of their block of flats from **private** landlords.

I have to warn you that this chapter is rather a bulky one, and contains rather a large quantity of complex technical concepts. Much of the technicality stems from one simple fact: if the owner of a fee simple estate allows another person to make use of his land, that transaction **may** be a lease; alternatively it may be only a licence. Differentiating between leases and licences has given rise to a quite considerable amount of case law.

Other causes of the complexity of this chapter stem from matters we have already touched upon. In **Chapter 1** we noted the differences between fixed-term leases and periodic tenancies, while in **Chapter 5** we considered *Walsh* v *Lonsdale* and noted that leases may be either legal leases or equitable leases. These matters must now be considered in greater depth.

17.3   The Essential Requirements for a Lease

There are three essential requirements:

(a)   The estate must be of a duration permitted for a leasehold estate.

(b)   The grant must give exclusive possession.

(c)   The grant must have the correct formalities.

In *Street* v *Mountford* [1985] 2 All ER 289, the House of Lords held that (subject to minor exceptions) a transaction which fulfils these three requirements **must be a lease** even if the parties say (in the relevant document) that the transaction is something else, e.g., a licence.

17.4   Duration of Leases

Leases can either be for a **fixed term**, or they can be **periodic tenancies**.

17.4.1   FIXED-TERM LEASES

Here we are talking of leases for periods such as one month, three years, 99 years, 999 years. The vital feature of a fixed-term lease is that there is a fixed **maximum** duration. It is perfectly possible (indeed normal) for a lease to contain a forfeiture clause under which the landlord can terminate the lease prematurely if the tenant breaks any of the terms of the lease.

Some fixed-term leases also contain a 'break clause', which can be invoked by the tenant. Under such a clause the tenant has a right unilaterally to terminate the lease before it has run its full course. You will sometimes see '21 year leases with seven year breaks'.

The lease in principle lasts 21 years, but the tenant has the option to terminate the lease after 7 or 14 years.

Leases for **uncertain maximum periods** are not permitted. In *Lace* v *Chandler* [1944] KB 368 leases 'for the duration of the war' were held to be invalid. This caused widespread panic, as such grants were (at the time) common. Parliament therefore rushed through an ingenious piece of legislation, the Validation of Wartime Leases Act 1944. This Act was retrospective, and converted grants 'for the duration of the war' into leases for a fixed-term of 10 years, with a proviso that either landlord or tenant could terminate the lease once the war ended by giving a month's notice.

The House of Lords recently applied the *Lace* v *Chandler* principle in *Prudential Assurance* v *London Residuary Body* [1992] 3 All ER 504. The former London County Council had, in 1930, granted a lease of property fronting the busy Walworth Road. The lease was on terms that 'the tenancy shall continue until the . . . land is required by the council for the purposes of the widening of [the road]'. The rent was £30 per annum. The road widening never took place. The House of Lords held that there was not a valid fixed-term lease. For reasons which will appear at **17.4.2**, the House found that there was a yearly periodic tenancy.

Alan has just been appointed manager of Bruddersford Town football club. He knows that he is likely to be sacked if the team plays poorly. He wants to take a lease of a house in Bruddersford from Charley, a keen Bruddersford supporter. Alan and Charley envisage that the lease will be for 'as long as Alan remains manager'. What sort of lease would meet their requirements? (A clue is the Validation of Wartime Leases Act 1944!)

Alan and Charley should agree on a fixed-term lease for some very long period (e.g., 40 years), but include a clause that should Alan cease to be manager either party can terminate the lease by (say) one month's notice.

17.4.2 PERIODIC TENANCIES

Here we are talking of weekly, monthly, yearly, quarterly tenancies, etc. The practical effect of a periodic tenancy is that it continues indefinitely until terminated by one or other side giving the appropriate notice. Why, then, do periodic tenancies not infringe the rule that a leasehold estate must have a fixed maximum duration? At least three different explanations have been given:

(a) A periodic tenancy is a lease for one period which goes on renewing itself automatically.

(b) A periodic tenancy is a lease for one period which goes on extending itself automatically.

(c) A periodic tenancy is a lease because its maximum duration is 'capable of being rendered certain' by the giving of the appropriate period of notice.

In *Prudential Assurance* v *London Residuary Body* (see **17.4.1**) the House of Lords clearly favoured explanation (a), **so this must be regarded as the correct one**.

The period of notice to terminate a periodic tenancy is prima facie one period, to expire at the end of a period. Thus, e.g., suppose on 1 January Les grants a monthly tenancy to Tom. Tom now decides he wants to leave. He must give (at least) one month's notice to expire on the last day of a calendar month.

SAQ 93

Suppose today is 15 February. If Tom gives Les one month's notice that he is quitting the property, when will that notice expire?

The answer is that the notice will expire at midnight at the end of 31 March. You should note that in practical terms this means that if Tom in fact moves out on (say) 16 February, he must still pay the rent until the end of March.

The parties to a periodic tenancy can agree that the requisite notice should be less than one period, but not more. Thus, e.g. in a half-yearly tenancy they could agree to it being terminable on giving three months' notice. They could not agree to a year's notice.

A special rule operates for yearly tenancies. In the absence of contrary agreement the period of notice is (anomalously) six months, though the parties can expressly agree to any period of notice up to one year.

It **used to be thought** that a party to a periodic tenancy could agree to conditions restricting his right to terminate the tenancy. In *Re Midland Railway's Agreement* [1971] 1 All ER 1007, the Railway (in 1922) granted a fairly standard half-yearly tenancy of some spare ground at Luton, but agreed not to terminate the tenancy until the land was required for railway purposes. This condition was held valid by the Court of Appeal, and binding on British Rail, who wanted to terminate the tenancy in order to let the land at a higher rent.

This case, and another very confusing case, *Ashburn Anstalt* v *Arnold* [1988] 2 All ER 147, were both (on this point) overruled by the House of Lords in the *Prudential Assurance* case. In *Prudential Assurance* the Court of Appeal had held that the tenants had a yearly tenancy, but subject to a condition that the tenancy could not be terminated until the land was required for the road-widening scheme. The House of Lords held that parties to a periodic tenancy cannot restrict their basic right to terminate the tenancy by giving the appropriate notice.

17.4.3 SPECIAL PROBLEMS CONNECTED WITH THE DURATION OF LEASES

17.4.3.1 'Leases for lives'

Traditionally life estates are created as part of a strict settlement and are governed by the Settled Land Act 1925, which we considered in **Chapters 11** and **12**.

The 1925 legislators had a problem with a practice which existed in some parts of the country. Landlords in some areas used to grant to tenant-farmers not fixed terms, but a life estate in return for the tenant paying a rent and/or premium. (A premium is a capital sum paid for the grant of a lease.) Clearly it would have been totally wrong to bring such transactions within the Settled Land Act 1925.

Section 149(6) of the Law of Property Act 1925 is designed to convert such 'leases for life' transactions into fixed-term leases.

Study s. 149(6) in *Cases and Materials* (17.1.3.1); is this sub-section confined to 'leases for life'?
(You will see that the word 'fine' appears in this subsection. Do not be confused. Where the 1925 legislation uses the word 'fine' it does not mean a monetary criminal penalty. Rather, the word 'fine' in the context of leases is an old-fashioned word for 'premium'.)

Unfortunately s. 149(6) is drafted in an unnecessarily wide way, and catches the following three types of transaction:

    (a) A lease at a rent and/or premium granted for a life or lives.

    (b) A lease for a fixed period determinable on life or lives.

    (c) A lease for a fixed period determinable upon marriage.

All the three types of transaction are converted into leases for a fixed term of 90 years. However, once the relevant death or marriage has occurred either the landlord or the tenant (or their personal representatives) can terminate the lease by giving a month's notice to expire on one of the traditional quarter days. The 'traditional quarter days' are Lady Day (25 March), Mid-Summer (24 June), Michaelmas (29 September) and Christmas.

Section 149(6) works perfectly well when applied to transactions of type (a) above. (Remember the Validation of Wartime Leases Act 1944 and **SAQ 92**.) However, the applicability of s. 149(6) to transactions of types (b) and (c) creates a trap for the foolish landlord.

Suppose in 1992 Laurie leases Blackacre to Terry at £500 per year rent, 'for 10 years or until Terry's death, if earlier'. Terry is a healthy young man of 20. Laurie expects the lease to expire in 2,002. But it is converted by s.149(6) into a 90-year term, and Laurie will not be able to give notice to terminate the lease until Terry dies, which may not be for a very long time. (And the rent remains fixed at £500 per year!)

In 1993, Harry leased a house to Wassilla, a spinster aged 22, 'for five years or until her earlier marriage'. Harry is looking forward to getting the house back in 1998. Wassilla has just joined a religious group which required her to take a vow that she would never marry. Advise Harry.

Harry is caught by s. 149(6). He will have to hope that Wassilla changes her religious views, as otherwise he (or his personal representatives) will not be able to terminate the lease until either Wassilla dies or she achieves the age of 112!

17.4.3.2 Perpetually renewable leases

The essence of such a lease **was** that the tenant took a fixed term of X years, but every time X years expired he had the option to renew the lease for a further X years. Thus, **provided the tenant remembered** to renew every time X years expired, he could keep the land indefinitely.

Prior to 1926 a perpetually renewable lease would be created by including in a fixed-term lease a clause like the following: 'This lease shall be renewable by the tenant at his option on exactly the same terms and conditions, including this provision.' The crucial words are of course, 'including this provision'. Had they been omitted, the lease would have been renewable just **once**.

As a result of s. 145 of the Law of Property Act **1922**, a perpetually renewable lease is not possible after 1925. Section 145 does not, however, invalidate leases containing the kind of clause just quoted. Far from it! Section 145 converts any purported grant of a perpetually renewable lease into a lease for 2,000 (sic) years. The tenant (only) has the option to terminate the lease by 10 **days'** notice every time the lease would have been due for renewal had it been allowed to take effect as a perpetually renewable lease.

Read the extracts from *Caerphilly Concrete v Owen* [1972] 1 All ER 248 in *Cases and Materials* (17.1.3.2). This case dramatically demonstrates that s. 145 is a trap for foolish landlords. Why is that?

The landlords discovered that they had leased their land for 2,000 years at a very low rent!

17.4.3.3   Tenancy at will

A tenancy at will is a very insecure arrangement, because either side can terminate it at a moment's notice. It is particularly unattractive from the point of view of the tenant at will, as he can be thrown out without any prior warning.

In modern conditions, tenancies at will are relatively rare. One does, however, exist where a landlord has allowed somebody to take possession of his land intending him to be a tenant, but, probably because the execution of a formal lease has been forgotten, or the formal lease is for some reason invalid, no estate or interest has been granted to the tenant. (It is, however, also possible deliberately to create a tenancy at will, as in *Manfield v Botchin* [1970] 2 QB 612.)

If a tenant at will starts paying rent on a regular basis, the tenancy at will is automatically converted into a periodic tenancy. This rule, which we consider at **17.7.2** and which the House of Lords applied in the *Prudential Assurance* case, goes a long way to mitigating the extremely insecure position of tenants at will.

One other point. In *Heslop v Burns* [1974] 3 All ER 406, a fairly wealthy person allowed two friends to occupy rent-free a house he owned. The Court of Appeal held that such a friendly arrangement (made without intent to create legal relations) regarding the occupation of a house or flat is nowadays to be treated as a **licence,** not as a tenancy at will.

17.5   Some Concepts Related to the Law of Leases

It is convenient to deal with certain miscellaneous points at this stage. I would stress that what follows is a bare outline of certain matters which you need to know to be able to understand the basic principles of the law of leases and also certain of the cases on the distinction between leases and licences.

17.5.1   TENANCY AT SUFFERANCE

This occurs where a tenant's lease has expired but he (**unlawfully**) continues in possession without the landlord's express agreement or express disagreement. The tenant is said to 'hold over'. If the landlord **expressly disagrees** with the ex-tenant staying, the ex-tenant is simply a trespasser, who should leave immediately. If the landlord **expressly agrees** to the tenant staying in possession, he is a tenant at will.

(Like a tenancy at will a tenancy at sufferance will automatically be converted into a periodic tenancy if the 'tenant' starts paying rent on a regular basis.)

17.5.2   PROTECTED TENANCY

This is a lease (granted prior to 15 January 1989) of a 'dwelling house' (which concept includes a flat) within the scope of the Rent Acts. If the lease terminates (even after 15 January 1989) then normally the tenant can lawfully stay in possession as a **statutory tenant**. (He will not be a tenant at sufferance.)

17.5.3 STATUTORY TENANCY

A statutory tenant technically has no estate or interest in the house or flat he is still occupying. He has a right given **by the statute** (a right which cannot be transferred) to continue to occupy the property notwithstanding the termination of his lease. Statutory tenancies are usually thought of as arising under the Rent Acts. It is worth noting that they could also arise under the Agricultural Holdings Acts, when a lease of a farm terminated but the tenant-farmer was allowed by the Acts to retain possession.

17.5.4 SECURE TENANCIES

Under the Housing Act 1980 public sector lettings such as council houses are **secure tenancies**; they are outside the Rent Acts and the Housing Act 1988, but the public sector secure tenant enjoys similar security of tenure to his private sector counterpart under the old Rent Acts. For lettings after 14 January 1989, the public sector tenant is better off.

17.5.5 ASSURED TENANCIES

Under the Housing Act 1988 (as a general rule), no new protected tenancies can arise. All private landlords of houses or flats are now able to grant **assured tenancies**. The assured tenant has some degree of security of tenure, but there are no controls on the rent charged.

17.5.6 ASSURED SHORTHOLD TENANCIES

A private landlord can also grant an **assured shorthold tenancy**. This is a fixed-term lease of a house or flat for at least six months. The tenant has no security of tenure once the fixed period expires; there are rather weak controls on the amount of rent. This form of letting is proving to be very popular with landlords, especially those who let to undergraduate students.

17.6 The Distinction Between Leases and Licences

The distinction is very important because:

(a) As leases are property rights (an estate or interest in land), they are in principle freely alienable, i.e. they can be sold, given away or left by will. A licence is a right personal to the licensee and cannot be assigned. (Suppose I was going away for a few weeks, and allowed a friend of mine to occupy my flat rent-free in my absence. That would be a 'licence'. It would obviously be wrong for my friend to transfer his right to a third party.)

(b) As leases are property rights, they in principle bind third-party purchasers of the landlord's reversion. Licences generally do not bind purchasers of the land over which the licence is exercisable. (Exceptionally a licence could bind a purchaser if a licensee acquired by his activities on the land a proprietary estoppel or a constructive trust interest. See **1.4.7** and **1.4.8**.)

(c) Leases are subject to security of tenure legislation such as the Rent Acts; licences are generally outside the scope of such legislation.

As you will see if you quickly flip through the next few pages of this text, there have been in recent years a lot of cases on the lease/licence distinction. Almost all of them relate to point (c) just mentioned. In almost all of them a landowner has granted a right to occupy his land, but tried to make the arrangement a licence, not a lease, so that he avoids the Rent Acts or other similar legislation.

17.6.1 EXCLUSIVE POSSESSION AS THE FOUNDATION OF THE LEASE/LICENCE DISTINCTION

Street v *Mountford* [1985] 2 All ER 289

Read the extracts from this case in *Cases and Materials* (17.2.1). You should note how Street (who was a solicitor) carefully drafted the agreement to avoid using words which suggested that the transaction was a lease.

Most land law teachers welcomed the decision of the House of Lords in *Street* v *Mountford*, as it both simplified and clarified the law. Most of the essential facts of this case are set out in the opening paragraph of Lord Templeman's speech:

> By an agreement dated 7 March 1983, the respondent Mr Street granted the appellant Mrs Mountford the right to occupy the furnished rooms numbers 5 and 6 at 5, St Clements Gardens, Boscombe, from 7th March 1983 for £37 per week, subject to termination by 14 days' written notice and subject to [quite elaborate] conditions set forth in the agreement.

I need only add that the agreement was called a 'licence', but nevertheless undoubtedly granted Mrs Mountford exclusive possession. When the case was decided by the Court of Appeal, it held that as 'the [subjective] intention of the parties' was that there should be a licence, that was all Mrs Mountford had. She did not have any form of lease protected by the Rent Acts.

This decision of the Court of Appeal was blasted off the face of the earth ('overruled' is too mild a word) by the unanimous decision of the House of Lords. (Lord Templeman gave the only speech.) The House held that whether a transaction is a lease or a licence depends (with minor exceptions) entirely on whether or not there is **exclusive possession**. The 'intent of the parties' and the label the parties attach to the transaction is irrelevant. As none of the minor exceptions was applicable, Mrs Mountford had a lease which was protected by the Rent Acts.

An 'old' decision of the Court of Appeal in *Addiscombe Gardens* v *Crabbe* [1958] 1 QB 513 is clearly correct in the light of *Street*. The Court of Appeal applied *Street* in *Family Housing Association* v *Jones* [1990] 1 All ER 385. In both these Court of Appeal cases a transaction described very carefully as a licence **but which granted exclusive possession** was held to be a lease.

17.6.2 THE MEANING OF EXCLUSIVE POSSESSION

If there is no exclusive possession granted to the 'grantee' then the transaction is a licence. The test for exclusive possession is:

Has the grantee been given the general control of the property?

This test stems from the nineteenth-century case of *Wells* v *Hull Corporation* (1875) LR 10 CP 402. In that case Hull Corporation owned a 'dry dock' used by shipowners to repair their ships. The corporation 'let' the dock to shipowners on terms which included provisions:

(a) that the corporation was responsible for opening and shutting the dock gates to allow ships to sail in and out;

(b) that the shipowner should clean out the dock at the end of each day's work under the supervision of the corporation's employees.

The court held that the shipowner was not granted 'general control' of the dock. Therefore the 'letting' to the shipowner was in fact only a licence.

17.6.2.1 *Shell-Mex* v *Manchester Garages* [1971] 1 All ER 841

In this case Shell granted the use of a filling station it owned to the garage company for one year. The agreement included a provision under which Shell retained control over the layout of the premises. It could move the pumps and the (extensive) underground storage tanks. The arrangement was held to be only a licence. (Although this case and *Marchant* v *Charters*, discussed next, are still correct in their result, some of Lord Denning's remarks in them about 'intent of the parties' are clearly wrong in the light of *Street* v *Mountford*.)

17.6.2.2 *Marchant* v *Charters* [1977] 3 All ER 918

Read this case in *Cases and Materials* (17.2.2). Do you consider that the result of this case is fair and sensible?

It has always been accepted that a 'lodger' does not have exclusive possession and therefore is only a licensee. In *Marchant* v *Charters* the 'grantee' was not a lodger in the traditional sense but occupied a 'service flat'. The grantor provided daily cleaning and regular changes of bed linen. The grantee was found to be only a licensee.

17.6.3 RETENTION OF KEYS BY THE GRANTOR

The mere fact that a grantor retains keys to the premises does not as such negate the existence of a lease. Lord Donaldson, MR, in *Aslan* v *Murphy* [1989] 3 All ER 190, explained:

It is not a requirement of a tenancy [i.e. lease] that the occupier shall have exclusive possession of the keys to the property. What matters is what underlies the provision as to keys. Why does the owner want a key, want to prevent keys being issued to the friends of the occupier or want to prevent the lock being changed?

A landlord may well need a key in order that he may be able to enter quickly in the event of emergency; fire, burst pipes or whatever. He may need a key to enable him or those authorised by him to read meters or to do repairs which are his responsibility. None of these underlying reasons would of themselves indicate that the true bargain between the parties was such that the occupier was in law a lodger [i.e. licensee]. On the other hand, if the true bargain is that the owner will provide genuine services which can only be provided by having keys, such as frequent cleaning, daily bed-making, the provision of clean linen at regular intervals and the like, there are materials from which it is possible to infer that the occupier is a lodger [licensee] rather than a tenant.

17.6.4   POSSESSORY LICENCES AFTER *STREET* v *MOUNTFORD*

The constantly recurring theme of the decision in *Street* v *Mountford* is that whether a transaction is a lease or a licence depends on whether exclusive possession is granted. However, almost at the end of his speech, Lord Templeman says this:

Sometimes it may be difficult to discover whether, on the true construction of an agreement, exclusive possession is conferred. Sometimes it may appear from the surrounding circumstances that there was no intention to create legal relationships. Sometimes it may appear from the surrounding circumstances that the right to exclusive possession is referable to a legal relationship other than a tenancy. Legal relationships to which the grant of exclusive possession might be referable and which would or might negative the grant of an estate or interest in the land include occupancy under a contract for the sale of the land, occupancy pursuant to a contract of employment or occupancy referable to the holding of an office. But where as in the present case the only circumstances are that residential accommodation is offered and accepted with exclusive possession for a term at a rent, the result is a tenancy.

In practice it therefore appears that there are, after *Street* v *Mountford*, four types of situation where somebody can have 'exclusive possession' of property but have only a licence. Put another way, there are four exceptions to the general rule laid down in *Street* that 'exclusive possession means that there is a lease'.

17.6.4.1   Acts of generosity or friendship where there is no intent to create legal relations

We have already noted *Heslop* v *Burns* [1974] 3 All ER 406, where a licence was held to exist (see **17.4.3.3**). I do not think there is any doubt that that decision is still correct after *Street*. Slightly more debatable is the decision of the Court of Appeal in *Rhodes* v *Dalby* [1971] 2 All ER 1144

Two men were **long-standing friends**. One owned a bungalow, but was going abroad for two years. The two men signed a document, described as 'a gentleman's agreement' not intended to create legal relations. Under that agreement the friend staying in this country took possession of the bungalow during the two-year absence. He agreed to pay a quite high 'rent' for being able to live in the bungalow. This arrangement was found to be a licence.

ACTIVITY 51

Read the extracts from *Rhodes* v *Dalby* in *Cases and Materials* (17.2.4.1). I personally think that the case is (after *Street*) correctly decided. Do you agree?

(I think the crucial fact was that the two men were friends **before** they signed the agreement.)

17.6.4.2   Service occupancies

It is perfectly possible for an employer to grant to an employee a formal lease over a house situated close to the place of work. However (and this is unaffected by *Street* v *Mountford*), if an employer, without executing a formal lease, allows an employee to live in the employer's accommodation so that he can readily be available for work at any time, the employee has a form of licence known as a 'service occupancy'. This is the case whether or not the employee is obliged by his contract of employment to live in the accommodation: *Crane* v *Morris* [1965] 3 All ER 77.

ACTIVITY 52

Can you think of types of workers who often have service occupancies?

Caretakers, agricultural workers, and members of the police, armed forces and fire brigade often have 'service occupancies'. A rather more unusual case is *Norris* v *Checksfield* [1991] 1 WLR 1241. In that case a coach mechanic had been granted the use of a bungalow close to the depot. The Court of Appeal held that he was a service occupier, not a tenant!

17.6.4.3   Occupancy by virtue of an office

This point is most likely to affect clergymen, who (you may be surprised to learn) do not usually have contracts of employment. Clergymen are only licensees of their manses, vicarages, presbyteries, etc.

17.6.4.4   Occupancy prior to the completion of a contract for sale

From time to time a purchaser who has **contracted** to buy a piece of land is allowed by the vendor to take possession of the property even though the sale has not yet been completed by a conveyance or land transfer.

In the past, it was sometimes said that such a purchaser in possession 'ahead of completion' was a tenant at will. *Street* v *Mountford* confirms that this view is not correct. Rather, the purchaser is to be regarded as a licensee.

17.6.5   FLAT-SHARING AGREEMENTS

In recent years there have been a number of cases where the facts have followed a similar sort of pattern. Two (or more) people are together looking for a flat or house to share. They find a 'landlord', who refuses to grant them a lease. Instead he grants each of them a separate 'non-exclusive' licence. Each licence includes a clause under which the grantor can introduce into the property other person(s).

17.6.5.1   *Somma v Hazelhurst* [1978] 2 All ER 1011

In this case H and S (a cohabiting couple) had each signed on the same day a separate agreement granting each the use of a bed-sitting room to be shared with a person 'to be introduced'. The Court of Appeal rejected the argument that the two transactions should be read together, and should be regarded as together granting exclusive possession and therefore creating a lease. In the view of the Court of Appeal, two licences had been created.

In the light of later cases, this decision is undoubtedly wrong. It was disapproved of in very strong terms by the House of Lords in *Street v Mountford*. Lord Templeman said of *Somma v Hazelhurst*:

> The agreements [sic] signed by H and S constituted the grant to H and S jointly of exclusive possession at a rent for a term for the purposes for which the room was taken and the agreement [sic] therefore created a tenancy.

17.6.5.2   The 1988 cases

In 1988 the House of Lords gave judgment on the same day in two cases raising the 'non-exclusive licence' issue.

Antoniades v Villiers [1988] 3 All ER 1058
In this case V1 and V2 (a cohabiting couple) each signed on the same day an agreement giving them the right to use a **small** flat. Clause 16 of each agreement provided: 'The licensor shall be entitled at any time to use the rooms together with the licensee and permit other persons to use all of the rooms together with the licensee.'

The House of Lords, led by Lord Templeman, took a very robust approach. The practical realities had to be looked at. The two documents read together granted exclusive possession and therefore created a lease. Moreover clause 16 should be ignored. It had been inserted by the grantor as a 'pretence', in an effort to show that V1 and V2 did not together have exclusive possession. Nobody would expect the grantor to exercise the 'right' conferred on him by clause 16.

ACTIVITY 53

In a radio interview a few years ago, Lord Templeman (whose first name is Sydney) admitted that he had been given the nickname 'Sid Vicious' by some lawyers. He mentioned, as one of the reasons for the nickname, his judgments in lease/licence cases. Why then 'Vicious'? (His judgment in *Bilson* v *Residential Apartments*, see 20.6.2, is further evidence of why he got the nickname.)

After reading some of his judgments on the lease/licence issue, you will realise that Lord Templeman is very tough on landlords who try to get round legislation designed to protect tenants.

AG Securities v *Vaughan* [1988] 3 All ER 1058
AGS owned a four-bedroomed flat. Each of the four occupiers had signed a non-exclusive licence. Each licence was signed on a different date, was for a different period, and was at a different rent. Was this one lease or four licences?

The House of Lords held that a lease had **not** been created. There were four separate licences.

You own a house, the use of which you are willing to grant to full-time students. In mid-September you are approached by a group of four respectable law students, who want accommodation for the forthcoming academic year. They want a lease to last to the following early July. You would rather give them 'non-exclusive licences'. How do you achieve your objective?

To achieve your objective you grant them four separate non-exclusive licences, to begin and end on different dates. For example:

(a)   Licence A would run from 20 September to 1 July.

(b)   Licence B would run from 23 September to 4 July.

(c)   Licence C would run from 18 September to 6 July.

(d)   Licence D would run from 25 September to 5 July.

17.6.6 'PRETENCE' CLAUSES DESIGNED TO NEGATE EXCLUSIVE POSSESSION

We have already seen that in *Antoniades* v *Villiers* (**17.6.5**) the grantor inserted the highly artificial clause 16 in an effort to fool the courts into thinking that V1 and V2, even taken together, did not have exclusive possession. The robust approach taken by Lord Templeman in *Antoniades* was applied by the Court of Appeal in two cases it decided together in 1989, *Aslan* v *Murphy* and *Duke* v *Wynn* [1990] 3 All ER 130.

In the first case, A granted to M the use of a tiny basement room. The licence included a term that A could introduce another occupant. It also included another provision that M had no right to use the room between 1030 and 1200 hours. Both these clauses were found to be 'pretences', and M was held to be a tenant.

In the second case D granted to Mr and Mrs W (who had two children living with them) a three-bedroom house for two years. D again reserved the right to introduce other occupiers to the property. This clause was found to be a 'pretence'. D had no genuine intention of introducing other person(s) to the house. The Ws were held to have a lease.

17.7 Formalities for Leases

There are three kinds of formality possible for a lease:

(a) Legal leases arising by express grant.

(b) Legal leases arising by operation of law.

(c) Equitable leases arising by virtue of a contract or an informal grant.

17.7.1 LEGAL LEASES BY EXPRESS GRANT

Normally to create a lease which is valid as a **legal lease** a deed is required. Section 54(2) of the Law of Property Act 1925 creates an important exception. Under this provision no special formality is required to create a legal lease if it satisfies **all** the following conditions (even an oral grant will suffice):

(a) The lease is for a period not exceeding three years. (This includes periodic tenancies.)

(b) The lease is at the best rent reasonably obtainable.

(c) No premium ('fine') is charged for the grant of the lease.

(d) The lease takes effect in possession immediately.

17.7.2 LEGAL LEASES BY OPERATION OF LAW

This applies only to periodic tenancies. A periodic tenancy will arise automatically where a tenant at will (or at sufferance) commences paying rent calculated on a periodic basis. (It is in effect presumed that the parties intended a periodic tenancy; see e.g. the case of *Martin* v *Smith* (1874) LR 9 Ex 50.)

What the 'period' (weekly, monthly, etc.) is for the periodic tenancy depends on the period by reference to which the rent is calculated, looking at all the evidence available. Usually the period by reference to which the rent is calculated is also the period by reference to which it actually has to be paid: £x per week will mean a weekly tenancy; £y a month will mean a monthly tenancy, and so on. In the recent case of *Prudential Assurance* v *London Residuary Body* [1992] 3 All ER 504 (see **17.4.1**), the House of Lords held, applying the principle we are currently considering, that as the rent had been fixed at £30 per annum, a yearly tenancy had arisen.

A problem might seem to arise if, for example, the evidence shows that informally the parties had agreed to a rent of £600 per annum, payable in monthly instalments. As the rent is **calculated** on an annual basis, there would in this example be a yearly tenancy.

A periodic tenancy by operation of law will not arise if the parties have expressly agreed that the arrangement between them should remain a tenancy at will. Neither will one arise where a prospective lessee has been let into possession, starts paying rent, but continues to negotiate with the landlord for the grant of a fixed-term lease: *Javad* v *Aqil* [1991] 1 All ER 243.

Hitherto I have never owned a car. I have therefore allowed Tom to keep his car in the garage attached to my house. There is nothing in writing, but Tom pays me £100 per month rent. I have now bought a car, and therefore want Tom out of my garage. How much notice must I give?

Assuming that Tom has had exclusive possession, he will have a monthly periodic tenancy. He will therefore be entitled to a month's notice to quit.

17.7.3 EQUITABLE LEASES

Re-read 5.5.3.4 and 5.5.4 regarding the creation of equitable leases. Note particularly the rulings in *Walsh* v *Lonsdale* and *Parker* v *Taswell*.

As a result of *Walsh* v *Lonsdale* it is sometimes said that 'an agreement for a lease is as good as a lease'. This is rather misleading, as there are in fact important differences between legal leases and equitable leases:

(a) A person's right to treat an agreement or an informal grant as an equitable lease depends on his being able to obtain specific performance. (Remember *Coatsworth* v *Johnson* at **5.5.4.1**.)

(b) Where the reversion is unregistered title, the equitable lease is registrable as a land charge. (Class C(iv) estate contract).

(c) Where the reversion is registered title, an equitable lease cannot be an overriding interest within the Land Registration Act 1925, s. 70(1)(k), but can of course fall within s. 70(1)(g). If not within s. 70(1)(g), the equitable lease will need 'protection' as a minor interest.

(d) An equitable lessee is not a 'purchaser of a legal estate' for the purposes of the Land Charges Acts or the old doctrine of notice. (A legal lessee is a 'purchaser of a legal estate'.)

(e) An assignee of an equitable lease is apparently not directly bound by the obligations in the lease. (It seems that the doctrine of 'privity of estate', which we consider in **Chapter 19**, does not apply to equitable leases.)

(f)   Section 62 of the Law of Property Act 1925 (which relates to the implied grant of easements and profits and which we discuss in **Chapter 24**) does not apply to equitable leases.

17.7.4   EQUITABLE LEASE AND LEGAL PERIODIC TENANCY EXISTING CONCURRENTLY

I now come to a point which students often find puzzling. As a result of a single informal transaction, a tenant may actually have **simultaneously both a legal periodic tenancy and an equitable lease** over the same piece of land.

Suppose L and T informally agree (in a document which does not amount to a deed) to a 10-year lease of Blackacre at £500 per annum rent. T takes possession and pays the rent. **At law** T will have a yearly periodic tenancy by operation of law; **in equity** T will have a 10-year lease. Applying the usual principle that where law and equity are in conflict, equity should prevail, it is the equitable lease which will govern the rights of the parties.

The legal periodic tenancy will not be totally invalid; **rather it will lie dormant**. If, the equitable lease should fail for any reason such as 'unclean hands' (remember *Coatsworth* v *Johnson*) or non-registration as a land charge, the legal periodic tenancy will become operative.

SAQ 97

In 1991 Carolyn and Dinah entered into a written agreement (which was not in the form of a deed) whereby Carolyn agreed to let to Dinah a field in which Dinah proposed to keep rabbits. The agreement was to last for 10 years. The rent was fixed at £60 per month. The field is unregistered title.

Dinah promised that she would not allow her rabbits to escape into neighbouring fields remaining in Carolyn's possession. Numerous rabbits have escaped into Carolyn's fields, causing damage to her crops of lettuces and carrots. Recently Carolyn sold all her fields, including the one occupied by Dinah, to Edwina. Advise Edwina, who wants Dinah to vacate the field immediately.

Dinah originally had an equitable lease, but it certainly will not be binding on Edwina. Even assuming that Dinah registered her equitable lease as a land charge, she clearly has 'unclean hands', and therefore has now lost her claim to an equitable lease.

However, Dinah still has her monthly **legal periodic tenancy**. Edwina will therefore have to give her a month's notice before she can gain possession of the field.

17.8 Conclusion

In this rather lengthy and involved chapter I hope to have achieved two things. First, you should now have enough understanding to be able to decide whether a particular transaction is a lease or whether it is something else. If it is a lease, you should be able to identify what type it is. Secondly, you should have a foundation of knowledge upon which we can build in the next three chapters.

17.9   End of Chapter Assessment Question

'Whether a transaction under which someone acquires the right to use another's property is a lease or a license depends largely, but not exclusively, on whether the transaction grants 'exclusive possession'.

Discuss.

See *Cases and Materials* (17.5) for a specimen answer.

CHAPTER EIGHTEEN

OBLIGATIONS IN LEASES

18.1 Objectives

By the end of this chapter you should:

■ be familiar with the concept of a rent review;

■ be familiar with the various rules which govern the liabilities of landlords and tenants to repair leased premises;

■ be able to explain the wide range of remedies which a tenant can deploy against a landlord who is in breach of an obligation to repair the leased property;

■ be able to explain the law applicable where the landlord wishes to sue the tenant for breach of a tenant's covenant to repair;

■ be familiar with the rules governing qualified covenants against assigning, sub-letting and parting with possession of premises, and in particular how the Landlord and Tenant Act 1988 has made things (in this area) easier for tenants.

18.2 Introduction

This is another chapter in which I necessarily have to paint with a rather broad brush. Leases (particularly long leases of commercial properties such as shops, offices and factories) are often very elaborate documents containing pages and pages of detailed obligations, many imposed on the tenant, some imposed on the landlord. We cannot possibly consider all the possible duties which a lease might impose. Instead we will concentrate on the three most common (and important) kinds of obligations in leases, namely rent, repairs, and covenants relating to assigning and sub-letting.

18.3 Rent – Certain Basic Points

18.3.1 FORM AND PAYMENT OF RENT

Rent need not be in money, but could be in kind, such as 'five hundred bottles of champagne a year'. In practice, the rent agreed upon at the commencement of a lease almost always takes the form of a regular money payment (£600 per year, £20 per week, etc.). Unless the parties agree otherwise, rent is payable 'in arrear', i.e. at the end of each year, week, etc. However, landlords almost always insist on payment in advance, at the beginning of each year, week, etc.

18.3.2   RENT REVIEWS

Whole encyclopaedias have been written on this topic! Ask anyone who is a surveyor. The first point to realise is that, **unless the parties agree otherwise,** the rent agreed on at the beginning of a lease remains the same throughout its duration. Nowadays, of course, long-term leases usually contain a provision to protect landlords from the ravages of inflation. It is possible to put in a clause 'index-linking' the rent, but this is relatively rare.

Consider why index-linking of rents has never really caught on.

The value (and changes in value) of a property (and therefore the rent it will fetch) can vary widely according to the type of property and its location. Even in a recession, there may be local 'booms' for particular kinds of property. Imagine that Blogtown gains a reputation for small-scale high-tech industry. There is consequently a shortage of small factory units. Rents for such units go up, even though elsewhere in Blogtown there are offices and shops standing empty.

Usually, in long fixed-term leases, there is a 'rent review clause'. Most modern rent review clauses provide for the landlord to claim a higher rent every five years, though there is no special magic in 'five' years; other periods, such as every seven years, are encountered.

Rent review clauses usually operate in the following way:

(a) The landlord must serve notice on the tenant claiming a higher rent, and proposing what the new rent should be. The lease usually provides that this notice must be served some time (e.g. six months) before the new rent becomes payable.

(b) The tenant can accept the new rent, or make a counter-proposal.

(c) If the parties cannot agree a new rent, the matter is referred to an arbitrator. Usually the lease provides for the arbitrator to be appointed by the president of the Royal Institution of Chartered Surveyors (RICS).

In the 1970s there was a lot of litigation involving landlords who had been late in claiming a rent review. In some cases landlords claimed a review even though the first date for payment of the new rent was past, and the tenants were continuing to pay the old rent.

The House of Lords ended the controversy with a very pro-landlord decision, *United Scientific Holdings Ltd* v *Burnley Borough Council* [1977] 2 All ER 62. Their Lordships held that 'time is not of the essence' with a rent review clause. This means that if the landlord is late in claiming a rent review, prima facie that does not matter. The landlord can still insist on a higher rent, and if necessary have it fixed by the arbitrator, even though he forgetfully allowed the review date to slip by. Their Lordships reasoned that in modern economic conditions, tenants with long leases of shops, offices, factories, etc. expect the rent to go up every few years. It would be wrong to allow tenants to benefit from landlords' forgetfulness.

There are two exceptions to the general principle in *United Scientific Holdings Ltd* v *Burnley Borough Council*:

(a)   The parties can always expressly agree in the lease that 'time shall be of the essence'; if the landlord is late claiming the review, that is his hard luck. This point is illustrated by *Weller* v *Akehurst* [1981] 3 All ER 411.

(b)   There could be an **estoppel**. If a landlord delayed a very long time in claiming a review and the tenant reasonably assumed that the old rent would remain in force and acted on that assumption, then the landlord could be estopped from claiming a review. But mere delay does not give rise to an estoppel.

In *Amherst* v *James Walker Goldsmiths and Silversmiths* [1983] 2 All ER 1067 Amherst was the landlord of a shop, and James Walker Ltd, the well-known 'High Street Chain', was the tenant. Amherst claimed a rent review four years late. Amherst succeeded in his claim. The crucial point was that the rent on one shop was 'a drop in the ocean' for a big firm like James Walker.

Consider how you would alter the facts in *Amherst* v *James Walker* to produce a situation where the court would hold that there was an estoppel preventing a late claim for a rent review.

Suppose 'big' James Walker own the freehold to a spare shop which they lease to 'little' Mr Amherst. Walkers forget to claim a rent review. After waiting two years Amherst (reasonably) concludes that the rent is not going to go up. So in fixing the prices he charges customers in his shop, he (very reasonably) assumes that his rent is going to stay the same until the next review date. This would estop Walkers from presenting a late claim for a rent review.

18.4   Repairs

18.4.1   LIABILITY TO REPAIR – GENERAL

Usually the lease itself will contain a clause, either:

(a)   placing liability to repair the property on the landlord; or

(b)   (common in long leases) placing liability to repair on the tenant; or

(c)   dividing the responsibility between landlord and tenant. For example, it is quite common to see leases where the landlord promises to do 'external' repairs and the tenant promises to do 'internal' repairs.

The form of repair clause adopted is a matter for negotiation between the parties. If the parties have not expressly agreed on the issue of repairs then (except where the Landlord and Tenant Act 1985 applies) the following (rather inadequate) common law rules apply:

(a) A fixed-term lessee is liable for 'permissive waste', i.e. he must maintain the property in the condition it was in at the commencement of the lease.

(b) A periodic tenant is under no liability to repair, but must use the property in a responsible manner.

You should note that except where the Landlord and Tenant Act 1985 applies, there are normally no implied duties to repair placed on the landlord. However in *Barrett* v *Lounova (1982) Ltd* [1989] 1 All ER 351, the Court of Appeal was faced with a lease of a dwelling house (dating from 1941) under which the tenant covenanted to do all **internal** repairs. The Court held that, in order 'to give business efficacy to the agreement', there was an implied obligation on the landlord to do **external** repairs.

Nevertheless, it is still possible to have a situation where, because of the drafting of the lease, when a defect arises in the leased premises neither landlord nor tenant is under a duty to the other party to repair it. For example, in long fixed-term leases you will often see a covenant under which the tenant agrees to do the repairs 'fair wear and tear excepted'. If a defect arises in the premises which is fair wear and tear (see **18.4.4** on that issue), the tenant is not liable to repair the defect; but neither is the landlord liable to make good the defect.

18.4.2 THE LANDLORD AND TENANT ACT 1985

The Housing Acts 1957 and 1961 imposed on landlords of 'dwelling houses' (i.e. houses and flats) obligations which applied **notwithstanding any agreement to the contrary**. These Acts have now been consolidated into the Landlord and Tenant Act 1985.

18.4.2.1 Sections 8 to 10 of the 1985 Act (derived from 1957 Act)

Sections 8 to 10 of the 1985 Act are of limited significance, because they apply only to lettings at not more than £52 per annum, (£80 per annum within London). They do not apply to lettings for three or more years.

Section 8 provides that the dwelling must be kept 'fit for human habitation'. The standards are strict, detailed matters being set out in the Act. (You should look at s. 10, set out in *Cases and Materials* **(18.2.2)**). However, as the rent limits for ss. 8–10 are so absurdly low, these provisions have only limited relevance today. Nevertheless, carefully consider the following question:

I own a derelict house in Nottingham. Four students desperate for accommodation approach me. (As it happens, two are studying building, one is studying quantity surveying and the other interior design.) They say, 'Lease your house to us for two years at one penny a week rent, and we will do it up for you. We can put up with the discomfort!' Advise me.

At first sight, it seems like a very good idea for all five of us. However, if I charge only one pence a week I will caught by ss. 8 to 10 of the 1985 Act and **I will be liable to do all the repairs!** I must therefore ensure that I charge at least one pound and a penny per week rent. We would also need to get the consent of the county court to exclude ss. 11–14: see below.

18.4.2.2 Sections 11–14 of the 1985 Act (derived from 1961 Act)

Sections 11 to 14 of the 1985 Act apply to all lettings of dwellings for not more than seven years; also to lettings for more than seven years if the landlord has an option to terminate within the first seven years. (It is possible for the parties to agree that ss. 11 to 14 shall not apply, but only if the consent of the county court is obtained in advance. Applications to the court for such consent are relatively rare.)

Under ss. 11 to 14, the landlord must:

(a)   keep in repair the structure and exterior of the house (including drains, gutters and external pipes) (*Quick* v *Taff Ely BC* [1985] 3 All ER 321 indicates complications which can arise;)

(b)   keep in repair and proper working order the installations in the home for the supply of water, gas and electricity, for space heating and the heating of water;

(c)   (added by s. 116 of the Housing Act 1988) in the case of blocks of flats, keep in repair 'common parts' such as lifts and staircases.

18.4.3 THE CRUCIAL PRINCIPLE IN *O'BRIEN* v *ROBINSON*

The principle in this case applies whenever a landlord is under an obligation to do repairs, whether that obligation is imposed by the terms of the lease or by the Landlord and Tenant Act 1985.

In *O'Brien* v *Robinson* [1973] 1 All ER 583 a tenant was injured when the ceiling of his flat suddenly and unexpectedly caved in upon him. His claim for damages was dismissed by the House of Lords. Their Lordships held that a landlord can be liable for disrepair only if either:

(a)   he knows of the need for repair; or

(b)   he has 'had information about the existence of a defect . . . such as would put him on enquiry as to whether works of repair were needed'.

SAQ 99

What is the moral of this case for tenants who are concerned about the condition of their premises?

If your landlord is liable to do the repairs, tell him of any defect or possible defect the moment it arises. Until he has been told of the defect, the landlord cannot be made liable for any damage suffered by the tenant as a result of the disrepair.

(If a landlord is liable to do repairs he will in practice expressly reserve a right to enter the premises to carry out the repairs. The House of Lords has assumed that such an express right entitles a landlord to take complete possession temporarily, if temporary complete possession is necessary to carry out the repairs: *Heath* v *Drown* [1972] 2 All ER 561.)

18.4.3.1 Landlord's covenant to repair common parts

The Court of Appeal has recently held that where a landlord covenants with a tenant to repair property which the landlord retains **in his possession** (e.g., in particular he promises to repair the common parts of a block of offices or flats) the principle in *O'Brien* v *Robinson* does not apply. A landlord must make good defects in the property he retains, whether or not he knew that there might be a defect and whether or not the tenant(s) have complained (*British Telecom* v *Sun Life Assurance* [1995] 4 All ER 44).

18.4.4 MEANING OF EXPRESS COVENANTS TO REPAIR

(The same principles apply whether it is a landlord's covenant or a tenant's covenant.)

Leases often use phrases such as 'good tenantable repair', 'substantial repair', 'satisfactory repair', etc. However, it seems that the adjectives are superfluous, and add nothing to the basic meaning of 'repair'.

The duty to repair was expressed thus by Professor Cheshire:

> After making due allowance for the locality, character and age of the premises at the time of the lease, he must keep them in the condition in which they would be kept by a reasonably minded owner. (*Cheshire and Burn*, 15th edn, p. 404.)

The standard of repair is fixed at the commencement of the lease. In *Anstruther-Gough-Calthorpe* v *McOscar* [1924] 1 KB 716, a 95-year lease was granted in 1825 of three houses. They were, in 1825, brand new, and in a very pleasant position on the then edge of the built-up area of London. By the time the lease expired in 1920 the area (in the vicinity of Kings Cross station) had become very 'run down'. In an action by the landlord against the tenant for breaking the covenant to repair, the Court of Appeal held that **even in 1920** the tenant should have maintained the property to the **1825** standard!

Just pause for a few moments and consider the possible financial implications of *Anstruther-Gough-Calthorpe* v *McOscar* for tenants who hold under long leases.

The rule applied in that case is of course extremely harsh on tenants of long leases who have covenanted to repair. That is why a tenant's promise to repair is nowadays often subject to the proviso **'fair wear and tear excepted'**. If such a proviso is included the tenant will not have to make good the natural ageing of the premises.

However, as Talbot J. explained in *Haskell* v *Marlow* [1928] 2 KB 45 at 59, the 'fair wear and tear exception' may not be much protection for tenants in some kinds of situations:

The tenant is bound to do such repairs as may be required to prevent the consequences flowing originally from wear and tear from producing others which wear and tear would not directly produce. For example, if a tile falls off the roof, the tenant is not liable for the immediate consequences, but if he does nothing and in the result more and more water gets in, the roof and walls decay and ultimately the top floor, or the whole house, becomes uninhabitable, he cannot say that it is due to reasonable wear and tear.

18.4.5   THE REPAIR/RECONSTRUCTION DISTINCTION

An obligation to 'repair' extends to replacing defective subsidiary parts of a building, but not to complete reconstruction of the building. In *Ravenseft Properties* v *Davstone Ltd* [1979] 1 All ER 929, Forbes J restated the test thus:

> . . . it is always a question of degree whether that which the tenant[/landlord] is being asked to do can properly be described as repair, or whether on the contrary it would involve giving back to the landlord[/tenant] a wholly different thing from that which he [leased].

In *Lister* v *Lane* [1893] 2 QB 212 the tenant did not have to reconstruct the whole house when the foundations became unsafe. However, in *Lurcott* v *Wakely* [1911] 1 KB 905, the tenant had to replace the front wall of a house, and in *Ravenseft Properties* v *Davstone Ltd* [1979] 1 All ER 929 a property company had to replace the external stone cladding on the whole of a block of flats.

'Repair' includes painting only in so far as painting is necessary to prevent deterioration of woodwork.

18.4.6   REMEDIES FOR BREACH OF LANDLORD'S EXPRESS COVENANTS TO REPAIR

(In the following discussion, you should never forget the principle in *O'Brien* v *Robinson* that a landlord becomes liable only if he knew or ought to have known of the defect: see 18.4.3.)

If a landlord is in breach of a covenant to repair, then the most usual remedy for the tenant is to sue for damages. However, in the last 25 years both the courts and Parliament have been busy expanding the remedies available to tenants against recalcitrant landlords who fail to do repairs which they know need doing.

18.4.6.1   No rent-strikes, *but* . . .

A tenant cannot simply go on 'rent-strike'. He cannot say to the landlord, 'I am not paying the rent until you do the repairs'. The tenant can, however, carry out the repairs himself (or employ contractors to do the work) and deduct the cost from future instalments of rent: *Lee-Parker* v *Izzet* [1971] 3 All ER 1099.

Suppose that the rent is £50 per week. The tenant spends £1,000 on repairs. If he invokes *Izzet's* case, what does he say to the landlord or his rent-collector?

He can say, 'See you in 20 weeks' time'.

I must, however, warn you that this **'do-it-yourself'** remedy has its limitations. First, a tenant contemplating employing builders to do the repairs should ensure that he gets several quotations before engaging contractors to do the repairs. Secondly, this remedy is not much good where a landlord has allowed a whole block of offices or flats, leased to individual tenants, to fall into a bad state of disrepair. Repairing the whole block is likely to be beyond the resources of an individual tenant, and even beyond the resources of the tenants acting jointly.

18.4.6.2   Specific performance for breach of a repairing obligation

Where the property is a dwelling house the Housing Act 1975, s. 125 specifically authorises the courts to award specific performance of the landlord's obligation to repair. (This is notwithstanding the fact that the tenant is still in possession of the property to be repaired.)

In any proceedings in which a tenant of a dwelling alleges a breach on the part of his landlord of a repairing covenant relating to any part of the premises in which the dwelling is comprised, the court may, in its discretion, order specific performance of that covenant, whether or not the breach relates to a part of the premises let to the tenant and notwithstanding any equitable rule restricting the scope of that remedy, whether on the basis of lack of mutuality or otherwise.

Read the extracts from the case of *Jeune* v *Queen Cross Properties* [1973] 3 All ER 97, set out in *Cases and Materials* (18.2.6.2); note that this case was decided before the enactment of the section just quoted. Why were the plaintiffs so keen to get a decree of specific performance?

18.4.6.3   Appointing a receiver

In recent years there have been increasing problems with recalcitrant private landlords of blocks of flats and blocks of offices failing to carry out their repairing obligations. Often the premises involved are 'up-market'.

In 1983 somebody hit upon the bright idea of invoking s. 37 of the Supreme Court Act 1981 to appoint a receiver: *Hart* v *Emelkerk* [1983] 3 All ER 15. Mention of the word 'receiver' probably makes you think of insolvent companies; but 'receivers' have their uses in land law! We shall come across them again in the law of mortgages (**Chapter 30**).

In the present context, 'appointing a receiver' works as follows:

(a)   The court appoints a responsible professional person to act as receiver.

(b)   The landlord must hand over management (though not of course ownership) of the block to the receiver.

(c)   Rents are now payable to the receiver, not to the landlord.

(d)   The receiver uses the money from the rents to pay for the repairs.

The remedy under s. 37 of the 1981 Act does unfortunately have its limitations as illustrated by the facts of *Evans* v *Clayhope Properties Ltd* [1987] 2 All ER 40. Suppose the block requires very extensive repairs, costing more than the total of several years' rent. Such a situation is far from unknown. Appointing a receiver under s. 37 is no good. The receiver cannot enter into long-term repair contracts binding on the landlord. Neither can he mortgage the block to finance the repairs.

(On a rather different point, s. 37 cannot be invoked against a local authority landlord which fails to repair its housing stock: *Parker* v *Camden L.B.* [1985] 2 All ER 141. This is because s. 111 of the Housing Act 1957 unequivocally vests the management of local authority housing in the local authority.)

18.4.6.4   Appointing a receiver-manager

The tenants of a privately owned block of flats (but not offices) have now been given a new stronger 'receiver' remedy against landlords who fail to do repairs. They can apply for the appointment of a receiver-manager under ss. 21 to 24 of the Landlord and Tenant Act 1987. It would **appear** that under s. 24 (unlike under the 1981 Act) the court could:

(a)   authorise the receiver-manager to mortgage the block to pay for repairs; and/or

(b)   require the landlord to pay repair bills incurred by the receiver-manager.

18.4.6.5   Local authorities taking action against private landlords

Where a house, flat, or block of flats is in disrepair, the local district council can serve a notice on the landlord requiring specified repairs. If the landlord fails to comply, the council can enter the property, carry out the repairs, and charge them to the landlord. (See the Housing Acts 1957–88.)

18.4.6.6   Measure of damages against landlords

If a tenant sues the landlord for damages, it seems that the tenant can recover, in addition to the cost of repairs actually done by the tenant:

(a)   compensation for any injury to health suffered;

(b)   the cost of alternative accommodation if the disrepair is such as to render the premises uninhabitable.

Read the extracts from *Calabar Properties* v *Stitcher* [1983] 3 All ER 759 in *Cases and Materials* (18.2.6.6). What would be the position if landlords were in breach of a covenant to repair a shop, with the result that (potential) customers considered the premises unsafe?

I think that the tenant could sue for loss of profits.

18.4.7 DAMAGES AGAINST A TENANT IN BREACH OF REPAIRING OBLIGATIONS

You should remember that in some leases, particularly long-term ones, the tenant undertakes to do the repairs. If the tenant fails to do repairs he has promised to do, then normally the landlord can recover from the tenant the cost of repairing the property. However, the landlord's right to damages may be limited or eliminated by s. 18 of the Landlord and Tenant Act 1927:

> Damages for a breach of a covenant to repair . . . shall in no case exceed the amount (if any) by which the value of the reversion in the premises is diminished . . . . In particular no damage shall be recovered for a breach of covenant to repair if it is shown that the premises would at or shortly after the termination of the tenancy have been or be pulled down. . . .

Thus, if on the expiry of the lease the landlord is going to demolish the premises, or reconstruct the premises to such an extent that their state of repair is immaterial, the landlord will not be able to claim any damages from the tenant for his breach of the covenant to repair.

A rather disturbing situation faced the judge in *Hibernian Properties* v *[A Very Bad Tenant]* [1973] 2 All ER 1117. The very bad tenant (VBT) leased a row of houses in Liverpool from Hibernian. VBT undertook to do the repairs. VBT failed so miserably in this task that Liverpool City Council public health officials came along, condemned the properties as unfit for human habitation, and made the houses the subject of a compulsory purchase order. The houses were then demolished.

Hibernian were paid compensation by Liverpool City Council limited to 'the site value'. That meant that they received no compensation for the buildings. They therefore sued VBT for damages. VBT pleaded the second sentence of s. 18 of the 1927 Act as a defence: 'The property has been pulled down. Therefore no damages are payable.' The judge boldly rejected this defence, holding that the words 'by the landlords' must be implied into s. 18 after the words 'pulled down'.

The identity of VBT is **totally irrelevant to this decision.** The decision would have been the same if VBT had been a big plc, or Charley Farns-Barnes, or you or me.

Can you guess the identity of VBT?

In fact VBT was Liverpool City Council itself.

(The Leasehold Property Repairs Act 1938 is also relevant to cases where the tenant is liable to do repairs. It can be properly understood only after I have explained forfeiture of leases, which I will do in **Chapter 20.**)

18.5 Covenants Against Assigning, Sub-letting and Parting with Possession

18.5.1 INTRODUCTION

A lease is of course a property right, an estate in land. It therefore follows that, prima facie, a lessee can:

(a) assign his lease, i.e. transfer the lease to somebody else, retaining no rights whatsoever;

(b) sub-lease (when a person sub-lets he creates a lease out of his lease – refer back to my Redacre example at **4.6.2**);

(c) part with possession to a licensee, e.g., to a friend, or to an employee occupying the property under a 'service occupancy' (see **17.6.4.2**).

However, I should immediately add that modern leases often restrict the lessee's right to assign, sub-let or part with possession. **As a generalisation:**

(a) Short-term leases and periodic tenancies (particularly of flats/houses) usually contain 'absolute covenants' under which the tenant is totally banned from assigning, sub-letting or parting with possession.

(b) Medium-term lettings (say 10 to 50 years) usually contain a 'qualified covenant', under which the tenant can assign, sub-let or part with possession (the whole or part of the premises) only if the landlord gives his consent.

(c) Very long-term leases (e.g., a 99-year lease of a flat) usually contain no restrictions on the right to assign, sub-let or part with possession.

It must be stressed that 'qualified covenants' are particularly common where the premises are of a commercial nature, e.g. shops, offices or factories. Landlords of commercial premises have found that **it is not a good idea** to insert into a commercial letting an 'absolute covenant'. The insertion of an absolute covenant into a commercial letting would substantially reduce the amount of rent the tenant was willing to pay.

18.5.2 ABSOLUTE COVENANTS

The covenant creates an absolute ban on all transactions. However, an assignment or sub-letting in defiance of the ban **does** convey or create an estate in the land. Breach of the covenant will merely entitle the landlord to damages, and to forfeit the lease, assuming the lease contains a forfeiture clause: *Peabody Fund* v *Higgins* [1983] 3 All ER 122.

A landlord can **waive** observance of an absolute covenant so as to permit a transaction in favour of a person he considers desirable. But a decision by a landlord to withhold his waiver cannot be challenged, however unreasonable, sexist, or racist the landlord is being.

Suppose in 1993 I leased a house to Hamish Macdonald (a Scot**sman**) for five years. The lease contained an absolute covenant against assigning, sub-letting or parting with possession. Hamish has now decided to buy a house. He comes to me with Trudi Jones, a perfectly respectable Welsh**woman**: 'Please can I assign my lease to Trudi?'

Now I **can** say 'Yes', and waive the absolute covenant. But if I say, 'No, I don't like the colour of her hair' or 'I don't like the Welsh' or 'I don't like women as my tenants', my decision to withhold my waiver cannot be challenged. (As we will see in a moment, the position would be very different if I had inserted only a 'qualified covenant' into the five-year lease.)

18.5.3 QUALIFIED COVENANTS

Where there is a qualified covenant, a tenant can assign, sub-let, or part with possession only if he gets the landlord's consent.

The Landlord and Tenant Act 1927 s.19(1)(a), is applicable to qualified covenants but not to absolute covenants. It provides:

> [A covenant against] assigning, underletting [i.e. sub-letting], charging or parting with possession of demised premises without licence or consent . . . shall . . . be subject to a proviso that such licence or consent is not to be unreasonably withheld.

Section 19(1)(a) operates 'notwithstanding any express provision to the contrary'. Thus a landlord who wants to retain the freedom to veto assignments or sub-lettings on whatever grounds he pleases (colour of hair etc.) should insert an absolute covenant. But always remember that tenants of commercial premises are unlikely to accept an 'absolute covenant', or do so only in return for a considerable reduction in rent.

18.5.4   WHEN IS A CONSENT UNREASONABLY WITHHELD?

There is not much statutory guidance on this issue. However:

(a)   The Race Relations Acts and the Sex Discrimination Act provide that a consent withheld on grounds of race or sex is unreasonably withheld.

(b)   The Law of Property Act 1925, s. 144 prohibits the charging of a premium for the giving of consent to an assignment or a sub-letting.

What, then, if a landlord said to a tenant, 'I will agree to your proposed transaction if you give me £10,000 pounds', but the tenant says 'I will not pay'?

The landlord would be threatening to break s. 144, and therefore withholding consent because the £10,000 was not forthcoming would clearly be unreasonable.

Apart from the statutory provisions just discussed, whether or not the landlord's veto is reasonable is primarily a question of fact. That has not prevented an enormous amount of case law developing, the effect of which was summarised and clarified in *International Drilling Fluids Ltd* v *Louisville Investments(Uxbridge) Ltd* [1986] 1 All ER 332. Except in one (obvious) respect, this case appears unaffected by the Landlord and Tenant Act 1988 (an Act we will discuss after we have considered the case).

The Court came up with seven numbered propositions. My comments on those propositions I have placed in square brackets:

1.   The purpose of a covenant against assignment [sub-letting, etc.] without the consent of the landlord, such consent not to be unreasonably withheld, was to protect the lessor from having his premises used or occupied in an undesirable way, or by an undesirable tenant or assignee.

[(a) It is clearly reasonable for a landlord to veto a proposed assignee/sub-tenant/ licensee who is of bad character, e.g., one who has a criminal record.]

(b) It is clearly reasonable for a landlord to object to a transaction which will depreciate the value of his reversion. The leading cases are *Norfolk Capital Group* v *Kitway Ltd* [1976] 3 All ER 787, and *Bickel* v *Duke of Westminster* [1975] 3 All ER 801. In both cases a long lease of a house was vested in a limited company. It was proposed to assign the lease to a human tenant who would be able to take advantage of various pieces of protective legislation not available to 'artificial persons'. This fact would have the effect of reducing the value of the landlords' fees simple in reversion. It was held that the landlords were reasonable in vetoing the assignments.

(c) It is clearly reasonable for the landlord to object where the proposed assignee/ sub-tenant proposes using the premises for unsuitable purposes. For example, using a house in a narrow street for a business which will create a lot of parking problems. Refer also to the court's proposition number 5.]

2. As a corollary to [proposition 1], a landlord was not entitled to refuse his consent to an assignment on grounds which had nothing whatever to do with the relationship of landlord and tenant in regard to the subject matter of the lease. [For example, 'I don't want the lease assigned to him because he has just run off with my wife'. Such an attitude would clearly be unreasonable.]

3. (**Overruled by the Landlord and Tenant Act 1988.**) The onus of proving that consent had been unreasonably withheld was on the tenant.

4. It was not necessary for the landlord to prove that the conclusions which led him to refuse consent were justified, if they were conclusions which might be reached by a reasonable man in the circumstances.

5. It might be reasonable for the landlord to refuse his consent to an assignment on the ground of the purpose for which the proposed assignee intended to use the premises, even though that purpose was not forbidden by the lease. [Refer back to note (c) under proposition 1.]

6. 'On the question whether it was permissible to have regard to consequences to the tenant if consent to the proposed assignment was withheld there was a divergence of authority. . . . A proper reconciliation of the two streams of authority could be achieved by saying that while a landlord needed usually only to consider his own relevant interests, there might be cases where there was such a disproportion between the benefit to the landlord and the detriment to the tenant if the landlord withheld his consent to an assignment that it was unreasonable for the landlord to refuse consent.'

[There have been a lot of cases in recent years where a tenant of business premises has been anxious to sell the **business**. The lease of the premises is of course an important asset **of the business**. If a landlord is unwilling to approve a particular prospective purchaser of the business as assignee of the lease, the prospective purchaser is not going to buy the business.]

7. Subject to the preceding propositions, it was in each case a question of fact, depending upon all the circumstances, whether the landlord's consent was being unreasonably withheld.

Consider whether it would be reasonable for a landlord to object to a proposed assignee on the ground that the assignee would use the premises for a business which competes with a similar business carried on by the landlord. (For example, 'Your proposed assignee is a greengrocer; so am I'.)

This point is controversial. The (first instance) case of *Premier Confectionery* v *London Commercial Sale Rooms* [1933] Ch 904, suggests that the landlord would be in the right. But I would argue that this case is wrong, as the landlord's reason for the veto has nothing to do with the landlord and tenant relationship (proposition 2 in *International Drilling*).

18.5.5 SEEKING THE LANDLORD'S CONSENT TO A PROPOSED TRANSACTION

If a tenant has a proposed transaction (assignment, sub-letting or parting with possession) he must always first ask the landlord for his consent (in writing), even if he thinks that there could not possibly be any reasonable objection. If the landlord vetoes a proposed transaction (or fails to reply within a reasonable time) there are four courses of action open to the tenant:

(i)   to concede that the landlord has a good argument and abandon the proposal;

(ii)   to abandon the proposal, but claim damages under the Landlord and Tenant Act 1988;

(iii) to go ahead with the proposed transaction, risking proceedings for damages (and forfeiture if the lease contains a forfeiture clause);

(iv)   to seek a declaration from the court that the consent is being withheld unreasonably; (the tenant may well now add a claim for damages under the 1988 Act).

18.5.6 LANDLORD AND TENANT ACT 1988

The Landlord and Tenant Act 1988 represents a shift in the law in favour of tenants. Until 1988, the onus of proof that the landlord was withholding his consent unreasonably was on the tenant. Moreover landlords frequently delayed their decisions for inordinate periods. Landlords who did eventually say 'Yes' often imposed stringent conditions. The overall effect of the 1988 Act is in my view:

(a)   to put pressure on landlords to make a decision on the tenant's application without unreasonable delay;

(b)   to ensure that landlords who veto transactions have really good grounds for doing so;

(c)   to ensure that landlords, if they impose conditions, impose only sensible ones.

Section 1 of the 1988 Act provides:

> . . .
>
> (3) Where there is served on the [landlord] a written application by the tenant for consent to [a] transaction, he owes a duty to the tenant within a reasonable time—
>   (a) to give consent, except in a case where it is reasonable not to give consent,
>   (b) to serve on the tenant written notice of his decision whether or not to give consent specifying in addition—
>   (i) if the consent is given subject to conditions, the conditions,
>   (ii) if the consent is withheld, the reasons for withholding it.
>
> (4) Giving consent subject to any condition that is not a reasonable condition does not satisfy the duty under subsection (3)(a) above.
>
> . . .
>
> (6) It is for the [landlord]—
>   (a) if he gave consent and the question arises whether he gave it within a reasonable time, to show that he did,
>   (b) if he gave consent subject to any condition and the question arises whether the condition was a reasonable condition, to show that it was,
>   (c) if he did not give consent and the question arises whether it was reasonable for him not to do so, to show that it was reasonable,
>
> and, if the question arises whether he served notice under that subsection within a reasonable time, to show that he did.

Section 4 places further pressures on landlords. It makes a landlord who breaks any of the duties laid down in the Act liable in damages to the tenant. Thus, for example, a tenant who was unable to sell his business because of his landlord's delaying tactics in giving consent, might have a claim for hefty damages.

The Law Commission says of these reforms:

> Reversal of the burden of proof should have the effect in practice that the landlord will have to concentrate his mind on his reasons before he makes his decision on the tenant's application for consent. This, together with our recommendation that the tenant should be given a written statement of reasons and that the landlord should be liable in damages for delay or unreasonable witholding, should have the conveyancing advantage of reducing considerably the delays that are liable to occur at present in dispositions of tenancies.

Consider why the Landlord and Tenant Act 1988 should make it easier for tenants of business premises (e.g., a shop) to sell their businesses.

With shops and other small businesses, the (long) lease over the shop or other premises is often the business's most valuable asset. If a shopkeeper who wants to sell up and retire cannot sell (i.e., assign for consideration) his lease, he obviously will not be able to sell his business. The 1988 Act will make it easier to sell the lease.

18.6   Section 22 of the Landlord and Tenant (Covenants) Act 1995

(The main provisions of this new Act, most of which are pro-tenant, are dealt with in the next chapter.) Section 22 of the 1995 Act is a pro-**landlord** provision, which applies to qualified covenants against assignment of leases of commercial properties (offices, shops, factories etc.) commencing **after** 1995. It has no application to sub-letting or parting with possession.

Section 22 was inserted into the 1995 Act at the insistence of big commercial landlords (property companies, institutional investors etc.) who are very concerned that leases should not be assigned to tenants who will be unable to pay rent, do repairs etc. Where s. 22 applies, a landlord can tighten his control over the assignment of a lease by including in the lease a specific clause stipulating that the landlord is entitled to withhold his consent in given circumstances. A witholding of consent in those circumstances will not be unreasonable.

For example, the lease states 'The Landlord will not consent to an assignment if the assignee fails to provide a bankers' reference that he will be able to pay the rent'. A potential assignee who is in fact financially very sound forgets to provide the reference. The landlord's veto will automatically be reasonable and not open to challenge under the 1927 and 1988 Acts.

However, there are limits on what I call 'section 22 clauses'. The clause cannot leave the decision as to whether circumstances exist justifying a landlord's veto to the landlord's subjective opinion. For example, a clause 'The Landlord will not agree to an assignee unless he is satisfied that the assignee can pay the rent' is not allowed. However it is permitted to have a clause which entrusts a decision to an independent third party, e.g., 'The landlord will not agree to an assignee unless the assignee can produce satisfactory evidence that he can pay the rent. In the event of a dispute as to whether the evidence is satisfactory, the matter shall be resolved by an arbitrator appointed by the president of the RICS.'

18.7   Surrender Clauses

In long leases (particularly of commercial properties) you will occasionally find a provision under which before asking for consent to assign or sub-let, the tenant must offer to surrender the lease to the landlord. (A lease is 'surrendered' where it is terminated early by mutual agreement of landlord and tenant.) Such surrender clauses have been held valid by the Court of Appeal: *Bocardo SA* v *S and M Hotels Ltd* [1979] 3 All ER 737.

(The decision in *Greene* v *Church Commissioners* [1974] 3 All ER 609, is correct only in so far as it holds that such a clause, being technically an option to repurchase the lease, is registrable as a land charge. (It would be a minor interest if the lease were registered title.))

Surrender clauses might enjoy renewed popularity as a way of avoiding the Landlord and Tenant Act 1988. (Where the landlord does not like the look of the proposed new tenant, he will accept the surrender.) The presence of such a clause does, however, have the effect of depressing the amount of rent the landlord is able to charge under the lease.

18.8   Conclusion

The law relating to obligations between landlord and tenant is often attacked as being too heavily biased in favour of landlords. Critics point to decisions such as *United*

Scientific Holdings, O'Brien v *Robinson* and *Anstruther-Gough-Calthorpe* v *McOscar*. They also cite the rule banning rent-strikes should the landlord fail to do the repairs, pointing out that in many American states such strikes are permitted.

My own view is that pro-landlord bias is gradually disappearing. Over the last 25 years, both the courts and Parliament have done a lot to redress the balance by, for example, the Landlord and Tenant Act 1988. And just look again at the sections in this chapter dealing with the greatly expanded remedies which tenants (particularly of residential properties) have if their landlords are in breach of a duty to repair. The decision in *Calabar* v *Stitcher* is perhaps of particular importance (see **Activity 60**).

The real problem with the law discussed in this chapter is, in my view, the piecemeal way in which it has been developed. This produces anomalies. For example, why on earth should the 'receiver' remedy created by ss. 21 to 24 of the Landlord and Tenant Act 1987 be confined to residential properties?

What is needed is a complete and organised statutory code of obligations between landlord and tenants. The Law Commission has been proposing something along these lines ever since 1975. But like all other proposals for major structural reform of land law, this proposal just gathers dust.

CHAPTER NINETEEN

THE RUNNING OF COVENANTS IN A LEASE

19.1   Objectives

By the end of this chapter you should:

■ be familiar with the concepts of 'privity of contract' and 'privity of estate', and be able to explain how they apply to the law of leases;

■ be able to distinguish between covenants which 'touch and concern the land' and those which do not touch and concern;

■ appreciate the position of a sub-tenant *vis-à-vis* a head landlord;

■ appreciate the new principles laid down in the Landlord and Tenant (Covenants) Act 1995 and applicable to leases granted after 1995.

19.2   Introduction

In the preceding chapter we rather assumed one point which is often not in fact true. We assumed that the persons involved in any disputes or potential disputes over obligations in a lease were the **original** landlord and tenant. Especially with long-term leases, this is often not the case.

As we saw at **18.5**, a tenant who no longer wants to use the land he has leased can (subject to the terms of his lease) assign (i.e. transfer) that lease to a third party. Alternatively, he can sub-let the whole or part of the property to a sub-tenant, provided the sub-tenancy is shorter in duration than the head lease. One day shorter will suffice. Equally a landlord is free to sell his fee simple reversion, though (except in unusual situations such as in *Hollington* v *Rhodes*) the purchaser will take the fee simple subject to the tenant's leasehold estate.

The issues discussed in this chapter can be summarised in the form of a question. If a tenant assigns his lease, or sub-lets, and/or a landlord sells his fee simple, who is now entitled to enforce the various terms of the lease, and against whom can they be enforced?

Before addressing these questions I must warn you that the Landlord and Tenant (Covenants) Act 1995 makes important changes in the law. But (subject to one exception) the changes only apply to leases granted on or after the commencement date of the new Act, which is 1 January 1996. I am therefore going to start by explaining the 'old' law which will continue to govern all pre-1996 leases. I will then turn to consider the 'new' law.

19.3   Privity of Estate – Introduction

Figure 3 (you will see similar diagrams in text-books) sets out the story of the letting of Black House. We will need to consider that story in some detail.

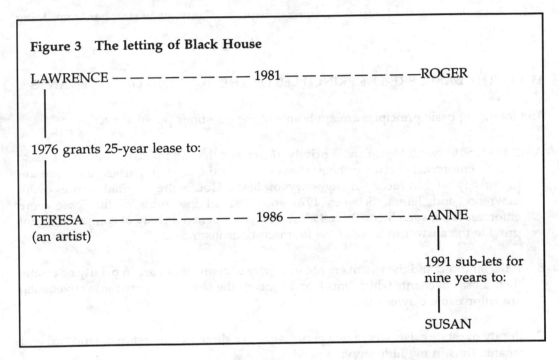

Figure 3   The letting of Black House

LAWRENCE — — — — — — — — 1981 — — — — — — — —ROGER

1976 grants 25-year lease to:

TERESA — — — — — — — — — 1986 — — — — — — — — ANNE
(an artist)

1991 sub-lets for
nine years to:

SUSAN

There are four stages in the recent history of Black House:

(a)   In 1976, Lawrence leased the house to Teresa for 25 years.

(b)   In 1981, Lawrence sold the fee simple reversion to Roger.

(c)   In 1986, Teresa assigned the lease to Anne.

(d)   In 1991, Anne sub-let the house to Susan.

By the terms of the lease agreed back in 1976, Lawrence covenanted to keep the property in good repair.

Teresa covenanted:

(i)   to pay £500 per annum rent;

(ii)   to use the property only for residential purposes;

(iii)   to paint the landlord's portrait every five years.

I will immediately add that covenant (iii) is a very odd one to find in a lease. It really has nothing to do with the lease. In technical phraseology, it does not 'touch and concern the land'.

Suppose that today the following problems have arisen:

1. Roger is very vain and wants Teresa and/or Anne to paint his portrait.

2. The rent is a long way in arrears. Can Roger sue for that rent (logically the answer should be 'Yes') and, if so, whom can he sue — Anne, Teresa, or Susan?

3. To the great annoyance of Anne and Susan, the property is in disrepair. Who can enforce the repairing covenant? Who can the covenant be enforced **against**?

4. Susan is using the house for business purposes. Can anyone stop her from doing so?

19.3.1   THE BASIC PRE-1996 PRINCIPLES OF THE RUNNING OF COVENANTS

The following basic principles are applicable to the questions posed above:

A   If the landlord and tenant are in **privity of contract** then all the covenants in the lease will be enforceable between them. However, only the original parties to a lease are in 'privity of contract'. (In my story of Black House the original parties were Lawrence and Teresa. Between 1976 and 1981 all the terms of the lease were enforceable between them. Since 1981 a lot has happened. Privity of contract will not provide the answer to three of the four questions just posed.)

B   If the landlord and the tenant are not in privity of contract but are in **privity of estate**, then those covenants which 'touch and concern the land' (but only those covenants) are enforceable between them.

C   Privity of estate exists where two persons are in a **direct relationship** of landlord and tenant. Thus in my little story:

(a)   Between 1981 and 1986 there was privity of estate between Roger and Teresa.

(b)   Between 1986 and 1991 there was privity of estate between Roger and Anne.

(c)   From 1991 onwards there is (still) privity of estate between Roger and Anne; in addition there is a separate privity of estate (and contract) between Anne and Susan.

SAQ 102

Why is there no privity of estate between Roger and Susan?

Roger and Susan are not in a **direct** landlord and tenant relationship. Anne (as it were) is in the way! The point I am trying to illustrate in this **SAQ** is absolutely crucial. If you did not get it right, think very carefully before proceeding to **Activity 64**.

ACTIVITY 64

Try to apply the principles A, B and C set out above to the four problems (numbered 1 to 4) which have now arisen regarding the lease of Black House:

1.

2.

3.

4.

I hope your answers are similar to what now follows.

1. **The portrait painting** As indicated earlier, the covenant to paint the portrait does not 'touch and concern the land'. A covenant which does not touch and concern is called 'a personal covenant'. Personal covenants which have been inserted into a lease normally remain enforceable only between the original parties. Thus Roger cannot insist on having his portrait painted. Assuming that Lawrence has remembered what was agreed 20-odd years ago, he could insist that Teresa paint his (Lawrence's) portrait.

2. **The arrears of rent** A covenant to pay rent does touch and concern the land. It follows that as there is privity of estate between Roger and Anne, Roger can (and normally would) sue Anne for those arrears. (For reasons which I will mention later at **19.5**, he could alternatively sue Teresa, assuming he can find her.)

3. **The repairing covenant** A repairing covenant also touches and concerns the land. At the current time it is Susan who is personally suffering from the disrepair of the house. However, there is no privity of estate between Susan and Roger. It is only Anne who can enforce the repairing covenant against Roger.

4. **The use of the house for business purposes** As there is privity of estate between Roger and Anne, but not between Roger and Susan, you are probably thinking that Roger can sue Anne, but not Susan, on the covenant to use the house for residential purposes only.

On the basic principles of the law of leases, this would be correct. Unfortunately there is an added complication which will work to Roger's advantage. Roger, although he cannot sue Susan under the basic **law of leases**, may have a case against her under **the law of restrictive covenants**. I will return to this point at **19.9.2**.

19.4   Which Covenants Touch and Concern the Land?

The tests traditionally applied are:

■   'Does the covenant affect the landlord **qua** landlord or the tenant **qua** tenant?' ('Qua' means 'in his capacity as'.)

or

■   'Does the covenant have some direct connection with the landlord and tenant relationship?'

If you are thinking that these tests are somewhat vague and uncertain in their operation, then I agree with you. Moreover, the courts have not always been consistent in applying these tests. If confronted with some new covenant not covered by existing case law you should apply the tests, but you should also consider whether the covenant is analogous to a covenant on which there is already a court decision. I summarise below the important court decisions.

19.4.1   COVENANTS BY LANDLORDS WHICH DO TOUCH AND CONCERN

■   A covenant to repair, also to reconstruct or repaint.

■   A covenant granting the tenant an option to renew the lease.

■   A covenant to supply the land with fresh water. (I would suggest that this decision would apply to covenants to provide 'services' such as gas and electricity.)

19.4.2   COVENANTS BY LANDLORDS WHICH DO NOT TOUCH AND CONCERN

■   A covenant granting the tenant an option to purchase the freehold reversion.

■   A covenant in the lease of a public house under which the landlord brewery promised not to supply beer to other pubs within a half-mile radius: *Thomas* v *Hayward* (1869) LR 4 Ex 311.

19.4.3   COVENANTS BY TENANTS WHICH DO TOUCH AND CONCERN

■   Covenants to pay rent.

■   Covenants to pay rates or other taxes payable with respect to the land leased.

■   Covenants to repair, repaint etc.

■   Covenants relating to the use for which the premises may be put.

■   'Tie clauses' under which the tenant of a pub or filling station can sell only the landlord's brand of beer or petrol. (See *Clegg* v *Hands* (1890) 44 Ch 503, which makes an ironic contrast with *Thomas* v *Hayward*.)

19.4.4   COVENANTS BY TENANTS WHICH DO NOT TOUCH AND CONCERN

Interestingly, examples are hard to find. One which is noteworthy is *Gower* v *Postmaster-General* (1887) 57 LT 527. This was a covenant by a tenant to pay rates on land **not comprised** within the lease. (This case could perhaps be extended by analogy to, say, a covenant to carry out building work on land other than that comprised in the lease.)

19.5   Liability of Original Parties After Assignment

It is extremely important for you to realise that in all leases granted prior to 1996 the original contractual liability of a party to a lease lasts for the full duration of the lease. That is why in my Black House story at **19.3**, Roger could sue Teresa, the original tenant, for the arrears of rent.

An original tenant of (say) a 50-year lease can be sued for arrears of rent run up by an assignee many years after he has parted with the lease. Or he can be sued for 'breaching' a repairing covenant, even though he has now no control over the premises. This point is of particular concern to small traders who 'sell up and retire'. They sometimes find that a peaceful retirement is rudely interrupted by a hefty claim for damages.

In *Arlesford Trading* v *Servansingh* [1971] 3 All ER 113, Arlesford were not the original landlords, but, like Roger in the Black House story at **19.3**, purchasers of the reversion. The Court of Appeal, confirming earlier cases, held that a purchaser of a reversion automatically acquires the right to enforce the original tenant's contractual liability for covenants which touch and concern the land. Thus people like Servansingh (or Teresa in our story) can be chased for damages by landlords of whom they may well have never heard.

19.5.1   INDEMNITIES BETWEEN ASSIGNEES OF A LEASE

The rules I am about to discuss go **a little way** towards mitigating the harshness on original tenants of the rules set out above.

In various contexts (including the present one) the law gives to a **defendant** to legal proceedings a 'right of indemnity'. This is a right, having paid damages to the plaintiff, to reclaim those damages from a third party.

Figure 4 represents the following story:

   (a)   In 1950, L granted a 99-year lease to A.

   (b)   In 1960, A assigned the lease to B.

   (c)   In 1970, B assigned the lease to C.

   (d)   In 1980, C assigned the lease to D.

   (e)   In 1990, D assigned the lease to E.

   (f)   E has now run up arrears of rent.

Figure 4   Assignments of a lease

L
|
1950
|
A — 1960 — B — 1970 — C — 1980 — D — 1990 — E (who is not paying the rent)

In this situation L has a choice of whether to sue A (on the original tenant's contractual liability) or E under the privity of estate rule. L can recover only one lot of compensation; he will choose to sue whoever has the most money. **Suppose L decides to sue A.**

A, having paid L, will have two, alternative rights of indemnity:

- At **common law** a right against the tenant in possession at the time of the breach (E in this story).

- Under the **Law of Property Act 1925 s. 77(1)**, a right against the person to whom he assigned the lease (B in this story).

Suppose A decides to claim indemnity from B. B pays up:

B can then claim indemnity from C (s. 77(1)) or E (common law).

B decides to claim indemnity from C. C pays up.

C can then claim indemnity from D or E.

C decides to claim indemnity from D. D pays up.

D can claim indemnity from E.

Will it be worth while D taking proceedings against E?

I very much doubt it. E is the one who is behind with the rent, and everyone else has avoided suing him, so it looks as though he has got little or no money.

ACTIVITY 65

It follows from the answer just given to SAQ 103 that D will (probably) end up footing the bill. Do you think this is fair?

I personally think that this is fair. It was **D** who brought the financially unsound party (**E**) into the story, so it is D who should bear the loss.

19.6   Position of Covenants which do not Touch and Concern

Suppose that Toni is the tenant of the Spotted Cow. She holds the property on a long lease from Lovely Ales plc. The lease includes a covenant under which Lovely Ales promise not to supply their beer to other pubs within a quarter-mile radius. As mentioned at **19.4.2**, such a covenant does not 'touch and concern' the land.

Alice is contemplating taking an assignment of the lease of the Spotted Cow. She wants to get the benefit of the 'local monopoly' in Lovely Ales beer. As the 'local monopoly' does not 'touch and concern the land', it will not **automatically** pass to Alice on the assignment of the lease. But it will pass if the deed assigning the lease **includes a special express clause** assigning the benefit of the 'local monopoly' covenant. So Alice should ensure that such a special clause is inserted into the assignment.

Alice should, however, be warned of one thing. If Lovely Ales sell their business to another brewery, the successor brewery will not be bound by the 'local monopoly' covenant.

The point of this Spotted Cow story is this. The benefit of a covenant which does not touch and concern the land can be passed on to an assignee of a lease, but only if there is a separate express assignment of the benefit of the covenant. However, the burden of a covenant which does not touch and concern is enforceable only against the original covenantor, Lovely Ales plc in my example.

19.6.1   POSITION OF OPTIONS TO PURCHASE THE REVERSION

Anybody who is an assignee of a lease which contains an option to purchase the landlord's reversion is almost certainly going to want to obtain that option as well as the lease itself. A covenant by the landlord granting a tenant an option to purchase the reversion does **not**, however, touch and concern the land. Nevertheless, the assignee can get what he wants, provided he remembers that the option (as well as being a covenant) is an independent equitable interest in the land. Consequently:

(a)   If the reversion is unregistered title, the option should be registered as a land charge. It comes within the very broad definition of an 'estate contract', class C(iv). Registering the option as a land charge will make the option binding on a purchaser of the reversion.

(b)   If the reversion is registered title, then it will usually be an overriding interest under the Land Registration Act 1925, s. 70(1)(g) (*Webb* v *Pollmount*).

(c) If you are purchasing a lease which includes an option to purchase the reversion, you should ensure that the deed assigning the lease also includes a separate clause assigning the option.

19.6.2 POSITION OF OPTIONS TO RENEW THE LEASE

A covenant by a landlord giving a tenant an option to renew the lease **does** touch and concern the land. However, in *Phillips* v *Mobil Oil* [1989] 3 All ER 97, the Court of Appeal created a yet further complication by holding that, if the reversion is unregistered title, such an option is registrable as a class C(iv) land charge. A tenant of a filling station who had not registered his option to renew as a land charge was thus not able to exercise it against a purchaser of the freehold reversion.

What if the fee simple in reversion to Phillips's lease had been *registered* title?

If the reversion were registered, the tenant's option would normally be an overriding interest within s. 70(1)(g), applying the principle in *Webb* v *Pollmount*. (Provided Phillips had been 'in actual occupation' there would be no need for him to enter a notice or lodge a caution.)

Lion Petrols plc owns the freehold in Blogford Garage. Its title is unregistered. In 1995 it granted a five-year lease of the garage to Tony. The lease contains a clause giving the tenant a right to purchase the freehold. Ali now wants to take an assignment of the lease; he particularly wants to ensure that he will (if he can raise the finance) be able to exercise the option. Advise Ali. (There are two points you should make.)

First, Ali should ensure that the option has been registered as a land charge. Secondly he should insist that the deed assigning him the lease includes a separate provision assigning to him the benefit of the option.

SAQ 106

The 1995 lease of Blogford Garage (predictably) includes a clause that the tenant must not sell brands of Petrol other than Lion's. Will Ali be bound by this 'tie clause'?

Of course he will. There will be privity of estate between Lion and Ali, and courts consistently have held that 'tie clauses' touch and concern the land (see **19.4.3**). (See also *Regent Oil* v *Gregory (Hatch End)* [1965] 3 All ER 673.)

19.7   The Landlord and Tenant (Covenants) Act 1995

It will be some time before the changes introduced by this Act have a large-scale impact, as it only applies to post-1995 leases. In recent years, the press (even the tabloids) has been full of sob stories about former original tenants who have assigned their leases but who many years later have been sued for breach of covenant (e.g. arrears of rent) by the landlord under what has (perhaps misleadingly) been dubbed the 'privity of contract' rule. There were widespread calls for the law to be changed so that the original tenant would not be liable for breaches of covenant which happened after he had assigned the lease.

The 1995 Act was eventually passed against opposition from landlords. They argued that they carefully select **original** tenants, and let only to persons of sound financial standing who will be able to pay the rent for the full duration of the lease. An assignee of a lease is selected by the assignor. An assignee may not be of the same sound financial standing as the original tenant.

Landlords did, however, extract two important concessions from Parliament. The first was s. 22, already discussed in the previous chapter. The second is 'authorised guarantee agreements' (discussed below in **19.7.3**).

19.7.1   ALL COVENANTS IN A LEASE NOW 'TOUCH AND CONCERN THE LAND'

I will start with perhaps the most surprising change made by the 1995 Act. Section 2 effectively abolishes the distinction between covenants which 'touch and concern' and those 'personal covenants' which do not. **Any covenant** entered into by a tenant **actually written into a lease** granted after 1995 will be enforceable by the current landlord against the current tenant under the doctrine of privity of estate, and similarly **any** covenant entered into by a landlord and written into the lease will be enforceable by the current tenant against the current landlord under the doctrine of privity of estate.

ACTIVITY 66

Reconsider the 'Spotted Cow' example I gave earlier in 19.6 of this text, on the assumption that the lease to Toni commenced in 1996. What would be the position when Toni assigns the lease to Alice?

If Toni assigns the lease to Alice, Alice will now automatically get the benefit of the 'local monopoly' clause. A separate assignment of this clause is no longer required. More important still, if Lovely Ales sell their business to another brewery, the local monopoly **will be enforceable** against the successor brewery.

Reconsider also the situation in **SAQ 105** on the assumption that the lease of Blogford Garage was granted in 1996. Ali need no longer insist that there be a special clause in the assignment transferring to him the option, but he should still ensure that it has been registered as a land charge.

19.7.2   ORIGINAL TENANT'S LIABILITY CEASES ON ASSIGNMENT

Section 5 is the key provision in the 1995 Act. It basically provides that an original tenant cannot be liable for breaches of covenant which occur after he has assigned the lease. However, an original tenant will still be liable if the assignment is itself in breach of covenant, or if the assignment occurs 'by operation of law' on death or bankruptcy of the original tenant.

19.7.3   AUTHORISED GUARANTEE AGREEMENTS

This is a major concession to landlords, spelt out in s. 16 of the Act. If a tenant needs a landlord's consent to assignment (whether under an absolute or qualified covenant against assigning) then the landlord can give his consent on condition that the tenant guarantees that the person to whom he is assigning will perform the tenant's covenants in the lease.

It must be stressed that this guarantee, when given by the assignor tenant, lasts only as long as the original assignee is the tenant of the property. Suppose:

(a)   L in 1996 grants a 99 year lease to T.

(b)   In 1998 T assigns the lease to U, with T entering into an authorised guarantee agreement.

(c)   In 2000 U assigns to V, who in 2005 falls into arrears of rent or breaks some other kind of covenant.

T is not liable on the guarantee. His liability ceased in 2000, when U assigned to V.

19.7.4   CESSATION OF ORIGINAL LANDLORD'S LIABILITY

An original landlord who disposes of his reversion still remains liable on the covenants he entered into (e.g. relating to repair). However, ss. 6 to 8 of the new Act provide a procedure under which he can be released from this continuing liability. The ex-landlord must serve notice on the tenant at the latest four weeks after he has assigned his reversion. The landlord is automatically released from his covenants once four weeks have elapsed from service of the notice, unless the tenant objects. If the tenant does object, the landlord is only released if a County Court decides that such a release would be reasonable.

19.7.5   NOTICE TO TENANT OR GUARANTOR OF ARREARS

Section 17 is the one significant provision which applies to pre-1996 leases as well as new leases. If a landlord wants to recover arrears of rent (or service charges) from an original tenant or somebody who has entered into an authorised guarantee agreement, then the landlord must serve a warning notice within six months of the arrears arising.

19.8   Position of Equitable Leases

A tenant under an equitable lease can assign the lease and the rights thereunder. However, the court in *Purchase* v *Lichfield Brewery* [1915] 1 KB 184, held that the doctrine of privity of estate does not apply to equitable leases. This decision has been much criticised, but it has probably stood too long to be overruled. **It appears to be unaffected by the 1995 Act**.

One particular consequence of the inapplicability of privity of estate to equitable leases is that an assignee of an equitable lease cannot be sued by the landlord for rent or breach of other obligations in the lease. Liability for the rent and other obligations in the lease remains solely with the original tenant.

ACTIVITY 67

An assignee of an equitable lease is nevertheless well-advised to ensure that the tenant's obligations in the equitable lease are carried out. Why is that?

I hope you have remembered that the very right to treat an informal transaction or contract as an equitable lease depends on the availability of specific performance. If there is a substantial breach of these obligations, the right to specific performance will be lost, and consequently there will no longer be an equitable lease. (If you have forgotten this point, look back at **5.5.4.1**, especially the discussion of *Coatsworth* v *Johnson*.)

19.9   Position of Sub-Tenants and Head Landlords

As we have already seen, there is no privity of estate between a head landlord and a sub-tenant. In my story at **19.3**, there was no privity of estate between Roger and Susan. It follows that the terms of the head lease are not, as a general rule, enforceable by or against a sub-tenant. A sub-tenant should, however, be wary of the two points discussed below.

19.9.1   FORFEITURE CLAUSES

A sub-tenant should as far as possible ensure that all terms of the head lease which are enforceable by **forfeiture** are in fact observed. If the head lease is forfeited, any sub-lease derived from it is automatically destroyed as well. But you should note the possibility of the sub-tenant claiming relief under s. 146(4) of the Law of Property Act 1925. I will discuss s. 146 in **Chapter 20**.

19.9.2   RESTRICTIVE COVENANTS IN THE HEAD LEASE

Here we have another awkward anomaly in the law. In my story at **19.3** it was indicated that Roger may be able to enforce the 'residential purposes only' covenant against Susan under the law of restrictive covenants. I want to stress two points:

(a) A landlord's reversionary estate counts as 'dominant land'.

(b) A restrictive covenant contained in a lease which is unregistered title is not registrable as a land charge. **Whenever created** such a covenant is subject to the doctrine of notice.

The practical consequence of this is that a head landlord can enforce restrictive covenants in the lease against a sub-tenant, despite the absence of privity of estate, where:

(a) the **lease is unregistered title and the sub-tenant has notice** of the restrictive covenants (usually the sub-tenant will have notice of the restrictive covenants in the head lease as the head tenant will, for his own protection, at least tell the sub-tenant about them); or

(b) the **lease is registered title.** Restrictive covenants in registered leases are automatically binding on sub-tenants by virtue of the Land Registration Act 1925, s. 23(1)(a) and (2).

19.10   Conclusion

The best way of concluding this chapter is to return to the Black House example at **19.3**.

What difference would it make to the four problems listed at **19.3** if, instead of sub-letting to Susan, Anne had assigned the lease to Susan? (The diagram now looks as shown in Figure 5.

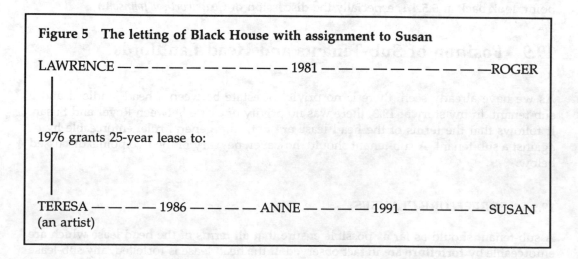

Figure 5   The letting of Black House with assignment to Susan

LAWRENCE — — — — — — — — — 1981 — — — — — — — — — —ROGER

1976 grants 25-year lease to:

TERESA — — — — 1986 — — — — ANNE — — — — 1991 — — — — — SUSAN
(an artist)

Your solutions to the problems posed in **19.3** should now be as follows:

1. With respect to the 'purely personal' portrait painting covenant, the answer is as before. The covenant remains enforceable by Lawrence (only) against Teresa (only).

2. Roger can sue either Teresa or Susan (but not Anne) for the arrears of rent. But you should note that if he chooses to sue Teresa, Teresa can claim an indemnity from Anne (s. 77(1)) or Susan (Common Law).

3. On our revised version of the story, Susan is in privity of estate with Roger, and this will work to her advantage. Susan can sue Roger for the disrepairs.

4. Roger can sue Susan invoking the privity of estate principle. There is no need for him to invoke the (rather technical) rule regarding restrictive covenants.

If you now compare the answers to the four problems with those following **Activity 64**, you will see that a lot does turn on whether the transaction between Anne and Susan is a sub-letting (a lease created out of a lease) or an assignment (a transfer of the existing leasehold estate).

In answering examination problems in the area of law covered in this **and/or the next chapter**, some students often get confused between assignments and sub-lettings. This is fatal to their chances of getting good marks. To help avoid the confusion, here are two tips:

(a) As we did with Black House, always draw a diagram to illustrate the facts of the problem.

(b) In that diagram **always** use **vertical** lines for leases and sub-leases, and **horizontal** lines for assignments and sales of freehold reversions.

19.11   End of Chapter Assessment Question

In 1980 Lisa leased (by deed) a house to Tommy for 40 years. The lease includes the following covenants:

(a)   the tenant should pay £2,000 per year rent;

(b)   the tenant should not use the house for any purpose other than as a private dwelling;

(c)   the tenant should not assign, sub-let or part with possession except with the landlord's consent.

The lease does not contain a forfeiture clause.

Lisa believes that Tommy intends to assign or sub-let to Percy. She is alarmed at that prospect, as Percy uses a number of houses in the area as branches of his very extensive accountacy practice.

Advise Lisa:

(i)   as to the possible legal consequences if she withheld her consent to an assignment or sub-letting to Percy;

(ii)   as to her position if she gave her consent to an assignment or sub-letting, but subsequently wishes to enforce covenants (a) or (b).

See *Cases and Materials* **(19.7)** for a specimen answer.

CHAPTER TWENTY

TERMINATION OF LEASES

20.1 Objectives

By the end of this chapter you should:

■ appreciate the various ways in which a lease may be terminated;

■ be able to both explain and distinguish between the two very different concepts of **waiver** of forfeiture and **relief** from forfeiture;

■ be familiar with the basic principles of section 146 of the Law of Property Act 1925;

■ be able to explain the basic principles of the Leasehold Property (Repairs) Act 1938.

20.2 Introduction

There are various ways in which a lease can come to an end (see **20.3**). Most of the ways in which a lease can terminate (e.g., notice or expiry) are self-explanatory; only one of them, forfeiture, requires extended consideration.

As you have probably guessed, forfeiture of a lease occurs where the landlord cancels a lease because the tenant has broken a provision in that lease. If a long-term lease is forfeit, that could be a disaster for the tenant, particularly if the rent is low relative to the value of the property. It is therefore not surprising that the law has placed quite severe restrictions on a landlord's right to forfeit a lease. However, as we shall see, those restrictions have become rather complex, and (possibly) too protective of tenants.

20.3 Ways in Which Leases May Terminate

20.3.1 NATURAL EXPIRY

This occurs where a fixed-term lease runs out and requires no further explanation here.

20.3.2 GIVING OF NOTICE

A lease may be terminated:

(a) by either the landlord or the tenant giving notice to terminate a periodic tenancy; or

(b) by the tenant invoking a 'break clause' in a fixed-term lease. A 'break clause' is
     in effect an option to terminate the lease early.

20.3.3 MERGER

A merger occurs where the tenant buys the landlord's reversion. The former lease then
comes to an end.

20.3.4 SURRENDER

A lease is surrendered where it is terminated by mutual agreement between landlord
and tenant. (I should stress that, except where there is a break clause or the lease has
been 'frustrated' (see **20.3.5**), a tenant cannot unilaterally give up a fixed-term lease he
no longer wants.)

20.3.5 FRUSTRATION

If you have not yet studied the doctrine of frustration, or are perhaps 'rusty' as to what
it involves, read *Distance Learning Text: Contract Law*, 5.6. Concentrate on the issue of
what sorts of events do/do not constitute frustration. There is no need for you to
consider the consequences of a contract being frustrated.

A contract is 'frustrated' when something unanticipated happens, the fault of neither
party, which makes the performance of the contract radically different from that which
was originally agreed. In *National Carriers* v *Panalpina* [1981] 1 All ER 161, the House of
Lords ended many years of controversy by holding that this law of contract rule of
'frustration' **does apply** to leases.

In January 1974, the defendants took a 10-year lease of a warehouse. In May 1979 the
local authority closed the only access road to the warehouse. The closure was likely to
last 20 months. The tenants refused to pay any further rent, arguing that the lease was
frustrated by the lack of road access. Their Lordships held that:

(a) the doctrine of frustration did apply to leases; but

(b) a 20-month interruption in the enjoyment of a 10-year lease was not such a drastic
     change in the rights of the parties as to amount to a frustrating event terminating
     the lease.

Unfortunately their Lordships did not indicate how long an interruption there would
have to have been to have terminated the lease.

ACTIVITY 69

Traditionalist land lawyers (like me) do not like *Panalpina*, and would have preferred the House of Lords to have followed old cases (going back to the seventeenth century) which held that leases cannot be frustrated. Consider why we think like this.

The *Panalpina* decision is productive of a lot of uncertainty. Suppose that the blockage of the access road had lasted several years. The lease would be frustrated, but **exactly when**? This question is important as the lease, and therefore the tenant's liability for rent, would terminate on the **exact date** of frustration.

20.3.6 FORFEITURE

This is a topic which requires extended consideration.

20.4 Forfeiture of Leases

20.4.1 THE NEED FOR A FORFEITURE CLAUSE

Obligations in leases are usually phrased as covenants, e.g., T covenants to pay the rent or T promises to do the repairs. Where the tenant's obligations in a lease are phrased as covenants, the landlord has the right to forfeit for breach by the tenant of one of his obligations only if the lease contains an express forfeiture clause ('right of entry'). Moreover, that forfeiture clause must extend to the breach which has in fact occurred.

I should immediately add that virtually every lease in existence today includes a very widely drawn express forfeiture clause which can be invoked if the tenant breaks **any** of his obligations. In the case of non-payment of rent, it is usual for the forfeiture clause to allow a period of 'grace'. For example, it is common for a lease to provide that the landlord can forfeit for non-payment of rent, but only if the rent is 30 days (or one month) in arrears.

(If, which nowadays is unlikely, an obligation in a lease is phrased as a condition, e.g., 'I grant you this lease provided that the premises are kept in good repair', no forfeiture clause is necessary. The landlord automatically has a right of entry for breach of the condition.)

20.4.2 MODES OF FORFEITURE

Traditionally there have been two alternative ways in which a landlord can forfeit a lease:

(a) **Peaceable** re-entry. This should be resorted to only if the property has been abandoned, or if it is absolutely clear that the tenant will leave of his own free will.

(b) Court proceedings for forfeiture. Such proceedings are usually essential because the Criminal Law Act 1977, ss. 6 to 13 (replacing the Forcible Entry Act 1381), make it a crime to re-possess property by force.

'Peaceable re-entry' is rarely used nowadays to forfeit a lease. In giving the leading speech in the House of Lords in *Billson* v *Residential Apartments* [1991] 3 All ER 265, Lord Templeman described peaceable re-entry as a 'dubious and dangerous method of determining [a] lease'. The decision of the House in this case (see **20.6.2**) will further discourage the use of peaceable re-entry.

For reasons which will emerge at **20.4.3**, peaceable re-entry should never be used to forfeit a lease of an occupied dwelling house.

20.4.3 FORFEITURE OF A LEASE OF A DWELLING HOUSE

First, a little bit of a digression. In the last 30 or so years, there has been an enormous problem with landlords 'harassing' tenants (cutting off electricity, creating loud noises at night, etc.) in an effort unlawfully to drive those tenants out of the houses or flats they have leased.

The 'harassment' of tenants is made **criminal** by the Protection from Eviction Act 1977, s. 1, but that provision did not create a civil claim for damages or an injunction. (But see s. 2 below.) However, under ss. 27 and 28 of the Housing Act 1988, a statutory tort has been created of harassing a 'residential occupier'.

The central point, though, for our present purposes is s. 2 of the Protection from Eviction Act 1977:

> Where any premises are let as a dwelling on a lease which is subject to a right of re-entry or forfeiture it shall not be lawful to enforce that right otherwise than by proceedings in the court while any person is lawfully residing in the premises or part of them.

This section effectively renders it impossible to forfeit a lease of an occupied dwelling by peaceable re-entry.

20.5 Waiver of Forfeiture

Waiver of forfeiture must not be confused with **relief** from forfeiture. The essence of 'waiver' is that the **landlord**, because of his conduct, is deemed to have forgiven the tenant and renounced his claim to forfeiture. (The landlord can still pursue a claim for damages.)

Relief from forfeiture (discussed at **20.6**) occurs where **the court** decides that although the tenant has broken the terms of the lease, he (the tenant) should be allowed to keep the lease. In effect **the court** shows mercy and forgives the erring tenant.

Waiver will occur where:

(a) the landlord knows of the breach; and

(b) with that knowledge, he does some unequivocal act, known to the tenant, which would indicate to a reasonable onlooker that he (the landlord) regards the lease as still subsisting.

The most frequently occurring 'unequivocal acts' are where the landlord either demands or accepts rent for a period after the breach. If the landlord distrains for rent, that is an 'unequivocal act' irrespective of when the rent in question was due. Another example of an 'unequivocal act' would be where the landlord enters into negotiations to renew the lease on its expiry, or offers to vary the terms of the existing lease.

A landlord has knowledge of facts constituting a breach if they come to his attention, or to the attention of any of his agents. If agent One has knowledge of a breach and agent Two sends out a rent demand, there is a waiver. The case of *Central Estates (Belgravia)* v *Woolgar (No. 2)* [1972] 3 All ER 610 illustrates many of the points just discussed.

Study carefully the extracts from *Woolgar's* case in *Cases and Materials* (20.3). (I must immediately stress that this case raised issues both of waiver and relief from forfeiture, and it is crucial not to get the two issues confused.)

Woolgar, an OAP and a First World War veteran, was tenant of a long lease (due to expire in 1993) of a sizeable house in central London. He had a fall from grace, and was convicted of using the premises as a (homosexual) brothel. In view of his past exemplary record he was granted a conditional discharge by the magistrates.

The landlords decided to forfeit the lease for breach of the covenant in the lease prohibiting illegal user, and served on Woolgar the warning notice required by s. 146 of the Law of Property Act 1925 (see **20.6.2**). (We will discuss this section later.) The landlords were anxious to forfeit the lease as the property would be **much more valuable** to them with vacant possession. (Sometimes property used as brothels or drug-dens gets stigmatised. That does not seem to have happened in *Woolgar's* case.)

A minor official of the landlords then made a fatal mistake – he sent to Woolgar a rent demand for a future instalment of rent. The Court of Appeal unanimously found that this rent demand waived the breach, even though:

(a) it was sent out in error;

(b) Woolgar had not been in any way misled by the demand. Even after the demand was sent he still personally believed that he was going to be thrown out of his home. The Court stressed that the test for an 'unequivocal act' was not what the tenant subjectively thought; rather it was an objective test of what a **'reasonable onlooker'** would think. The reasonable onlooker always considers rent demands as indicating that the landlord intends to allow the lease to continue.

In *Blackstones Ltd* v *Burnetts* [1973] 3 All ER 782 Burnetts had a lease from Blackstones of premises in central London. There was a qualified covenant against sub-letting. Burnetts obtained Blackstones' consent to sub-let to two people, A and D, trading in partnership. However Burnetts actually sub-let to a **different** person, Flat Finders Ltd. (A and D were the directors of that company.)

The landlords' solicitors heard of what had happened. The solicitors seem to have been ignorant of the very basic principle of company law that a company is a **separate person** from its shareholders and directors. They sought counsel's opinion as to whether there had been breach of the qualified covenant against sub-letting. (Clearly there had been such a breach.) While this opinion was awaited, a clerk in the landlords' office sent out a rent demand for the next quarter's rent. The rent demand was held to have waived the breach.

What is the moral for landlords of the two cases just discussed?

If you want to forfeit a lease, give clear instructions to all your agents (and not just to your specialist rent-collectors) that they must neither send out rent demands nor accept rent paid without a demand being sent. (If the landlord's rent files are computerised, the computer should be programmed to warn that no rent should be demanded/accepted. If he still has manual files, a red warning marker should be placed in the file.)

20.6   Relief from Forfeiture

Where a tenant claims relief from forfeiture, he will normally do so by counterclaiming for relief in the landlord's proceedings to terminate the lease. The tenant could bring a separate action 'for relief', but that is unlikely as it would mean unnecessary additional costs.

20.6.1   RELIEF FROM FORFEITURE FOR NON-PAYMENT OF RENT

Such relief from forfeiture was traditionally governed by equity, but has now been incorporated into statute (currently the Supreme Court Act 1981, s. 38).

Three conditions must be fulfilled for relief to be granted:

(a)   the tenant must pay all the arrears of rent;

(b)   the tenant must pay all the landlord's costs;

(c)   it must appear just and equitable to grant relief.

You may already know that it is a general rule of English litigation that the loser of court proceedings pays both sides' costs. Point (b) above is a perfectly sensible **exception** to this rule. The tenant 'wins' relief, but he must pay the landlord's legal costs as part of the price of winning.

It is fair to say that if points (a) and (b) above are satisfied the court will in normal circumstances automatically conclude that it is 'just and equitable' to grant relief. Point (c) really means that the court has a discretion to refuse relief even though the tenant pays off all the arrears of rent and the landlord's costs.

ACTIVITY 71

Can you think of situations where a court might refuse relief despite the fact that the tenant has cleared the arrears and paid all the landlord's costs?

The court might well refuse relief if the circumstances are such that the tenant is very likely to fall into serious arrears of rent again. It might also refuse relief if the tenant is in serious breach of other obligations in the lease as well as rent, e.g. had broken covenants regarding the user of premises.

Another (related) aspect of 'condition (c)' above is that in exceptional cases the court can grant relief on conditions which do not relate to payment of rent. Suppose the tenant is rather neglecting the property. The court could grant relief on condition that the property be put into good repair: *Belgravia Insurance* v *Meah* [1964] 1 QB 430.

Relief against forfeiture for non-payment of rent has one further oddity. Unlike relief where court proceedings have been taken under s. 146 of the Law of Property Act 1925 (see **20.6.2**) the court has the power to grant relief to the tenant even **after** the landlord has repossessed the property! The tenant can claim this 'late relief' up to six months after the landlord's repossession. But I should stress that this late relief requires the expense of separate court proceedings brought by the tenant, and that the court would not grant this late relief if the landlord had already let the property to a new tenant.

20.6.2 FORFEITURE FOR BREACH OF COVENANT OTHER THAN RENT

This is governed by s. 146 of the Law of Property Act 1925. Section 146(1) provides:

> A right of re-entry or forfeiture under any proviso or stipulation in a lease for a breach of any covenant or condition in the lease shall not be enforceable, by action or otherwise, unless and until the lessor serves on the lessee a notice—
> (a) specifying the particular breach complained of; and
> (b) if the breach is capable of remedy, requiring the lessee to remedy the breach; and
> (c) in any case, [where the landlord wants compensation] requiring the lessee to make compensation in money for the breach;
> and the lessee fails, within a reasonable time thereafter, to remedy the breach, if it is capable of remedy, and to make reasonable compensation in money, to the satisfaction of the lessor, for the breach.

Section 146(2) provides that the court can, in its discretion (in the landlord's forfeiture proceedings or in separate proceedings commenced by the tenant), grant relief from forfeiture. The general rule under s. 146(2) is that a tenant cannot claim relief once a landlord has actually repossessed the property. But this general rule applies only if the landlord forfeits **by court proceedings**.

In *Billson* v *Residential Apartments* [1991] 3 All ER 265, the House of Lords held that where the landlord forfeited a lease by **peaceable re-entry**, the tenant could, **after** the landlord has re-occupied the property, commence court proceedings to get the property back. Their Lordships stressed that there is no fixed time limit on such an application for relief after peaceable re-entry. However, if the tenant delayed a long time before claiming relief, that would be a factor to be considered by the court when exercising its discretion whether or not to grant relief.

Why will the decision in *Billson* further discourage the use of peaceable re-entry to forfeit leases?

If a landlord forfeits by court proceedings under s. 146, he knows that once he has taken possession under the court order there is no possibility of the tenant's lease being restored. If he forfeits by peaceable re-entry, he is subject to the risk that (perhaps years later) the court will give the lease back to the tenant.

20.6.2.1 The four stages required by s. 146 for forfeiture by court proceedings

■ The landlord must serve a carefully drafted warning notice on the **current** tenant: *Old Grovebury Estates* v *Seymour Plant Sales (No. 2)* [1979] 3 All ER 504.

■ The landlord must then wait 'a reasonable time' before commencing forfeiture proceedings. If during this time the tenant 'remedies' the breach, the landlord cannot claim forfeiture.

■ Assuming (as is usually the case) the breach is not remedied within a 'reasonable time', the landlord can issue a writ claiming forfeiture.

■ When the landlord's forfeiture case reaches court, the tenant can beg the court to grant him relief. The court is most likely to grant relief either where the breach (e.g., disrepair) has now at last been put right, or where the landlord has not been substantially harmed by an 'irremediable' breach.

20.6.2.2 The s. 146 notice must be drafted correctly

The notice must spell out in detail what breaches the landlord is relying on. For example, it is not sufficient to say, 'the property is in disrepair'. If the breach is capable of remedy, the landlord must specifically include a clause in the notice demanding the breach be put right.

If the s. 146 'warning' notice has not been drafted correctly, any court proceedings commenced by the landlord will be abortive, even if the tenant is clearly a sinner who should be thrown out. In such a case the landlord would have to serve another (this time correctly drafted) s. 146 notice and start all over again.

20.6.2.3 Remediable or irremediable breaches?

This is a very important distinction for three reasons:

(a)   The need to draft the s. 146 notice correctly. (There have been a number of cases where the landlord has drafted his s. 146 notice on the assumption that the breach is irremediable, but the court has ruled that the breach was 'remediable'. The landlord's forfeiture proceedings were therefore dismissed.)

(b)   The length of the 'reasonable time' which must elapse between service of the s. 146 notice and the commencement of proceedings for possession.

   (i)   Where the breach is remediable, then the landlord must wait at least three months.

   (ii)   Where the breach is irremediable, a fortnight's delay between service of notice and commencement of proceedings generally suffices. Two days was held to be insufficient in *Horsey Estates* v *Steiger* [1899] 2 QB 79, at 91.

(c)   The court is **more likely** to grant relief where the breach is capable of remedy.

Breaches of **positive covenants**, e.g., repairing and painting covenants, are generally capable of remedy. This is confirmed by the decision in *Expert Clothing* v *Hillgate House* [1985] 2 All ER 998, especially at 1008. In that case the breach consisted of a failure to reconstruct the premises by an agreed date. The Court of Appeal held that the breach was 'remediable' by the tenant belatedly doing the reconstruction. Slade LJ said:

> Nevertheless, I would, for my part, accept the submission of counsel for the defendants that the breach of a positive covenant (whether it be a continuing breach or a once and for all breach) will ordinarily be capable of remedy. As Bristow J pointed out in the course of argument, the concept of capability of remedy for the purpose of s. 146 must surely be directed to the question **whether the harm that has been done to the landlord by the relevant breach is for practical purposes capable of being retrieved**. In the ordinary case, the breach of a promise to do something by a certain time can for practical purposes be remedied by the thing being done, even out of time. (Emphasis added.)

Breaches of **negative covenants** are generally incapable of remedy. In *Scala House* v *Forbes* [1973] 3 All ER 308, it was held that breach of a covenant against sub-letting was irremediable. The case of *Glass* v *Kencakes* [1964] 3 All ER 807 is difficult.

Read the extracts from *Glass* v *Kencakes* in *Cases and Materials* (20.4.2.1), keeping in mind two things. First, the situation in that case of an innocent tenant being put in breach of covenant by an evil sub-tenant is not unusual. Secondly, the case was decided before the Court of Appeal decision in *Woolgar*.

In *Glass*, L let to T, the lease including a covenant against illegal/immoral user. T sub-let to S, who, without T's knowledge, used the premises for prostitution. L served a s. 146 notice on T in terms which assumed the breach was incapable of remedy. T in turn served a s. 146 notice on S. The sub-lease was declared forfeit. The judge held that T had remedied his (arguably technical) **breach** of the head-lease by getting rid of S **before the property became tainted with a stigma**.

20.6.3   RELIEF FOR BREACHES WHICH ARE INCAPABLE OF REMEDY

Glass v *Kencakes* was decided before the Court of Appeal's decision in *Central Estates* v *Woolgar*. I have already told you the facts of that case (see **20.5**) and the court's ruling on the waiver issue. Woolgar also (in the alternative) claimed relief from forfeiture. The Court of Appeal held that relief could be granted even where the breach was **irremediable**, which it clearly was in Woolgar's case.

Moreover a majority of the court (had it not already decided the waiver issue in Woolgar's favour) would have granted Woolgar relief. The majority was clearly impressed by three facts: (i) Woolgar's hitherto exemplary character; (ii) his genuine repentance; (iii) the fact that if there was a forfeiture the landlord's fee simple (now with 'vacant possesion') would substantially **increase** in value.

If a case like *Glass* v *Kencakes* recurred today (an innocent head-tenant prejudiced by the nefarious activities of a sub-tenant) how do you think that the court would deal with the case?

I think the court would deal with the matter by granting relief to the head tenant, without worrying whether the breach was capable of remedy.

20.6.4   RELIEF TO SUB-TENANTS

If a head lease is forfeited, then all sub-leases created out of that head lease are destroyed as well. Situations thus arise from time to time where a sub-tenant who has faithfully fulfilled all the conditions of the sub-lease is nevertheless imperilled by the failure of the head tenant to perform an obligation in the head lease. (**Contrast *Glass* v *Kencakes* at 20.6.2.3.**)

A sub-tenant who is imperilled by the head tenant's failure to pay the rent under the head lease can (in theory) claim relief in equity. This remedy is unlikely to be invoked nowadays for two reasons:

(a)   The lease of the (unsatisfactory) head tenant is preserved by the sub-tenant's efforts in paying off the arrears, yet the head tenant may well again fall into arrears.

(b)   If the sub-lease is of part of the property, relief cannot be confined to that part. (In one old case the head lease consisted of 100 houses. Each house was sub-let to a separate individual tenant. The head tenant fell into arrears of rent. One of the sub-tenants applied to the Court of Chancery for relief. He was told he could have relief, but only if he paid off the arrears of rent under the head lease with respect to all 100 houses. I would imagine that was beyond his resources!)

20.6.4.1   Section 146(4) of the LPA 1925

Today, sub-tenants may seek relief under **s. 146(4) of the Law of Property Act 1925**. This provision applies to all breaches of covenants, **including** (unlike the rest of s. 146)

non-payment of rent. (Mortgagees of leases can also seek relief under s. 146(4) where a mortgaged lease is threatened with forfeiture, and in modern conditions this is very important.)

As you will see if you study it in *Cases and Materials* **(20.4)**, the drafting of s. 146(4) is somewhat obscure. However the courts have managed to make sense of it. A good example is *Chatham Empire* v *Ultrans* [1961] 2 All ER 381.

Section 146(4) works in the following way. If the court decides that the head lease should be forfeited but that the sub-tenant should be protected, the head lease is destroyed by court order. The ex-sub-tenant is granted a new head lease for a period not exceeding that unexpired under the old sub-lease. If the old sub-lease was of part of the property, the new head lease will relate to that part only. The court has a discretion as to the detailed terms of the new head lease.

Where a mortgagee of a lease claims relief, and the court decides that the lessee himself does not deserve relief, the court orders the old lease to be destroyed. A new (head) lease is granted in its place to the **ex-mortgagee**. The mortgagee now becomes a lessee.

20.7   Leasehold Property Repairs Act 1938

This statute was passed because of a problem with 'shark' landlords in the 1930s who were inducing tenants to **surrender** long leases of poorly repaired property by threatening them with heavy claims for damages.

The landlord would first write to the tenant saying something like, 'Dear Tenant. Your house/shop is in shocking repair. We are going to sue you for £X,000 damages'. This terrified the tenant. (Many of the tenants affected were small businesses suffering from the effects of the Depression.)

A few weeks later another letter would arrive, in terms, 'Dear Tenant, if you agree to surrender your lease we will forget about our claim for damages'. The tenants were usually only too glad to accept the invitation. The practical outcome was that the landlord had succeeded in terminating the lease while by-passing the elaborate procedure laid down in s. 146 of the Law of Property Act 1925.

The 1938 Act applies to all leases for more than seven years with at least three years to run. Where the Act applies, a landlord cannot enforce a repairing covenant by forfeiture or **damages** unless he first serves a s. 146 notice.

In addition to the usual particulars, the warning notice must inform the tenant that he has 28 days in which to serve a 'counter-notice' claiming the protection of the Act. If this counter-notice is served (as usually it is), the landlord cannot take any further steps to enforce the repairing covenant unless he first gets the permission ('leave') of the court. This leave is generally given only if there is a pressing need for immediate repairs. Indeed the House of Lords has recently held that:

> . . . save in special circumstances, the landlord must prove (on the balance of probabilities) that the immediate remedying of a breach of the repairing covenant is required in order to save the landlord from substantial loss or damage which the landlord would otherwise sustain. (*per* Lord Templeman in *Associated British Ports* v *C H Bailey Plc* [1990] 1 All ER 929).

(If you get a chance to read this case, read first the **penultimate** paragraph of the speech. You will then understand the real reasons underlying this very protracted litigation.)

20.7.1   SEDAC INVESTMENTS V *TANNER* [1982] 3 All ER 646

This case threw up a peculiar problem. A very bad tenant (a local Conservative Club) covenanted to do the repairs but allowed the building to get into a dangerous state. The landlords (under pressure from the local authority) did the repairs themselves. The landlords then sued, but found their claim for damages blocked by the 1938 Act. There was no longer any pressing need for repairs!

A somewhat similar situation arose in *Hamilton* v *Martell Securities* [1984] 1 All ER 665, except that the lease expressly provided that if the landlord should carry out repairs the tenant would indemnify the landlord for the cost. It was held that the 1938 Act did not prevent an action being brought on this **indemnity** clause.

What is the moral for landlords of the decisions in *Sedac Investments* and *Hamilton* v *Martell*?

When drafting new leases where the tenant will be liable to do the repairs, always include an indemnity clause similar to that in *Hamilton* v *Martell*.

20.8   Reform of Forfeiture of Leases

The Law Commission, in 1986, proposed radical reform of this complex area of law.

Read the summary of the Law Commission's proposals in *Cases and Materials* (20.6), and then re-read the extracts from the decision in *Billson* v *Residential Apartments*, remembering that the House of Lords in that case in December 1991 overruled a Court of Appeal decision made in February 1991. Also refer back to my remarks at 20.6.4.1 regarding s. 146(4) and in particular to the question of relief for mortgagees. Then consider the following questions, bearing in mind that 1991 was the depths of the recession and that a General Election was expected in the spring of 1992:

(a) What had less scrupulous landlords been doing from February to December 1991?

(b) Which wealthy organisations were particularly upset by these activities of these less scrupulous landlords?

(c) **What would Parliament have been forced to do if Lord Templeman and his colleagues had ruled in favour of the landlords?**

My own answers would be as follows:

(a) What was happening was that landlords were staging 'dawn raids'; i.e. peaceably re-entering deserted buildings before the tenants arrived. The landlords thought that (courtesy of the Court of Appeal) they had thereby forfeited the lease(s) **and deprived the tenants, sub-tenants and mortgagees** of their right to seek relief.

(b) The answer to this question lies in the answer to (a). Financial institutions (especially the big banks) had lent money to tenants who were now in severe financial difficulties because of the recession. The banks had taken mortgages of the tenants' leases to secure the loans, but these mortgages were being destroyed by the dawn raids.

(c) Had the House of Lords ruled the other way in *Billson*, the big banks would have been screaming at the government for immediate reform. With an election pending, the government would have been forced to dust off the 1986 Law Commission Report and tell Parliament, 'We do not have time to argue the details. We must immediately enact these proposals'.

20.9 Conclusion

The preceding paragraph, as well as relating to **Activity 73**, is also the first part of my conclusion, so I will not repeat it.

The second part is to remind you of an examination question I asked a few years ago. Candidates were invited to discuss the following proposition:

A landlord who wants to forfeit a lease is often faced with a long and tortuous process. During that process he dare not collect any rent. And the proceedings for forfeiture may well end with the court forgiving the erring tenant.

I think you will have realised that I am in broad agreement with this proposition, and (as I hinted at **20.2**) the law is arguably too protective of tenants. It is certainly not surprising that when the Court of Appeal in *Billson* appeared to open a door to landlords to circumvent one of the protections for tenants, many landlords rushed through only to find that door slammed shut by the House of Lords.

Lord Templeman and his colleagues took the heat off the government, but certainly did not eliminate the need for wholesale reform of this area of law.

20.10   End of Chapter Assessment Question

In 1982 Letitia leased (by deed) a shop to Tamsin for 40 years. The lease includes a covenant under which the tenant undertakes to ensure that the shop is not used for illegal purposes. Rent is payable quarterly and in advance to Letitia's agent Rocky. The lease also includes a forfeiture clause which can be invoked if the tenant breaks any of the covenants.

In 1994 Tamsin lawfully assigned the lease to Ann. In early 1995 Dandy, one of Ann's shop assistants, took advantage of the fact that Ann did not normally arrive at the shop until 9.30 a.m. He started an early morning 'side-line' selling cocaine. After only a month Ann found out about the illegal trade. She immediately dismissed Dandy and reported his activities to the police. Last week Dandy was convicted of drug-trafficking.

Letitia has just read of Dandy's conviction in the local newspaper. She has decided to endeavour to forfeit the lease. She tells you, 'The rent under the existing lease is ridiculously low; if I can get Ann out a new tenant would be willing to pay three times as much'.

Advise Letitia.

See *Cases and Materials* (20.8) for a specimen answer.

CHAPTER TWENTY-ONE

ADVERSE POSSESSION AND THE LIMITATION ACTS

21.1 Objectives

By the end of this chapter you should:

■ appreciate the role adverse possession plays in English land law;

■ be able to explain the meaning of the concept;

■ appreciate fully the legal difficulties which arise where adverse possession is taken against land subject to a trust;

■ appreciate fully the legal difficulties which arise where adverse possession is taken against a leaseholder;

■ be able to explain all the varied legal ramifications which arise where adverse possession is taken against a proprietor of registered land.

21.2 Introduction

Adverse possession is a short but vital topic. If the concept did not exist, then the English system of **unregistered** title would be impossible to operate.

The basic concept is not difficult to understand. Moreover, land lawyers have been greatly helped by a modern Court of Appeal decision involving a very striking set of facts which both clarified and simplified the law.

Though I think you will find the early part of this chapter straightforward, I should warn you that difficulties will begin to mount when we consider, first, adverse possession against land which is subject to a lease and, secondly, adverse possession against land which is registered title.

ACTIVITY 74

Read *Bucks C.C.* v *Moran* [1989] 2 All ER 225 in *Cases and Materials* (21.1). This is a case where the adverse possessors (Moran and his predecessors) succeeded in gaining ownership of quite a large patch of land. Most adverse possession cases are not nearly

as spectacular. **What do you think is the most common type of situation where the rules of adverse possession have to be applied?**

The most common type of case for applying the adverse possession rules is encroachment between neighbours, e.g. where a boundary fence is moved.

21.3   Possession Gives a Right to Sue Trespassers

First consider the following propositions:

■ Ownership is often defined as 'the best right to possess'.

■ Possession of land, or any other property, is itself evidence of ownership of that land or property. The longer the possession the better the evidence of ownership.

When a purchaser investigates title to unregistered land he is merely checking that the vendor and his predecessors have been in control of the land for a sufficiently long time to make his claim to ownership safe (see **2.5**).

We all have heard the phrase 'Possession is nine-tenths of the law'. In the context of land law, this cliché is correct! A person in possession of land, though he has no title to it, can nevertheless defend that possession by legal proceedings against **anyone but the true owner**.

Suppose that Anthea is the owner in fee simple of Wasteacre. In 1990 Bertram seized possession of Wasteacre and has remained in possession ever since. Now (1996-7) Charlotte (a total stranger with no connections to Anthea) is trying to interfere with Bertram's possession, or even to evict Bertram from Wasteacre. If Bertram sues Charlotte for trespass, who will win?

Bertram will win. It will be no defence for Charlotte to say, 'But it is not Bertram's land'.

21.4   The Limitation Act 1980

Section 15(1) of the Limitation Act 1980 replaces legislation dating back many centuries. The practical effect of this provision (and its predecessors) is to declare that in appropriate circumstances possession shall be ten-tenths of the law!

No action shall be brought by any person to recover any land after the expiration of twelve years from the date on which the right of action accrued to him or, if it first accrued to some person through whom he claims, to that person.

Under a provision which is now tucked away in sch. 1, para. 8(1) of the 1980 Act, a 'right of action' accrues to the owner of a piece of land when a stranger takes 'adverse possession' of the land against him.

The practical effect of what I have said so far is as follows:

(a) Once adverse possession has started, the adverse possessor can defend his possession against all but the original owner.

(b) Once adverse possession has continued for 12 years, the adverse possessor can defend his possession against all **including** the original owner.

SAQ 112 has already illustrated proposition (a). Suppose now that Bertram remains in continuous adverse possession against Anthea for many more years. In the year 2002 proposition (b) will become operative and Bertram will have a title to Wasteacre which he can assert against the whole world, **including Anthea**. That title will be based on his long possession of the land.

Looked at from another angle, at the end of the 12 years' adverse possession the original owner's title (Anthea's title to Wasteacre in my example) is completely extinguished. The adverse possessor has a completely new (fee simple) title based on his long adverse possession. You should note, however, that it is not correct to say that in the year 2002 Anthea's title is transferred to Bertram.

Anthea may well, after 2002, retain title deeds to 'her' fee simple title to Wasteacre, but those deeds will be worthless scraps of paper.

21.4.1 'SQUATTERS'

Unfortunately the word traditionally used by lawyers for any person who takes adverse possession is 'squatter'. This word, used in its time-honoured legal sense, is both broader in meaning and less emotive than the present-day colloquial usage.

21.4.2 COMMENCEMENT OF ADVERSE POSSESSION

Adverse possession commences when the adverse possessor displaces the original owner. As was emphasised in *Bucks C.C.* v *Moran*, the adverse possessor **must take control of the land with the intention of excluding everyone else from the land**. As I have said already, the most common cases of adverse possession today are encroachments between neighbours, e.g. where a boundary fence is moved. However, every few years we do seem to get a (reported) case where an adverse possessor successfully 'annexes' to his own property a quite large chunk of land. *Bucks C.C.* v *Moran* is a good illustration of this type of case. Another striking case is *Treloar* v *Nute* [1977] 1 All ER 230. In that case the plaintiff and the defendant were adjoining farmers. The plaintiff (an elderly lady) had about one-seventh of an acre of waste ground about which she totally forgot. The defendant and his father in effect took over the ground. They levelled it off (there had been a deep gully). They then used it for various purposes, such as an informal motor-bike trials course and as a rubbish dump. Eventually the defendant started to build a bungalow on the ground. At that point Mrs Treloar woke up: 'Hey that's my land you're building on!'

The defendant and his father were able to prove that they had been using the ground for more than 12 years. Mrs Treloar's title to the land was extinguished. Nute (junior) had a new title based on adverse possession. The Court of Appeal therefore gave judgment for Nute.

21.4.3 THE 'ADVERSE' IN ADVERSE POSSESSION

For a long period of possession to extinguish an original owner's title, the possession must be 'adverse' to the original owner's title. This means that the possessor's occupation of the land must be **inconsistent** with the title of the original owner. Thus, during the running of a lease, a tenant cannot be in adverse possession against his landlord with respect to the land comprised in the lease. A tenant's possession is not in any way inconsistent with or in conflict with the landlord's ownership of the fee simple.

What if a tenant fails to pay the rent? Does that make his possession 'adverse'?

Failure to pay rent does not make the tenant's possession 'adverse'. The tenant's lease is derived out of the landlord's freehold, and is not in conflict with that freehold, irrespective of whether or not the tenant pays rent. (However, the right to an instalment of rent is time-barred after a six-year delay in collecting that instalment.)

Trustees of land can never be in adverse possession against their beneficiaries. This is because there is no inconsistency between the trustees' **legal** title and the beneficiaries' **equitable** interests.

Suppose A, B, C, D, and E are tenants in common of Highhouse, but only A and B are trustees of the legal title. A and B get nasty and shut C, D, and E out of the house. They keep C, D, and E locked out for more than 12 years. Are the rights of C, D, and E 'time-barred'?

Even if the unhappy state of affairs continues for 50 years or more, C, D, and E will never be 'time-barred'; their rights cannot be extinguished by the trustees' decision to keep possession of the house exclusively for themselves.

One other significant point is that a purchaser of land who takes possession prior to completion of the contract of sale is not in adverse possession unless and until the contract of sale is rescinded. A purchaser's 'estate contract' equitable interest is in no way inconsistent with the vendor's ownership of the legal fee simple: *Hyde* v *Pearce* [1982] 1 All ER 1029.

21.4.4 THE 'APPARENTLY ABANDONED PLOT' PROBLEM

In *Treloar* v *Nute* (see **21.4.2**) Mrs Treloar had totally forgotten about the land in dispute. The facts of that case are to be contrasted with the line of cases I am now going to discuss. I must mention this line of cases even though the Court of Appeal has recently held them to be overruled by legislation.

These cases held that where a landowner had a piece of land which he left vacant but for which he had future plans, a third party who occupied the land was not in adverse possession until either the owner abandoned his plans or the stranger did acts which rendered those plans impossible. The first case in the line appears to be *Leigh* v *Jack* (1879) 5 Ex Div 264. However, it was two mid-twentieth-century cases which caused considerable consternation.

In *Williams Brothers Ltd* v *Raftery* [1957] 3 All ER 593 the plaintiffs purchased in 1937 a piece of waste ground at the back of their factory. They hoped to expand their premises onto this ground, but they were prevented from doing so, first by the War, and then by the refusal of planning permission.

In 1940, the defendant came along, saw the waste ground, and started 'to dig for victory', that is he used the ground as a vegetable patch. Having helped to defeat Hitler, he then kept greyhounds on the land, erecting kennels and fencing. In 1957 the plaintiffs suddenly claimed possession of the ground. The defendant claimed he had gained a title to the ground by adverse possession.

A director of the plaintiffs testified that they had always retained their expansion 'plans', and that they had always hoped that the town planners would change their minds. (He did not produce any actual drawings, maps or diagrams.) The Court of Appeal held that in view of the fact that the 'plans' for the ground had been 'retained' and that the defendant had done nothing to render them impossible, the defendant never had adverse possession of the land.

In *Wallis's Cayton Bay Holiday Camp* v *Shell-Mex* [1974] 3 All ER 575 the defendants acquired one and one-third acres of land in the middle of a field for the purposes of a new filling station. This one and one-third acres adjoined the site of a proposed new road, but neither the road nor the one and one-third acres were marked off by boundary markers. All a passer-by would see (looking from, say, the top of a double-deck bus) was an arable field no different from its neighbours. The field belonged to Wallis's, which farmed both it and adjoining fields through a subsidiary company.

For eleven and a half years Wallis's farming activities extended to the one and one-third acres. Then the local authority abandoned the scheme for the new road. Shell promptly wrote to Wallis's offering to sell the one and one-third acres. Wallis's did not reply. (Why they did not reply relates to another point of adverse possession law with which we will deal with at **21.7**.) Instead they carried on their farming for eight more months, and then claimed that they had got title through adverse possession.

The Court of Appeal ruled that as Shell had only recently abandoned their plans, there had been only a few months', not 12 years', adverse possession. Shell therefore won.

Lord Denning further confused matters by holding that people like Wallis's and Raftery were 'by a legal fiction' deemed to have had an implied licence to occupy the land. As they were there 'by permission', they could not be **adverse** possessors.

The decisions in *Williams Brothers* and *Wallis's* cases were heavily criticised by many (including myself) as undermining the whole concept (and utility) of adverse possession. Consider why we said that.

The practical result of the *Williams Brothers* and *Wallis's* cases was that whether or not there was adverse possession depended not upon the activities of the alleged adverse possessor, **but upon the state of mind of the original owner.**

21.4.5 *BUCKINGHAMSHIRE COUNTY COUNCIL v MORAN*

The following statutory provision (first enacted in 1980) was designed to overrule the *Williams Brothers* and *Wallis's* line of cases. (Now sch. 1, para. 8(4) of the consolidating Limitation Act 1980.)

> For the purpose of determining whether a person occupying land is in adverse possession of the land it shall not be assumed by implication of law that his occupation is by permission of the person entitled to the land merely by virtue of the fact that his occupation is not inconsistent with the latter's present or future enjoyment of the land.

This is not the clearest of statutory provisions, and it seems to aim only at Lord Denning's 'implied licence' idea. However the Court of Appeal in *Bucks C.C. v Moran* [1989] 2 All ER 225 held that this provision **did** overrule the broader principle 'recognised' in *Williams Brothers* and *Wallis's*.

Moran extended his garden onto land which he knew was owned by the County Council; he knew they intended to build a road on it. In giving a judgment holding that Moran was an adverse possessor and that the County Council had lost their title, Slade LJ said:

> If in any given case the land in dispute is unbuilt land and the squatter is aware that the owner, while having no present use for it, has a purpose in mind for its use in the future, the court is likely to require very clear evidence before it can be satisfied that the squatter who claims a possessory title has not only established factual possession of the land, but also the requisite intention to exclude the world at large, including the owner with the paper title, so far as is reasonably practicable and so far as the processes of the law will allow.

Thus, in cases where the owner of the original 'paper' title has retained plans for the land, it will be perfectly possible for his title to be destroyed by adverse possession. It will be a question of fact whether, despite the 'paper' owner retaining plans known to the alleged 'squatter', the latter has done sufficient to establish adverse possession.

21.5 Adverse Possession and Tenants

21.5.1 WHAT IF AN ADVERSE POSSESSOR DISPLACES A TENANT?

In the discussion so far we have assumed that the adverse possessor has displaced a fee simple owner. What, however, if the land in question has been leased to a tenant, and it is the tenant who is displaced by the adverse possessor? The principles applicable were restated by the House of Lords in *Fairweather* v *St Marylebone Property Co.* [1962] 2 All ER 288. (To avoid confusion, **do not yet read** this case or the extracts from this case set out in *Cases and Materials*. There is a major, added complication which it is best to ignore until the end of this chapter.)

Back in 1893, a landlord (L) owned the fee simple in a house and an adjoining shed. In that year he granted a 99-year lease of the house and shed to T. T left the shed derelict. In 1920 a neighbour (M) took adverse possession of the shed. M and his successor, Fairweather, maintained the adverse possession until the dispute arose in 1959.

In 1959, St Marylebone bought from L the fee simple to the house and shed. By agreement between St Marylebone and T, the 99-year lease was 'surrendered', i.e. terminated by mutual agreement. This of course gave St Marylebone an immediate right to occupy the house. They then sued Fairweather, claiming possession of the shed.

Fairweather argued that because of the adverse possession he had acquired title to the rest of the term of the leasehold estate over the shed; the landlord (he said) could not claim the land until 1992! This neat, logical argument was not accepted by the House of Lords. Why not?

(a)   A tenant's right to occupy land leased to him is lost after 12 years' adverse possession against him. Thus from 1932 onwards, T could not claim possession of the shed from M or (later) Fairweather.

(b)   Where there has been 12 years' adverse possession it is wrong to say that the adverse possessor acquires the estate of the person he has displaced. Rather the adverse possessor has a completely new title. Thus Fairweather had **not** acquired T's leasehold estate over the shed lasting until 1992.

(c)   Instead, Fairweather had a defective title to the land; defective in the sense that in certain circumstances (see (e) below) he could be ousted by the landlord.

(d)   Where (under proposition (a) above) the tenant has lost the right to occupy the land to an adverse possessor, the lease is not totally destroyed. It continues to have a **notional existence** between landlord and tenant.

(e)   When this 'notional lease' is terminated by agreement between the landlord and tenant, by forfeiture or by the expiry of the originally agreed period, the landlord gains an immediate right to claim possession of the land from the adverse possessor.

(f)   The landlord will be 'time-barred' only if he allows 12 years to elapse from the termination of the notional lease without bringing proceedings against the adverse possessor.

In the *St Marylebone* case the plaintiffs sued almost immediately after the termination of the notional lease. Thus Fairweather, who thought he had got the shed until 1992, was evicted some 30 years earlier than he had anticipated.

I hope that you have already realised that anybody who (like Fairweather) maintains adverse possession against a tenant, even for well over 12 years, is going to be in a very insecure position. If the notional lease is terminated in any way, the adverse possessor can expect almost immediate eviction.

ACTIVITY 76

Consider the following situation. Suppose in 1975, Lawrence, the owner in fee simple of Dull Shack, leased Dull Shack to Terry for 99 years at a nominal rent. In 1977, Terry became a permanent invalid, and forgot all about his lease of Dull Shack. Lawrence did not bother to collect the nominal rent.

In 1980, Nina, a neighbour, took adverse possession of Dull Shack, using it for general storage purposes. She has continued in adverse possession ever since. Terry has recently remembered his lease of Dull Shack, and he also is informed that Nina is in adverse possession. What can he do to get Dull Shack back? (There are two, alternative answers.)

(a)   Terry should approach Lawrence, and suggest the following 'deal'–

(i)   Terry surrenders the lease to Lawrence.

(ii)   Lawrence sues Nina for possession.

(iii) Having got possession Lawrence grants a fresh lease to Terry.

I would expect Lawrence to charge a price for his cooperation.

(b)   An alternative 'deal', which involves less trouble to Lawrence, is as follows–

(i)   Terry buys Lawrence's fee simple in reversion.

(ii)   This (seemingly) brings about a termination of the 'notional lease' by 'merger'. (The same person cannot be both landlord and tenant!)

(iii) In his new capacity as owner of a fee simple, Terry sues Nina for possession. As this fee simple has not been extinguished by adverse possession, Terry should win.

21.5.2 THE PROBLEM OF A TENANT ENCROACHING ON ADJOINING LAND

Figure 6

Westacre		Centreacre		Eastacre

In 1976, Leonora leased Centreacre to Thomas for 21 years. In 1978, Thomas moved both the eastern and western fences of Centreacre a few feet so as to encroach upon Westacre and Eastacre. The original fee simple in Westacre belongs to Leonora. The original fee simple in Eastacre belongs to Norman.

The fences have remained in their 1978 position. In effect Thomas has for the last umpteen years maintained adverse possession of two strips of land. Since 1990, no one will have been able to claim those strips from him. But what happens in 1997, when his lease expires?

The principles applicable in this kind of situation were restated in *Smirk* v *Lyndale Developments Ltd* [1975] 1 All ER 690. Where a lessee encroaches upon other land, the encroachment is presumed to be an extention in the 'locus' of the lease. This means that the tenant is presumed merely to be expanding the area granted to him. This is so whether the land encroached upon belongs to a stranger or to the lessee's landlord.

Consider, therefore, what the answer is to our 'Thomas' problem. Remember that there are two separate strips of land to think about.

Applying the law set out in *Smirk* v *Lyndale* to our example of Thomas, the outcome is not favourable to him! When his lease expires in 1997 he will not be able to retain either of the two strips. Leonora will regain the strip Thomas 'pinched' from Westacre. She will also get the strip which Thomas 'pinched' from Norman's Eastacre.

Thomas's only hope of retaining one or both of the strips is if he can rebut the presumption that he is expanding the area of his lease. It seems that to rebut the presumption he would have to show that he was treating the land encroached upon as distinct from the land leased.

Suppose that the lease of Centreacre contained a covenant that Thomas would not keep dogs on the land. Suppose that on the strip 'pinched' from Westacre he has since 1978 kept kennels full of Alsatians, Rottweilers etc., (or, if you like, Chihuahuas and Pekinese). I think that Thomas will be able to claim that he has a permanent title to the western strip. He will be able to tell Leonora that she cannot have this strip back. His dogs (of whatever breed) will not have to move to a new home!

21.6   Adverse Possession Where Land is Held in Trust

The following rules apply whether land is held under a strict settlement or under a trust for sale.

It is essential to consider the equitable interests under the trust separate from the legal estate:

(a) An equitable interest in possession is time-barred after 12 years' adverse possession of the land.

(b) An equitable interest in remainder or reversion is time-barred after—

    (i) 12 years from the adverse possession starting; **or**
   (ii) six years from the equitable interest coming into possession,
              whichever is later

(c) The legal estate is not time-barred until all equitable interests under the trust have been time-barred.

Suppose Mauveacre has since 1976 been held in trust for Anthea for life, remainder to Bertram in fee simple. (It does not matter whether the trust is a strict settlement or a trust for sale. It does not matter whether the legal title is vested in Anthea as life tenant or in independent trustees.)

Suppose that Squarm took adverse possession of Mauveacre in 1981 and has maintained adverse possession ever since. Anthea died in early 1995:

(1) Anthea's equitable life interest was 'time-barred' back in 1993. See rule (a) above.

(2) Bertram's equitable fee simple will not be time-barred until 2001. See rule (b)(ii) above.

(3) The legal estate (whoever has got it) will also be time-barred in 2001. See rule (c) above.

Suppose now that Anthea had died in 1986, only five years after adverse possession had commenced.

(a) In what year was Bertram's equitable interest time-barred?

(b) In what year was the legal estate time-barred?

Bertram's equitable interest was time-barred in 1993, applying rule (b)(i). Applying rule (c), the legal estate was also time-barred in 1993.

21.7 Time Starts Running Afresh by Acknowledgement of Title

If an adverse possessor, with time running in his favour, acknowledges the original owner's title, time stops running in his favour. A new 12-year period starts from the date of the acknowledgement of title.

By 'acknowledgement of title' is meant any direct or indirect recognition by the adverse possessor of the original owner's title, provided it is in writing and signed by the adverse possessor and addressed to the original owner.

In *Edginton* v *Clark* [1963] 3 All ER 468, the adverse possessor wrote to the original owner of the land offering to buy. The adverse possessor was held to have acknowledged title.

21.7.1 ACKNOWLEDGEMENT OF TITLE MADE BY PERSON IN WHOSE FAVOUR TIME HAS ALREADY RUN IS OF NO EFFECT

Suppose that in 1982, Squirt took adverse possession of Greenacre, the original owner of which was Oswald. Squirt has maintained adverse possession ever since. In 1995, Oswald writes to Squirt offering to 'sell' Greenacre. Squirt immediately writes back, 'Dear Oswald, I am interested in buying Greenacre from you, I will go and see my solicitor'. What will the solicitor advise?

Squirt's solicitor will advise him that Oswald's title was time-barred in 1994. What about the letter? Fortunately for Squirt, it was sent too late!

Squirt's position must be contrasted with that of the defendant 'Tillson' in *Colchester Borough* v *Smith* [1992] 2 All ER 561. Tillson had been (apparently) in adverse possession of the plaintiff's land for well over 12 years. Despite that fact, the plaintiff began proceedings for possession against him. These **earlier** proceedings were **compromised** on the terms:

(a)   that Tillson accepted that the plaintiff still owned the land;

(b)   that the plaintiff granted Tillson a lease of the land.

In **later** proceedings for possession brought on the expiry of the lease, Tillson claimed that he had a freehold title by virtue of adverse possession. The Court of Appeal ruled that Tillson was bound by the earlier compromise and therefore was estopped from disputing the plaintiff's title to the freehold.

21.7.2 NATURE OF TITLE ACQUIRED UNDER LIMITATION ACTS WHERE TITLE ADVERSELY POSSESSED AGAINST IS UNREGISTERED

When time runs out there is not an automatic 'statutory conveyance' of the original owner's title to the adverse possessor. In the Squirt-Oswald example in **SAQ 116**, Oswald's fee simple in Greenacre was destroyed in 1994. Squirt has a completely new fee simple based on his long possession of Greenacre.

An adverse possessor does, however, take 'his' land subject to third-party rights such as easements, profits and restrictive covenants. This was made clear in *Re Nisbet and Potts Contract* [1906] 1 Ch 386, which also held that an adverse possessor was not a 'purchaser' for the purposes of the doctrine of notice. Neither will an adverse possessor be a purchaser for the purposes of modern legislation such as the Land Charges Acts.

21.8 Adverse Possession Where the Title Possessed Against is Registered Land

It will be best to begin with two preliminary comments. First, you may be surprised that the law relating to adverse possession applies where the land is registered land. Many foreign lawyers familiar with continental systems of land registration would share your surprise. The very fact that adverse possession applies to registered land further undermines the efficiency and accuracy of our system of land registration.

Secondly, it is only in the last 25 to 30 years that there have been (outside London) large numbers of registered titles. This probably explains why there is very little case law on the impact of adverse possession on a registered title.

21.8.1 THE THREE CRUCIAL POINTS WHEN CONSIDERING ADVERSE POSSESSION AGAINST A REGISTERED TITLE

21.8.1.1 Section 75(1) of the Land Registration Act 1925

This provides:

> The Limitation Acts shall apply to registered land in the same manner and to the same extent as those Acts apply to land not registered, except that where, if the land were not registered, the estate of the person registered as proprietor would be extinguished, such estate shall not be extinguished but shall be deemed to be held by the proprietor for the time being in trust for the person who, by virtue of the said Acts, has acquired title against any proprietor . . .

Dopey was the original owner in fee simple of Greyacre. In 1982 Squall took adverse possession and has maintained it ever since. Now if Dopey's fee simple in Greyacre was unregistered, that fee simple would have been destroyed in 1994. Squall gets a new fee simple based on his long possession.

What if (ever since he acquired the land in 1980) Dopey was registered proprietor of Greyacre?

Applying s. 75(1), if Dopey is registered proprietor in fee simple of Greyacre, his fee simple is not destroyed in 1994. Rather he holds that fee simple under a 'bare trust' in trust for Squall, who has a new equitable fee simple.

21.8.1.2   Section 70(1)(f) of the Land Registration Act 1925

This provision makes the rights of an adverse possessor an overriding interest. Therefore Squall's equitable fee simple would automatically bind a purchaser of Dopey's legal title. I do not think the purchaser will be too happy!

21.8.1.3   Rectification of the register

Although s. 70(1)(f) of the Act gives him considerable security, an adverse possessor in whose favour time has already run can apply for rectification of the register. Provided there is sufficient proof of the adverse possession, the Registrar must rectify the register. This rectification in effect transfers the legal fee simple from the original owner (Dopey) to the adverse possessor (Squall). The original owner (Dopey) is not compensated in any way.

21.9   Adverse Possession Against the Registered Proprietor of a Lease

This is a tricky area of law. You should carefully distinguish two situations from each other.

21.9.1   TWELVE YEARS' ADVERSE POSSESSION BUT NO RECTIFICATION OF THE REGISTER

Suppose adverse possession is taken against a lessee and maintained for 12 years, but the adverse possessor does not bother to have the register rectified. (It is quite possible that the adverse possessor does not know that he can apply for rectification.) As a result of s. 75(1) of the Land Registration Act 1925 (see **21.8.1**), the registered proprietor of the lease will hold that lease on trust for the adverse possessor.

Suppose further that the registered proprietor of the lease, notwithstanding the existence of this trust, 'pulls the *St Marylebone* trick' (see **21.5.1**). He surrenders the lease to the landlord, who sues the adverse possessor for immediate possession.

ACTIVITY 78

Now you should read the extracts from *St Marylebone* set out in *Cases and Materials* (21.7.1). You will see that in my earlier explanation of the case at 21.5.1 one important fact was omitted. What was it?

I deliberately omitted to tell you that the 99-year lease was registered title! The House of Lords, however, considered this to be irrelevant, deciding the case under principles (already discussed) which it considered to be applicable equally to both unregistered and registered titles.

Counsel for Fairweather did argue that when the legal lease was surrendered, such a surrender could not destroy Fairweather's **equitable** rights. Indeed, he could have argued that the surrender was a breach of trust and therefore did not destroy the equitable interest under the trust!

Their Lordships rejected the argument, based on s. 75(1), that the equitable rights of Fairweather were not destroyed by the surrender. Lord Denning (of all people) dismissed the s. 75(1) provision as merely 'machinery so as to apply the Limitation Acts to registered land'.

I think that if a case like *St Marylebone* were to occur today the House of Lords would reconsider its decision on the s. 75(1) point. It would hold that the surrender was a breach of the trust imposed by s. 75(1), and that therefore it did not destroy the adverse possessor's equitable rights.

I think the House would reconsider for two reasons. First, it is now appreciated (as it was not 30 years ago) that there can be substantive differences between property rights in registered land and property rights in unregistered land. The House of Lords itself realised this in 1980 in *Williams and Glyns Bank* v *Boland* (do you remember my 'tale of two fields' at **10.3.5**?).

Secondly, the result of *St Marylebone*, when put alongside the result in *Spectrum Investments* v *Holmes* (discussed below), is very anomalous.

21.9.2   TWELVE YEARS' ADVERSE POSSESSION AND THERE IS RECTIFICATION OF THE REGISTER

Adverse possession is taken against a lessee and maintained for 12 years. The adverse possessor **then does have the register rectified** and becomes the registered proprietor of the lease. Later the **original lessee** purports to surrender the lease to the owner of the fee simple. The owner of the fee simple sues for possession.

This is exactly what happened in *Spectrum Investments* v *Holmes* [1981] 1 All ER 6. The judge (Browne-Wilkinson J, now Lord Browne-Wilkinson) held that the original tenant ceased to have any estate in the land once the register was rectified. Thus the 'surrender' of the lease was totally ineffective. The fee simple was still subject to the lease vested in the (former) adverse possessor.

Consider what an adverse possessor should do if he has maintained adverse possession for 12 years (or more) against a registered proprietor of a leasehold estate.

Just in case *St Marylebone* is still correct on the s. 75(1) point, any adverse possessor who has maintained adverse possession for 12 years against a registered lease should **rush off** and apply to have the register rectified in his favour. Once rectified, the '*St Marylebone*' trick cannot be played against him.

The rectification of the register does, however, have a drawback for the (former) adverse possessor. It seems that he will be brought into privity of estate with the landlord, and therefore become liable on the covenants, e.g., he will be liable to pay the rent.

21.10 Conclusion

I hope you now see why at the beginning of this chapter I indicated that adverse possession is a basically simple concept which brings with it complex ramifications. The *St Marylebone* case (in particular) gives rise to a lot of difficulties. (It is incidentally the one House of Lords land law case which I personally think was wrongly decided.)

Should the concept be abolished? Many non-lawyers consider that the concept of adverse possession is absurd. 'It's legalised theft.' (Actually, land cannot be stolen.) What arguments are there in defence of it? As I previously stated, the concept is essential to the proper operation of **unregistered** title. By destroying stale claims to ownership, the concept ensures that the person who (together with his predecessors in title) has been in control of unregistered land for a lengthy period is indeed the owner.

This argument cannot be applied to **registered** land. The only arguments which can justify applying adverse possession to registered land are socio-economic and perhaps controversial. Land is a scarce commodity, and 'people' like Mrs Treloar, Williams Brothers Ltd and Buckinghamshire County Council should not allow land to lie derelict. By contrast, people like Messrs. Nute (father and son), Raftery and Moran should be rewarded for their efforts.

21.11   End of Chapter Assessment Question

Edwina holds an 80 year lease (granted in 1965) over Greenacre and a freehold title to Redacre. The two plots adjoin and Edwina uses most of the land for her business as a scrap merchant. However she has left vacant part of the land ('Grey Land'). Grey Land is partly within Greenacre and partly within Redacre.

In 1982 Freda, the owner of nearby Great House, started to cultivate Grey Land as an ornamental garden. Freda admits that, 'I have known all along that Grey Land belongs to Edwina'. Indeed in 1995 Freda wrote to Edwina offering to buy Grey Land. (Edwina did not reply to this letter.)

Edwina's business is now expanding, and she wishes to regain possession of Grey Land.

Advise Edwina.

See *Cases and Materials* (21.9) for a specimen answer.

CHAPTER TWENTY-TWO

RECTIFICATION OF THE REGISTER OF TITLE

22.1 Objectives

By the end of this chapter you should:

■ be familiar with the basic grounds upon which the register of title can be rectified;

■ be able to explain the very limited circumstances in which rectification can be obtained against a registered proprietor in possession;

■ be able to advise on the circumstances in which a registered proprietor against whom rectification is ordered can be awarded compensation ('indemnity');

■ be able to identify the (limited) circumstances in which a claimant for rectification who is refused rectification can be awarded compensation ('indemnity').

22.2 Introduction

Rectification of the register is a short but not unimportant topic. It is natural to deal with it immediately after adverse possession. As I indicated in the previous chapter, if somebody maintains adverse possession against a registered proprietor for the requisite period, usually 12 years, he can apply to have the register rectified. On the register being rectified, the original owner ceases to have a legal title and the (former) adverse possessor acquires a legal title.

Rectification of the register is not, however, confined to adverse possession situations. The Land Registry is nowadays an enormous organisation, so the occasional error is bound to occur. Cases where crooks and fraudsters have got themselves registered as owners of land to which they are not entitled are also not unknown.

22.3 The Statutory Framework

In the case of *Norwich and Peterborough Building Society v Steed* [1993] 1 All ER 330, the Court of Appeal emphasised that the courts' powers to order rectification of the register are strictly confined to the grounds set out in s. 82 of the Land Registration Act 1925.

The basic grounds for rectifying the register are set out in s. 82(1) of the Land Registration Act 1925. If, however, rectification of the register is sought against a 'registered proprietor in possession' (most potential rectification cases which are not adverse possession will fall into this category), the conditions in s. 82(3) **will also have to be satisfied**.

22.3.1   THE BASIC GROUNDS FOR RECTIFICATION

22.3.1.1   Rectification by court order

The Land Registration Act 1925, s. 82(1), provides that the register may be rectified:

(a)   . . . where a court . . . has decided that any person is entitled to any estate right or interest in or to any registered land or charge, and as a consequence of such decision such court is of opinion that a rectification of the register is required, . . .

(b)   . . . where the court, on the application . . . of any person who is aggrieved by any entry made in, or by the omission of any entry from, the register, or by any default being made, or unnecessary delay taking place, in the making of any entry in the register, makes an order for the rectification of the register.

22.3.1.2   Rectification by court order or by the registrar

Section 82(1) of the 1925 Act further provides that rectification of the register may take place:

(c)   In any case and at any time with the consent of all persons interested;

(d)   Where the court or the registrar is satisfied that any entry in the register has been obtained by fraud;

(e)   Where two or more persons are, by mistake, registered as proprietors of the same registered estate or of the same charge;

(f)   Where a mortgagee has been registered as proprietor of the land instead of as proprietor of a charge . . .

(g)   Where a legal estate has been registered in the name of a person who if the land had not been registered would not have been the estate owner;

(h)   In any other case where by reason of any error or omission in the register, or by reason of any entry made under a mistake, it may be deemed just to rectify the register.

The above looks a very intimidating list. However, I should immediately add that para. (g) is by far the most important, and is the only one which needs extended discussion.

Paragraph (g) covers two very important, and very differing situations. We consider them in **22.3.2** and **22.3.3** below.

22.3.2   RECTIFICATION FOR ADVERSE POSSESSION

If Oliver was owner of Dullacre, unregistered title, and adverse possession was maintained for 12 years against him, Oliver would on the expiry of the time limit cease to own the legal title to Dullacre. If Dullacre were registered title, Oliver would continue to hold the legal title notwithstanding the 12 years' adverse possession against him. He would, of course, be subject:

(a)   to the 'trust' in favour of the adverse possessor created by s.75(1) of the Land Registration Act 1925 (see **21.8.1**);

(b)   to a claim for rectification against him under s. 82(1)(g).

22.3.3 RECTIFICATION WHERE THERE IS 'DOUBLE CONVEYANCING'

'Double conveyancing' occurs where somebody owns a piece of land, conveys that land to one person, and then later purports to convey **the same land** to somebody else.

Consider the following example of 'double conveyancing' on the assumption that all the titles involved are unregistered. X owned the freehold to Greenfield; Greenfield included a small area known as Greypatch.

In 1987, X sold Greypatch to Y; the legal estate to Greypatch was conveyed to Y. It would be the normal practice for Y to ensure that the fact of the sale of Greypatch was endorsed upon the title deeds to Greenfield. Y (perhaps he was a 'do-it-yourself conveyancer') failed to do so. In 1994, X (purportedly) conveyed the whole of Greenfield, including Greypatch, to Z. Who owns Greypatch?

The answer is (of course) Y. X, having given up ownership of Greypatch to Y, cannot convey it to Z.

What if compulsory registration intervenes between the two conveyances?

Change (slightly) the facts of SAQ 118. Suppose in 1988 the district in which Greenfield is situated became an area of compulsory registration of title, and in 1994 Z applied for registration as proprietor of the whole of Greenfield. Z presented to the registry a perfect set of title deeds for the whole of Greenfield. What will the registry do?

The registry will of course grant Z an absolute title to Greenfield, including Greypatch. Z will therefore become legal owner of Greypatch. Y will lose his title to Greypatch, but he could seek rectification under s. 82(1)(g) of the 1925 Act.

22.3.4 RECTIFICATION AGAINST A REGISTERED PROPRIETOR IN POSSESSION

Section 82(3) of the Land Registration Act 1925, which is designed to protect 'registered proprietors in possession', will apply in most cases where rectification is sought under s. 82(1). (For a case, not involving adverse possession, where s. 82(3) did not apply, see *Argyle Building Society* v *Hammond* (1984) 49 P and CR 148.)

Section 82(3) was amended in 1977 to give even greater protection to the registered proprietor in possession. Pre-1977, there were four headings under which a registered proprietor in possession could lose his title through rectification. Since 1977, there have been only three. Moreover, the first of the surviving three headings was changed in 1977 in a manner favourable to existing registered proprietors.

I believe it actually helps to understand the present position if we also examine the pre-1977 law.

22.3.4.1   Registered proprietor 'to blame' for the wrong registration

Pre-1977

Section 82(3)(a) provided for rectification against a registered proprietor in possession where:

> [the proprietor] has caused or substantially contributed, by his act, neglect or default, to the fraud, mistake or omission in consequence of which such rectification is sought;

This provision was applied in *Re 139 Deptford High Street* [1951] 1 All ER 950.

Read the extracts from this case in *Cases and Materials* (22.1.2.1). What caused the registry to make an error?

Prior to 1948, No. 139 was unregistered title. In 1948, V sold No. 139 to P. The conveyance, which had no plan attached, described the land as 'all that shop and dwelling house situate and known as 139, High Street, Deptford in the County of London'. P applied for first registration.

It appears that V, P, their respective legal advisers, and the Land Registry all thought that No. 139 included a small piece of disused land at the back next to the railway. P was registered as proprietor of the dwelling house/shop **and the land at the back**. In fact this land really 'belonged to' British Railways. The registration thus deprived the railway of that small piece of land. When the railway found out, it sought rectification of the register.

To succeed against P the railway not only had to prove a case under s. 82(1)(g), it also had to prove a case under s. 82(3)(a).

Rectification was granted. The judge ruled that P was caught by s. 82(3)(a), because P had 'contributed' to the error at the registry. P had done so by putting forward documents for registration which were inaccurate in that they appeared to include the disused ground which in fact belonged to the railway. It did not matter that P had been neither fraudulent nor negligent in putting forward inaccurate documents. It did not matter that P neither knew nor ought to have known that 'number 139' did not include the disused ground at the back.

Post-1977

Section 82(3)(a) has now been amended to give greater protection to a registered proprietor in possession. Under the new provision rectification can be granted only where '. . . the proprietor has caused or substantially contributed to the error or omission **by fraud or lack of proper care'** (emphasis added).

What if a case like *Re 139 Deptford High Street* were to occur today; would rectification be granted?

Rectification of the register would be refused. A registered proprietor in possession who had obtained registration by putting forward inaccurate document(s) would now be caught under the s. 82(3)(1)(a) only if either:

(a) he knew that the document(s) were inaccurate (that would be a case of fraud); or

(b) he ought to have known that the documents were inaccurate (that would be a case of 'lack of proper care').

22.3.4.2 Void disposition in favour of a registered proprietor

Pre-1977

Section 82(3)(b) used to provide for rectification of the register against a proprietor in possession:

> [where] the immediate disposition to [the registered proprietor] was void, or the disposition to any person through whom he claims other than for valuable consideration was void.

Under this provision, rectification could be obtained against a proprietor who had been registered on the strength of a conveyance or land transfer which was **void** because it was a forgery, or because it was vitiated by fundamental mistake. It did not matter whether the proprietor knew or ought to have known that the document was invalid.

Post-1977

Section 82(3)(b) was the 'heading' completely removed in 1977.

About the time of the First World War there was a notorious criminal at work in London. He operated in the following way:

(a) **He would find a wealthy spinster who owned her own house.**

(b)   He would marry her.

(c)   He would forge a conveyance or land transfer of her house in his favour.

(d)   On the strength of the forgery, he got himself registered as proprietor of the house.

(e)   He would murder the lady by drowning her in the bath.

And so on . . .

When he was caught, the personal representatives of the unfortunate ladies sought and obtained rectification of the register against the crook under s. 82(3)(b). How would such a case be dealt with today (under s. 82) if the facts were to recur?

Anybody who obtains registration today by putting forward a 'void' document (e.g. a forgery) which he knew or ought to have known was invalid would still be caught by s. 82(3)(a). Clearly the crook knew that the conveyances and land transfers he was putting forward for registration were forgeries.

22.3.4.3   Unjust not to rectify the register

Section 82(3)(c) provides for rectification against a registered proprietor in possession:

> [where] for any other reason, in any particular case, it is considered that it would be unjust not to rectify the register against [the registered proprietor].

Three points should be made about this provision:

(a)   It is clear from its context and wording (particularly the use of a double negative) that this provision should be used only in a case where it is absolutely clear that justice demands that the register be rectified.

(b)   This provision was not changed in 1977.

(c)   There has been only one case of significance involving this provision (*Epps* v *Esso* [1973] 2 All ER 465). In that case, Templeman J, applying the no-nonsense approach for which he (as Lord Templeman) has become famous, refused rectification. The approach adopted by Templeman J in *Epps* is very much in line with the approach adopted by Parliament in 1977 when it amended s. 82(3).

ACTIVITY 81

Read the extracts from *Epps* v *Esso* in *Cases and Materials* (22.1.2.2). You should note carefully both the arguments Templeman J rejected and those he accepted.

The figure below illustrates the area of land involved in *Epps* v *Esso*.

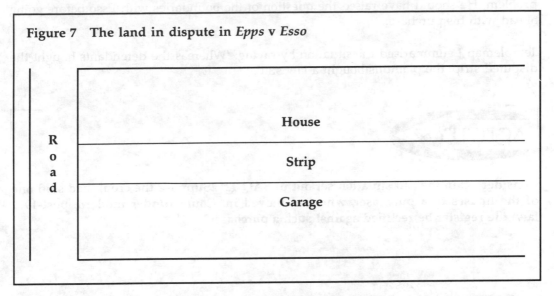

Figure 7 The land in dispute in *Epps* v *Esso*

From **1935 to 1955**, C had owned the whole of the relevant area, situated in Gillingham, Kent.

In **1955**, C's personal representatives conveyed the house **and strip** to Edna Jones. She covenanted to erect a wall between the strip and the garage, but failed to do so. The existing fence between strip and house remained *in situ*. The strip therefore appeared to 'belong to' the garage.

In **1957** Gillingham became an area of compulsory registration.

In **1959**, C's personal representatives conveyed the garage and strip to Ball. Ball applied for first registration, and was registered as proprietor of both garage and strip. There was thus a 'double conveyancing' situation (see **2.2.3.3**). But as Ball, the second purchaser, had become registered proprietor of the strip, he had legal title, and not the first purchaser, Edna Jones. (This is the same as Greypatch in **SAQ 118**.)

Since **1959** the strip has been in use as part of the garage. In **1964**, Ball sold the garage including the strip, to Esso; Esso became registered proprietor.

In **1968** Edna Jones's personal representatives sold the house **and purported to sell the strip** to Epps, but the Land Registry refused to register him as proprietor of the strip. He applied for rectification. Epps's only hope lay in s. 82(3)(c).

Templeman J regarded as totally irrelevant the following two arguments:

(a) Epps was a 'little man' claiming rectification against a huge organisation. A strip 11 feet by 80 feet was a lot of land for Epps; to a multinational like Esso it was tiny.

(b) That the rules governing the grant of 'indemnity' (i.e. compensation) were much more generous to Esso than to Epps. If rectification had been granted against Esso, it would have got full compensation at a 1973 valuation. If rectification was refused, Epps would seemingly get no compensation. (See **22.4.2**.)

Templeman J was of the view that, 'Justice in the present case lies wholly with the defendants'. He applied what I call 'a comparative conveyancing care' approach. When Esso purchased the garage, both the register and the physical layout of the site indicated that the strip was part of the garage. When Epps purchased the house the title deeds said that the strip was part of the house. But the fact that no brick wall had been erected, and the physical appearance of the site, should have warned him that there was a problem. He should have raised the question of the boundaries with Esso before going ahead with his purchase.

Templeman J summarised the situation by saying: 'Whereas the defendants bought the disputed strip, the plaintiffs bought a law suit'.

Consider again the sad situation set out in SAQ 121. Suppose the crook had sold one of the houses to a purchaser, who had moved in. Could (under modern, post-1977 law) the register be rectified against such a purchaser?

First, the personal representative of the deceased women would not have an overriding interest, so the heading at **23.3.4.4** below would not apply. That leaves either s. 82(3)(c) or s. 82(3)(a). I would submit that the personal representatives would succeed in getting rectification only if they could show that the purchaser knew or ought to have known that the crook had gained title by criminal activities (s. 82(3)(a)).

22.3.4.4   Rectification 'for the purpose of giving effect to an overriding interest'

This heading was unaffected by the 1977 changes. As a registered proprietor is in any event bound by an overriding interest, he cannot really object if the register is rectified to give effect to that interest.

22.4   Indemnity

22.4.1   INDEMNITY FOR A REGISTERED PROPRIETOR WHERE RECTIFICATION IS GRANTED

In practice, rectifications of the register are not that common, and that is something which I think should remain the case. (Templeman J in *Epps* v *Esso* was clearly of the same view.)

In those cases where rectification is ordered, s. 83 of the Land Registration Act 1925 becomes relevant. **Prima facie**, a registered proprietor against whom rectification is granted is entitled to an indemnity, i.e. compensation. He will get the value of the estate or interest he loses, valued as at the date of rectification. (The building society in *Argyle B.S.* v *Hammond* would have obtained full indemnity under this rule.)

A registered proprietor rectified against will, however, get no indemnity whatsoever if:

(a)   rectification is to give effect to an overriding interest; (*Re Chowood* [1933] Ch 574); or

(b)   the applicant for indemnity has caused or substantially contributed to the error by fraud or lack of proper care (s. 83(5)).

Exception (a) above is clearly logical. A proprietor is in any event bound by an overriding interest. He thus loses nothing when the register is rectified against him. In *Re Chowood*, an adverse possessor had gained title to part of a piece of land of which Chowood Ltd was registered proprietor. The adverse possessor obtained rectification of the register. Chowood Ltd was held not to be entitled to any indemnity. The adverse possessor had an overriding interest under the Land Registration Act s. 70(1)(f), and Chowood lost nothing as a result of the rectification.

Exception (b) above is the current law, but has been criticised as being rather harsh. A registered proprietor who was perhaps only 'slightly careless' loses all claim to compensation if the register is rectified. It has been suggested that such a proprietor should be awarded partial compensation, i.e. a percentage of the full value of the land.

(There is an analogy here from the law of tort. Prior to 1945 a victim of (say) a road accident partly or largely caused by the defendant's negligence but himself partly to blame, could not recover **any** damages. The Law Reform (Contributory Negligence) Act 1945 allows the court to award the victim an appropriate percentage of the damages he would have recovered if he had been innocent of all blame. It could be said that the law relating to indemnity when the register is rectified is in a 'pre-1945' state!)

22.4.2   INDEMNITY FOR A PERSON WHO IS REFUSED RECTIFICATION

Section 83(6) of the 1925 Act is designed to provide for the payment of indemnity where the restrictive provisions of s. 82(3) lead to rectification being refused despite some error in the registry. This form of indemnity is supposed to protect somebody like Epps (see **22.3.4.3**). However, there are two drawbacks:

Re-read the latter part of the judgment of Templeman J in *Epps, Cases and Materials* (22.1.2.2) and try to identify those drawbacks.

You should have identified the following drawbacks:

(a)   The land 'lost' is valued at the date the error occurred. (In *Epps* v *Esso* this would be 1959, not 1973.)

(b)   By s. 83(11) of the Land Registration Act 1925, this kind of claim for indemnity must be brought within six years of the error in the register occurring. Epps did not bring his claim until 1971, so he was too late to claim any compensation. Epps was out of time!

22.5   Conclusion

It does seem that a rectification of the register for reasons other than adverse possession is a relatively rare occurrence. This is fortunate. If rectifications were frequent, much of the purpose and value of registration of title would be lost. The whole purpose of land registration is to guarantee the security of titles. It is therefore not surprising that Parliament (s. 82(3) and the changes made in 1977) and the courts (*Epps* v *Esso; Norwich and Peterborough Building Society* v *Steel*) have reinforced the policy of limiting cases for rectification.

It may also be seen as encouraging that the Land Registry faces relatively few claims for indemnity. This is at least partly due to the efficiency of the registry. But critics would argue that the rules for indemnity are **too** restrictive. Epps rightly lost his claim for rectification. But it was tough that he did not get any compensation either.

22.6   End of Chapter Assessment Question

The Aberconwy District (Llandudno, Conwy, Llanrwst etc.) became an area of compulsory registration of title on 1 December 1988.

In 1987 Geoffrey purchased a small piece of land 'Lomasacre' situated in Aberconwy. Lomasacre formed a small part of the vast 'Brooke Estate' owned by John. Geoffrey did his own conveyancing; as a result no indorsement referring to the sale off of Lomasacre was placed on the deeds to the Brooke Estate.

Geoffrey has only visited Lomasacre on one occasion since he purchased it; on that occasion he dumped some rusting railings on part of the land.

Last week John sold the whole of the Brooke Estate to Malcolm; Malcolm believes that Lomasacre is part of the land he has purchased. He has successfully applied for registration as proprietor of the whole of the Brooke Estate.

Discuss.

See *Cases and Materials* (22.4) for a specimen answer.

CHAPTER TWENTY-THREE

THE ESSENTIAL CHARACTERISTICS OF EASEMENTS

23.1 Objectives

By the end of this chapter you should be able to:

■ appreciate the wide variety of rights which can exist as easements;

■ explain the (somewhat ill-defined) limits on the type of right which can be an easement;

■ distinguish between dominant and servient land.

23.2 Introduction

This chapter, and the two which follow it, deal with the law of easements. It will be rather short, but perhaps not very satisfying. In it we will be considering the question, 'What kinds of rights does the law recognise as easements?'. As I hinted in the objectives set out above, we can give only a vague answer to that question.

23.3 Preliminary Considerations

Re-read 1.4.3 on easements. Also re-read 1.4.2 on restrictive covenants and 1.4.4 on profits à prendre. You should note that quite a wide variety of rights can exist as easements, but be careful not to confuse easements with either restrictive covenants or with profits.

SAQ 122

What do a right of way, a right of support, a right of light, and a right to use a neighbour's toilet have in common?

They are all rights which English law recognises as easements.

In continental legal systems the concept equivalent to easements is 'servitudes'. Modern continental systems, such as those in France and Germany, have a clear list of types of servitude, and no new types of servitude can be recognised. English law is more flexible. There is no exhaustive list of types of easement, and since the Second World War new types of easement have been recognised. In particular:

(a)   the right of the occupants of one flat to use the toilet in a neighbouring flat: *Miller v Emcer Products Ltd* [1956] 1 All ER 237;

(b)   the right of owners of houses situated around a 'private square' to use the private garden in the middle of the square for relaxation purposes: *Re Ellenborough Park* [1955] 3 All ER 667;

(c)   the right of owners of a factory to use a neighbouring airfield. The easement allowed visitors to the factory to fly their private aircraft in and out of the airfield: *Dowty Boulton Paul* v *Wolverhampton Corporation (No. 2)* [1973] 2 All ER 491.

Courts do not have a completely free hand to recognise (some would say 'invent') new easements. In *Phipps* v *Pears* [1964] 2 All ER 35, the Court of Appeal refused to accept as an easement the (alleged) right of one building to be protected from the weather by another building.

Any alleged easement (whether it is of a new type or one of the existing, well-recognised categories) must comply with the four broad principles which I am about to discuss in **23.4** to **23.7** below.

23.4   There must be a Dominant and a Servient Tenement

As I explained in **Chapter 1 (1.4.3)**, an easement can exist only if it is attached to ('appurtenant to') a piece of dominant land. Suppose Gillian owns Wideviews Farm, situated in rural Derbyshire. She executes a deed in favour of Wendy (a keen walker) granting Wendy the right to use a path which crosses the farm. Wendy owns no land whatsoever. Though the right granted by the deed will give Wendy a lot of pleasure, it is certainly not an easement.

23.5   The Easement Must Accommodate the Dominant Tenement

Suppose that in my Wideviews Farm example Wendy actually owns a house, but that house is situated in London, 150 miles away. The right to use the path across Wideviews is expressed to be for the benefit of Wendy's London house.

SAQ 123

Can Wendy's right be an easement?

It will not be an easement. A right to be an easement must 'accommodate' the dominant land; it must have some direct beneficial impact on the dominant land itself. It must not merely be for the grantee's personal benefit.

For an easement to accommodate the dominant land it is not essential that the dominant and servient land be contiguous, although they must be sufficiently near each other for the easement to be of direct benefit to the dominant land. In *Pugh* v *Savage* [1970] 2 All ER 353, there was a 'right of way' over one field to get to another field, but a third field lay between the servient and dominant fields. The right of way was held to be a valid easement.

In *Hill* v *Tupper* (1863) 159 ER 51 a rather different problem arose. The Basingstoke Canal Company owned the canal and some land on the banks of the canal. They leased the land on the banks of the canal to Hill for the purposes of a boatyard. The lease included a clause granting Hill the exclusive right to put pleasure boats on the canal. Tupper nevertheless started placing his pleasure boats on the canal.

Hill sued Tupper, claiming that his 'pleasure boat monopoly' was an easement. If the court had accepted that claim, it would have meant that the pleasure boat monopoly was a property right which could be protected by suing **anybody** who interfered with it. The court however held that the pleasure boat monopoly was **not** an easement. The monopoly did not 'accommodate' the land leased to Hill; rather it was for the benefit of Hill's business. (Hill's only remedy was to sue the canal company for breach of contract.)

SAQ 124

Suppose that in *Hill* v *Tupper*, the lease from the canal company granted Hill a right to cross the canal to get to and from his boatyard, but that right was being obstructed by Tupper's boats. Would Hill have been able to sue Tupper?

Yes, Hill will be able to sue Tupper. The right to cross the canal would be a right of way (albeit over water), and therefore Hill would have an easement, a property right which can be protected by suing **anybody** who interferes with it.

23.6   The Tenements must not be Owned and Occupied by the Same Person

Gillian owns Stouttree Farm. Stouttree Farm includes Distantfield. To get to Distantfield from the public road, Gillian drives her tractor along a track across Nearfield, which is also part of her farm. Clearly in this situation there is no question of there being an easement. A landowner such as Gillian cannot have an easement over her own land!

Suppose, however, that Gillian leases Distantfield to Horace for 10 years. The lease includes a clause that Horace shall have a right of way across Nearfield to gain access to Distantfield. This clause will create a (leasehold) easement. The two fields are, of course, **still owned** (in fee simple) by the same person, but they are **not occupied** by the same person.

23.7   'An Easement must be Capable of Forming the Subject Matter of a Grant'

What this really means is that the law is rather cautious towards any claim for a new type of easement not previously recognised. A number of criteria may be applied if some new type of easement is claimed. (The court may also consider whether a new alleged easement is analogous to any established easement. In the 'right to use a toilet' case at **23.3** the Court of Appeal was influenced by an old case which had decided that a right to use a neighbour's kitchen could amount to an easement.)

23.7.1   AN EASEMENT MUST BE CAPABLE OF REASONABLY EXACT DEFINITION

In *Harris* v *De Pinna* (1886) 33 Ch D 238, the court, applying this principle, held that there could be no easement for a general flow of air to a timber-drying shed. Similarly, there cannot be an easement for 'a beautiful view'.

An easement of light, under which a dominant building is entitled to natural light coming across the servient land, is not an exception to this rule. Where a dominant building has an easement of light over servient land, the dominant building is not entitled to an unlimited amount of natural light coming across the servient land. The House of Lords made this point clear in *Colls* v *Home and Colonial Stores* [1904] AC 179, where it was held that where there is an easement of light, 'The light reaching the windows [of the dominant building] must be such as is sufficient according to the usual notions of mankind for the comfortable enjoyment of the building, bearing in mind the type of the building and its locality'. (For a modern case applying this test, see *Allen* v *Greenwood* [1979] 1 All ER 819.)

The existence of an easement of light over a piece of land restricts the kind of buildings which can be placed on that land. Putting a building upon the servient land does not infringe the easement of light provided the natural light which remains once the building is erected is still sufficient to satisfy the test laid down in *Colls* case.

23.7.2   AN EASEMENT MUST NOT INVOLVE ANY EXPENDITURE BY THE SERVIENT OWNER

There appears to be one exception to this general rule. In rural areas you may come across the 'spurious easement' of fencing. Under this 'easement' the dominant farmer has the right to insist that the servient farmer maintain the boundary fence between their properties. Courts have repeatedly stressed that this fencing 'easement' is anomalous, and that no other exceptions to the 'no expenditure rule' will be tolerated.

The easement of **support** is not an exception to this rule. Easements of support are, of course, common, often existing where there are semi-detached or terraced buildings. Where an easement of support exists, it is the right of the dominant building not to have support from the servient building **deliberately withdrawn**. Thus, if the servient owner knocks down the servient building, with the result that the dominant building collapses, the dominant owner's rights have been infringed.

SAQ 125

What if the servient building simply falls down because of neglect by the servient owner?

The dominant owner has no claim for infringement of his easement. (He can, however, enter the servient land and, at his own expense, reconstruct the support he was getting!)

Where a private **right of way** exists, the servient owner is under no liability to maintain the way. However, the dominant owner has the right to carry out repair works.

23.7.3 AN EASEMENT MUST NOT BE SO EXTENSIVE AS TO AMOUNT TO A CLAIM TO JOINT POSSESSION OF THE SERVIENT LAND

The essence of an easement is that it is a right to make use of somebody else's land, not a claim to joint possession of that land. In *Copeland* v *Greenhalf* [1952] 1 All ER 809 the alleged servient property was a long strip of land about 150 feet long and 20 feet wide. The servient owners used the strip to gain access to their orchard.

The alleged dominant owners were 'wheelwrights', i.e. vehicle repairers. For many years they parked vehicles awaiting repair on the strip. These vehicles often occupied a large part of the strip, but the wheelwrights were always careful to leave a gap through which the 'servient owners' could pass to get to their orchard.

The wheelwrights eventually claimed that they had a prescriptive easement to park their vehicles on the strip.

ACTIVITY 85

Read *Copeland* v *Greenhalf* in *Cases and Materials* (23.4.2), noting carefully why the judge rejected the wheelwrights' claim.

The claim was rejected because the wheelwrights were in effect claiming joint possession of the land. Such a claim was (in effect) 'too big' to be an easement.

(Another interesting case is *Grigsby* v *Melville* [1973] 1 All ER 385, where, applying *Copeland* v *Greenhalf*, an alleged right to store goods in a cellar was held not to be an easement.)

In *Miller* v *Emcer Products* [1956] 1 All ER 237 (the right to use a toilet case), the Court of Appeal approved of, but distinguished, *Copeland* v *Greenhalf*. Romer LJ stated:

> In my judgment the right had all the requisite characteristics of an easement. There is no doubt as to what were intended to be the dominant and servient tenements respectively, and the right was appurtenant to the former and calculated to enhance its beneficial use and enjoyment. It is true that during the times when the dominant owner exercised the right, the owner of the servient tenement would be excluded, but this in greater or lesser degree is a common feature of many easements (for example, rights of way) and does not amount to such an ouster of the servient owner's rights as was held to be incompatible with a legal easement in *Copeland* v *Greenhalf*.

In the more recent case of *London and Blenheim Estates* v *Retail Parks* [1993] 1 All ER 307, the deputy High Court judge, Paul Baker QC (in *obiter dicta*) accepted that there could be an easement to park vehicles on a piece of (servient) land provided the servient land was sufficiently large. (This point was not considered when the case went to the Court of Appeal.) He said:

> The essential question is one of degree. If the right granted in relation to the area over which it is to be exercisable is such that it would leave the servient owner without any reasonable use of his land, whether for parking or anything else, it could not be an easement though it might be some larger or different grant.

Suppose you take a lease of one office in a large block, and that lease gives you the exclusive use of a numbered parking space in the basement car-park. Could this parking right be an easement?

Clearly not, but you could argue that you have 'exclusive possession' of the numbered space and that therefore you have a lease of the space.

23.7.4 NEW TYPES OF *NEGATIVE* EASEMENTS

The law is very cautious when it comes to a claim for a new type of *negative* easement.

It appears that easements can be classified as either **positive** easements, or **negative** easements. Easements such as rights of way or rights to use an airfield are **positive**. The essence of a positive easement is that the benefits of the easement are enjoyed by occupants of the dominant land performing some activity such as walking across the servient land or, in *Miller* v *Emcer Products*, using the toilet.

Rights of **light** and **support** are **negative** easements. The dominant land (or building) just sits there and passively enjoys the light or support it gets 'from' the servient land or building.

The effect of a negative easement is often severely to hamper the development of the servient land. The law is thus reluctant to recognise new types of negative easements. This was a major reason why the Court of Appeal in *Phipps* v *Pears* [1964] 2 All ER 35, refused to accept as an easement the (alleged) right of one building to be protected from the weather by another building.

23.8   Access to Neighbouring Land Act 1992

I should briefly mention this new piece of legislation. It is perfectly possible for an easement to exist granting the owners of the dominant property a right to go on the servient land in order to carry out maintenance and repairs to the dominant property. Such an easement is particularly useful where a building is constructed right up to the boundary with the servient property.

Unfortunately such easements for 'access for repairs' are not particularly common. Until recently a building owner who wanted to go on to neighbouring land to carry out repairs to his own building had (in the absence of an easement) to rely on getting permission from the neighbour. Some neighbours can be extremely unreasonable.

The 1992 Act was designed to solve this problem, but I must stress that it does **not** create a statutory form of easement. Rather, it allows a landowner, who needs access to a neighbour's land to carry out maintenance/repair work on his own property, to get a county court order authorising him to go on to the neighbour's land. There is, however, no automatic right to an order for access:

> An order can only be made where the works are reasonably necessary to preserve land [that includes, of course, buildings] and where they cannot be carried out, or would be substantially more difficult to carry out, without the access. Even where these requirements can be established, an order will not be made where the court concludes that it would be unreasonable to make an order due to the degree of interference caused to the neighbour's use or enjoyment of the land or due to any hardship which would be caused to the neighbour. . . .' (MacKenzie and Phillips, *A Practical Approach to Land Law*, 5th edn, p. 298)

When making an access order the court can impose conditions as to days/times, and as to other matters such as insurance.

23.9   Conclusion

The 1992 Act is a rare statutory intervention in an area of law which has otherwise been left to be developed by the courts.

The common law has not drawn up a fixed list of easements. This has the disadvantage of uncertainty, but has the great advantage of flexibility. The English law of easements can react to new technology, such as aircraft and computer cables, without the need to invoke the slow processes of the legislature.

CHAPTER TWENTY-FOUR

EXPRESS AND IMPLIED GRANT OF EASEMENTS

24.1 Objectives

By the end of this chapter you should be able to:

■ explain the basic rule for interpreting express grants (and reservations) of easements;

■ recognise the situations in which implied grant of an easement is likely to be alleged;

■ explain **and distinguish between** the four different rules for the implied grant of easements.

24.2 Introduction

This chapter (at **24.3** and **24.4**) starts with some very straightforward 'black letter' law. But I must warn you that when we reach the question of implied grant of easements (**24.5**), matters become very complex. Some (arguably rather strange) rules have developed under which a vendor (or lessor) of land creates easements over land he retains in his possession even though those easements **are not expressly mentioned** in the conveyance (or lease).

24.3 Creation of Easements (and Profits) – Legal or Equitable?

An easement or a profit is a legal interest in land provided that:

(a) it is created (expressly or impliedly) by deed, by statute or by prescription; **and**

(b) its duration is of a fee simple absolute in possession or a term of years absolute.

24.4 Express Grant and Reservation of Easements (and Profits)

There is an 'express reservation' of an easement in the following kind of situation. Bloggs owns the fee simple in Dominantacre and Servientacre. He sells Servientacre to Cluggs. Bloggs is anxious that he should have a right of way over Servientacre to get to

Dominantacre. He thus includes a clause in the conveyance of Servientacre 'reserving' an easement of way over Servientacre to get to and from Dominantacre.

The interpretation of express grants and express reservations of easements sometimes gives rise to difficulties. In *St. Edmundsbury Board of Finance* v *Clarke (No. 2)* [1975] 1 All ER 772 the Church of England originally owned a church and churchyard, and the adjoining rectory and rectory grounds. In 1945, the Church of England sold the rectory and its grounds to Clarke.

The only access to the church building was across the rectory grounds, so the conveyance to Clarke included an express reservation of an easement of way along an existing track across the rectory grounds to and from the church. Unfortunately this reservation did not make it clear whether this right of way was 'on foot only', or whether vehicles could use the track. Clarke, to the great inconvenience of weddings, funerals etc., insisted that the right of way was 'on foot only'.

Evidence established that in 1945 there had been at the churchyard end of the track two solid gateposts only about four feet apart. This fact proved fatal to the Church's claim.

The Court of Appeal held:

(a)   When interpreting an express grant or reservation of an easement, the physical circumstances of the pieces of land at the time of the grant or reservation had to be taken into account.

(b)   If, **but only if**, the doubts were not resolved by looking at the physical circumstances, the court should give the benefit of the doubt to the dominant owner and construe the grant in his favour.

The Court (applying rule (a) above) concluded that the narrow gap through the gateposts which existed back in 1945 meant that the right of way was on foot only. In view of the physical facts in 1945, rule (b) (which the Church was trying to invoke) was not applicable.

24.5   Implied Grant of Easements (and Profits)

Implied grant of easements is a complex topic. This is largely because there are four separate headings (**24.5.1** to **24.5.4** below) under which easements can be implied.

The common feature of all four headings is that originally the dominant and servient tenements were in common ownership; the dominant land is then sold off (or leased).

If certain conditions are satisfied then the grant of an easement over the servient land retained by the vendor/lessor is **implied** as one of the terms of the conveyance (or lease). As we shall see, such a result may be very convenient for the purchaser (or tenant), but very inconvenient for the vendor (landlord), who finds that he has 'impliedly' granted an easement over the land he retains.

24.5.1   WAYS OF NECESSITY

Such an easement would arise on the sale of a 'land-locked' parcel of land, i.e. a vendor sells a part of his land which has no direct access to the public highway system. The purchaser of the isolated 'land-locked' plot acquires an implied easement to cross the vendor's retained land. The vendor can fix the route of the easement, but it must be a reasonably convenient route, and once selected it cannot be varied.

The way of necessity can be used only for those purposes for which the dominant land was being used at the time the necessity arose (i.e. at the time the land became isolated). In *Corporation of London* v *Riggs* (1880) 13 Ch D 798, Riggs acquired a 'land-locked' piece of farm-land in the middle of Epping Forest. Epping Forest was (and still is) the property of the **City** of London. Riggs started building 'tea rooms' on his land. It was not disputed that Riggs had a 'way of necessity' to and from his land. However, he could use the way for farming purposes only. Neither contractors building the tea-rooms, nor his future clientèle, could use the way.

24.5.2 INTENDED EASEMENTS

If dominant land is granted for a particular purpose known to the grantor, any easement over land retained by the grantor which is **absolutely essential** in order for that purpose to be carried out is implied into the grant. The leading modern case involved a situation where the dominant land was leased for a particular purpose, but the principle would equally apply where land was sold for a specific purpose known to the grantor.

Read *Wong* v *Beaumont Property Trust* in *Cases and Materials* (24.2.2). Pay particular attention to the terms of the lease granted to Blackaby. At the time of the original grant of the lease, did anyone realise the need for a ventilating shaft?

In *Wong* v *Beaumont Property Trust* [1964] 2 All ER 119 a landlord had granted a lease of the basement of premises it owned to Blackaby. He covenanted:

(a) to run the premises as a 'popular restaurant';

(b) to comply with the Public Health Regulations;

(c) to eliminate 'all noxious smells'.

Blackaby's attempts to run the premises as an English restaurant were a miserable failure. He assigned the lease to Wong, who converted the restaurant to Chinese food, with resounding success. However, the tenant upstairs complained about the dreadful 'noxious smells' coming from the basement. Public Health Officers were called in. They told Wong that unless a ventilation shaft was run from the basement up the back of the above-ground floors of the building, Wong would have to close down.

The landlord refused to let Wong put up the ventilating shaft, so Wong commenced proceedings, claiming that he had an easement entitling him to put up a shaft. The county court judge found as a fact that, **at the time the lease was granted to Blackaby**, a ventilating shaft was necessary for the restaurant to function successfully and eliminate smells. The fact that neither of the original parties realised this need was irrelevant. Wong therefore was held entitled to his ventilation shaft. The Court of Appeal affirmed this conclusion.

24.5.3 THE RULE IN *WHEELDON* v *BURROWS*

The two rules for implied grant of easements discussed at **24.5.1** and **24.5.2**, involve creating an easement as if 'out of thin air'. Before the sale (or lease) of the dominant land there is not the slightest sign of there being an easement in favour of the dominant land. Remember that in *Wong* v *Beaumont*, before and at the time of the original lease, nobody had even dreamed of a ventilation shaft down to the basement.

The rule in *Wheeldon* v *Burrows* (1879) 12 ChD 31 operates in a very different way. The rule requires that before the dominant land was sold (or leased) by the person who originally owned both pieces of land, a 'nebulous right' already existed in favour of what became the dominant land. If certain conditions are fulfilled then, on the sale or lease taking place, the 'nebulous right' is converted into an easement.

There are two (rather different) types of nebulous right to which the *Wheeldon* v *Burrows* rule applies. These are called 'quasi-easements' and 'privileges'.

24.5.3.1 Quasi-easements

Two plots are in common ownership. The common owner exercises over one plot for the benefit of the other plot a right which could have been an easement had the two plots been in separate ownership.

For example, Farmer Giles owns two fields, Closefield and Awayfield. Whenever he needs to go to Awayfield, he gains access to it by using a worn track across Closefield.

Or take another example. Bloggs owns a house and a large front garden to the south of his house. Underneath the garden there are drains, pipes and cables, all leading out to the road. Bloggs also enjoys lovely sunshine streaming in over his garden to the windows of his house.

24.5.3.2 Privileges

Two plots are in the common ownership of L. L leases one of those plots to T. L later grants to T a revocable licence exercisable over the land he retained. That licence benefits the land leased, and could have been granted as an easement.

For example, L owns Smallhouse and (adjoining) Largefield. Smallhouse fronts on to a minor road. L leases Smallhouse to T. There is no mention in the lease of easements over Largefield. T originally used the minor road to get to and from Smallhouse, but this road is very circuitous. **As a friendly gesture**, L says to T, 'To save your shoe-leather take a short cut across my Largefield'. T gladly accepts the invitation.

Or take another example. L owns two terraced houses. L leases one of the houses, which has only an outside toilet right at the bottom of the garden, to T. L, some years after granting the lease says to T, 'You can use my inside toilet if you like'.

(Note that in both of these examples L has granted a gratuitous licence **which he could revoke at any time.**)

24.5.3.3 The almost magical conversion of 'nebulous rights' into easements

Under the rule in *Wheeldon* v *Burrows*, three conditions must **all** be satisfied before a 'nebulous right' is converted into an easement upon the sale (or lease) of the dominant land:

(a) Immediately prior to the grant, the 'nebulous right' was used for the benefit of what becomes the dominant land.

(b)   The 'nebulous right' was 'continuous and apparent'.

(c)   The 'nebulous right' must be 'necessary for the reasonable or convenient enjoyment' of the (alleged) dominant land.

With respect to point (b) above, a 'nebulous right' is 'continuous and apparent' provided that it is regularly used and provided there is **physical evidence** on the plot of land involved of the existence of the right. For example, there might be a worn track leading across the 'servient' land towards the 'dominant' land. Even such matters as drains could be 'apparent' if there were such things as gratings and man-hole covers on the 'servient' land.

The simplest illustration of *Wheeldon* v *Burrows* is *Borman* v *Griffith* [1930] 1 Ch 49.

Read *Borman* v *Griffith* in *Cases and Materials* (24.2.3.1). It may help your understanding of this case if you draw a diagram to illustrate the facts of the case.

In *Borman* v *Griffith*, James owned a sizeable country estate. The estate included a mansion leased to Griffith for the purposes of a school. Running across the estate from the mansion to the main road was a properly made up private driveway. On that private driveway was a smaller house known (somewhat confusingly) as 'The Gardens'.

In 1923, James agreed to lease 'The Gardens' to Borman, a poultry farmer. This agreement said nothing about access to 'The Gardens'. However, at the time of the agreement James was constructing an alternative access route to 'The Gardens'. In wet weather this alternative route proved impassable for the lorries which served Borman's business. The lorries therefore used the main driveway, despite opposition from Griffith.

The judge held, applying *Wheeldon* v *Burrows*, that an easement to use the driveway was to be implied into the 1923 agreement. He held that the three elements of the rule were satisfied. You should note in particular that for element (c), Borman had to show only that a right to use the driveway was 'necessary for the reasonable or convenient enjoyment' of the dominant land. He did not have to show the stricter standard of 'absolute necessity' which is required for an easement to arise under the 'intended easements' rule applied in *Wong* v *Beaumont* (see **24.5.2**).

You should also note that Borman had only an agreement for a lease (i.e. an equitable lease) over 'The Gardens'. Fortunately for him, this did not matter. The rule in *Wheeldon* v *Burrows* is applicable not only to conveyances and legal leases, but also to contracts for sale and equitable leases.

In the Court of Appeal case of *Goldberg* v *Edwards* [1950] Ch 247, the claim for an easement under *Wheeldon* v *Burrows* failed. Unlike *Borman* v *Griffith* (which involved a 'quasi-easement' type of nebulous right), *Goldberg* v *Edwards* involved a 'privilege'.

Edwards owned a main building, together with an annex at the back of the main building. He leased the annex to Goldberg. That lease included an express grant of a right of way permitting all visitors to the annex to gain access using an open yard at the side of the main building. While this first lease was still in force, Edwards gave permission for visitors to the annex to pass through the hallway of the main building. (That way, they did not get wet!)

The first lease expired, but Goldberg was granted a new lease, with the same express clause regarding using the open yard at the side. The new lease made no express mention of the hallway, but Goldberg claimed that the new lease impliedly granted him an easement to use the hallway.

Goldberg's claim under *Wheeldon* v *Burrows* failed, because the Court of Appeal ruled that a right to use the hallway, while it had its advantages, was not 'necessary for the reasonable or convenient enjoyment' of the annex.

In giving judgment on the *Wheeldon* v *Burrows* claim the Court of Appeal stressed two points rather ignored by certain textbooks:

(i)   Implied grant under *Wheeldon* v *Burrows* can apply to 'privileges' as well as to 'quasi-easements'.

(ii) All three conditions ((a) (b), and (c) above) must be satisfied before an implied easement can arise under *Wheeldon* v *Burrows*. (Some books **wrongly** suggest that it is sufficient to prove **either** condition (b) or (c).)

24.5.3.4   All three conditions must be satisfied for an easement to arise under *Wheeldon* v *Burrows*

By a strange coincidence, two very recent decisions of separate divisions of the Court of Appeal confirm that for an easement to arise under *Wheeldon* v *Burrows*, all three conditions must be fulfilled.

In both cases the (alleged) dominant owners bought a house in the country, and claimed an implied grant of a right of way across land retained by the vendor. In both cases there was an alternative means of access to the house. Both cases were 'quasi-easement' cases where prior to the sale the vendor had used the 'nebulous right' to gain access to the house. In both cases the 'right' (prior to the sale) was continuous and apparent. Both cases therefore turned on the 'necessary for reasonable or convenient enjoyment point'.

In *Wheeler* v *Saunders* [1995] 2 All ER 697 the alternative route was virtually just as convenient as the one being claimed by implied grant. A court presided over by Staughton LJ therefore rejected the claim to an implied easement.

In *Millman* v *Ellis* [1995] Conveyancer 346, by contrast, the alternative route was dangerous and would involve making a detour. A court presided over by Sir Thomas Bingham MR held that a claim under *Wheeldon* v *Burrows* succeeded. Moreover the claim succeeded even though the (dangerous) alternative route was by virtue of an easement expressly granted by the vendor, in the conveyance of the house, over other land which he retained.

24.5.4   SECTION 62 OF THE LAW OF PROPERTY ACT 1925

The material part of s. 62 reads:

> A conveyance of land shall be deemed to include . . . all . . . liberties, privileges, easements, rights and advantages whatsoever, appertaining or reputed to appertain to the land . . .

This statutory provision first appeared in the Conveyancing Act 1881. It is very probable that Parliament did not intend it to be a rule under which new easements could be **created**. Almost certainly the original purpose behind what is now s. 62 was simply to reaffirm the common law rule that where a parcel of land is 'dominant' to an existing easement or profit, a conveyance of that dominant land **automatically** passes the right to enjoy the easement or profit to the new owner.

The courts have, however, given s. 62 a strange interpretation, under which a conveyance or lease of land may convert an existing 'privilege' type of 'nebulous right' into a full easement.

The best illustration of how s. 62 operates to create an easement is the decision of the Court of Appeal in *Wright* v *Macadam* [1949] 2 All ER 565.

Read *Wright* v *Macadam* in *Cases and Materials* (24.2.4.1). One striking thing about this case is that the dispute concerned a very trivial matter giving rise to a very important point of law!

In *Wright* v *Macadam* [1949] 2 All ER 565 the defendant leased a top-floor flat to Mrs Wright. While this first lease was still running, Macadam gave Mrs Wright permission to store her coal in a coal-shed situated in the garden to the small block of flats.

When Mrs Wright's first lease ran out, it was renewed for a further period. At the time of renewal **nothing was said about the coal-shed**. Later, during the running of the second lease, Macadam demanded that Mrs Wright pay one shilling and sixpence (7.5p) per week for the use of the coal-shed. She refused.

The Court of Appeal held that, on the renewal of the lease to Mrs Wright, there was implied into the renewed lease an easement to store coal in the coal-shed. The crucial point (fatal from Macadam's point of view) was the existence of the privilege **at the time the lease was renewed**. The statutory magic of s. 62 therefore converted Mrs Wright's privilege into a full easement.

If on the expiry of Mrs Wright's first lease, Macadam had leased the flat not to Mrs Wright but to a third party, s. 62 would have created an easement in favour of that third party.

What if Macadam had sold the flat in fee simple to a third party?

The third party would have acquired an easement (in fee simple!) to store coal in the coal-shed. I think Macadam would have been very unhappy at such a result.

24.5.4.1   The breadth of the s. 62 principle

I should stress that for s. 62 to convert a 'privilege' into an easement, all that is necessary is that the 'privilege' exists at the time of the relevant conveyance (or lease). Under the s. 62 rule there is no requirement that the 'privilege' be 'continuous and apparent'. Neither is there any requirement that the privilege be 'necessary for the reasonable or convenient enjoyment' of the dominant land.

The facts of *Goldberg* v *Edwards* were set out at **24.5.3.3**. The claim for an implied easement under *Wheeldon* v *Burrows* failed in that case.

Goldberg also relied on s. 62. Did he win under that heading?

Despite losing on the *Wheeldon* v *Burrows* issue, Goldberg won the case; he was held to have acquired (on the renewal of his lease) an implied easement to use the hallway under s. 62!

What is the moral for landlords of cases such as *Wright* v *Macadam* and *Goldberg* v *Edwards*?

(a)   Do not ever give your tenants any friendly permissions to make use of land you retain in your possession.

(b)   If you have been so foolish as to give such a friendly permission, revoke it (**in writing**) before the lease expires.

Either way, there will then be no 'privilege' on which s. 62 can work its statutory magic. (See also **24.7.**)

24.5.4.2   The limits on s. 62

Although s. 62 appears as a rule very dramatic in its effects, there are two important limitations upon its scope.

■ **Section 62 can operate only where there is a 'conveyance'.** A legal lease counts as a 'conveyance', but neither an equitable lease nor a contract for sale are 'conveyances' for the purposes of s. 62.

■ **Section 62 applies only to convert 'privileges' into easements.** Unlike *Wheeldon* v *Burrows*, s. 62 cannot apply to 'quasi-easements'. The House of Lords made this point clear in *Sovmots Investments* v *Secretary for the Environment* [1977] 2 All ER 385, at 391, approving *Long* v *Gowlett* [1923] Ch 177 at 198.

Why was s. 62 of no help to Borman in *Borman* v *Griffith*?

I hope you identified two reasons. First, Borman had only an equitable lease. Secondly (though this point is not expressly mentioned in the judgment), the case clearly involved a quasi-easement, to which s. 62 is inapplicable.

24.5.4.3   *Graham* v *Philcox*

This case, reported at [1984] 2 All ER 621, added a new way in which s. 62 can operate. This new way is in addition to what we have already discussed.

The material facts of the case were that L owned a large garden with a house at one end of that garden. In 1960, L leased the house to T. This lease included an express grant to T of a right of way over the garden **for the duration of the lease**. In 1975 (while T's lease was still running), L sold the fee simple reversion in the house to G. The 1975 conveyance made no mention of a right of way. The Court of Appeal held that s. 62 implied into the 1975 conveyance the grant to G of a fee simple easement of way over the garden.

The practical effect of this case appears to be that if the landlord of Blackacre grants to a lessee of Blackacre a full easement over Retainedacre for the duration of the lease, and then the landlord sells the freehold to Blackacre, there will be implied into the conveyance of Blackacre a freehold easement over Retainedacre!

24.5.4.4   Section 62 and profits à prendre

Unlike the other three forms of implied grant which we have been discussing, it appears that s. 62 could apply so as to imply a **profit** into a conveyance (or lease).

Suppose that Larry owns a house and an adjoining meadow. He leases the house to Teresa for 10 years. Teresa is a keen horsewoman, and when Larry discovers that fact he says to her, 'Seeing we are now good friends you can pasture your horse in my meadow'. Teresa accepts the invitation.

When the lease of the house runs out, Larry sells the fee simple in the house to Penny. The conveyance makes no mention of horses, but Penny now produces her horse and says to Larry, 'I have got the right to put my horse in your meadow'. It would appear that Penny is correct in this assertion. She has a fee simple **profit** to pasture one horse in the adjoining meadow.

24.6   Implied Reservation of Easements

This could occur only under the 'way of necessity' and 'intended easements' rules (see **24.5.1** and **24.5.2**). (Section 62 and *Wheeldon* v *Burrows* cannot operate 'in reverse' to create easements by implied reservation.)

Suppose that Muggins owns Nearacre and Faracre. He foolishly sells Nearacre, with the result that Faracre becomes 'landlocked'. Muggins is lucky. He will have a 'way of necessity' over Nearacre to get to Faracre. (You must remember, however, the principle in *Corporation of London* v *Riggs* at **24.5.1**.)

Suppose that Wang owns a building which includes a basement. He leases the above-ground floors to Bloggs on a 50-year lease, but he retains the basement. He opens a restaurant in the basement. The tenant of the upper floors complains, and the environmental health officers say that the restaurant has to have a ventilation shaft up the back of the above-ground floors. Can Wang claim an easement?

It would seem that Wang will be able to claim an easement for a ventilation shaft by implied reservation only if he can show that at the time the 50-year lease was granted Bloggs (sic) knew that Wang intended to run a restaurant in the basement: *Re Webb's Lease* [1951] 2 All ER 131 (see also **24.5.2**).

24.7   Exclusion of the Rules Providing for Implied Grant (and Reservation)

The rules for implied grant (and reservation) which we have just discussed at some length depend upon 'the presumed agreement of the parties'. (You may, like me, find this surprising, but the point is an important one.)

It is perfectly permissible and indeed quite common for solicitors drafting contracts for sale (and contracts for leases) to include a clause in the contract excluding the rules relating to implied grant. Thus, in particular, a vendor or lessor of land who retains other land in the vicinity can, by careful drafting, avoid being saddled with easements which would otherwise arise 'by implication'.

SAQ 131

Refer back to *Graham* v *Philcox* discussed at 24.5.4.3. There L found himself saddled with a fee simple easement of way over the garden he retained. What should L's solicitor have done to avoid that result?

L's solicitor should have included in the contract for sale of the house in 1975 a clause to the effect, 'On the conveyance of the house, no easements over the garden shall be implied under s. 62, "the rule in *Wheeldon* v *Burrows*" or any other rule'. (Out of extreme caution, a similar clause should also be included in the conveyance itself.)

24.8   Compulsory Purchase and the Rules for Implied Grant

In *Sovmots Investments* v *Secretary for the Environment* [1977] 2 All ER 385, the House of Lords held that as the rules for implied grant and reservation of easements are founded on 'presumed agreement', the rules can have no application to land acquired under a compulsory purchase order.

24.9   Simultaneous Sales or Bequests

Suppose Alec owns Greenacre and Blueacre. He simultaneously grants Greenacre to Brian and Blueacre to Charles. It appears that *Wheeldon* v *Burrows* can operate in favour of Brian and/or Charles, but the other rules of implied grant, such as s. 62, can have no application.

24.10   Conclusion

This whole chapter could be concluded in seven words: 'Make sure you draft your documents correctly.' As the Church of England discovered (*St Edmundsbury* v *Clarke*, see **24.4**), even an **expressly** created easement may prove to be incorrectly drafted.

I would strongly suggest that the most important part of this chapter is **24.7**, together with **SAQ 131** and its answer. The strange magic-like rules of implied grant benefit people such as Wong, Borman, Wright and Goldberg, quite possibly in ways they did not really anticipate. Equally, people like Beaumont, Griffith (no doubt worried about the safety of his pupils) and the owners of the garden in *Graham* v *Philcox* find that they have 'impliedly granted' easements which may substantially depreciate the value of their land. Careful drafting of contracts, leases and conveyances would have avoided such disasters.

CHAPTER TWENTY-FIVE

PRESCRIPTION FOR EASEMENTS (AND PROFITS)

25.1 Objectives

By the end of this chapter you should be able to:

- explain the general principles common to all forms of prescription, and in particular the concept 'user as of right';

- distinguish between the three forms of prescription;

- appreciate why common law prescription is unlikely to be a very useful rule in modern conditions;

- appreciate why the simple 'lost modern grant' rule can be used only as a last resort;

- appreciate the complexities of the Prescription Act 1832.

25.2 Introduction

The basic concept of prescription is not too difficult. Suppose John owns Remotehouse, situated next to Largefield, which is owned by Keith. The road from Remotehouse to the nearest shops is very circuitous. John therefore decides to take a short cut across Largefield. John **does not get any permission** from Keith. However, he uses 'his' short-cut very regularly and in broad day-light, and Keith makes no attempt to stop John.

John's open and regular use of the short-cut across Largefield does not alter the fact that every time he goes on Largefield he is a trespasser. At any time Keith could say to John, 'Stop crossing my field; if you don't stop I will sue you for an injunction and damages!'.

Suppose, however, that John continues to use the short-cut openly and without any objection from Keith for **20** years. Subject to some very complex rules, 20 years is the normal 'prescription period'. That means that (in principle) after 20 years' use of his short-cut, John acquires an easement to cross Largefield. He ceases to be a trespasser, and Keith can no longer stop him. Put more crudely, John's use of the short-cut (as a trespasser) for 20 years creates for himself (and for Remotehouse) an easement of way across Largefield.

25.3   The Complexities of Prescription Law

The example given at **25.2**, though a good way to start the discussion, rather oversimplifies the law of prescription. I wish the law was simply that '20 years' user gives you a prescriptive easement (or profit)'! But that is not the case. Unfortunately there are no less than three forms of prescription for easements and profits:

(i)   common law prescription;

(ii)   lost modern grant;

(iii) the Prescription Act 1832.

If somebody (such as John in my Remotehouse example) is claiming a prescriptive easement (or profit) he will suceed only if:

(a)   he can satisfy certain important rules which are common for all three forms of prescription, **and**

(b)   he can satisfy the specific rules governing **any one** of the three forms of prescription.

25.4   Rules Common to All Three Forms of Prescription

User, to be prescriptive, must be 'as of right'.

I hope you noticed that in my Remotehouse example at **25.2** I said that John crossed Largefield openly, and without either permission or opposition from Keith. I said those things so as to ensure that John's user was 'as of right'. User is only 'as of right' if it is *nec vi, nec clam, nec precario*, i.e. 'without force, without secrecy and without permission'.

25.4.1 WITHOUT FORCE

If in my Remotehouse example John had had to force his way across Largefield, his user would not have been prescriptive.

In this context, 'force' has been given a very wide meaning, and the courts have ruled that user, to be prescriptive, must not be contentious in any way. Thus, fisticuffs man-to-man, the breaking down of barriers and the climbing over of fences are all 'forcible' user and therefore not prescriptive.

The courts have also held that user in face of express oral or written protests from the alleged servient owner should be deemed to be 'forcible', even though there is no actual violence. Thus if Keith constantly wrote to John saying, 'Get off my land!', John could not acquire a prescriptive easement.

25.4.2 WITHOUT SECRECY

User, to be prescriptive, must be open; 'such that a reasonable person in the position of the alleged servient owner, diligent in the protection of his interests, would have a reasonable opportunity of discovering the right asserted'.

ACTIVITY 90

Read the leading case of *Lloyds Bank* v *Dalton* [1942] 2 All ER 352, in *Cases and Materials* (25.2.2). If you had been the owner of the servient dye-works, would you have known about the outhouse?

In *Lloyds Bank* v *Dalton*, Dalton owned the servient building, which was a large dye-works. The dominant building was a small outhouse which claimed a prescriptive easement of support against the dye-works. The outhouse had, for well over 20 years, leant against a wall of the dye-works. That wall was a blank wall without any windows.

The outhouse could therefore not be seen from the works, neither could it be seen from the public road. The court nevertheless rejected Dalton's contention that there was 'secret' user. A reasonable owner would surely go around his premises from time to time. A reasonable owner would therefore at some stage have discovered the outhouse.

Lloyds Bank v *Dalton* should be contrasted with *Liverpool Corporation* v *Coghill* [1918] 1 Ch 307. Coghill ran a chemical factory which worked 24 hours a day. For many years Coghill poured borax effluent into the corporation's sewers. Coghill always did so in the 'wee small hours'. This was not out of any deliberate intent to conceal what it was doing. Discharging effluent at night suited its 'production cycle'.

The Court of Appeal held that Coghill could not claim a prescriptive right. Its user was in law 'secret', even though there was no deliberate attempt at concealment.

25.4.3 WITHOUT PERMISSION

User must not depend on permission or consent. Even an oral permission is sufficient to negate prescription. Normally, once a user is permissive, it will always be permissive, i.e. a permission to use is normally regarded as lasting indefinitely. If, however, a permission were revoked but user still continued, the continued user would be 'as of right'.

Where the servient owner knows that user is going on, and simply tolerates such user without ever giving express permission, then that user is 'as of right': *Mills* v *Silver* [1991] 1 All ER 449.

25.4.4 USER MUST BE CONTINUOUS

In *Hollins* v *Verney* (1884) 13 QB 304, especially at 315, the alleged dominant owner had used the right of way only three times in the last 20 years. The Court of Appeal rejected the claim for a prescriptive easement. It held that user must be sufficiently regular so that a reasonable servient owner would know some right was being asserted. (You should note that this is in effect much the same rule as is applied in 'secrecy' cases.)

25.4.5 USER MUST BE BY OR ON BEHALF OF A FEE SIMPLE AGAINST A FEE SIMPLE

This is a peculiar rule which has become firmly embedded into English common law (see, for example, the case of *Simmons* v *Dobson* [1991] 4 All ER 25), though not into other versions of the common law (e.g., Irish law). English law insists that a prescriptive easement or profit **can be only of fee simple duration**. This apparently simple rule creates complications where either:

(a)   the person carrying out the user as of right is a lessee rather than a fee simple owner; or

(b)   the servient land has at any time been leased (or settled).

Four consequences flow from this rule:

(i)   A tenant cannot prescribe for an easement against his own landlord. For example, Leonard owns the fee simple in Blackacre and Whiteacre. He leases Whiteacre to Tamsin for 999 years. Tamsin immediately starts to cross Blackacre to get to Whiteacre. She and the successors to her lease continue to do so 'as of right' for hundreds of years. A prescriptive easement cannot arise.

(ii)   *A fortiori*, one tenant of a landlord cannot prescribe for an easement against another tenant of the same landlord. See *Simmons* v *Dobson*.

(iii)   If a tenant prescribes 'as of right' against a third party, any resultant right enures to the benefit of the landlord's fee simple.

(iv)   A period of user **entirely** against a lessee or life tenant of the servient land cannot be prescriptive. However, if user **commences** against a fee simple owner in actual possession, it does not matter if the servient land is subsequently leased.

ACTIVITY 91

Consider the old case of *Palk* v *Shinner* (1852) 118 ER 215 (*Cases and Materials*, 25.2.5), which illustrates the last two points above. Palk leased his land to various tenants. From 1820 onwards, the tenants crossed Shinner's land 'as of right' to reach the land leased to them. From 1821 onwards, Shinner's land was leased to X. User as of right by the tenants continued until the dispute broke out in about 1850. What do you think was the result of the case?

The court gave judgment for Palk, holding that his tenants were to be regarded as acting on his behalf (point (iii)). Palk thus acquired a fee simple easement. Moreover, as the user as of right had commenced against Shinner personally (a fee simple owner in actual possession) it did not matter that the servient land had **subsequently** been leased (point (iv)).

What would be the position if Shinner had leased his land to X in 1818?

The claim to a prescriptive easement would fail, as the user as of right would have been **entirely** against a lessee.

25.5 Prescription at Common Law

For reasons which will quickly become apparent, a claim for an easement or a profit by 'prescription at common law' is very rarely successful. The theory of this form of prescription is that once upon a time a deed was executed by the then servient owner in favour of the then dominant owner, granting the relevant easement or profit. However, this deed was granted so long ago that its execution is 'outside the scope of legal memory'.

Unfortunately legal memory is elephantine, and stretches back to 1189 (the year of the accession of Richard I). In effect, if you claim a prescriptive easement (or profit) at common law, you have boldly to assert that you and your predecessors have been exercising the right ever since 1189.

Fortunately you do not have to produce evidence of user covering the whole of the last 800 or so years. If 20 years' user is proved, user right back to 1189 will be presumed. But the presumption can be rebutted by showing any of the following facts:

(a)   at some time since 1189 the right was not exercised; or

(b)   at some time since 1189 the right could not have been exercised; or

(c)   at some time since 1189 dominant and servient plots were in common ownership.

Thus a servient owner faced with a claim for prescription at common law will look round for rebutting evidence from elderly inhabitants or ancient records. Suppose the current owner of Westacre is claiming at common law a prescriptive easement of way over neighbouring Eastacre. The owner of Eastacre will be delighted if he can find some very senior citizen who says something like, 'When I was a little girl my mum worked at Westacre and nobody got to it by crossing Eastacre. They always used the track across Northacre'. Or perhaps it will be, 'When I was a little boy Eastacre was very swampy and impossible to cross. I remember because I once fell in; dad gave me a right walloping'.

Ancient records will be just as effective. Proof that for a few years *circa* (say) 1400 the same person owned both Westacre and Eastacre, will be enough to defeat the common law claim.

25.6 Prescription by Lost Modern Grant

The utility of common law Prescription is largely destroyed by the absurd '1189 rule'. However, the old, pre-1875 courts invented a legal doctrine called 'lost modern grant'.

This doctrine was designed to allow prescription for easements and profits where there was strong evidence of at least 20 years' 'user as of right' but it was clear that user had commenced 'in modern times'. Modern times was any date after 1189!

Lost modern grant is a 'legal fiction'. A legal fiction occurs where the court 'finds as a fact' something everyone knows is really not true, and then decides the case on the basis of that 'fact'. The essence of 'lost modern grant' is that the court 'finds as a fact' that a deed was executed 'in modern times' granting the easement (or profit) claimed, but that deed has been lost.

In the days when civil cases (including land disputes) were tried by juries, 'lost modern grant' caused judges (particularly trial judges) a lot of trouble. Suppose that the owner of Northacre was claiming a prescriptive easement of way across Southacre, and that it did appear that for many years the owners of Northacre had indeed been crossing Southacre to get to their land. The trial judge would have to direct the jury along the following lines:

> Gentlemen; if you find that there is convincing evidence that the owners of Northacre have been 'as of right' crossing Southacre for at least 20 years, I **instruct** you to find as a fact that a deed was executed granting a right of way but that deed has somehow been mislaid.

Some nineteenth-century juries, sworn to 'well and truly try' the case, were understandably worried by this instruction. Nevertheless, in 1881 the House of Lords in *Dalton* v *Angus* (1881) 6 App Cas 740, reaffirmed the validity of the lost modern grant rule.

Two developments in the twentieth century have greatly improved the situation. First, land law disputes are no longer tried by jury; they are tried by a judge alone. A judge is not going to be worried by the apparent absurdity of finding as a fact something no one really believes to be true. Secondly, this area of law has been much simplified by two modern Court of Appeal decisions, *Tehidy Minerals* v *Norman* [1971] 2 All ER 475 and *Oakley* v *Boston* [1975] 3 All ER 405.

ACTIVITY 92

Read the extracts from *Tehidy Minerals* in *Cases and Materials* (25.4). Be particularly careful to ensure that you have understood the facts correctly.

Tehidy Minerals involved a claim for a prescriptive profit of grazing on a part of Bodmin Moor. In January 1920 a group of farmers started grazing their sheep on the servient land. They continued to do so 'as of right' until October 1941, when the land was requisitioned by the War Office for military training. The farmers continued to graze their sheep on the land, but it was conceded that this post-1941 grazing was by permission. (Permission came first from the War Office and then, after the land had been derequisitioned, from the servient owners.)

The farmers successfully claimed under 'lost modern grant' a prescriptive profit of pasture on the basis of their 1920 to 1941 user. The Court of Appeal held that a 'presumption' of lost modern grant arose where the claimant produced strong evidence of 20 years' user as of right. If there is such evidence then 'the deed which has got lost' is assumed to have been executed:

(a)   at the earliest, immediately before user as of right commenced;

(b)   at the latest, **20 years before** user as of right ceased.

The Court held that it is not sufficient to rebut the 'presumption' of lost modern grant for the servient owner to show that the grant never **in fact** took place. The presumption of lost modern grant can be rebutted (and the claim for the profit or easement therefore defeated) only by showing that **throughout the period (a) to (b).** ('the relevant period') the grant was **legally impossible.** There would be 'legal impossibility' if, say, throughout 'the relevant period' the land had been requisitioned, or vested in a person who had no power to grant profits or easements.

In *Tehidy Minerals*, the relevant period for the presumed grant was January 1920 to October **1921** (sic). During those 21 months there was no question of a grant being legally impossible. Hence the farmers' victory.

In the later case of *Oakley* v *Boston*, a differently constituted Court of Appeal applied the rules in *Tehidy Minerals*, but held against the claimant for an easement. The evidence was that there had been user as of right of an alleged right of way from 1914 to 1962. After that there had been insufficient user.

In *Oakley* v *Boston*, what was 'the relevant period' at some time during which the presumed grant would supposedly have taken place?

Applying *Tehidy Minerals* v *Norman*, the presumed grant would be some time between 1914 and **1942**.

There was, however, one crucial fact in *Oakley* v *Boston* which I have not yet mentioned. The alleged servient land had been, until **1952**, 'glebe land'. Glebe land is land vested in the local vicar (of the Church of England) not in his personal capacity but in his official capacity as an 'ecclesiastical corporation sole'.

The Court of Appeal first held (interpreting some very obscure nineteenth-century legislation governing the Church) that a vicar **owning land in his official capacity as an 'ecclesiastical corporation sole'** had no power to grant easements.

What, therefore, was the result of the case?

As throughout 'the relevant period' when the supposed grant could have taken place it was 'legally impossible', the claim for a prescriptive easement invoking lost modern grant failed.

25.7   Prescription under the Prescription Act 1832

Look at the Prescription Act 1832 as set out in *Cases and Materials* (25.5). Do *not* (at this stage) even attempt to understand the provisions.

I am sure you will agree that this Act is far too complex and very badly drafted. The House of Lords came to that conclusion in 1841, but nothing has ever been done to reform or repeal the Act.

The complexity of the 1832 Act is to be contrasted with the relative simplicity of the 'lost modern grant' rule as restated in *Tehidy Minerals* (see 25.6). I would like to be able to say to students, 'Forget the Prescription Act, rely on lost modern grant'. I cannot say that for two reasons:

(a) The courts have repeatedly held that lost modern grant, being a 'legal fiction', can be relied upon only if the other forms of prescription (common law and the 1832 Act) fail.

(b) The complexities of the Act produce the result that there are quite a few situations which the Act covers which are not covered by the other two forms of prescription.

25.7.1   SHORTER AND LONGER PERIODS UNDER THE ACT

Study ss. 1 and 2 of the 1832 Act in *Cases and Materials* (25.5) to try to discern if there is some kind of pattern linking the two sections.

If you study ss. 1 and 2 of the Act, you will eventually realise that the Act makes some kind of distinction between 'shorter periods' and 'longer periods'. The shorter periods are 20 years' user as of right for easements, and 30 years for profits. The longer periods are 40 years' user as of right for easements, and 60 years for profits.

Where a claim for an easement or a profit is based on 20 or 30 years' user as of right, the claim will not 'be defeated or destroyed by showing only that such right, profit, or benefit was first taken or enjoyed at any time prior to such period of [twenty] thirty years, but such claim may be defeated in any other way by which the same is now liable to be defeated'.

Where a claim for an easement or a profit is based on 40 or 60 years' user as of right, 'the right thereto shall be deemed absolute and indefeasible'.

We will return to the differences between the shorter and longer periods at **25.7.3**. For the moment it is sufficient to say that most cases will be covered by the shorter periods. It will be relatively rare that a dominant owner will want to rely on the longer periods.

25.7.2   THE 'NEXT BEFORE ACTION' AND 'WITHOUT INTERRUPTION' RULES

Section 4 of the 1832 Act introduces **for the purposes of the Act** (but not for the other forms of prescription) two very strange rules.

25.7.2.1   The 'next before action' rule

> Each of the respective periods of years hereinbefore mentioned shall be deemed and taken to be the period next before some suit or action wherein the claim or matter … be brought into question.

What this really means is that the period of 'user as of right' relied on by the dominant owner for the purposes of the 1832 Act must be a period ending when the dispute between the parties arises. The dispute 'arises' when the writ in the court case is issued. (It does not matter whether it is the servient owner suing as plaintiff claiming that there is no easement or profit or the dominant owner suing as plaintiff claiming a prescriptive easement or profit.)

If there is a period (however long) of 'user as of right' **followed by a gap when there is no user,** and then after this gap the writ is issued, the Prescription Act 1832 is no help to the dominant owner. He will have to rely on one of the other forms of prescription.

This point is illustrated by the facts of *Oakley* v *Boston* (see **25.6**). The judge found as a fact that regular user as of right ceased in 1962. The writ in the case was not issued until 1972. Because of the 10 year gap in activity the alleged dominant owner had no chance under the 1832 Act. Similarly in *Mills* v *Silver*, the dominant owners could rely only on lost modern grant, since the user as of right had been from 1922 to 1981 but the writ was not issued until 1987.

25.7.2.2   The 'without interruption' rule

> No act or other matter shall be deemed to be an interruption within the meaning of the statute, unless the same shall have been or shall be submitted to or acquiesced in for one year after the party interrupted shall have had or shall have notice thereof and of the person making or authorising the same to be made.

This rule always reminds me of the children's riddle, 'When is a door not a door? When its ajar'. The riddle I pose to you is, 'When is an interruption not an interruption?'. The answer is 'When we are dealing with the Prescription Act 1832 and the interruption has lasted less than a year'.

Suppose that in 1968, Tom, the owner of Greenacre, started (as of right) to cross Fred's Brownacre to get to and from Greenacre. In 1988, for about six months, the path across Brownacre was blocked by Fred. Fred then removed the blockage and Tom recommenced his user as of right. Fred has once again blocked the path.

If Tom immediately issues a writ claiming a prescriptive easement, will he win the case?

Yes, he will win. He will be able to show nearly 30 years' user 'next before action'. The six months' interruption is not an interruption for the purposes of the 1832 Act. (The result would be different if back in the late-1980s, Fred had blocked the path for 15 months.)

In **SAQ 135** I indicated that Tom immediately issued a writ when his path was blocked a second time. This was to avoid the (fatal for the dominant owner) gap between user as of right and commencement of legal proceedings.

Actually an immediate writ is not essential. The 'without interruption' rule in effect creates an exception to the 'next before action' rule. Provided legal proceedings are commenced **within a year** of the date when the interruption first actually occurred, a dominant owner will be able to rely on user as of right continuing up to that date of actual interruption. (In our Tom and Greenacre example, Tom would lose if he delayed more than a year before issuing his writ.)

25.7.2.3 Interruption of user as of right in the twentieth year
The strange quirks of s. 4 were demonstrated as early as 1841 in the House of Lords case of *Flight* v *Thomas* (1841) 8 ER 91. In that case the dominant owner had enjoyed his easement as of right for 19 years and 11 months. He was then interrupted by an obstruction. He waited a few months before issuing his writ. Thus 20 years had elapsed from the commencement of his user as of right, but he had not yet been 'interrupted' for one year.

What do you think was the result of the case?

The dominant owner was held to have a prescriptive easement. The practical result of this decision is that enjoyment for 19 years and a bit (even one day) will be sufficient to give a prescriptive easement under the 1832 Act, provided that the dominant owner times the issue of his writ correctly. Similar principles would apply where one of the longer periods of prescription was being relied on and the interruption occurred in the thirtieth, fortieth or sixtieth year of user as of right.

In January 1977, David started to cut across Greenacre to get to Yellowacre, and has done so ever since. Suppose it is now March 1996. What should Shane, the owner of Greenacre, do to stop David gaining an easement?

Shane should immediately issue a writ against David. David will have only 19 years' (and a bit) user 'next before action', and therefore any claim for a prescriptive easement is bound to fail.

Suppose, in March 1996, Shane does not issue a writ but instead puts up a fence barring David's way. What should David do?

David should 'lie low' until February 1997, and then issue a writ claiming that he has a prescriptive easement. He should win, as the writ will be more than 20 years after user as of right commenced, but the 'interruption' will not have lasted one year.

25.7.3 DIFFERENCES BETWEEN LONGER AND SHORTER PERIODS UNDER THE PRESCRIPTION ACT 1832

25.7.3.1 Oral permissions

When enacting the longer periods of prescription, the 1832 Act (ss. 1 and 2) states that after 40 or 60 years' user, 'The right thereto [to the easement or profit] shall be deemed absolute and indefeasible, unless it shall appear that the same was taken and enjoyed by some consent or agreement expressly made or given for that purpose by deed or writing'.

User, to be prescriptive under the Prescription Act 1832, must (in principle) be 'as of right'. Thus the reference to 'consent . . . by deed or writing' seems very confusing. It would appear (though this has never been firmly decided by the courts) that for the longer periods of prescription the strange wording of the statute creates a small **exception** to the general rule that user to be prescriptive must be 'as of right'. It seems that if there has been 40 (or 60) years' user originally based on a purely **oral** permission, but that permission has not been renewed in the last 40 or 60 years, the user is prescriptive.

Suppose that in 1954 Stephen, the owner of Bluefield, gave oral permission to Daphne, the owner of Redfield, allowing Daphne to cross Bluefield to get to Redfield. That permission has never been renewed and Daphne has been crossing Bluefield for the last 40-something years. Although normally a permission lasts indefinitely (see **25.4.3**), an oral permission **given more than 40 years ago is ignored**. Thus Daphne acquires a prescriptive easement of way under the longer period.

If Stephen had renewed the oral permission at any time in the last 40 years (say in 1963) Daphne would lose her claim for a prescriptive easement: *Gardner* v *Hodgson's Kingston Brewery* [1903] AC 229 and *Healey* v *Hawkins* [1968] 3 All ER 836.

25.7.3.2 Periods excluded from computation by s. 7 of the 1832 Act

Section 7 of the 1832 Act applies only with respect to the shorter (20- or 30-year) prescription periods:

> Provided also, that the time during which any person otherwise capable of resisting the claim . . . shall have been or shall be an infant, idiot, non compos mentis, [feme covert], or tenant for life . . . shall be excluded in the computation of the periods hereinbefore mentioned . . . .

This section creates a special rule designed to protect **servient** owners who are under a 'disability'. In effect a period of user against a person under one of the disabilities listed in s. 7 is not to count towards the 20 (30) years. The 'disabilities' are insanity, being under age, and being a life tenant. Being a 'feme covert' (married woman) was a disability until 1882!

Suppose in 1970, W commenced user as of right of a pathway over X's land. From 1977 to 1985, X was insane. W (if he continues the user as of right) does not acquire any right under the Act until . . . ?

The answer is 1998. One way of looking at this is to say that the eight years of the insanity has to be added to the normal prescription period of 20 years to produce a total period of 28 years.

Suppose that, in the example in **SAQ 138**, between 1980 and 1983 (while X was insane) user as of right was prevented by a barbed wire fence. W's claim for a prescriptive easement will fail. Section 7 is purely for the protection of servient owners. An 'interruption' occurring during the period of the disability cannot be ignored!

25.7.3.3 Periods excluded from computation by s. 8 of the 1832 Act

This provision applies only to the 40-year period of prescription for easements. (It has no application to profits.)

To try to help make sense of the provision, I have split it into three parts below. (You will also see that I have written the word 'easement' in the second line, although in the official edition of the 1832 Act the word used is 'convenient'. The word 'convenient' makes no sense: it is thought that it is a misprint for 'easement'.)

> Provided always, that when any land or water upon, over, or from which any such way or other [easement] watercourse or use of water shall have been or shall be

enjoyed or derived hath been or shall be held under or by virtue of any term of life, or any term of years exceeding three years from the granting thereof,

the time of enjoyment of any such way or other matter as hereinbefore mentioned, during the continuance of such terms, shall be excluded in the computation of the said period of forty years,

in case the claim within three years after the end or sooner determination of such term be resisted by any person entitled to any reversion expectant on the determination thereof.

Section 8 operates in a way somewhat similar to s. 7 (see 25.7.3.2). However, carefully notice:

(a) that the 'disabilities' are that either the servient land has been leased for a period of more than three years, or that the servient owner was a life tenant. (See the last words of the first part of the section.)

(b) A servient owner can invoke the special protection given him by s. 8 only if proceedings disputing the easement are commenced within three years of the lease or life tenancy expiring. (See the third part of the section.)

Suppose Alf commenced user as of right of a path over Blackacre in 1950 and has continued ever since.

From June 1953 to June 1993, the servient land was subject to a strict settlement under which Leonard was the life tenant.

What is the position under the 1832 Act if in March 1996 either Alf commences an action claiming an easement, or the (new) servient fee simple owner commences proceedings against Alf?

The servient owner would win in proceedings based on the 1832 Act; he would be able to invoke the protection of s. 8, and therefore a claim under the longer 40-year period would fail.

What if legal proceedings (begun by Alf or the servient owner) were not commenced until July 1996?

The servient owner would be too late to invoke the protection of s. 8, as more than three years would have elapsed since the expiry of the life tenancy. Alf would win under the longer period provided by the 1832 Act.

25.7.3.4 The requirement that user be 'against a fee simple' does not apply to the longer periods of prescription

(See **25.4.5**, for the general rule.)

Continue the example I have been just discussing in Activity 96 and SAQ 139. Suppose the servient land was settled from June 1943 to June 1993, and that Alf's user as of right commenced (as before) in 1950. Further suppose that it is now March 1997, and Alf has just issued a writ claiming a prescriptive easement under the 40 year period. Will he win?

Normally, the fact that user as of right commenced against a life tenant or lessee is fatal to a claim for a prescriptive easement. But when dealing with the 40-year period under the 1832 Act, the usual rule about 'user [commencing] against a fee simple' does not apply. So Alf will succeed in a claim under the 40-year period despite commencing his user against a life tenant.

Use the same example as in Activity 97, except that the servient (fee simple) owner issued a writ against Alf sometime in 1996. Who will win this case?

Provided he issued his writ before June 1996, the servient owner will win, as he will be protected by s. 8. If the servient owner delayed to the latter half of 1996 he would lose, as he would be outside the three-year period for 'resisting' given by the last part of s. 8 (see **25.7.3.3**).

25.7.4 PRESCRIPTION FOR EASEMENTS OF LIGHT

This is governed by s. 3 of the Prescription Act 1832. Section 3 was designed to make it easier to acquire a prescriptive easement for light. Unfortunately, it is, if anything, now too easy for a building to acquire a prescriptive easement of light over an adjoining vacant plot of land. The rules under s. 3 differ quite substantially from the normal rules governing prescription.

25.7.4.1 User under s. 3 need not be as of right

This was established in *Morgan* v *Fear* [1907] AC 425. The only aspect of user as of right applicable to s. 3 cases is that a **written** permission will debar a claim. Thus, if a dominant owner kept on demolishing obstructions to his light which appeared on the servient land, he could acquire a prescriptive easement! (He would, however, be liable for trespassing on the servient land when carrying out his demolition work.)

25.7.4.2 The normal rules about user 'by or on behalf of a fee simple against a fee simple' do not apply

Under s. 3 of the 1832 Act, a tenant can prescribe against his own landlord, or against a fellow tenant of his own landlord. (Yet apparently any easement which arises under s. 3 is in fee simple!)

25.7.4.3 Rights of Light Act 1959

In 1959, there were still some war-time bomb-sites which had not been redeveloped. It was suddenly realised that it had been nearly 20 years since 'the blitz', and that if there was not special legislation, prescriptive rights of light would be acquired over bomb-sites. Such rights of light would severely limit redevelopment.

The 1959 Act included temporary provisions which are now only of historic interest. The prescription period was extended to 27 years if the action related to an infringement occurring before 1 January 1963.

The Act also included permanent provisions (of an almost comical nature) which remain in force today.

Prior to the Second World War, if you owned land over which there was a risk that a neighbour would acquire a prescriptive easement of light, you erected enormous hoardings on your land to block out his light. With the advent of modern planning law, this is no longer possible.

The 1959 Act creates a procedure for erecting **imaginary** buildings on one's land. You do not need planning permission to erect your imaginary building, and you should make your imaginary building very large!

You, 'the potential servient owner', register an imaginary obstruction on your land in the **local** land charges register kept by the District Council. Registration is equivalent to an obstruction acquiesced in for one year, and the registration lasts only one year.

To be safe, how often should you register under the 1959 Act?

To be on the safe side, you should make a registration every **19** years. In that way your neighbour can never acquire a prescriptive easement of light.

If an imaginary obstruction is erected under the 1959 Act, the dominant owner may want to claim that he already has an easement of light and that the 'obstruction' has come too late. The 1959 Act allows him to sue as if his light were actually obstructed!

25.8 Conclusion

It has to be said that the English law of prescription is extremely complex, and is clearly in need of simplification and reform. Perhaps our only consolation when we consider the complexities of the law is that (especially with the 1832 and 1959 Acts) there are aspects which are faintly comical.

There have been suggestions that the whole law of prescription should be abolished. Why should somebody, by trespassing for a long enough time, acquire a **property** right to do something which previously was unlawful? On the other hand, if you have been doing something for a very long time totally unchallenged, do you not feel that you have the right to do it?

My own personal view is that a very simple and effective reform would be for Parliament to repeal the 1832 and 1959 Acts (without replacement), to abolish prescription under the '1189' common law rule, and to abolish all prescription for easements for light. That would leave just 'lost modern grant' to govern all remaining cases. (In practice these remaining cases will involve rights of way, grazing, or (occasionally) support.)

25.9 End of Chapter Assessment Questions

1. Last month Finnegan, owner of Blackacre and Whiteacre, two neighbouring farms, sold and conveyed Blackacre to Milligan. The conveyance contained no provision relating to easements and profits.

Advise Milligan regarding the following:

(a) The only direct access to Blackacre is a narrow footpath insufficiently wide to accommodate motor traffic. Milligan wishes to make use of the private driveway which runs from Blackacre through Whiteacre and leads into the adjoining public highway.

(b) Some drains run from Blackacre under Whiteacre. Milligan wishes to make use of those drains.

(c) Cyrus, the owner of Redacre, an adjoining farm, claims that he can continue to graze his sheep on a hill-side forming part of Blackacre where sheep from Redacre have been grazed 'as long as anyone can remember'.

2. In 1973 Louise acquired the freehold to Grand House. Grand House adjoins West Field, the freehold to which was then owned by Nellie. Over the years Nellie has leased West Field to Olive for short periods.

On acquiring Grand House, Louise immediately leased it to Terry for 70 years. Soon after taking the lease, Terry started to pasture the five sheep he owned in West Field, and to take a short cut across West Field to get to the nearest station. He continued both of these activities until September 1995, without any objection from Nellie or Olive.

In September 1995 Patel acquired the freehold to West Field from Nellie, and immediately ordered Terry not to make any further use of West Field. Initially Terry complied with this demand, but now both he and Louise are threatening legal action.

It is now January 1996. Advise Patel.

See *Cases and Materials* (25.7) for specimen answers.

CHAPTER TWENTY-SIX

RESTRICTIVE COVENANTS – THE BASIC PRINCIPLES

26.1 Objectives

By the end of this chapter you should be able to:

■ distinguish **restrictive** covenants from positive covenants;

■ explain the rules which govern the running of the **burden** of restrictive covenants;

■ appreciate the true significance of s. 56 of the Law of Property Act 1925.

26.2 Introduction

(Re-read **1.4.2** which deals with restrictive covenants.)

In this and the ensuing two chapters, we study a very confusing area of law. The material in this chapter (except perhaps the case of *Wrotham Park*, see **26.6**) is relatively straight-forward, but **Chapter 27** will be an entirely different matter. To help give you some confidence in this area, we start with another little story; one designed to give you some idea of the issues which we will be facing in this and the following chapters.

26.3 Restrictive and Positive Covenants Distinguished

Suppose Alfred owns in fee simple two adjoining high class residences, Blueacre and Redacre. He plans to retain Blueacre for his own home, and to sell Redacre to Bert. Alfred wishes to maintain 'the tone of the area'. In the conveyance of the fee simple in Redacre, Alfred induces Bert to covenant:

(a) that he will keep Redacre in good repair, and repaint every five years (a **positive** covenant);

(b) not to carry on any business in Redacre (a **negative** covenant).

These covenants are expressed to be for the benefit of Blueacre rather than just for Alfred's personal benefit. (We say that the covenants are 'annexed' to Blueacre.)

Suppose Alfred sells Blueacre to Charles. In principle Charles can enforce the covenants against Bert. He can enforce both the positive and the negative covenants against the

original covenantor. (In *Smith* v *River Douglas Catchment Board* [1949] 2 All ER 179, the defendants promised a farmer, for the benefit of his farm, to maintain the banks of a river. A later purchaser of the farm was held entitled to enforce this promise.)

Suppose that Bert now sells Redacre to Donald. **Can Charles sue Donald on the covenants?**

With respect to the **negative** 'no businesses' covenant, the answer is (in principle) **yes**. This 'no businesses covenant' is a restrictive covenant, governed by the elaborate law which we are about to discuss.

With respect to the **positive** 'repair and repaint' covenant, the answer is **no**. It is a principle of English law that the **burden** of a positive covenant relating to a piece of land cannot 'run with the land'. The covenant to repair and repaint is enforceable only against the original covenantor, Bert. It cannot be enforced against Donald, a purchaser of the fee simple.

This rule, that 'positive covenants cannot run with the burdened land', has been much criticised, but was recently re-affirmed by the House of Lords in *Rhone* v *Stephens* [1994] 2 All ER 65.

 ACTIVITY 99

Suppose that Alfred, instead of selling Redacre to Bert, had granted him a 999-year lease charging a large premium and a nominal rent. Bert later assigned the lease to Donald. Could Charles enforce the repair and repaint covenant against Donald?

If you did not know the answer to this question, refer back to **19.3**. A repair and repaint covenant contained in the 999-year lease would be enforceable by Charles against Donald under the doctrine of privity of estate.

26.3.1 RESTRICTIVE COVENANTS LAW DIVIDES ITSELF INTO THREE PARTS

(a) Issues relating to the running of the burden of covenants with the servient land.

(b) Issues relating to the running of the benefit of covenants with the dominant land.

(c) Developers trying to 'escape' from restrictive covenants burdening their land.

Issue (a) is straightforward and is discussed below. Issue (b), dealt with in **Chapter 27**, is notoriously complex: the courts (particularly in the last 40 years) have created a total mess. Issue (c), dealt with in **Chapter 28**, is also quite complex, but has an element of excitement about it!

26.4 Passing the Burden of a Restrictive Covenant

Three conditions must be fulfilled before the obligation to observe a restrictive covenant will pass to a successor in title to the servient land.

26.4.1 THE COVENANT MUST BE NEGATIVE IN SUBSTANCE

The test is that the observance of the covenant must not necessitate expenditure on the part of the servient owner. A covenant 'not to allow this building to fall into disrepair' is of course positive, and not a restrictive covenant.

On the other hand, a covenant 'to keep Xacre as an open space uncovered by buildings' (the covenant involved in the 1847 case of *Tulk* v *Moxhay* (1848) 2 Ph 774, which in effect invented this whole area of law) is a restrictive covenant.

26.4.2 THE COVENANT MUST BE MADE WITH AN INTENT TO BURDEN THE SERVIENT LAND

The nineteenth-century lawyers who 'invented' restrictive covenants drew a distinction between:

(a) a covenant intended to bind only the covenantor; and

(b) a covenant intended to throw a continuing burden on the land itself and thereby bind all subsequent owners of the land.

Only the latter type of covenant is a valid restrictive covenant.

Nineteenth-century covenants usually included phraseology like, 'I Charley Farns-Barns covenant on behalf of myself and my successors in title . . .'. This long-winded phraseology is no longer necessary, as the point is now covered by a **'word-saving'** provision, s. 79(1) of the Law of Property Act 1925.

Read s. 79(1) in *Cases and Materials* (26.2.2); for future reference, compare it with its obvious sister provision, s. 78(1).

Section 79(1) is a word-saving provision which in effect provides that covenants which relate to the covenantor's land are **deemed** to be made on behalf of his successors in title **unless** the contrary appears from the terms of the covenant. Thus anybody who makes a covenant about the use of his land is presumed to intend that the covenant will be a **permanent burden** on the land irrespective of its ownership. In the unlikely event that it is desired that covenant should bind only the original covenantor and not his successors, this will have to be expressly stated.

26.4.3 THE COVENANT MUST BE MADE TO PROTECT DOMINANT LAND RETAINED BY THE COVENANTEE

In *London County Council* v *[Mrs] Allen* [1914] 3 KB 642 the LCC sold a large amount of land to Mr Allen, a builder. With respect to one small part of the land, Mr Allen covenanted not to build upon it. This small parcel was intended as an open space for the local residents. The LCC retained no other land in the vicinity.

Mr Allen sold the small parcel to his wife, who commenced building work. The LCC sought an injunction against Mrs Allen, which was refused. The Council had no dominant land, so it could not claim it had the benefit of a restrictive covenant. (Nowadays the Council would use town planning law to curb Mr and Mrs Allen's activities.)

A rather different problem arose in *Newton Abbot Co-operative Society Ltd* v *Williamson and Treadgold* [1952] 1 All ER 279. Originally, a Mrs Mardon owned two shops in the small central Devon town of Bovey Tracey. The shops were about 50 yards apart on opposite sides of the street.

In 1923, Mrs Mardon sold one of the shops. In the conveyance of that shop there was imposed a restrictive covenant which said that no ironmongery was to be sold from the shop. The restrictive covenant did not identify the dominant land. However, the shop across the road retained by Mrs Mardon sold . . . ironmongery!

The judge held that there was a valid restrictive covenant which bound a subsequent purchaser of the shop sold by Mrs Mardon in 1923. Although the dominant land was not expressly identified in the conveyance which contained the restrictive covenant, it could be identified by examining the geography of the locality. That, in the view of the judge, was sufficient.

 ACTIVITY 101

What would have been the legal position if the shops had been 500 yards apart in a large city?

You might well argue that there would be no valid restrictive covenant, as it would not be possible confidently to identify the dominant land.

26.5 Restrictive Covenants as Equitable Interests

Restrictive covenants were in effect first 'invented' in the mid-nineteenth century by the pre-1875 Court of Chancery. The common law courts never recognised them. Thus, historically, all restrictive covenants are equitable interests, and this was confirmed by s. 1 of the Law of Property Act 1925. It follows that:

(a) Where the servient estate is unregistered title, a pre-1926 restrictive covenant is still subject to the doctrine of notice.

(b) Where the servient estate is unregistered title, a post-1925 restrictive covenant is registrable as a land charge.

(c) Where the servient estate is registered title, the restrictive covenant must be protected by entry on the register of a notice or caution.

26.6   Remedies to Enforce a Restrictive Covenant

The fact that a restrictive covenant is always only an equitable interest means that the principal remedy to enforce a restrictive covenant against a successor in title to the servient land is an injunction; there is no **automatic** right to damages.

In restrictive covenant cases the court has a discretion as to the remedy it can grant. The court may award damages instead of or in addition to an injunction. The discretion which the court has on matters of remedies is well illustrated by the decision in *Wrotham Park Estate Ltd* v *Parkside Homes* [1974] 2 All ER 321.

Read *Wrotham Park Estate Ltd* v *Parkside Homes* in *Cases and Materials* (26.3). However, it is important to realise that the case raised two issues. The first was, 'Did the current plaintiff have the right to enforce the restrictive covenant?', a point I deal with in Chapter 27. In this chapter I deal only with the second issue: 'What remedy should be granted to the plaintiff?'

In 1935, the Wrotham Park Estate, then owned by the Earl of Strafford, extended to about 4,000 acres. In that year the Earl sold 47 acres out of the Estate. This land was subject to a restrictive covenant 'not to develop the . . . land for building purposes except in strict accordance with plans [approved by the owners of Wrotham Park Estate]'. The covenant was expressed to be for the benefit of the 'Wrotham Park Estate'.

This sort of restrictive covenant is quite common. The dominant owners do not want totally to prevent development of the servient land; they just want to ensure that the development is 'good class', not low grade, development.

The plaintiff company later acquired Wrotham Park Estate. The defendant, Parkside Homes, acquired a small part of the servient land. The defendant obtained planning permission **from the local authority** to build 13 'middle class' houses on this land. It did not, however, submit its plans to the plaintiff for approval. It believed (for reasons which will be explained at **27.3.1.3**) that the plaintiff was not entitled to enforce the covenant.

In January 1972, the defendant started to lay foundations. On 14 February, the plaintiff issued a writ claiming an injunction to restrain building. The plaintiff, however, then made a mistake. It did not apply for an 'interlocutory', i.e. temporary, injunction to restrain the development pending a full trial of the dispute.

The defendant carried on building, and by the date of the trial before Brightman J (July 1973) the 13 houses were complete and 13 married couples had purchased them and moved in.

Brightman J held (for reasons which I will explain in the next chapter) that the plaintiff was entitled to enforce the restrictive covenant. The plaintiff, having won on that issue, took the attitude, 'The defendant has acted in defiance of our rights. There is a danger that the tone of the area will go down. The only way our rights can be protected is if the court makes an order (a "mandatory injunction") that the houses be demolished'.

Brightman J refused to grant such an order: 'It would, in my opinion, be an unpardonable waste of much needed houses to direct that they be pulled down.' He thus exercised his 'discretion' to refuse an injunction. But he also 'in his discretion' decided to award the plaintiff damages. How much damages should he award?

The houses themselves were of good quality, situated in an area (Potters Bar) which is prime 'commuter belt' for London. The existence of these houses did not in any way lower the tone of the area. There was every reason to suppose that if the defendant had complied with the covenant and submitted plans to the plaintiff, the plaintiff would have approved them.

You may be thinking that the judge awarded nominal damages, but this would be allowing the defendant 'to get away with it'. Brightman J took note of a fact which you may find surprising but which is perfectly true. The dominant owner to a restrictive covenant is often willing to execute a deed releasing the servient land from the covenant. However, the dominant owner usually requires that he be paid a consideration (some would say 'bribe') for releasing the covenant. He often asks for a percentage of the profit the defendant will make from developing the (ex)-servient land.

Brightman J (correctly in my view) decided to award the plaintiff the 'price' it could **reasonably** have asked for releasing the covenant. The plaintiff suggested 50 per cent of the defendant's profits on the 13 houses. The judge awarded 5 per cent! The total profit was estimated at £50,000, thus the plaintiff got £2,500.

This award of damages by Brightman J in *Wrotham Park* has been criticised in some quarters, but in the recent case of *Jaggard* v *Sawyer* [1995] 1 WLR 269, the Court of Appeal approved it and applied it to a situation where a single house had been built in a garden in breach of a restrictive covenant. As in *Wrotham Park*, damages were awarded on the basis of what a reasonable dominant owner could have asked for releasing the covenant.

26.7 The Benefit of Restrictive Covenants – Identifying the Original Covenantees

It is perfectly possible to enter into a restrictive covenant for the benefit of a number of original covenantees. For example, a restrictive covenant is entered into in favour of several landowners all with land adjacent to the servient land.

Suppose Ernest owned Centreacre and Eastacre. Centreacre is surrounded by Eastacre, Northacre, Westacre, and Southacre. Northacre is owned by Norman, Westacre by William, and Southacre by Stephen. All five parcels of land are farmland.

Ernest sells Centreacre to Celia. In the conveyance of Centreacre Celia covenants, for the benefit of Eastacre, Northacre, Westacre, and Southacre, that Centreacre will be used for agricultural purposes only. Thus clearly there are four original covenantees and four parcels of dominant land.

Prior to the Conveyancing Act 1881 there was a problem with the kind of arrangement just described. There was an old common law rule that only people who actually executed a deed could claim benefits under the deed. In our example only Celia and Ernest would execute the deed containing the restrictive covenant. Thus at common law only Ernest could claim to be an original covenantee and only Eastacre was dominant land. This, of course, was contrary to what Ernest and Celia intended.

The inconvenient old common law rule was abolished by what is now s. 56 of the Law of Property Act 1925. Under that section, any person identifiable at the time the deed is executed and intended to have the benefit of a covenant is an original covenantee, whether or not he executed the deed containing the covenant.

In our example, under the modern law, who are the original covenantees, and what is/are the dominant land(s)?

I hope you deduced that Ernest, Norman, William, and Stephen are **all** original covenantees. Eastacre, Northacre, Westacre, and Southacre are separate parcels of dominant land.

26.8   Conclusion

In this chapter you should have learnt three things of importance: the circumstances in which a restrictive covenant is enforceable against the servient land; the remedies available to a dominant owner when a restrictive covenant is infringed; the identification of the original covenantees. We are now in a position to move on to **Chapter 27**, in which we consider the various ways in which the right to enforce a restrictive covenant can pass from an original covenantee (in the example just considered, Ernest, Norman, William, and Stephen were all original covenantees) to a successor in title to that covenantee's land.

CHAPTER TWENTY-SEVEN

THE PASSING OF THE BENEFIT OF RESTRICTIVE COVENANTS

27.1   Objectives

By the end of this chapter you should be able to:

■ explain how the concept of annexation of restrictive covenants operated prior to the controversial decision in *Federated Homes*;

■ appreciate the impact of the Court of Appeal decision in *Federated Homes* (assuming it is correctly decided);

■ explain the rules regarding assignment of restrictive covenants;

■ explain the concept 'building scheme';

■ appreciate why the Law Commission is highly critical of the current state of the law.

27.2   Introduction

I want you to think back to the law of easements for a moment. If an easement is appurtenant to a parcel of dominant land, then that easement automatically 'runs' with the dominant land. This means that anybody who acquires the dominant land can automatically enjoy the benefit of the easement.

I wish I could make a similar simple statement about the benefit of restrictive covenants. Unfortunately that is impossible. The law as to when a successor to dominant land acquires the right to enforce a restrictive covenant benefiting that land is extremely complex.

Indeed, there are three **alternative** sets of rules. If, but only if, a successor to the dominant land can bring himself within **one** of these sets of rules, he will be able to enforce the restrictive covenant. The sets of rules are:

(a)   Annexation.

(b)   Assignment.

(c) 'Building scheme'.

These sets of rules originally were developed in the nineteenth and early-twentieth centuries. Until the Second World War the rules (though already quite complex) were clear and strictly enforced. Their strict enforcement sometimes meant that a purchaser of dominant land did not get the benefit of an existing covenant intended to benefit that land. But the law had the **great merit of certainty.**

That certainty has been destroyed by some extremely short-sighted decisions of the courts, most notably the Court of Appeal decision in *Federated Homes Ltd* v *Mill Lodge Properties Ltd* [1980] 1 All ER 371. The modern decisions show an alarming trend to bend or change the old rules in favour of persons **claiming to be dominant owners**.

This trend makes life very difficult for servient owners generally. If a person owns land which is subject to a restrictive covenant, it is sometimes very difficult to work out who the dominant owners are and thus who, if anyone, is entitled to sue if the covenant is broken.

27.3 Annexation

The essence of annexation is easy to follow. If the benefit of a restrictive covenant is annexed to Blackacre then (*cf.* an appurtenant easement) the right to enforce the covenant passes on to all successors in title to Blackacre.

Unfortunately, considerable confusion has been introduced into this area of the law by the judgment of the Court of Appeal in *Federated Homes Ltd* v *Mill Lodge Properties Ltd*. In my view this case was wrongly decided, and ought to be overruled by the House of Lords.

In any event, even if *Federated Homes* is correct, that case cannot apply to covenants entered into pre-1926. This is confirmed by the decision in *Sainsburys* v *Enfield Borough Council* [1989] 2 All ER 817. Thus we must first consider the law ignoring *Federated Homes*, and then endeavour to explain the effect of the case.

27.3.1 THE TRADITIONAL VIEWPOINT ON ANNEXATION

According to the traditional view (ignoring *Federated Homes*), annexation can be achieved only by drafting the document containing the restrictive covenant to **express** an intention to benefit a defined piece of land, rather than merely to benefit the original covenantee.

To achieve annexation to (say) Blackacre, drafting using one of the following methods should be employed. (Even today competent solicitors always use one of these formulations.)

■ 'This covenant is entered into for the benefit of Blackacre.'

■ 'This covenant is entered into for the benefit of Jones in his capacity as owner of Blackacre.'

■ 'This covenant is entered into with Jones and his successors in title to Blackacre.'

ACTIVITY 103

Now have another look at s. 78(1) of the Law of Property Act 1925 in *Cases and Materials* (27.1), again comparing it with its sister provision, s. 79(1) in *Cases and Materials* (26.2.2).

Section 78(1) has, like its sister, traditionally been viewed as a 'word-saving' provision inserted to ensure that there were no doubts about the effectiveness of the first two formulas above. (Unfortunately, I shall have to return to s. 78 later.)

The traditional approach to annexation is best exemplified by *Renals* v *Cowlishaw* (1879) 11 Ch D 866. The conveyance of the servient land said that the restrictive covenant was entered into for the benefit of the vendors, 'their heirs, administrators and assigns'. That phrase implied the existence of dominant land, but the conveyance did not identify any dominant land. That omission was fatal.

The Court of Appeal held that there had been no annexation.

A modern case, *Jamaica Mutual Life Assurance* v *Hillsborough* [1989] 1 WLR 1101, also involved a situation where the dominant land was not expressly identified. The Privy Council was applying Jamaican (**not English**) law, and held that in **Jamaica** annexation can be achieved only by an express clause in the document creating the restrictive covenants.

27.3.1.1 Annexation to the whole or to each and every part?

On the traditional view of the law, a restrictive covenant which is annexed to 'Blackacre' is presumptively annexed **only to the whole of Blackacre**. This presumption can be rebutted if the conveyance includes some phrase such as 'this covenant is annexed to Blackacre and each and every part thereof'.

When drafting a restrictive covenant for the benefit of a large piece of land, the solicitor acting for the dominant owner needs to decide whether:

(a) to annex the covenant only to the whole of the dominant land; **or**

(b) to annex the covenant to 'each and every part of the dominant land'.

Each alternative has its advantages and disadvantages.

27.3.1.2 The disadvantages of annexation only to the whole of the dominant land – the 'small plot-big plot' situation

Any annexation only to the whole may be ineffective if the servient land is small and the dominant land is (relatively) very large. This is because the dominant owner must prove that **the whole of the large** dominant land benefits from the covenant. The leading case is *Re Ballard* [1937] 2 All ER 691.

Figure 8   The dominant and servient land in *Re Ballard*

The then owners of the Childwickbury Estate sold 16 acres on the edge of the Estate, but subject to a restrictive covenant that the land sold should be used for agricultural purposes only. This covenant was expressed to be for the benefit of 'the whole of the Childwickbury Estate'. Childwickbury extended to 1,700 acres.

The judge held that there was no valid annexation. For annexation to be valid, the current owners of Childwickbury would have to have proved that **all 1,700 acres** were benefited by the 'agriculture only' covenant. In the judge's view, those parts of Childwickbury close to the 16 acres were benefited, but those further away were not.

ACTIVITY 104

Read the extracts from *Re Ballard* in *Cases and Materials* (27.2.1.2), and consider what the position would be if the covenant had been entered into 'for the benefit of Childwickbury and each and every part thereof'.

There would have been a valid annexation to those parts of Childwickbury close to the 16 acres, but not to those parts further away. There would have been a valid annexation to those parts south-west of the circular line in **Figure 8**, but not to those north-east thereof. (Where exactly the 'circular line' should be drawn, of course, might be subject to fierce dispute!)

27.3.1.3   The modern trend in 'small-plot big-plot' cases

In recent years the courts have been much more willing to find as a fact that a covenant on a very small piece of land does benefit the whole of a large plot. (Such findings of fact were made in *Marten* v *Flight Refuelling* [1961] 2 All ER 696 at 706; *Earl of Leicester* v *Wells-next-the-Sea UDC* [1972] 3 All ER 89, and in *Wrotham Park Estate* v *Parkside Homes* [1974] 2 All ER 321.)

ACTIVITY 105

Re-read the extracts from *Wrotham Park Estate* v *Parkside Homes* in *Cases and Materials* (26.3). We are now dealing with the first issue raised in the case, i.e. whether the plaintiff had the right to enforce the covenant. What was the decision of the court on this matter?

You will recall that in *Wrotham Park Estate* v *Parkside Homes*, a covenant over 47 acres was annexed to the whole of a large estate extending to 4,000 acres. Was that annexation valid? The plaintiff called expert evidence from surveyors that the covenant over 47 acres could benefit all 4,000 acres. The defendant called expert evidence that the covenant could not possibly benefit all 4,000 acres. I am sure that judges from earlier generations would have laughed at the plaintiff's evidence and found that there was no valid annexation. Such judges would have dismissed the proceedings, and the issue of remedies discussed at **26.6** would not have arisen.

However Brightman J held:

> There can be obvious cases where a restrictive covenant clearly is, or clearly is not, of benefit to an estate. Between the two extremes there is inevitably an area where the benefit to the estate is a matter of personal opinion where responsible and reasonable persons can have divergent views.

In other words, if there is conflicting evidence as to whether the whole of the large plot benefits from the covenant, the decision should go in favour of annexation to the whole of the large piece of land. Thus the owners of Wrotham Park got the benefit of the doubt. The covenant was held to be validly annexed to the whole of their land and they could enforce the covenant.

27.3.1.4   Annexation destroyed on sub-division of the dominant land

If there is a valid annexation to (only) the whole of a dominant piece of land, then that annexation is destroyed on the sub-division of the dominant land: *Russell* v *Archdale* [1962] 2 All ER 305.

You should understand this principle if you consider **Figure 9** and the accompanying example.

Figure 9   Annexation destroyed where dominant land sub-divided

Westacre	Eastacre

Suppose the owner of Eastacre enters into a restrictive covenant expressed to be for the benefit of (only) the whole of Westacre. While Westacre remains all in one piece there is no problem; successive owners of Westacre can enforce the covenant. But if Wally, the current owner of Westacre, sells the northern half of the plot to (say) Norma, the right to enforce the covenant will **not** pass by virtue of annexation to Norma.

If Wally then sold the southern half of Westacre to Sally, Sally would not get the benefit of the covenant by virtue of annexation either. As I said before, the division of the land **destroys** the annexation.

ACTIVITY 106

Consider what the position would be if the annexation had been to 'Westacre and each and every part thereof'.

The splitting of the land would **not** have been fatal to annexation. Both Norma and Sally would acquire the right to enforce the covenant.

27.3.1.5 The disadvantage of annexation to each and every part

When the dominant land is sub-divided, the number of owners entitled to enforce the covenant is bound to increase; with a large dominant area the number of dominant owners could initially be one, but later be enormous. Consider the situation represented by the figure below.

Figure 10   Annexation to each and every part of Bigpots Estate

The Duke of Dunstable owns the huge Bigpots Estate. He sells off 'south-west corner' (SWC), subject to a restrictive covenant banning building on the land. The covenant is annexed 'to the Bigpots Estate and each and every part thereof'. Subsequently the Duke sells off other small pieces of land (SP) near to south-west corner.

Sid, the current owner of south-west corner, asks the duke to cancel the 'no building' covenant. The duke agrees to do so 'for a consideration of £20,000'. Sid obtains planning permission, but the purchasers of the other small pieces near to south-west corner have acquired the right to enforce the covenant! Any one of them could enforce the covenant against Sid.

27.3.2 THE POTENTIAL EFFECTS OF THE *FEDERATED HOMES* CASE – A HIGHLY QUESTIONABLE NEW FORM OF ANNEXATION

It is possible to get tangled up in the facts of this case, so I am going to simplify the facts to their bare essentials.

I will start by making two comments on those facts. First, the restrictive covenant involved was of a rather unusual type. You may well ask, 'Should these sorts of covenant be allowed?'. I personally think they should be banned, but that is irrelevant! Under current law, they **are** allowed.

Secondly, it would appear that a large amount of money (profits from a large housing development) hung on the outcome of the case. The dispute arose because of bad drafting of the original restrictive covenant. One would think that solicitors acting for property developers would be punctilious in their drafting.

The story in the case starts with a firm called Mackenzie Hill Ltd owning a large amount of development land at Newport Pagnell (just north of Milton Keynes). It had outline planning permission to develop the land with 1,250 houses. It sold part of that land to Mill Lodge. The conveyance included a restrictive covenant:

> In carrying out the development of the . . . land the purchaser shall not build at a greater density than a total of 300 dwellings so as not to reduce the number of units [i.e. houses] which the vendor might eventually erect on the retained land under the existing planning consent.

Mackenzie Hill later sold the land they retained in the area to Federated Homes. The Court of Appeal had (*inter alia*) to decide whether the above clause effected an annexation so that on the sale of the 'retained land' the right to enforce the covenant passed automatically to Federated Homes.

ACTIVITY 107

Now read the extracts from *Federated Homes* set out in *Cases and Materials* (27.1), but do not panic if you do not yet understand the legal arguments.

The Court in *Federated Homes* held that the clause quoted achieved a **valid annexation**.

I am sure nineteenth-century judges would have decided otherwise. They would have held, 'No annexation, the covenant was not correctly drafted. The dominant land was not clearly identified'. Many twentieth-century lawyers (including me) argue that that should have been the decision in 1980.

The Court of Appeal (led by Brightman LJ) adopted an argument put forward in **one** textbook that s. 78 of the Law of Property Act 1925 created a new form of 'statutory annexation'. The court held that **by virtue of s. 78**, there was a valid annexation to 'the retained land'.

The Court rejected the commonly held view that s. 78 was (like its sister s. 79) a **'word-saving'** provision not designed to change substantive law. Instead the Court of Appeal put forward two alternative interpretations of s. 78.

(a) There is annexation where the covenant mentions the existence of dominant land, but that land can be identified only by looking at the surrounding circumstances.

or

(b) There is annexation whenever the covenantee retains land in the vicinity of the servient land, whether that land is mentioned in the restrictive covenant or not. (Annexation will then be to all the covenantee's land in the vicinity.)

Although the first view would have been sufficient to decide the case in favour of the plaintiffs, the Court appears to favour the second view.

27.3.2.1 *Federated Homes* and 'each and every part'

Brightman LJ caused yet further confusion with an *obiter dictum* directed at the issue of whether annexation is only to the whole of a piece of dominant land, or is to 'each and every part'. Ignoring all past decisions (including his own in *Wrotham Park*, see **27.3.1.3**) he was of the view that annexation is to be presumed to be to 'each and every part' unless the contrary is expressly stated.

27.3.2.2 The practical effect of *Federated Homes*

If correct, the decision in *Federated Homes* means that whenever a restrictive covenant has been entered into after 1925 that covenant is automatically annexed to (each and every part of) **all** land which the covenantee retains in the vicinity of the servient land. It does not matter that the conveyance containing the covenant does not identify the dominant land.

ACTIVITY 108

Consider the facts of the *Newton Abbot Co-op* case set out at 26.4.3. That case, as we shall see at 27.4.2, was decided on 'assignment' not 'annexation' principles. But try to apply the *Federated Homes* rule to the facts of *Newton Abbot Co-op*.

If *Federated Homes* is correct (and it is a big 'if') then on the facts of *Newton Abbot Co-op* there would be **an annexation** to the ironmongers across the road (and each and every part of it), even though those premises were not even hinted at in the restrictive covenant.

27.3.2.3 Drafting of restrictive covenants in the light of *Federated Homes*

In *Roake v Chadha* [1984] 3 All ER 503, the judge specifically upheld the effectiveness of a clause (**drafted in 1934**) which made it clear that the benefit of a set of restrictive covenants was not to pass by annexation, but only by express assignment. The judge rejected an argument that the benefit of the covenants had nevertheless been annexed by virtue of s. 78. He held that careful drafting had excluded the effect of s. 78.

Roake v *Chadha* confirms that the potential effects of *Federated Homes* can be avoided by careful drafting of covenants. But *Roake* v *Chadha* is of little comfort to **competent draftsmen** who have found the meaning of their pre-1980 drafts seemingly changed retrospectively by the Court of Appeal. (You should also bear in mind the Law Commission's comments which I quote at **27.6**.)

27.3.2.4 Why the House of Lords should overrule *Federated Homes*

Two recent Privy Council decisions applied Jamaican and Trinidadian law respectively. They make no reference either to s. 78 or *Federated Homes*. However, both these cases were decided on policy grounds totally overlooked by *Federated Homes*. It is submitted that the reasoning in these two cases undermines *Federated Homes* and indicates that the House of Lords, if it had the opportunity, would probably overrule that decision (You should also note the powerful arguments of the Law Commission quoted at **27.6**.)

Jamaica Mutual Life v *Hillsborough* [1989] 1 WLR 1101
In this case, the Privy Council held that, in Jamaica, annexation can be achieved only by an express clause identifying the dominant land. It seems that one of the reasons for the Privy Council's decision was the policy consideration that a person entering into a restrictive covenant ought from the outset to know for certain the identity of the dominant land(s). *Federated Homes* totally overlooked this enormously important consideration.

Emile Elias v *Pine Groves* [1993] 1 WLR 305
This case concerned an alleged building scheme. (Building schemes are discussed at **27.5**.) The Privy Council (advising through Lord Browne-Wilkinson) reaffirmed a long-standing principle first stated in 1909, that for a valid scheme the area of land covered by the scheme must be fixed before any land is sold off by the common vendor: 'In order to create a valid building scheme, the purchasers of all the land within the area of the scheme must know what that area is.'

Thus, in a building scheme, owners of land know the full extent of the dominant land. By contrast, somebody who buys land subject to restrictive covenants annexed under the *Federated Homes* principle is guessing at the identity of the dominant land.

27.4 Assignment of the Benefit of Restrictive Covenants

27.4.1 THE RULES FOR A VALID ASSIGNMENT

These rules are important in two types of situation:

■ Where the restrictive covenant has not been validly annexed to the dominant land.

■ Where the restrictive covenant has been annexed only to the whole of the dominant land, and that dominant land is sub-divided. (Remember that the sub-division destroys the annexation: see **27.3.1.4**.)

(It is worth noting that if *Federated Homes* is correctly decided (see **27.3.2**), then these assignment rules are not as important as they used to be. For example, the *Newton Abbot Co-op* case was decided applying assignment principles; but applying *Federated Homes*, there would be an annexation to the ironmongers across the road.)

Where assignment of the benefit of a restrictive covenant is under consideration, the rather elaborate rules in *Miles* v *Easter* [1933] Ch 611, especially at 632, apply. If a dominant owner is to be able to enforce a covenant under the assignment rules, four conditions must be satisfied:

(a) The covenant must be entered into for the benefit of 'ascertainable land'. It must be possible to identify the dominant land from the terms of the document containing the covenant, or (as in *Newton Abbot Co-op*) from the surrounding circumstances.

(b) This 'ascertainable land' must actually be benefited by the existence of the covenant. (In *Marten* v *Flight Refuelling* [1961] 2 All ER 696 and *Leicester* v *Wells-next-the-Sea* [1972] 3 All ER 77 it seems to have been assumed that where the 'ascertainable land' is a large area, the whole of that area must be benefited for the rules to operate. In each of these cases the judge found that a very large area was benefited by the restrictive covenants.)

(c) The assignee must have acquired at least part of the 'ascertainable land'. (In *Russell* v *Archdale* [1962] 2 All ER 305 and *Stilwell* v *Blackman* [1967] 3 All ER 514, it was held that a covenant annexed only to the **whole** of a piece of dominant land could be assigned on the sale of **part** of that dominant land.)

(d) Simultaneous with the conveyance of the land, the assignee must have been assigned the benefit of the restrictive covenant.

The basic idea underlying this last rule is that every time the dominant land is conveyed (or transferred in any way), the conveyance or other transfer document should include **an express clause** assigning the benefit of the restrictive covenant.

ACTIVITY 109

Suppose I am contemplating buying Downacre. It appears that Downacre is dominant to a restrictive covenant over Slowacre, but that the covenant has not been annexed to Downacre. What will I insist be put into the conveyance of Downacre?

I will insist that the conveyance to me of Downacre includes a special clause assigning me the benefit of the covenant.

SAQ 142

If I later sell Downacre to Penny, what will she insist I put in the conveyance to her?

She will, of course, insist that I include in the conveyance to her a special clause assigning the benefit of the restrictive covenant.

27.4.2 EXCEPTIONS TO THE RULE THAT THERE MUST BE AN EXPRESS ASSIGNMENT CLAUSE

The courts have created two exceptions to the rule ((d) at **27.4.1**) that every time the land which is dominant to an unannexed covenant is sold, the covenant passes only if there is an express assignment clause.

The first exception was recognised in *Northbourne* v *Johnstone* [1922] 2 Ch 309. In that case the contract for sale of the dominant land included a special clause promising that the vendor would assign to the purchaser an unannexed restrictive covenant. Somebody forgot to include the special assignment clause in the conveyance itself. The court nevertheless held that the purchaser had acquired the right to enforce the covenant. It applied the maxim 'equity looks on as done that which ought to be done' **to the contract**. The contract transferred to the purchaser the right to enforce the covenant.

The *Northbourne* exception is clearly correct. The same cannot be said of the second exception, which was created by the *Newton Abbot Co-op* case. At one stage in the history of the dominant ironmongers the current owner died, but her will made no mention of the unannexed covenant. Nor did the 'assent' of the shop signed by her executors. The judge nevertheless held that the current owners of the ironmongery could enforce the unannexed covenant.

In *Leicester* v *Wells-next-the-Sea* [1972] 3 All ER 77, the land dominant to the covenant was settled land. One life tenant died and was succeeded by another life tenant. The new vesting assent executed by the Settled Land Act trustees made no mention of the covenant, yet the new life tenant was held entitled to enforce the covenant.

The apparent effect of these two cases (on this point) is that if the dominant land devolves on death (rather than passing on sale) the new owner of the land can enforce the covenant without an express assignment in either the will, or the assent from the deceased's personal representatives.

These last two cases are a startling illustration of the sad trend I mentioned at **27.2**, i.e. that modern courts tend 'to bend or change the old rules in favour of persons claiming to be dominant owners'. You should note, too, that in these two cases the dominant owners in whose favour the rules were 'bent' were donees, not purchasers!

27.5 Building Schemes or Schemes of Development

If you go back to **1.4.2**, you will see a modern example of what conveyancers have traditionally called 'a building scheme'. If a building scheme has been validly created then all properties within the scheme are both servient and dominant land. All the current owners are both obliged to observe the covenants and are entitled to enforce them.

27.5.1 THE CONDITIONS REQUIRED FOR A VALID BUILDING SCHEME

To establish a building scheme a number of conditions must be satisfied. These conditions were laid down in *Elliston* v *Reacher* [1908] 2 Ch 374, at 384:

(a) At the outset the creator of the scheme (nowadays we would refer to him as 'the developer') sets up a scheme for a defined area of land. As the Privy Council reaffirmed in *Emile Elias* v *Pine Groves* [1993] 1 WLR 305 (see **27.3.2.4**), the area of the scheme must be fixed before any selling commences.

(b) The creator of the scheme sells off the land in 'plots' subject to restrictive covenants. The covenants must form part of an organised scheme for the whole area decided upon before selling commenced. The 'plots' may be empty sites ripe for development, or they may already have been built upon. (In the nineteenth century the creator of a building scheme would usually sell off vacant plots on which the purchasers would arrange for the construction of their houses in compliance with the covenants. In the twentieth century the creators are usually firms like Barratt or Wimpey selling off houses they have already constructed.)

(c) The creator of the scheme must have intended the restrictions on each plot to be for the benefit of the other plots. (He must have intended 'mutual enforceability'.)

(d) The original purchasers from the creator of the scheme must have realised that the covenants were to be mutually enforceable between the purchasers.

27.5.2 PROVING THAT THE CREATOR OF THE SCHEME INTENDED MUTUAL ENFORCEABILITY

Normally, the intention that the covenants should be mutually enforceable is apparent from documents drawn up when the scheme was first created.

In the nineteenth century the creator of a building scheme usually made his intentions clear by drawing up a 'mutual deed of covenant'. This was a document (often very long) which contained all the restrictive covenants and stated that the covenants were intended to be mutually enforceable. Each purchaser of a 'plot' was required to seal the 'mutual deed'. Thus, if there were 40 plots in the scheme, there would eventually be 41 seals on the mutual deed.

For an example of such a 'mutual deed', read the extracts from *Baxter* v *Four Oaks* [1965] 1 All ER 906, in *Cases and Materials* (27.4.2).

The enactment of s. 56 of the Law of Property Act 1925 (see **26.7**) means that there is no longer any need to use this cumbersome 'mutual deed' device. What happens nowadays is that the developer (Wimpey, Barratt, etc.) sells off each house subject to restrictive covenants, and the conveyance (or land transfer) of each house makes it clear that the covenants are entered into for the benefit of all the other houses on the estate. This is undoubtedly sufficient to create a 'building scheme'. This is illustrated by *Eagling* v *Gardner* [1970] 2 All ER 838.

27.5.3 PROVING INTENTION FROM THE CIRCUMSTANCES SURROUNDING THE ORIGINAL SALE

In *Elliston* v *Reacher* (the leading case on building schemes, see **27.5.1**) the intention that there was to be mutual enforceability was proved not by reference to documents, but by reference to the manner in which the original plots of land were advertised and sold.

In that case the building scheme was created in 1861. The plots were sold from an office in Ipswich, but the scheme itself was on 10 acres of land at Felixstowe, 12 miles away on the Suffolk coast.

Anybody entering the office in Ipswich would have seen on the wall a large plan of the scheme, with the restrictive covenants endorsed prominently on the plan. Potential purchasers of a plot could buy a copy of this plan (with the covenants listed) for 1s 6d. The covenants were of a kind designed to preserve the 'exclusive' nature of the area.

Now we all know that estate agents do their very best to sell properties. The prominent advertising of the restrictions was in effect saying to purchasers, 'Look what a high class area you are buying into!'. It was a natural inference from this advertising (drawn by all four judges who heard the case) that the creator of the scheme back in 1861 intended the covenants to be mutually enforceable.

The conclusion in *Elliston* v *Reacher* seems fair enough. But you should note that the dispute arose 45 years after the creation of the scheme; some of the original purchasers were still able to give evidence of what had happened. What if the dispute (which was over somebody wanting to build a hotel on one of the plots) had not arisen until 1990?

27.5.4   MODERN CASES EXPANDING THE BUILDING SCHEME PRINCIPLES

In *Elliston* v *Reacher* the courts perhaps 'stretched' the law a little bit in order to find the existence of a building scheme. (I think the judges should have insisted on the intent of mutual enforceability being spelt out in formal documentation.)

Two modern cases also betray this 'stretching' process. In *Baxter* v *Four Oaks* [1965] 1 All ER 906 there was a Victorian building scheme with one special feature. The common vendor had fixed the area of his scheme but had not divided his land into plots **before** commencing selling. Rather, he had sold each purchaser as much land as he (the purchaser) desired. (Remember that in those days the purchaser took a vacant site and then built his own house.)

Cross J held that the special feature of the case did not prevent there being a building scheme. (I am sure this is correct.) In *Baxter* there was an organised scheme of covenants for a defined area, and those covenants had been incorporated into a mutual deed of covenant.

The case which I think stretched things too far is *Re Dolphin's Conveyance* [1970] 2 All ER 664. In 1871, two sisters were tenants in common of the 30-acre 'Selly Hill Estate' on the (then) south-west edge of Birmingham. They started selling off sizeable parts of this estate. They then gave the remaining parts of Selly Hill to their nephew. He sold off further chunks of Selly Hill, until it had all gone by 1891.

As each chunk of Selly Hill was sold, restrictive covenants were imposed on the land. The purchasers (usually builders) promised to build only high class housing; each house was to have a minimum of a quarter of an acre of grounds.

On each sale the vendors (the sisters or the nephew) covenanted that if they sold further parts of Selly Hill, the same restrictive covenants would be imposed. The judge inferred from this promise by the vendors an intention that the covenants restricting the area to high-class housing were to be mutually enforceable.

The judge went on to hold that although:

(a)   there had been no scheme of restrictive covenants for the whole area decided upon before sale commenced; **and**

(b) the selling of the estate had been spread over 20 years;

there was nevertheless in his view a situation within the building scheme principle. Thus current owners of large houses on Selly Hill could enforce the covenants against Birmingham Corporation, who had bought other parts of Selly Hill for high-density council housing.

ACTIVITY 111

Is *Re Dolphin* correct, in view of the Privy Council cases discussed at 27.3.2.4?

Re Dolphin would appear to be inconsistent with the principle reasserted by the Privy Council in *Emile Elias*, that the total area of the scheme must be fixed before selling commences. It might well therefore be overruled by the Court of Appeal or House of Lords.

27.6   The Chaotic State of the Law on the Running of Benefits of Covenants

The Law Commission in its 1984 Report on Restrictive Covenants (Law Com. No. 127) sums up the situation at p. 30:

> A traveller in this area of the law, old though it is, walks on ground which is still shifting. Particularly striking examples come from the same two topics: the *Federated Homes* case has made radical and controversial changes in what was thought to be the law about annexation, and successive court decisions in recent years [in particular *Re Dolphin*] have altered the conditions thought to be essential for the establishment of a building scheme.

> Shifts in the law as interpreted by the courts may be wholly beneficial so far as future covenants are concerned, but they must of course apply equally to existing covenants and here their effects are much more mixed. If a landowner sought legal advice periodically about the enforcement of a particular covenant, he would have to be told different things at different times; and his lot would not be a happy one if he had acted in good faith on advice given one year only to find it invalidated the next.

> Before leaving the subject of uncertainty we would mention one particular instance in which the law . . . is productive of uncertainty in practice. There is at present no requirement that the instrument creating the covenant shall describe the benefited land clearly enough to enable it to be identified without extrinsic evidence.

The Law Commission proposes to forbid the creation of new restrictive covenants. There would be a new type of right in land, 'land obligations'. 'Land obligations' could either be negative or (subject to certain limits) positive.

Land obligations would be of two types:

(a) Neighbour Obligations;

(b)   Development Obligations (to be used in situations in which in the past a building scheme would have been created).

Whatever the form of the land obligation, one thing is crystal clear concerning the Commission's proposals. Any document(s) creating land obligations would have expressly to identify the intended dominant land. Thus, under the new law, there would be no room for decisions like *Newton Abbot Co-op*, *Federated Homes* and *Re Dolphin*.

27.7   Conclusion

'If you are going to buy land which is subject to a restrictive covenant, make sure that that land is situated in Jamaica or Trinidad, not in England or Wales.' Why might someone say that?

If you buy Jamaican or Trinidadian land then, thanks to the recent, enlightened decisions of the Privy Council, you will know exactly who the dominant owners are. You will know the identity of the party who will want to enforce the covenants, or (as often happens) who will be willing to cancel those covenants on payment of a suitable sum.

Unless there has been some exceptionally careful drafting of the restrictive covenant(s) (remember *Roake v Chadha*), the purchaser of English or Welsh land will not know **for certain** who the dominant owners are. He may well be able to make an intelligent guess, but property owners demand certainty, not guesswork. That certainty would be (largely) achieved if the House of Lords overruled both *Federated Homes* and *Re Dolphin*. Legislation in the area of restrictive covenants (though desirable) is perhaps not essential.

CHAPTER TWENTY-EIGHT

ESCAPING FROM RESTRICTIVE COVENANTS

28.1 Objectives

By the end of this programme you should be able to:

■ appreciate the problems which restrictive covenants and the highly complex law governing them can cause for developers;

■ explain how s. 84(2) of the Law of Property Act 1925 can be used by a servient owner to establish a conclusive list of all dominant owners;

■ explain why s. 84(1) of the 1925 Act is logically and conceptually totally distinct from s. 84(2);

■ advise on and distinguish between the (quite complex) grounds set out in s. 84(1) for the discharge or modification of restrictive covenants.

28.2 Introduction

If somebody buys a piece of land and obtains planning permission to develop it, his plans may still be obstructed by the existence of a restrictive covenant(s) burdening that land. **The granting of planning permission does not authorise the breaching of restrictive covenants.** The facts of *Re Dolphin* (considered at 27.5.4) neatly illustrate this point. The Corporation had planning permission for their council houses, but the restrictive covenants still prevented the development.

There are various courses of action open to the determined developer whose plans are obstructed by restrictive covenants. The main purpose of this chapter is to consider those various alternatives. You will see that I identify five, but notice that the alternatives do to some degree overlap. I should also warn you that the final alternative, proceedings under s. 84(1) of the Law of Property Act 1925, is by far the most complex.

28.3 Carry on Regardless

Some developers may boldly say, 'Let's ignore those restrictive covenants,' and start work hoping that no 'dominant owner' will come along and object. In some types of situation there is little risk in doing this. In particular, you will sometimes come across 'building schemes' where the covenants to maintain the 'poshness' of the area generally have been ignored.

ACTIVITY 113

If some 'dominant owner' in such an area tried to enforce the covenants by seeking an injunction, what do you think would probably happen?

The court would refuse an injunction, applying the maxim, 'He who comes to equity must come with clean hands'. In plain English, somebody who is in serious breach of the rules of the scheme is not entitled to enforce the rules against others.

ACTIVITY 114

In contrast to Activity 113, suppose you are a dominant owner, 'your hands are clean', and the developer has just moved the bulldozers on to the servient land. Think back to the facts of *Wrotham Park*, at 26.6. Consider what you should do.

Like the plaintiff in *Wrotham Park* you should issue a writ without delay. But (unlike in *Wrotham Park*) you should immediately seek a temporary 'interlocutory' injunction pending a full trial of the dispute.

Obtaining such an injunction is now relatively easy as you have to show to a judge only that you have an **'arguable** case' that you are a dominant owner entitled to enforce the covenant. In view of the muddle and uncertainty in the law, it is not difficult for someone to put forward a plausible **claim** that he is a dominant owner.

28.4 'Doing a Parkside Homes'

This is merely a variant on the course of action already discussed at **28.3**, and is often adopted. In the *Wrotham Park* case the defendants believed (in my view, reasonably believed) that nobody was entitled to enforce the covenant against them. They did, however, have nagging doubts. (This is not an uncommon situation; it is yet another horrible side-effect of the chaotic law.)

Parkside Homes thus commenced their building work, **but took out an insurance policy** to protect themselves (and the purchasers of their houses) should anyone succeed in a claim that the covenant could still be enforced. As we know, a claim to enforce the covenant did (unexpectedly) succeed. The £2,500 damages awarded by Brightman J was paid (as his Lordship well knew) by the insurers.

28.5   Attempt to Buy Out the Dominant Owners

You must first realise that if there are (say) 10 dominant owners, then all 10 must be persuaded to give up their rights to enforce the covenant. If nine dominant owners say, 'OK' I will give up my rights,' but the tenth says, 'Over my dead body, even ten million pounds would not persuade me!', then that is enough to exclude this course of action.

You must also appreciate that as a result of the chaos caused by modern cases such as *Federated Homes*, *Wrotham Park*, and *Re Dolphin* (see **Chapter 27**), it is often impossible to be certain that you have 'persuaded' every dominant owner. Dominant owners have a habit of turning up and convincing sympathetic judges that they have a valid claim. It may therefore be necessary to insure against the possibility of other dominant owners appearing.

28.6   Take Proceedings under the Law of Property Act 1925, Section 84(2)

Section 84(2) is a ray of sunshine in the gloomy chaos created by cases such as *Federated Homes* and *Re Dolphin*.

Take a quick look through the whole of s. 84 as set out in *Cases and Materials* (28.4). You will immediately conclude that it is a very complex section which (unlike most of the 1925 legislation) has been heavily amended since 1925. Then specifically focus your mind on s. 84(2). Does it really fit in with the rest of the section?

The point I want to stress is that Parliament has put this sub-section in the wrong place. Section 84(2) is logically distinct from the sub-sections which both precede and follow it. Moreover it is logically **anterior** to the rest of s. 84, including s. 84(1). Parliament, when amending s. 84 in 1969, should have removed s. 84(2) from its unnatural position and renumbered it s. 83A.

Section 84(2) allows a servient owner to apply **to the High Court** for a declaration establishing a complete list of all the dominant owners. Any decision of the court produces a conclusive list which is binding on everyone in the whole world.

Suppose Stephen is a servient owner of Blackacre. He takes proceedings under s. 84(2) with respect to Blackacre. The court makes a declaration that Tom, Dick and Harriet (three close neighbours who were made parties to the court proceedings) are the dominant owners. Charley (a slightly more distant neighbour) turns up after the court's decision and says, 'Hey, I am a dominant owner as well!'. What will happen in any proceedings commenced by Charley?

Charley's claim must fail, **even though he was not a party to the s. 84(2) proceedings.**

Because the effect of an order under s. 84(2) is to destroy possible claims (like that of Charley) to be dominant owner, the courts have laid down a special procedure to be adopted in s. 84(2) cases: *Re Sunnyfield* [1932] 1 Ch 79 at 93, and *Re Elm Avenue* [1984] 3 All ER 632. The courts require that an applicant under s. 84(2) (Stephen in **SAQ 143**) circularises all nearby owners, just in case any of them claim to be 'dominant'. The circular must tell the nearby owners that proceedings are pending, and that they have a right to join in as parties to those proceedings if they so wish. The circular will also warn that everyone is bound by the result of the proceedings whether or not they join in.

Having obtained a court order under s. 84(2) giving an exhaustive list of the dominant owners, the servient owner may well attempt to persuade those dominant owners to release their rights. If one or more refuse to be persuaded, then the servient owner may well then make an application to the Lands Tribunal under s. 84(1). (See **28.7** below.)

In *Re Dolphin*, Birmingham Corporation applied to the High Court for an order under s. 84(2). This application is the case which is reported and which we considered at **27.5.4**. However, it is worth knowing that Birmingham Corporation, having established a (disappointingly long) list of dominant owners then applied to the Lands Tribunal for an order under s. 84(1). I believe that those proceedings were successful.

28.7 Commence proceedings in the Lands Tribunal under Section 84(1)

The essence of s. 84(1) of the Law of Property Act 1925, is that it gives to the Lands Tribunal the power to modify or discharge out of date restrictive covenants.

The Lands Tribunal is an important administrative tribunal, whose main role is to assess the compensation which should be paid when landowners are deprived of their land by a compulsory purchase order. (This is a function which bears little resemblance to dealing with restrictive covenants).

The Lands Tribunal has no jurisdiction to decide disputes as to who is/are the dominant owners. Thus unless an order has already been obtained from the court under s. 84(2) of the 1925 Act, an applicant under s. 84(1) to the Lands Tribunal has to concede even questionable claims by neighbours that they are dominant owners. (In the case of *Re Bass* which we discuss at **28.7.2.2**, it was questionable whether some of the objecting local residents were dominant owners. To speed things up, the applicants did not dispute the claims of these residents to be dominant owners.)

28.7.1   THE BIG CHANGE IN 1969

Prior to 1969, it was relatively difficult to get a restrictive covenant discharged or modified. In practice the introduction in 1969 of the new ground (aa) has considerably altered the law, and made life relatively easier for property developers.

Another quite substantial change made in 1969 is s. 84(1C). This makes it clear that 'modification' of a restrictive covenant includes removing one covenant and replacing it with a new one. Thus, for example, the Lands Tribunal could in appropriate circumstances remove a covenant saying 'agricultural purposes only' and replace it with one saying 'residential purposes only'.

28.7.2 THE GROUNDS FOR DISCHARGE OR MODIFICATION OF RESTRICTIVE COVENANTS

Under the Law of Property Act 1925, s. 84(1), the grounds on which a restrictive covenant may be discharged or modified are as follows:

(a) that by reason of changes in the character of the property or the neighbourhood or other circumstances of the case, . . . the restriction ought to be deemed obsolete;

(aa) that . . . the continued existence [of the restrictive covenant undischarged/unmodified] would **impede some reasonable user** of the land for public or private purposes;

(b) that [the dominant owner(s)] . . . have agreed, either expressly or by implication, by their acts or omissions, to the [restrictive covenant(s)] being discharged or modified;

(c) that the proposed discharge or modification will not injure the persons entitled to the benefit of the restriction.

28.7.2.1 The old grounds (a), (b) and (c)

These are relatively straightforward. Ground (b) is virtually academic. If all the dominant owners agree to a restrictive covenant being discharged or modified, they will normally execute a deed to that effect. Applying to the tribunal in such a case would be a waste of time and money. The only possibility for a ground (b) case seems to be where the dominant owners indicated that they would agree to a discharge but then refused to execute the formal deed.

Ground (a) would be invoked, e.g. where there was a restrictive covenant 'agricultural purposes only', but all the surrounding land had been built upon. Or suppose there was one house in a street which was subject to a 'residential purposes only' covenant, but all the other houses had been converted into offices.

Ground (c) cases are relatively rare. In one case there was a restrictive covenant on a shop that no alcohol should be sold from the premises. The purpose of such a covenant was to keep the area free from the evil of 'the demon drink'. The applicants, however, already had an off-licence a few doors away. They wanted to transfer that off-licence to the servient shop. The covenant was discharged under ground (c). The 'demon drink' was already in the area; moving the outlet would not make things worse for the dominant owners. (*Re Forgacs' Application* (1976) 32 P & CR 464 is another successful ground (c) case.)

28.7.2.2 New ground (aa)

This ground, introduced in 1969, may strike you as alarmingly vague. What on earth is 'some reasonable user'? However, this 'new' ground is further defined by s. 84(1A). Under ground (aa), two elements must be satisfied, though the first element consists of two alternatives:

(1) the restriction, in impeding 'some reasonable user', either –

(a) 'does not secure to [the dominant owner(s)] any practical benefits of substantial value or advantage . . .' **or**

(b) 'is contrary to the public interest';

and

(2) . . . money will be an adequate compensation for the loss or disadvantage (if any) which any [dominant owner] will suffer from the discharge or modification.'

In determining these issues, s. 84(1B) provides that:

> . . . the Lands Tribunal shall take into account the development plan and any declared or ascertainable pattern for the grant or refusal of planning permissions in the relevant area . . .

In relation to element (1)(a) above, a dominant owner may find his right taken away by the Lands Tribunal even though the effect of removing the restrictive covenant will be to depreciate the value of his land **somewhat**.

In relation to the alternative element (1)(b) above, a dominant owner might lose his right even though the depreciation in the value of his land is **substantial**. Some might say that (1)(b) is a developers' charter. An applicant under ground (aa) will argue that the 'public interest' requires his development. He will make statements like 'much needed homes', or 'this factory if built will create X hundred jobs in an area of high unemployment'.

An applicant under ground (aa) must, however, always also satisfy element (2) above. So if his new factory, bus depot, or whatever is going to make life unbearable for the dominant owner(s), the application should be refused.

It is also important not to misunderstand s. 84(1B). That provision is **not** referring to the fact that the applicant has (presumably) obtained planning permission to develop his individual plot of land; rather it is telling the tribunal to consider the general planning picture for the area within which the applicant's plot is situated.

Town planners usually 'zone' areas for different purposes. One area may be zoned (i.e. designated) for housing, another for industry, a third for recreational activities, and so on. It is this 'zoning' which the Lands Tribunal has to take into account in applying s. 84(1B).

28.7.2.3 *Re Bass's Application* **(1973) 26 P & CR 156**

ACTIVITY 116

Read this case in *Cases and Materials* **(28.5)**. Note carefully the seven-question analysis adopted by the Lands Tribunal in this well-publicised ground (aa) case, as it is widely accepted as correct.

The applicants had bought some land in 'inner-city' Birmingham which was 'zoned' for industrial use. They obtained planning permission to establish on the land what they called 'a trunker park'. In plain English, this meant a large depot for long-distance beer lorries. It was estimated that some 250 lorries a day would come in and out of the depot. The land was, however, subject to a 'residential purposes only' restrictive covenant. Local residents, claiming to be the dominant owners to this covenant, defeated Bass's application under ground (aa) to have the covenant removed.

The tribunal analysed the issues raised by ground (aa) applications into seven questions:

Q1   Is the proposed user reasonable?

Q2   Do the covenants impede that user?

Q3   Does impeding the proposed user secure practical benefits to the objectors?

Q4   If the answer to Q3 is yes, are those benefits of substantial value or advantage?

Q5   Is impeding the proposed user contrary to the public interest?

Q6   If no to Q4, would money be adequate compensation?

Q7   If yes to Q5, would money be adequate compensation?

Applying these questions to the facts the tribunal concluded:

Q1   Yes. Bass had obtained planning permission and the obtaining of such permission is usually conclusive proof that the user is a 'reasonable' one.

Q2   Clearly, yes!

Q3   Yes, the residents were spared all those lorries.

Q4   Yes, for the same reason. (I personally think that questions 3 and 4 will always go together.)

Q5   No! That was the crucial victory for the residents. Bass argued that if a landowner gets planning permission, this automatically proves that his plans are in the public interest. This argument was firmly rejected by the tribunal. The granting of planning permission merely indicates that the proposed development is **not against** the public interest.

Bass also argued that the establishment of their depot would benefit the economy of the area and create more jobs. The tribunal accepted this was true, but these benefits had to be balanced against the noise and congestion the lorries would cause. In the tribunal's view, these disadvantages outweighed the economic advantages.

The tribunal did not have to answer questions 6 and 7.

If the tribunal had had to consider questions 6 and 7, what do you think the tribunal would have decided?

I strongly suspect that the tribunal would have held that money was not adequate compensation for the residents for all the noise, stench etc.

28.7.2.4   *Re Banks' Application* (1976) P & CR 138: A successful 'AA' application

In this case the servient land adjoined the sea. The dominant land was a row of seven houses inland from the servient land and on a higher level than the servient land. The restrictive covenant prohibited building on the servient land, thus preserving a lovely view over the sea from the dominant houses.

The servient owner obtained planning permission to build a bungalow which would impinge **somewhat** on the view from the dominant houses. The application failed under s. 84(1)(c) but succeeded under ground (aa). The restrictive covenant was modified so as to allow the bungalow to be built, but the servient owner had to pay £2,000 compensation to each of the five dominant owners who had objected. (The case of *Gilbert* v *Spoor* [1982] 2 All ER 576, is also of interest.)

28.7.3   COMPENSATION FOR DOMINANT OWNERS

Where the Lands Tribunal discharges or modifies a restrictive covenant(s), it has a discretion to award compensation to the dominant owner(s).

In practice compensation is hardly ever awarded in cases succeeding under the 'old' grounds (a), (b), and (c). However, the tribunal usually does award compensation in ground (aa) cases. When awarding compensation it has a choice between two, alternative measures of compensation:

    (i)   'a sum to make up for any loss or disadvantage suffered by [the dominant owner] in consequence of the discharge or modification'; **or**

    (ii)   'a sum to make up for any effect which the restriction had, at the time when it was imposed, in reducing the consideration then received for the land affected by it'.

The first alternative is the 'natural measure of compensation' and is the one normally used.

You may find the second alternative difficult to follow. This second alternative recognises the fact that when a covenant is placed upon a piece of land, that covenant depreciates the value of that land. Suppose that in 1960 Blackacre was sold for £20,000 subject to a covenant 'no buildings'. If that covenant had not been imposed the price for Blackacre would have been £25,000. The compensation payable under the second alternative will be £5,000.

What are the practical objections to this 'second alternative' for assessing compensation?

If you are objecting, 'It is difficult to prove what the land would have been worth without the covenant, particularly if the covenant was imposed a long time ago', and 'This measure of damages is not inflation proof', then I agree on both points. That is why the tribunal normally uses alternative (a) when awarding compensation (as it did in *Re Banks*).

28.8 Conclusion

There are people who take the following attitude:

Restrictive covenants are a great nuisance to developers of land and bad for the economy of the country. They should all be abolished. We should trust the expertise of our town planners to protect us from undesirable developments.

Do you agree with these sentiments?

I personally cannot agree. There is (perhaps regrettably) widespread distrust of town planners and planning law. This stems in part from the fact (emphasised in *Re Bass)* that planning permission for a development will be granted unless that development is **contrary** to the public interest. But there is also the widespread fear that town planners too often favour 'the public good' rather than the interests and anxieties of individuals who object to a particular development.

If you are a dominant owner in relation to a restrictive covenant banning or controlling development, you have a **private law** right which **you** can assert against the servient owner. You are not dependent for your protection on the whims of 'faceless' officials. However, in fairly limited circumstances, proceedings under s. 84(1) of the 1925 Act may deprive you of your right.

From time to time there are suggestions that there should be further reforms to s. 84(1) to make it easier for servient owners to have awkward covenants removed or modified. I have some sympathy with this suggestion. At minimum, ground (aa) needs simplifying and the provisions for compensation need clarification.

But perhaps the oddest feature of s. 84(1) is the fact that the powers given by the provision are **not** given to the courts. This means that developers are often involved in wasteful duplicate litigation. Like Birmingham Corporation in *Re Dolphin*, they have to go first to the court under s. 84(2) and then to the Lands Tribunal under s. 84(1). A simple reform would be to give the High Court (and for less valuable properties, county courts) jurisdiction to make orders under s. 84(1).

28.9   End of Chapter Assessment Question

In 1870 Mark bought the fee simple in Broadacre. Broadacre was then 10 acres of poor quality farm land, so Mark decided to sell the land for high class housing.

From 1871 to 1875 he sold off the whole of Broadacre in 40 plots of approximately a quarter of an acre each. In each conveyance he imposed restrictive covenants which (inter alia) prohibited the building of more than one house on each plot.

Luke has just purchased 'Redgables', a house built in 1873 on one of the plots sold by Mark. He has obtained planning permission to build a second house in the garden of 'Redgables'.

Luke's plans have caused alarm amongst some of his neighbours, and they are threatening proceedings for an injunction, claiming that they are entitled to enforce the 'one house per plot' restrictive covenant.

Other neighbours have indicated to Luke that they support him, and that they are also considering applying for planning permission to build a second house in their gardens.

Advise Luke.

See *Cases and Materials* (28.7) for a specimen answer.

CHAPTER TWENTY-NINE

THE CREATION OF MORTGAGES

29.1 Objectives

By the end of this chapter you should be able to:

■ appreciate the historical development of the legal mortgage;

■ explain the way(s) in which legal mortgages can be created today;

■ explain how equitable mortgages can be created, both before and after 1989.

29.2 Introduction

Re-read 1.4.1 on mortgages. Note carefully the correct terminology. Remember, too, that it is borrowers who grant mortgages, not banks and building societies!

The English law of mortgages has been the product of a historical evolution spread over many hundreds of years. Despite some quite drastic changes made in 1925, there is (as we shall see) still a large amount of law (and terminology) which is explicable only by reference to that long evolution.

Furthermore, because it is the product of a slow historical evolution, almost the whole of the law of mortgages has developed around mortgages of land which is **unregistered** title. It is easiest if we first look (in this chapter and the three ensuing chapters) at the law as it applies to unregistered titles. **Most** of that law applies equally to registered titles. There are, however, some important legal differences between mortgages of registered titles and mortgages of unregistered titles. Those differences particularly relate to 'formalities' and to 'priorities'. It is best if I leave these differences to the very last chapter (**Chapter 33**), even though nowadays most mortgages of land are registered titles.

29.3 Form of a Legal Mortgage of a Fee Simple Pre-1926

The pre-1926 standard way of mortgaging a fee simple may strike you as rather surprising. The mortgagor conveyed to the mortgagee the whole fee simple in the land, but subject to a **proviso for redemption**, i.e. a clause that if the debt was repaid with the appropriate interest on a named date, the mortgagee was obliged to reconvey the fee simple to the mortgagor.

(I should stress that even with this 'old' form of mortgage, the mortgagor (borrower) usually retained possession of the land. Remember that all a mortgagee normally requires is security for his loan. He normally does not want the bother of managing the land on which his loan is secured.)

If the mortgagor duly repaid on the named date (**the legal redemption date**) but the mortgagee did not reconvey the fee simple, the mortgagor could sue the mortgagee at common law for damages, or in equity for an order (of specific performance) that the property should be reconveyed.

What happened if the mortgagor failed to repay on the agreed legal redemption date? The attitude of the common law was 'Tough!'. The mortgagor lost all right to the property, even if the property was worth far more than the debt owed, and even if the failure to repay on time was due to some kind of accident.

Equity was much more sympathetic to mortgagors. The Court of Chancery ruled that if the mortgagor at any time **after the legal redemption date** repaid the loan with interest up to the date of actual repayment, the mortgagor was entitled to reclaim the land; if necessary equity would order (by a decree of specific performance) the reconveyance of the fee simple.

Lawyers came to realise that equity had created an **equitable right to redeem** continuing indefinitely after the legal redemption date. This equitable right to redeem was (and still is) the automatic right of every mortgagor; it can be terminated only by a **foreclosure order**, or by the mortgagee exercising his power of sale. (These concepts I will discuss in **Chapter 30**.)

29.3.1 THE NOMINAL LEGAL REDEMPTION DATE

We now come to a point you may well find extremely strange. You may be thinking that the legal redemption date was (and is) fixed on the day when the parties anticipate that the loan will finally be repaid. So if Farns-Barnes borrowed £2,000 on 1 May 1900, the loan to be repaid in 10 years' time, you might expect the legal redemption date in any mortgage to secure the loan to be 1 May 1910.

However a very curious thing has happened to the legal redemption date. **The equitable right to redeem** (which always goes on indefinitely after the 'legal' redemption date) has become all important. It has consequently long been the practice to set the legal redemption date at some nominal date, usually six months after the date of the mortgage. In my Farns-Barnes example, the legal redemption date would normally be fixed on 1 November 1900, though nobody really expected Farns-Barnes to repay on that date.

Despite the fact that it is of such fundamental importance, the equitable right to redeem was (and still is) not normally mentioned in the mortgage deed.

29.3.2 MORTGAGOR RETAINING POSSESSION

It has long been the practice for mortgagees to allow mortgagors to remain in possession of the mortgaged property. Even today a mortgagee has **the right to take possession**. Mortgagees normally exercise that right only as a preliminary to enforcing their security by selling the property.

If a mortgagee did take possession, and held the property for a long period, equity would place on him a strict duty to 'account on the basis of wilful default'; a phrase which means that there is a duty to get the maximum income from the land. This rule (which I will explain more fully in **Chapter 30**), coupled with the fact that the mortgagee does not normally want the responsibility of looking after the land, effectively makes it not worth the mortgagee's while taking possession unless he wishes to enforce his security.

29.4   Legal Mortgages of Fees Simple after 1925

The 1925 legislation banned the traditional form of mortgage, the conveyance of the fee simple with a provision for reconveyance on redemption. The 1925 legislators organised things so that the mortgagor retained the fee simple, but granted the mortgagee as security for the loan either a very long lease, or a 'charge by way of legal mortgage'. Thus the 1925 legislation provides two ways of mortgaging a fee simple.

29.4.1 MORTGAGE BY LONG LEASE ('MORTGAGE BY DEMISE')

The mortgagor grants to the mortgagee a lease for a very long period (usually 3,000 years) subject to a proviso for **cesser on redemption**, i.e. a provision that on the debt being repaid on a named date the lease should automatically terminate. This named date is the legal redemption date and is still usually fixed at a nominal six months from the date of the creation of the mortgage. The equitable right to redeem remains all important.

Any attempt after 1925 to create a mortgage by conveyance of the fee simple is converted by the Law of Property Act 1925 s. 85(2) to a mortgage by demise for 3,000 years, with a proviso for cesser on redemption.

Any legal mortgage existing on 1 January 1926 which had been created by conveyance of the fee simple was automatically converted into a mortgage by demise for 3,000 years. The fee simple was automatically revested in the mortgagor.

29.4.2 CHARGE BY WAY OF LEGAL MORTGAGE

Study the basic format of this type of mortgage laid down by the Law of Property Act 1925, sch. IV, Form One, in *Cases and Materials* (29.2.2). Notice that the statutory form does not provide for a legal redemption date.

For this form of mortgage a deed is necessary, identifying the land in question and expressly declaring it to be charged by way of legal mortgage. The mortgagee has the same rights, powers and remedies **as if** he had taken a mortgage by 3,000-year lease, although strictly speaking he has no estate in the land, only a 'charge'. A legal redemption date is not necessary, although one is usually inserted providing for repayment at a nominal six months.

It is worth stressing that mortgages by long lease are virtually unknown today. All lenders nowadays use the modern 'charge by way of legal mortgage'. The mortgage deed is usually much more elaborate than the 'bare bones' set out in sch. IV of the 1925 Act.

29.4.3   INSTALMENT MORTGAGES

It should be borne in mind that the law of mortgages has largely developed around what is sometimes called the 'classic' mortgage'. A classic mortgage is one where it is envisaged that the whole debt will be repaid in one lump sum, like the Farns-Barnes example at **29.3.1**.

Many modern mortgages are, of course, instalment mortgages, where it is envisaged that the capital debt will be repaid in instalments over a long period of time. (Twenty-five years is the most common period, but there is no legal rule requiring that the period be 25 years.)

The general law of mortgages applies to instalment mortgages. An instalment mortgage must be by long lease or by charge by way of legal mortgage. It will in practice follow one of the following two patterns:

(a)   The borrower covenants to repay the whole debt on a nominal redemption date (say six months); there are then clauses providing for repayment by instalments if (as, of course, will be the case) there is no repayment on the redemption date.

(b)   There is no nominal redemption date; the borrower covenants to repay by instalments and there is a proviso that if he is a stated period in arrears (e.g., two months) the whole capital debt becomes repayable. Thus there is a 'floating' legal redemption date.

(If you are a mortgagor, it may at this stage be both interesting and useful to study the terms of your mortgage. But be warned. In 1904, one of the greatest judges of the day, Lord Macnaghten, commented, 'No one . . . by the light of nature ever understood an English mortgage of real estate'. Despite the changes made in 1925, this remains true.)

29.5   The Equity of Redemption

'Equity of redemption' is the phrase used for the sum total of the mortgagor's equitable rights with respect to the mortgaged land. The 'equitable right to redeem' is by far the most important of those rights.

Since 1925, a mortgagor owns both the legal estate and an 'equity of redemption'. The legal estate is of no intrinsic value, but the value of the equity of redemption is (roughly) the value of the property when unencumbered, minus the total debt outstanding. (Hence the expression, 'the equity in my house is £X,000'. Hence also the modern expression 'negative equity', where the amount of the debt exceeds the value of the property.)

An equity of redemption can be disposed of like any other interest in land. It can be sold, settled, leased, etc. It can itself be mortgaged, so as to create a second mortgage.

Prior to 1926, as a first legal mortgage was normally created by conveyance of the legal estate, the mortgagor retained only an equitable interest, and therefore second and subsequent (3rd, 4th, etc.) mortgages were necessarily equitable. After 1925, a series of legal mortgages is a quite normal phenomenon.

Pre-1926, a mortgagee, because he had the legal estate, had an automatic right to take possession of the deeds relating to that estate. Post-1925, a legal mortgagee has a statutory right to take possession of the title deeds, unless an earlier mortgagee has taken them. In practice a first mortgagee normally exercises the right to take possession of the deeds.

29.6   Mortgages of Leases

29.6.1   PRE-1926

A legal lease was mortgaged either:

(a) by assignment of the lease with a proviso for re-assignment on redemption; **or**

(b) by sub-lease with a proviso for cesser on redemption.

Even before 1926, method (b) was normally used. Why? (The answer is to be found in the law of leases: see 19.3.)

If the mortgage were by assignment, then the mortgagee would come into privity of estate with the landlord and therefore be liable for the rent and to perform other covenants entered into by the tenant.

29.6.2   POST-1925

A mortgage of a lease now takes the form of either:

(a) a sub-lease with a proviso for cesser on redemption; **or**

(b) a charge by way of legal mortgage.

If form (b) is used (as is invariably the case nowadays) then the mortgagee is in the same position as if he had taken a mortgage by sub-lease to run out one day before the term mortgaged. (Any attempt to mortgage a lease by assignment is converted into a mortgage by sub-lease, the sub-lease to run out **10** days before the lease mortgaged expires.)

29.7 Equitable Mortgages of Legal Estates

29.7.1 EQUITABLE MORTGAGES PRE-1989

ACTIVITY 123

Refer back to 5.5.3.4, regarding the creation of equitable interests in land. Consider how that section may be applied to informal mortgages.

Equity treated any transaction (other than one by deed) carried through with intent to create a mortgage as a contract for a mortgage, and therefore as an equitable mortgage. In particular, if a borrower deposited title deeds with a lender with intent that the property to which they related should be security for the loan, the depositing of the deeds was sufficient to create an equitable mortgage **even though no new document was executed.**

The following scenario used to be quite common. Bloggs goes to his bank manager to see whether he can arrange an overdraft. 'What security can you offer us?' asks the manager. Bloggs produces the title deeds to his house. The manager looks at them: '35 Blogtown Way; that must be worth at least £70,000,' he murmurs. 'Hand these deeds over to us and you can have an overdraft up to £50,000.' Bloggs hands over the deeds and the manager immediately authorises the overdraft. **Before anything has been signed** Bloggs has created an equitable mortgage.

In practice an equitable mortgage 'by deposit of title deeds' was almost always immediately followed by a document **recording** the terms of the loan (interest rates, length of time for repayment, etc.). Moreover, because of the rules governing mortgagees' statutory powers and rights this document was usually a deed, referred to as a 'memorandum under seal'.

29.7.2 COMPARISON OF LEGAL AND EQUITABLE MORTGAGES PRE-1989

With both a legal and an equitable mortgage the usual position was that a new deed was executed and the mortgagee took the existing title deeds to the property.

With a legal mortgage, the new deed was executed with the intent that it should **create** the mortgage; the existing title deeds were handed over for other reasons. (These reasons are to facilitate enforcement of the security should that be necessary, and to preserve the 'priority' of the mortgage.)

With an equitable mortgage, the new deed made it clear that it merely **recorded** a mortgage already created by deposit of the existing title deeds.

29.7.3   EQUITABLE MORTGAGES AFTER 26 SEPTEMBER 1989

ACTIVITY 124

Read the extracts from *United Bank of Kuwait* v *Sahib* [1995] 2 WLR 94, in *Cases and Materials* (29.3.1). That case involved a purported equitable mortgage of a registered title by deposit of the land certificate, but the same reasoning would apply to a post-1989 attempt to create an equitable mortgage by deposit of title deeds.

Although some lenders did not in 1989 immediately grasp this point, equitable mortgages by deposit of title deeds are no longer possible. This is because under s. 2 of the Law of Property (Miscellaneous Provisions) Act 1989, a contract to create an interest in land must be in writing. An equitable mortgage is technically such a contract. It is not now sufficient to have an oral transaction, such as a deposit of deeds, followed by a memorandum recording the transaction. Any post-1989 mortgages in this form are **void**; *United Bank of Kuwait* v *Sahib* confirms this point. Note that this case was affirmed by the Court of Appeal on 2 February 1996 (*The Times*), 13 February 1996).

To create an equitable mortgage after 26 September 1989, a written document will be required, signed by both parties, contracting to create or actually creating the mortgage. Thus, after 26 September 1989:

(a)   A legal mortgage must be by deed.

(b)   An equitable mortgage must be by a written document. This document will not be a deed, but must be signed by both parties and include all the terms of the mortgage.

29.8   Equitable Mortgages of Equitable Interests

Suppose that a life tenant wanted to mortgage his equitable interest under a settlement; or a tenant in common wished to mortgage his 'share' in a property.

Both before and after 1925, an equitable mortgage of an equitable interest is created by an assignment of that interest to the mortgagee, with a proviso for re-assignment on redemption. The mortgage must be in writing, to comply with the Law of Property Act 1925, s. 53(1)(c). (This type of mortgage is unaffected by the 1989 Act. Nowadays they seem to be relatively rare.)

29.9   Conclusion

Although there are still four more chapters on the law of mortgages to be considered, I hope that you are already beginning to appreciate the emphasis I placed on historical evolution in the introduction to this chapter. Historical evolution explains why, even after 1925, the form of a legal mortgage with its legal redemption date and (unstated) equitable right to redeem, defies common sense and 'the light of nature'.

As will be confirmed by later chapters, the legal evolution of the law of mortgages most certainly did not end in 1925. Indeed, as we have just seen, Parliament made quite a drastic change to equitable mortgages in 1989. In the next chapter we will see further modern contributions to the evolution, not just from Parliament, but also from the courts.

CHAPTER THIRTY

THE REMEDIES OF MORTGAGEES

30.1   Objectives

By the end of this chapter you should be able to:

■ explain and distinguish between the various remedies which mortgagees have to enforce their security;

■ appreciate why foreclosure (in its technical sense) is of limited significance today;

■ advise on the various restrictions which surround the mortgagee's power of sale;

■ explain the (limited) circumstances in which a mortgagee's claim for possession of a mortgaged property can be delayed;

■ appreciate the role receivers play in the law of mortgages.

30.2   Introduction

In this chapter we meet another area of law, steeped in history, but ill-adapted to the economic realities of the late-twentieth century. The continued existence of foreclosure (in its technical sense) can be explained only by history. The same is true of the **mortgagee's** (more or less automatic) right to take possession of the mortgaged property.

As you read through this chapter you may well be surprised (perhaps indeed worried) by an apparent pro-mortgagee bias in the law. But the big 'institutional' lenders (banks, building societies, etc.) will argue that they need to have means of enforcing their security **quickly and cheaply**. They will argue that stricter limits on mortgagees' remedies might benefit individual mortgagors, but would be against the economic interests of the country as a whole.

30.3   Remedies of Legal Mortgagees – An Overview

A mortgagee can always sue in contract to recover the debt owed, but there are four remedies for enforcing the security:

(a)   foreclosure;

(b) sale;

(c) taking possession;

(d) appointing a receiver.

The remedies of foreclosure and taking possession flow from the intrinsic nature of a mortgage. By contrast, the remedies of (b) sale and (d) appointing a receiver were originally conferred by express provision in the mortgage deed, but are now conferred on mortgagees by statutory provisions. Moreover, these remedies (unlike (a) and (c)) can be exercised without taking court proceedings. However, mortgagees who want to sell the property will (in modern economic conditions) almost certainly want to sell with vacant possession. They will therefore need a court order giving vacant possession before putting the property on the market.

A mortgagee can exercise any or all of the remedies (including an action in contract) in combination, provided the total amount recovered does not exceed the total capital and interest owed.

30.4 Foreclosure

I should stress that I am using the word 'foreclosure' in its narrow technical sense. (Sometimes the word is used by non-lawyers to mean **any action** taken by the mortgagee to enforce his security.) Understanding the concept of foreclosure is important to your understanding of the law of mortgages as a whole, even though, in modern conditions, foreclosures are relatively rare.

Foreclosure proceedings can be taken at any time after the legal redemption date is passed. The effect of a foreclosure order absolute **before** 1926 was that the legal estate already vested in the mortgagee was freed from the mortgagor's equity of redemption, which was destroyed by the order.

Since 1925, if a foreclosure order absolute is made it vests the legal estate in the mortgagee as well as destroying the equity of redemption. Thus the effect of foreclosure order is that someone who was a mortgagee becomes an outright owner.

ACTIVITY 125

Do you think that foreclosure will be an attractive remedy where there is substantial 'equity' in the property, for example where the property is worth £100,000 but the mortgage debt is only £50,000?

On what I have said so far, I will forgive you for answering this question 'Yes'. But now read on.

30.4.1 THE FORECLOSURE PROCESS

This will probably strike you as long and cumbersome, but the reason for the complexities is the desire to protect the mortgagor. Remember that if there is a foreclosure order absolute, the mortgagor loses **all** his rights.

A foreclosure order is made in two stages. A foreclosure order *nisi* directs a Master (a senior court official) to prepare an account setting out exactly how much is owed. It further provides that if the money owed is not repaid within a specified period (usually six months) after the account has been drawn up, the foreclosure shall become **absolute**. The order absolute vests the property in the mortgagee free from the rights of the mortgagor.

Even a foreclosure order absolute may be 're-opened' in exceptional circumstances, and the equity of redemption thereby revived. This might occur, for example, where some last-minute accident prevented repayment of the debt within the time-limit.

30.4.2 JUDICIAL SALE IN FORECLOSURE PROCEEDINGS

I hope that you are already beginning to appreciate why foreclosure is not very common today. You may, however, be thinking, 'Despite it being a long-drawn-out affair, foreclosure will be attractive where the mortgaged property is worth substantially more than the total debt'.

You would be wrong in thinking in this way. In any foreclosure proceedings the mortgagor (or any persons deriving title through him, such as a second mortgagee or the owner of a constructive trust interest) may apply to the court for an order of judicial sale in place of foreclosure. Although there is a discretion, a sale will generally be ordered where the value of the property is noticeably **greater** than the mortgage debt. Hence the fact that foreclosure is not much resorted to nowadays.

Foreclosure is sometimes resorted to in 'negative equity situations'. Why?

Although foreclosure is a slow process, where the value of the property is less than the mortgage debt there is seemingly no risk of an order for judicial sale. The mortgagee gets the property, and can sit and hope that (perhaps because of an improvement in the economy) the property will increase in value.

30.4.3 FORECLOSURE AND DWELLING HOUSES

If the mortgaged property is or includes **a dwelling house**, there is a further safeguard protecting the mortgagor. The court may adjourn foreclosure proceedings if the mortgagor is likely to be able within a reasonable time to pay 'any sums' due under the mortgage. This flows from the Administration of Justice Act 1973, s. 8(3), which extended to foreclosure the rules I discuss at **30.6.2.2**, restricting a mortgagee taking possession of a dwelling house.

30.5   The Mortgagee's Statutory Power of Sale

The relevant statutory provisions (Law of Property Act 1925, s. 101(1) and s. 103) draw a distinction between the statutory power of sale 'arising' and the statutory power becoming 'exercisable'. We will consider the significance of this distinction below.

30.5.1   WHEN DOES THE STATUTORY POWER ARISE?

Two (very straightforward) conditions must be satisfied:

(a)   the mortgage must be by deed; **and**

(b)   the mortgage debt must be due, i.e. the legal redemption date must be past.

30.5.2   WHEN DOES THE STATUTORY POWER BECOME EXERCISABLE?

The power (having first arisen) becomes exercisable if **any one** of three conditions is satisfied:

(a)   notice has been served on the mortgagor requiring repayment and three months have elapsed without the mortgagor repaying the whole debt; **or**

(b)   interest is at least two months in arrears; **or**

(c)   there has been a breach of a term of the mortgage other than one relating to repayment of capital and interest.

30.5.3   PROTECTION FOR PURCHASERS IN GOOD FAITH FROM MORTGAGEES

If a mortgagee attempts to convey the property before the power of sale has even arisen, any conveyance will be completely invalid.

Once the power has **arisen,** a mortgagee can convey a good title to a purchaser free of the mortgagor's rights, **whether or not the power has become exercisable.**

A purchaser in good faith from a mortgagee need satisfy himself only that the power of sale has arisen; he is under no duty to enquire whether the power has become exercisable.

What do you think is the rationale underlying the rule I have just stated?

The rule is eminently sensible from the point of view of the purchaser from the mortgagee. It is relatively easy for a purchaser to check if the power of sale has arisen; it would be very difficult for him to check whether the power has become exercisable.

It follows from this that if a mortgagee were to sell after the power had arisen but before it became exercisable, the mortgagor's only redress would be a claim for damages against the mortgagee. (Exceptionally, if a purchaser had actual knowledge of the fact that a power of sale had not become exercisable he would not be immune, as he would not be a purchaser in good faith.)

30.5.4   MORTGAGEE'S DUTIES ON SELLING THE PROPERTY

First, a word of warning. The proposition in some textbooks and cases that a 'mortgagee is not a trustee of his power of sale' is not really accurate in view of modern developments, especially the decision in *Cuckmere Brick* (see below).

A mortgagee can sell either by auction or by 'private treaty'. (By 'private treaty' is meant negotiating with buyers individually.)

Read the extracts from *Cuckmere Brick Co.* v *Mutual Finance Co.* in *Cases and Materials* (30.3.1), noting very carefully what the court said about the timing of the sale.

The Court of Appeal in *Cuckmere Brick Co.* v *Mutual Finance Co.* [1971] 2 All ER 633, held:

(a)   In deciding **when** to sell the mortgagee is entitled to consult his own interests to the total exclusion of the mortgagor's interests. Thus, he can sell at a time when the market for the type of property comprised in the mortgage is depressed.

(This point is confirmed by recent decisions of the Privy Council, for example *China and South Sea Bank* v *Tan* [1989] 3 All ER 839. Statements by Lord Denning and some textbooks that the mortgagee owes a duty of care to the mortgagor over the **timing** of the sale are undoubtedly wrong.)

(b)   Having decided to sell at a particular time, in conducting the sale a mortgagee owes a duty of care to the mortgagor to take reasonable care to obtain the best price reasonably obtainable at that time. If the mortgagee fails to obtain that best price, he will have to account for the difference. The onus of proving that the mortgagee is in breach of this duty of care is **on the mortgagor**. (This duty of care is owed only to the mortgagor. It is not owed to a person who has an equitable interest in the property under a constructive or resulting trust: *Parker-Tweedale* v *Dunbar Bank plc* [1990] 2 All ER 577.)

In *Cuckmere Brick*, a property company owned a sizeable vacant site on the edge of Maidstone. The company had planning permission to develop the site for houses or flats. The mortgagees exercised their power of sale. They sold by auction. The adverts for the auction mentioned that there was planning permission for houses, but not the permission for flats. Because of this omission the site did not fetch as high a price as it should have. The mortgagees had to account for this difference in price.

Under current law, can the mortgagee sell when the country is in the throes of a recession?

The answer is, of course, 'Yes'.

Consider whether a mortgagee should be placed under a duty to take care as to the timing of sale.

I would argue 'No', for two connected reasons. First a duty as to timing of sale would lead to endless litigation, with constant arguments like the following:

Mortgagor: 'You sold while the market was depressed; you should have waited for things to get better.'
Mortgagee: 'I was anxious to recover at least some of my money, and my economic advisers disagreed with the government's forecasts; my advisers said things would get worse.'

Secondly, 'a duty as to timing' would make lenders more cautious as to the **amount** they would be willing to lend on the security of a particular property. At the moment lenders often lend 80–90 per cent of the value of the property in the confident knowledge that they can enforce their security **at any time**.

30.5.5   CAN A MORTGAGEE SELL TO HIS 'FRIENDS'?

A mortgagee cannot sell to himself or to a nominee in trust for himself, or to his agent. He **can** sell to a company in which he has a substantial share-holding, but if the sale is challenged by the mortgagor **the onus of proof will be on the mortgagee** to show that reasonable efforts were made to obtain the best price: *Tse Kwong Lam* v *Wong Chit Sen* [1983] 1 WLR 1349.

30.5.6   POSITION OF PURCHASERS AND THE QUESTION OF PRICE

A purchaser from the mortgagee is under no duty to pay the best price. Provided he acts in good faith he will get a good title, even though the mortgagee should have obtained a higher price by taking greater care. It is not bad faith for a purchaser to consider that he has got a good bargain. It would be bad faith if the mortgagee and the purchaser conspired so that a deliberately low price was charged to the purchaser.

30.5.7   THE EFFECT OF SALE

The mortgagor's equity of redemption is destroyed as soon as the **contract** of sale is made; if the mortgagee has contracted to sell, the mortgagor cannot prevent completion by paying off the debt.

The conveyance by the mortgagee conveys the fee simple previously vested in the mortgagor free from the rights of the mortgagor and all subsequent mortgagees. These rights are all **overreached**. (I hope you noticed that we have here an exception to the ancient principle *nemo dat quod non habet* ('you cannot give what you have not got').)

The conveyance is in principle subject to any mortgages having priority over that of the vendor, although an earlier mortgagee may permit a later mortgagee to sell free from the earlier mortgage.

Suppose that Messyacre is worth approximately £130,000. It is subject to a first mortgage for £70,000 in favour of Freda, and to a second mortgage for £50,000 in favour of Stephen. Any sale by Stephen would be (in principle) subject to Freda's first mortgage. Thus Stephen is unlikely to get more than £60,000 on such a sale. Freda might, however, allow the sale to take place free from her rights. Stephen would obviously then get a price in the region of £130,000. Freda (under the rules I am about to discuss) would still get 'first dip' into the proceeds of sale.

30.5.8   DESTINATION OF PROCEEDS OF SALE

The mortgagee has always been regarded as 'trustee of the proceeds of sale'. Proceeds in the hands of a mortgagee must be applied in the following order:

(a)   In paying off the total debt (capital and interest) owed to any mortgagee earlier in priority who permitted the property to be sold free from his mortgage (Freda in the example at **30.5.7**).

(b)   In discharging any costs of sale and any attempted sale.

(c)   In discharging the total debt (capital and interest) owed to the mortgagee.

(d)   The balance (if any) must be paid to the mortgagee next in order of priority or, if none, to the mortgagor.

If there is a mortgagee later in priority than the one selling, but the seller pays the balance to the mortgagor, then the seller is in principle liable for any loss suffered by a later mortgagee. There will be no such liability if the seller **had no notice** of the later mortgage.

If the later mortgage has been registered as a land charge or entered on the register of title, the seller will automatically be fixed with notice of the later mortgage. A mortgagee should therefore search the Land Charges Register or the register of title (depending on whether the land is unregistered or registered) before paying surplus proceeds to the mortgagor.

If a later mortgagee receives surplus proceeds of sale from an earlier mortgagee, he must apply them as if they were proceeds of a sale effected by him.

30.6   Mortgagees Taking Possession

Why does a mortgagee have the right to take possession immediately the mortgage is made; 'before the ink is dry', as one judge once put it?

You should remember that in the past (pre-1926) a mortgagee had an **estate** in the mortgaged land, while nowadays his 'charge by way of legal mortgage' gives him rights equivalent to an estate. He can assert those rights at any time and say, 'give me control of what is (in effect) my land'.

The Court of Appeal has recently reaffirmed the validity of the principle that a mortgagee is entitled to possession at any time he chooses. In two cases a mortgagee was held entitled to assert its immediate right to possession of the mortgaged property, notwithstanding substantial counterclaims for unliquidated damages brought by the mortgagors which, if valid, would totally extinguish the mortgagors' debts: *Ashley Guarantee* v *Zacaria* [1993] 1 All ER 254; *National Westminster Bank plc* v *Skelton* [1993] 1 All ER 242.

In practice, of course, mortgagees are content to allow the mortgagor to keep possession, and will take possession only if things start going wrong. Some textbooks still suggest that the usual reason a mortgagee takes possession is to recover arrears of **interest**. In modern conditions this is not correct. Today a mortgagee taking possession merely to recover arrears of interest is rare, though not unknown. The usual reason for taking possession is in order to sell with **vacant possession**. The desirability of selling with vacant possession is so great that if a mortgagee's court proceedings for possession are in some way delayed, the sale is (speaking from a practical point of view) also delayed.

30.6.1   COURT PROCEEDINGS FOR POSSESSION BROUGHT BY A MORTGAGEE

In order to avoid possible prosecution under the Criminal Law Act 1967, a mortgagee seeking possession in practice always seeks a court possession order. Proceedings are normally brought in the Chancery Division, and as a general principle the court has no jurisdiction to adjourn proceedings to give the mortgagor an opportunity to repay the loan.

It must be stressed that as a general principle the mortgagee's right to possession is not in any way dependent on default by the mortgagor. It flows from the fact that a mortgagee has an estate in the land mortgaged, or rights equivalent to an estate.

30.6.2   MORTGAGEE TAKING POSSESSION OF A DWELLING HOUSE

Responsible lenders such as the big banks and building societies are reluctant to take possession proceedings. If such organisations took possession without good reason, it would be very bad for business!

Less responsible lenders do not worry about their reputations. In the late 1960s there was a rash of cases where less reputable mortgagees had taken possession (with a view to selling with vacant possession) of houses, even though there had been no default (or certainly no serious default) by the mortgagor.

30.6.2.1 The 1970 'reform'

In my view, Parliament should have enacted a clear, unambiguous and drastic reform applicable to all mortgages, and limiting mortgagees' rights to take possession to cases where there had been **serious default** by the mortgagor. Instead Parliament introduced special (but complex) rules applicable where the mortgaged property is or includes a dwelling house.

First, unless the house is within Greater London, a mortgagee's possession proceedings must be brought **in the county court**. This rule, which applies irrespective of the value of the house, is designed to avoid a provincial house-owner from being dragged off to London.

Secondly, and more importantly, s. 36 of the Administration of Justice Act 1970 gives the court a wide discretion to adjourn possession proceedings, or to make a possession order but suspend its operation. The idea is to give the mortgagor time to find the money and in the meantime protect him in his home.

Under s. 36, the power to adjourn or suspend exists if it appears to the court that it is likely that the mortgagor will be able to repay within a 'reasonable period', 'any sums due under the mortgage' (**i.e. the whole capital debt**).

The adjournment or suspension can be made on conditions, e.g., 'the possession order is made but suspended for one year on condition that the mortgagor repays the debt at X pounds per month'; or 'I adjourn the proceedings for six months provided you repay half the debt in two months' time and the other half before the six months is up'.

30.6.2.2 A further 'reform' in 1973

Section 36 originally proved rather ineffective, because judges, even in instalment mortgage cases, initially interpreted the phrase 'any sums due' to mean the whole capital debt. Parliament therefore enacted s. 8 of the Administration of Justice Act 1973, which operates where the mortgage in question is an instalment mortgage.

Under s. 8, an adjournment of possession proceedings or a suspended possession order can be granted if it is likely that within a reasonable period the mortgagor will be able to pay off arrears of instalments (if any) and meet any further instalments which fall due within that reasonable period.

Could you express this point in another (perhaps clearer) way?

The mortgagee will not get an order for immediate possession if the mortgagor can show that he is (within a reasonable period) likely to catch up with the instalments.

Any clause making the whole capital debt repayable if instalments are in arrears (see clause (b) quoted at **29.4.3**) is to be ignored when applying s. 8 of the 1973 Act.

But what is a 'reasonable period' for the court to allow the mortgagor to catch up with the instalments? Hitherto, the answer has been 'a year, two or three years at most'. But the Court of Appeal has now held in *Cheltenham and Gloucester BS v Norgan* (1995) 145 NLJ 1849, that with an instalment mortgage a 'reasonable period' can mean the full **duration of the mortgage**. In Norgan's case the mortgage was an instalment mortgage created in 1986 and repayable over 22 years. The court in effect held that Mrs Norgan would be entitled to the protection of s. 8 provided she could show that there was a reasonable prospect that she would have caught up by 2008! To put it mildly, this case represents a considerable shift in the law in favour of mortgagors. Mortgagees may well wish to challenge the decision in the House of Lords.

You should also notice that a person deriving title from the mortgagor of a dwelling house can ask the court to adjourn or suspend possession proceedings. In particular, this will include a spouse of the mortgagor with Class F rights of occupation.

Who else would count as 'deriving title' for the purposes of this legislation?

A cohabitee who had a constructive trust interest would certainly derive title, but so would a tenant of the mortgagor.

It should be stressed, however, that the spouse/cohabitee/tenant will have to show that he or she can within a reasonable period find the money to catch up with the instalments. Mrs Goddard, in *Hastings and Thanet Building Society* v *Goddard* [1970] 3 All ER 954, found out about her husband's arrears only when it was far too late for her to do anything about them.

30.6.3 DUTY OF MORTGAGEE IN POSSESSION TO ACCOUNT STRICTLY

The rules below apply only in those cases (relatively rare in the late-twentieth century) where a mortgagee takes possession **on a long-term basis**.

A mortgagee who takes long-term possession must use any income gained from the land (e.g. in particular rents from tenants) to pay off interest on the debt. Any surplus income is (at the mortgagee's option) either paid to the mortgagor, or put to reducing the capital debt.

One rule I have already mentioned (at **29.3.1**) I must now explain more fully. I have already said that if a mortgagee takes possession on a long-term basis, the mortgagee must account 'on the basis of wilful default'. This means that the mortgagee must manage the property to get the maximum income obtainable by reasonable methods. If he fails to get that maximum income, he will nevertheless be deemed to have received it. (The amount owed by the mortgagor will thus be reduced by the amount of extra income the mortgagee should have obtained.)

ACTIVITY 131

Read the extracts from *White v City of London Brewery* in *Cases and Materials* (30.4.2). (Note that a lot of cases concerning mortgages arose around the turn of the century, and quite a few of them involved public houses. In studying these cases, remember that in some respects economic conditions were different 100 years ago; in particular, interest rates were much lower.)

In *White v City of London Brewery* (1889) 42 ChD 237 a pub, originally a 'free' house, was mortgaged to a brewery, the mortgage (surprisingly) not containing a tie clause. The brewery took possession and leased the pub as a 'tied house'.

In those days a tied house was confined to one brewery's products and fetched a **lower** rent than a 'free' house, which can sell whatever brands of beer it wishes. In finalising the amount which White owed the brewery, the court ruled that the brewery had to account on the basis of the higher rent which a 'free house' would then have commanded. (The tie in the lease was to the mortgagees, but that is irrelevant.)

30.7 Power to Appoint a Receiver

This remedy is in practice exercised only where the mortgaged land is subject to leases, and the mortgagee wishes to intercept rent payable under those leases. It is a particularly attractive remedy where the mortgaged property is a block of flats or offices, or a row of shops.

Where a mortgagee appoints a receiver, the rents payable by the tenants must be paid by them to the receiver and not to the mortgagor. The power to appoint a receiver **arises** when the power of sale **arises**; it becomes **exercisable** when the power of sale becomes **exercisable** (see **30.5**). If there were a purported appointment of a receiver before the power arose, any payment of rent to the receiver would not discharge the tenant's obligations.

SAQ 147

Bearing in mind what was said at 30.5.3, what do you think would be the position if a receiver were appointed after the power to appoint had arisen but before it had become exercisable. Would rent paid to the receiver discharge the tenant's obligations?

The tenant would be in the clear. If the power to appoint has arisen, any payments by the tenant to the receiver are valid, whether or not the power has become exercisable.

Any money received by the receiver must be applied in the following order:

(a)   To pay rents, rates etc. payable with respect to the mortgaged estate.

(b)   To pay interest on any mortgages having priority over the appointor's mortgage.

(c)   To pay the receiver's commission (usually 5% of the gross receipts).

(d)   To pay insurance on the property.

(e)   To pay for repairs on the property, if the mortgagee so directs.

(f)   To pay the interest due to the appointing mortgagee.

(g)   If the mortgagee so directs, to reduce the capital debt (otherwise any surplus goes to the mortgagor).

In practice it is heads (f) and (g) which really matter from the mortgagee's point of view.

30.7.1   RECEIVER DEEMED TO BE THE MORTGAGOR'S AGENT

The mortgagee, exercising the power to appoint a receiver given by the Law of Property Act 1925, can choose whoever he likes to act as a receiver. He does not have to choose a professional person such as an accountant or surveyor. Yet the receiver is **deemed to be the mortgagor's agent**.

If a receiver defaults in any way (e.g., he runs off to Latin America with the rents he has collected), who bears the loss?

Although it is the mortgagee who appoints the receiver, it is the **mortgagor** not the mortgagee who will bear the loss.

This harsh rule, which means that the mortgagor takes the risk of the receiver's dishonesty or incompetence, is to be contrasted with the very strict 'wilful default' rule which operates if the mortgagee personally takes long-term control of the land (see **30.6.3**). Moreover, in *Downsview* v *First City Corporation* [1993] 3 All ER 626, the Privy Council has held that while the power to appoint a receiver must be exercised in good faith **only** for the purposes of enforcing the mortgagee's security, the mortgagee owes the mortgagor **no duty** to be careful in selecting the receiver appointed.

It is therefore not surprising that mortgagees rarely take long-term personal possession of mortgaged property. In cases where the capital of the debt is well-secured but there have been problems with interest payments, appointing a receiver may be a much more attractive remedy!

There is, however, one (arguable) advantage if a mortgagee takes personal possession of the land rather than appointing a receiver. If a mortgagee personally takes possession and remains in possession for 12 years without either acknowledging the mortgagor's title or receiving any payment from the mortgagor towards capital or interest, the mortgagor's rights are extinguished by the Limitation Acts. The mortgagee acquires an unencumbered title by virtue of adverse possession. If a receiver's appointment lasts more than 12 years (or even 112 years), this cannot affect the mortgagor's title. The receiver is agent of the mortgagor, and therefore cannot be in adverse possession against him.

30.8 Remedies of an Equitable Mortgagee

30.8.1 FORECLOSURE

Nowadays this remedy operates exactly as with a legal mortgage (see **30.4**).

30.8.2 SALE AND APPOINTING A RECEIVER

A pre-1989 equitable mortgage by deposit of title deeds accompanied by a memorandum under seal was 'made by deed' for the purposes of the statutory power of sale and other statutory powers, such as the power to appoint a receiver.

Where an equitable mortgage is not 'made by deed' there will be no statutory powers of sale or appointing a receiver. The mortgagee can apply to the court for an order of judicial sale, or for the court to appoint a receiver.

The Law Reform (Miscellaneous Provisions) Act 1989, s. 2, in effect requires all equitable mortgages to be made by a formal document. To incorporate the statutory powers of sale and appointing a receiver, that document will have to be a deed. In view of the 1989 Act, it is questionable whether equitable mortgages of unregistered titles will continue to be used. There seems to be no point in using them!

30.8.3 TAKING POSSESSION

It seems that an equitable mortgagee has no right to take possession of the property, unless the memorandum under seal (or other document) gives him the right, which it usually does.

30.9 A Lifeline to Mortgagors with Negative Equity

Read the important, recent case of *Palk* v *Mortgage Services Funding plc* in *Cases and Materials* (30.6). You may notice that, judged by the sums involved, the Palks were not an 'average' middle-class couple caught in the negative equity trap.

In *Palk* v *Mortgage Services Funding plc* [1993] 2 All ER 481 the Palks owned a house encumbered with a debt amounting to £358,000. They had found a prospective purchaser willing to pay just £283,000, and they wanted to sell the property and make up the difference out of their personal resources.

The mortgagee refused to agree to this, and took proceedings for possession. It was the mortgagee's intention not to sell the house until 'the market improved', and in the meantime to let the house to a tenant. It was clear that the rent obtainable **would be substantially less** than the interest continuing to accrue. Thus the amount owed by the Palks would steadily increase, as would the amount of 'negative equity'.

The Palks thus faced an ever-increasing debt and (presumably) eventual bankruptcy. They therefore applied for and obtained an order of sale under the **Law of Property Act 1925, s. 91(2)**, a hitherto little known provision of the 1925 Act which gives the court **a discretion** to order the sale of mortgaged property. In making the order for sale the Court of Appeal stressed that a mortgagee must not exercise its various powers in a manner wholly unfair to the mortgagor.

This case has received wide publicity; it shows that s. 91(2) allows an escape route for mortgagors caught by 'negative equity'. The mortgagors apply for a court order of sale, losing their house but staving off mounting arrears and possible eventual bankruptcy.

30.10 Conclusion

The decision in *Palk* has been widely welcomed. It is a breath of fresh air amidst a fog of rules which are increasingly ill-suited to the economic realities of the late-twentieth century.

It is very easy to advocate reform, but it is far more difficult to agree what those reforms should be. Most critics agree that nothing valuable would be lost if foreclosure were abolished and the mortgagee's right to possession restricted to cases where the mortgagor is in serious default. But other questions are more difficult. For example:

■ Should the mortgagee be under a duty as to the **timing** of sale?

■ Should (in the light of *Downsveiw*) restrictions be placed on who can be appointed a receiver?

■ Should (strengthening the rule in *Palk*) a mortgagor who has negative equity have an automatic right to cut his losses by having the property sold?

In considering these questions, remember that the big institutional lenders will argue that restrictions on their remedies to enforce mortgages will reduce their willingness to lend amounts up to almost the full value of the mortgaged property. If loans secured by a mortgage cease to be readily available, the whole economy of the country will suffer.

30.11   End of Chapter Assessment Question

In 1990 Bertha borrowed £40,000 from the Doorway Building Society. The loan is secured by a first legal mortgage of Bertha's freehold house 'Arkwrite Towers'.

In 1992 Bertha borrowed a further £20,000 from Princewest Finance Ltd secured by a second legal mortage on Arkwrite Towers. The interest on this loan is 23%, and Bertha has fallen into arrears with her repayments to Princewest.

(a)   Explain whether it will be possible for Princewest to take possession of and sell Arkwrite Towers, and how such a sale would affect the position of the Doorway Building Society.

(b)   If Princewest sells Arkwrite Towers at less than its open market value, consider whether Bertha would have any remedy against either:

   (i)   Princewest, or

   (ii)   the purchaser from Princewest.

(c)   How must Princewest apply the proceeds of any sale of Arkwrite Towers?

See *Cases and Materials* **(30.9)** for a specimen answer.

CHAPTER THIRTY-ONE

SPECIAL LEGAL RULES GOVERNING MORTGAGES

31.1   Objectives

By the end of this chapter you should be able to:

■ explain the (inadequate) statutory rules regarding insurance of mortgaged premises;

■ explain the statutory rules regarding the leasing of mortgaged land, and the position if that power of leasing is excluded;

■ appreciate the limits the law puts on mortgagees' attempts to delay redemption of a mortgage;

■ appreciate the concept of 'collateral advantages', and be able to distinguish between (i) the rules governing the validity of such advantages **prior** to redemption, and (ii) the rules governing their validity **after** redemption;

■ explain consolidation of mortgages.

31.2   Introduction

The contents of this chapter are (inevitably) something of a miscellany. But there is one general point which I can usefully make at this stage. Most of the law discussed in this chapter dates from the first 40 years of this century. This is true not just for the relevant legislation, which is still largely in its 1925 form, but also for the case law. Consequently, a law, developed for the economic conditions which prevailed at the beginning of this century, has to be applied to the very different conditions (in particular much higher interest rates) which prevail at the end of this century.

31.3   Fire Insurance of the Mortgaged Property

A mortgagee whose mortgage is 'made by deed' has a statutory power (Law of Property Act 1925, ss. 101 and 108) to take out fire insurance on the mortgaged property and add the premiums to the capital debt. The policy must be for an amount specified in the mortgage deed, but in the absence of a specific provision the amount **must not exceed two-thirds** of the cost of restoring the building in the event of total destruction.

The statutory power is excluded if:

(a) the mortgage deed specifically provides that there shall be no fire insurance;

(b) the mortgagor maintains a policy in accordance with the express terms of the deed;

(c) the mortgage deed says nothing about fire insurance, but the mortgagor with the mortgagee's consent keeps up a policy for at least two-thirds of the cost of restoration in the event of total destruction.

As you may already have guessed, the statutory power relating to insurance is totally inadequate for modern conditions.

 ACTIVITY 133

How do institutional lenders such as banks and building societies deal with this problem?

I hope you realised that they invoke exclusion (b). Most modern mortgages specifically require the mortgagor to maintain insurance cover (against all catastrophes, not just fire) to the **full value** of the property. Alternatively, they provide that the mortgagee will insure the property for its full value and add the premiums to the mortgage debt.

31.4 Leasing of the Mortgaged Property

Prima facie there is in every mortgage executed post-1881 a statutory power of granting a lease binding upon both parties to the mortgage (Law of Property Act 1925, s. 99).

This statutory power belongs to the mortgagee if he has taken possession, or if he has appointed a receiver; otherwise the power belongs to the mortgagor. **In practice modern mortgages usually exclude the mortgagor's power to grant leases, but not the mortgagee's.**

 ACTIVITY 134

Why do you think that modern mortgages usually exclude the mortgagor's statutory power to grant leases?

Because, despite the restrictions set out at **31.4.2** of this chapter, mortgagees fear that mortgagors will lease the property on terms which (particularly as to rent) will reduce the value of their security.

31.4.1 POSITION WHERE THE STATUTORY POWER IS EXCLUDED

If a mortgagor who remains in possession of the mortgaged property grants a lease, **it will not be binding on the mortgagee**. But the mortgagee could estop himself from claiming that the lease is not binding on him by words or conduct which would lead a reasonable man in the position of the tenant to conclude that the mortgagee does regard the tenant's rights as binding upon him.

Appointing a receiver does not give rise to an estoppel, as the receiver is deemed to be the mortgagor's agent. However, creating the impression that the mortgagee is now the landlord and the receiver is his agent would raise the estoppel. For example, in *Chatsworth Properties* v *Effiom* [1971] 1 All ER 604, the mortgagee wrote to the tenants saying, 'Do not pay your rent to your *former* landlord, but to the receiver we have appointed'. The mortgagee was held to be estopped, and bound by the tenants' leases.

31.4.2 POSITION WHERE THE STATUTORY POWER APPLIES

Where the statutory power to grant a lease applies, the following restrictions are imposed:

(a) No mining or forestry leases are allowed.

(b) Building leases may be granted for up to 999 years; otherwise the lease must not exceed 50 years.

(c) The lease must take effect in possession within 12 months.

(d) The lease must be at the best rent reasonably obtainable. A premium ('fine') must not be charged.

(e) The tenant must covenant to pay the rent. There must be a forfeiture clause for non-payment of rent if the rent is 30 days in arrear. (A lesser period of grace may be fixed.)

(f) The lease need not be by deed. The tenant should execute a counterpart, but failure to do so does not invalidate the lease.

31.5 The Rules of Equity Protecting the Equitable Right to Redeem

The equitable right to redeem cannot be excluded by the terms of the mortgage. In order to escape from this rule, attempts have been made from time to time to disguise a mortgage as some other transaction. However, equity treats any transaction which **in substance** is the grant of security for a loan as a mortgage.

For example, suppose Andrea conveys Greenacre to Betty for £w, but Betty immediately grants Andrea an option to repurchase the property in x years' time for £y. £y appears to be £w plus interest for x years. Equity will treat the transaction as a mortgage, with an equitable right to redeem continuing **after** x years have expired.

31.5.1 NO IRREDEEMABLE MORTGAGES

A mortgage granted by a human being cannot be made irredeemable. Moreover, it is the essence of a mortgage that having repaid the debt the mortgagor must get his property back free from all rights of the mortgagee. As the older cases say, there must be no 'fetters' or 'clogs' on redemption.

One consequence of this is that it is impossible to include, **as a term of the mortgage**, a provision giving the mortgagee an option to purchase the mortgaged property. But if, after the land has been mortgaged, the mortgagor **as a completely separate transaction** grants an option to the mortgagee, the option is valid.

It would also appear that, as a completely separate transaction, a mortgagor can sell or lease the land to the mortgagee: *Alec Lobb (Garages) Ltd* v *Total Oil* [1985] 1 All ER 303.

31.5.2 POSTPONEMENT OF REDEMPTION

Occasionally a mortgage is created which deliberately postpones the legal redemption date from the traditional six months, and in effect provides that the debt **cannot** be repaid until x years have run.

Most mortgagees are, of course, very pleased when the debt is repaid, so you may well be asking, why should a mortgagee want to postpone the right to redeem? There are two possible answers to this question. In some cases the mortgagee, who is in effect investing his money in the loan, may want to be sure that his investment continues for a longish period. He may not want the bother of finding a new investment if the mortgage debt is repaid.

The second answer lies in the well-known fact that when a brewery lends money to a publican, the mortgage will include a tie clause tying the publican's pub to the brewery. (A similar thing happens, of course, with petrol companies and filling stations.) By postponing the right to redeem, the brewery (or petrol company) hopes to prolong the duration of the tie as long as possible.

A postponement of redemption is valid only if on all the facts the postponement is not 'unconscionable or oppressive' to the mortgagor. If the postponement is void under this rule, the mortgagor can redeem at any time.

Read *Fairclough* v *Swan Brewery Ltd* in *Cases and Materials* (31.3.2). Notice that as the estate mortgaged was leasehold not freehold, that fact made the case easier for the judges to decide.

Where there is a mortgage of a lease, and the postponement is so great that the right to redeem is of very little value, the postponement is undoubtedly void. In *Fairclough* v *Swan Brewery Ltd* [1912] AC 565, a lease of a hotel with $17\frac{1}{2}$ years to run was mortgaged to a brewery, redemption being postponed until there was just six weeks to run on the lease. (The mortgage of course included a 'tie' to the brewery.) The Privy Council had no difficulty holding the postponement invalid.

Where there is a mortgage of a **fee simple** there is no set rule that a postponement for greater than x years is void, but for less than x years is valid. Whether the postponement is oppressive or unconscionable depends on the circumstances of each case. The relative economic strengths of the parties is all important. In *Esso* v *Harpers* [1966] 1 All ER 725, the Court of Appeal held a postponement for 21 years in the mortgage of a filling station to be void. (I am sure you have guessed that the mortgage included a 'tie' to Esso petrol. As the postponement of redemption was held invalid, Harpers could repay the mortgage and thereby free themselves from the 'tie'.)

Esso v *Harpers* should be contrasted with *Knightsbridge Estates* v *Byrne* [1938] 4 All ER 618. In that case a London property company mortgaged land to an insurance company (a 'big man' to 'big man' transaction). A postponement of redemption for 40 years was held to be valid. It was in all the circumstances perfectly fair that the insurance company stipulate that the mortgage continue as a long-term investment.

31.6   Collateral Advantages

A collateral advantage arises where a mortgagee stipulates that in return for his loan he shall get **as well as a normal rate of interest**, some other additional benefit.

The most common example of a collateral advantage is, as you may have guessed, a 'tie' to a mortgagee brewery, petrol company, etc. For other kinds of more unusual collateral advantages, see the cases of *Multi-Service Bookbinding* v *Marden*, *Bradley* v *Carritt* and *Kreglinger* v *New Patagonia Meat Company Ltd*, all of which we consider below.

Collateral advantages give rise to two distinct problems:

(a) Validity of the advantage while the loan remains outstanding.

(b) Validity of the advantage after redemption of the mortgage.

31.6.1   VALIDITY WHILE THE MORTGAGE SUBSISTS

A collateral advantage is in principle valid as long as the mortgage remains unredeemed. It is void only if:

(a) it is oppressive or unconscionable in nature; or

(b) it is in unreasonable restraint of trade; or

(c) it infringes the Consumer Credit Act 1974, ss. 137 to 139.

'Ties' are generally not oppressive or unconscionable, nor it seems are they in unreasonable restraint of trade, provided they cease on redemption and the right to redeem is not postponed beyond the traditional six months.

In *Multi-Service Bookbinding* v *Marden* [1978] 2 All ER 489, there was a rather interesting 'collateral advantage'. A clause provided for the capital repayments to increase proportionate to the decrease in value of the pound sterling against the Swiss franc ('the Swiss franc uplift'). This clause was held to be valid. Notice, however, that in this case the lender was a private individual anxious to preserve the capital value of his investment. An unscrupulous money-lender might not receive such sympathetic treatment.

The more simple device of index-linking capital repayments would also seem to be valid. See *Nationwide Building Society* v *Registrar of Friendly Societies* [1983] 1 WLR 1226. In any event, the Building Societies Act 1986 now specifically empowers **building societies** to grant index-linked mortgages (see ss. 10 to 23).

Where one party to a mortgage is an individual, the mortgage could fall foul of the Consumer Credit Act 1974, ss. 137 to 139. If an agreement is an 'extortionate credit bargain', the court can modify or set aside the terms of the agreement. A credit bargain is 'extortionate' if it:

(a) requires the debtor to make payments which are grossly exorbitant; or

(b) otherwise grossly contravenes ordinary principles of fair dealing.

These provisions apply even to building societies and other lenders exempted from the general provisions of the Consumer Credit Act 1974. They apply whatever the size of the loan.

Read *Davies* v *Directloans Ltd* in *Cases and Materials* (31.4.1). What were the crucial facts which led the court to uphold the abnormally high rate of interest?

In *Davies* v *Directloans Ltd* [1986] 2 All ER 783, the terms of a loan granted to a cohabiting couple to enable them to buy a house were held valid, even though the rate of interest charged was 21.6 per cent as against a (then) market rate of approximately 17 per cent. The couple's income was very uncertain (they were artists by profession), and they were therefore unable to borrow from institutional lenders. The high rate of interest was not therefore 'extortionate'.

(I should stress that details of the Consumer Credit Act 1974 go way beyond what I have just told you and are outside the scope of traditional land law syllabuses, and therefore outside the scope of this text.)

31.6.2 COLLATERAL ADVANTAGES AFTER REDEMPTION

A collateral advantage which forms **part of the terms of the mortgage** ceases to have effect on the redemption of a mortgage, even though it was intended that the advantage should continue after redemption.

What happens, on redemption of the mortgage, to a 'tie clause' tying the borrower to the lender's beer, petrol, or whatever?

A tie clause in a mortgage must cease on redemption: *Noakes* v *Rice* [1902] AC 24. (This rule regarding collateral advantages applies whether the collateral advantage (tie clause or whatever) is contained in the mortgage deed, or in some other document contemporaneous to the mortgage.)

The case of *Bradley* v *Carritt* [1903] AC 253 given prominence in most textbooks, is quite tricky. The mortgagor was the controlling shareholder of a tea company. The mortgagor was not the tea company itself, which of course is in law a separate person. The property mortgaged was the shares themselves. (Shares in companies are often mortgaged.)

The mortgagee was a tea-broker. The mortgage included a collateral advantage under which the mortgagor promised that the mortgagee should always remain broker to the company.

The mortgagor, having paid off the mortgage, was held, by the House of Lords to be released from this promise of permanent employment for the mortgagee.

ACTIVITY 137

If the collateral advantage had been allowed to continue after redemption, what would have been the position of the mortgagor and his shareholding?

He would never have been free to dispose of his shares. He would have had to have kept them so as to keep control of the company, and whom it employed!

31.6.3   A COLLATERAL ADVANTAGE AS AN INDEPENDENT AGREEMENT

A collateral advantage, even one appearing in the mortgage deed, may on occasion be treated as an **independent agreement** separate from the mortgage. If a collateral advantage is held to be an independent agreement it has continuing validity after redemption of the mortgage.

ACTIVITY 138

Read the extracts from *Kreglinger* v *New Patagonia Meat Company* in *Cases and Materials* (31.4.3). Remember that this is another 'big man' to 'big man' case, and that interest rates in those days were much lower than nowadays.

In *Kreglinger* v *New Patagonia Meat Company* [1914] AC 25 the meat company were mortgagors, while the mortgagees were a firm of woolbrokers. The mortgage contained a provision that for the next five years the company should not sell any sheepskins to any other person without first offering them to the woolbrokers at the best price obtainable elsewhere.

The idea of this clause was (in effect) to guarantee to the woolbrokers (the mortgagees) a supply of sheepskins for the next five years. The woolbrokers accepted a slightly reduced rate of interest in return for this guarantee. The mortgagor repaid the debt after only two years. The House of Lords held that the 'sheepskins clause' remained valid for the full five years, even though the mortgagors had redeemed the mortgage.

The distinction drawn by the House of Lords in *Kreglinger* between advantages which 'form part of the terms of the mortgage' and advantages which are 'independent agreements' is often criticised as very artificial. I agree with the critics. The 'independent agreement' rule is in reality a convenient way of distinguishing collateral advantages such as 'ties' imposed by the 'big man' on the 'small man', from fair advantages agreed to by parties of equal bargaining strength. *Kreglinger* was a case falling into the latter category.

31.7 Redemption of Mortgages

31.7.1 WHEN MAY REDEMPTION TAKE PLACE?

A mortgage may be redeemed:

(a) On the legal redemption date.

(b) At any other time expressly permitted by the terms of the mortgage.

(c) On the expiry of six months' notice of intention to repay.

(d) At any time, without notice, if the mortgagee is demanding repayment or attempting to enforce the security, or if the loan was intended to be temporary.

Notice, therefore, that unless situations (a), (b), or (d) apply, a mortgagor is not entitled as a matter of law suddenly to turn up at the mortgagee's door and say, 'Here is all the money I owe you'. Unless one of those situations apply, the mortgagee is entitled to six months' notice, or six months' interest in lieu of notice.

Having said that, I should mention that in practice institutional lenders such as banks and building societies are usually flexible in their approach to redemption, and are usually happy to accept repayment at less than six months' notice.

31.7.2 WHO MAY REDEEM?

The original mortgagor may redeem, together with any persons who derive title through him.

ACTIVITY 139

What sort of people 'derive title' through a mortgagor?

Undoubtedly this concept covers a spouse with rights of occupation in the mortgaged property under the Matrimonial Homes Acts, or anybody (e.g., a cohabitee) with a constructive trust interest in the property. It would also include a tenant of the mortgagor, even if his lease is not binding on the mortgagee.

31.7.3   THE EFFECT OF REDEMPTION

If a mortgage is repaid by the mortgagor himself, it is simply discharged. If it is repaid by a third party entitled to redeem then the mortgage is transferred to that third party; that (in effect) means that the third party assumes the role of mortgagee.

31.7.4   MACHINERY OF REDEMPTION

Where a mortgage is redeemed, the parties could execute a new deed discharging or transferring the mortgage (as the case may be). However, it is the normal practice to invoke Law of Property Act 1925, s. 115, under which the mortgagee indorses on or annexes to the mortgage deed a receipt for the debt, indicating who is paying the money. If the person named is the mortgagor, the mortgage is simply discharged; if the person named is a third party, the receipt will transfer the mortgage to him.

On redemption the title deeds should be handed back to the mortgagor or handed to the transferee (as the case may be). If the loan is repaid by the mortgagor, then before handing the title deeds back the mortgagee must search the Land Charges Register. If he thereby discovers a subsequent mortgagee, he must hand the title deeds to that subsequent mortgagee.

31.8   Consolidation of Mortgages

Consolidation of mortgages occurs where a mortgagee has two mortgages created by the same mortgagor, and insists that if one mortgage is redeemed the other mortgage is redeemed as well. This right of consolidation is of practical value where the mortgagor proposes to repay a well-secured loan, but to leave a poorly-secured loan outstanding. For example, Bloggs owns Blackacre and Whiteacre, both worth £50,000 and both mortgaged to the Muggtown Bank. The debt secured on Blackacre is £70,000; the debt secured on Whiteacre is only £15,000. Bloggs proposes to repay the £15,000 secured on Whiteacre.

The following conditions must be satisfied for consolidation to be effected:

(1)   At least one of the two mortgages must confer a right of consolidation. (Modern mortgages always include a clause entitling the mortgagee to consolidate.)

(2)   The legal redemption date on each mortgage must be past.

(3)   Both mortgages must have been made by the same mortgagor.

(4)   At some point of time (however long or short) both mortgages were in common ownership, and both equities of redemption were in common ownership.

Consider the following examples of condition (4) (assuming the first three conditions are satisfied):

X mortgages Brownacre to A and Greenacre to B. C acquires both mortgages. C is entitled to consolidate. He would no doubt wish to do so if the loan secured on Greenacre was for £70,000 but Greenacre is now worth only £50,000, while Brownacre is worth considerably more than the loan secured on Brownacre.

C would still be entitled to consolidate if subsequently the equity of redemption in Brownacre was sold to Y, and the equity in Greenacre was sold to Z. If (say) Y was compelled to pay off the mortgage on Greenacre, he would take the mortgage on Greenacre by transfer (for what it's worth!).

If (say) X had sold the equity in Blackacre to Y before C had acquired both mortgages, there could be no consolidation by C.

This consolidation rule is often criticised, and I agree with those (including now the Law Commission) who say that it should be abolished. The consolidation rule is a major reason why, in modern conditions, people are reluctant to buy a property subject to a mortgage which will **not** be discharged out of the proceeds of sale.

Why is consolidation a risk to somebody who buys an equity of redemption i.e. a property subject to an outstanding mortgage?

A person who buys land subject to a mortgage always runs the risk that the mortgage on his land will be consolidated with a mortgage of which he has never even heard. (Y, in our recent example, may never have heard of Greenacre!)

31.9 Conclusion

In the introduction to this chapter I stressed that the law has not kept pace with economic realities. I hope, however, that you have noticed that some of these rules, for example those relating to insurance and leasing, can and **often are** avoided by careful drafting of the mortgage. The parties 'contract out' of the awkward rules.

The parties cannot, however, 'contract out' of the (largely judge-made) rules regarding delaying redemption and collateral advantages. In an era when the phrase 'consumer protection' had not been even thought of, the judges realised that borrowers needed protection from oppressive terms which lenders might otherwise impose.

However, as the *Kreglinger* case perhaps demonstrates, these judge-made rules lack the flexibility of modern legislation such as the Consumer Credit Act or the Unfair Contract Terms Act. Moreover, these judge-made rules apply to all borrowers, whatever their wealth or status.

CHAPTER THIRTY-TWO

PRIORITY OF MORTGAGES OF UNREGISTERED TITLES

32.1 Objectives

By the end of this chapter you should be able to:

■ identify which mortgages are registrable as land charges and which are not;

■ appreciate the problems centred on s. 97 of the Law of Property Act 1925;

■ explain the priority rule which operates where an equitable interest is mortgaged;

■ advise as to when a further advance may be 'tacked'.

32.2 Introduction

As you know, a parcel of land can be (simultaneously) subject to several mortgages. Problems of priority will arise if the borrower defaults and it transpires that the total amount of money secured on the land exceeds its value.

Suppose Tom, Dick and Harriet have each lent Mathew £40,000. Each has taken a mortgage of Mathew's house, Mudstacks, to secure their loan. Mathew is in financial difficulties and Mudstacks is worth only £60,000. It follows that the mortgagee who comes first in priority will get paid in full. The mortgagee who comes second will get (roughly) only £20,000 from Mudstacks. The mortgagee who comes third in priority . . .

As you may have already guessed, the 'natural order' of priority between mortgages is order of creation. The mortgage which was created first has first claim, the mortgage created second has second claim, and so on. But as we shall see, that 'natural order' of priority between mortgages can be upset.

Priority of mortgages is one topic where it makes a considerable difference whether the land mortgaged is unregistered or registered title. The rules applicable where the land is unregistered are complex, and (in this respect at least) it is perhaps fortunate that unregistered titles are in quite rapid decline.

32.3 Priority of Mortgages where an Unregistered *Legal* Estate is Mortgaged

Very little depends nowadays on whether the mortgage(s) is (are) legal or equitable. The vital distinction (nowadays) is between mortgages registrable as land charges and mortgages which are not so registrable.

If a mortgagee **does** take possession of the title deeds to the land at the time the mortgage is created, the mortgage is **not** capable of registration as a land charge. (Remember that **normally** the mortgagee whose mortgage is created first takes possession of the title deeds. He is not, however, absolutely obliged to do so.)

If a mortgagee (whether legal or equitable) does **not** take possession of the title deeds to the land at the time the mortgage is created (probably this will be because another mortgagee already has them), the mortgage **is** registrable as a land charge. If legal, it will be a Class C(i) 'puisne mortgage'; if equitable it will be a form of 'general equitable charge', Class C(iii).

(If at the date of the mortgage the mortgagee takes the deeds but returns them to the mortgagor for any reason prior to redemption, this does not make his mortgage registrable as a land charge. Equally, if a mortgagee did not take the deeds at the outset, but obtained them later, his mortgage remains registrable.)

32.3.1 POSITION OF A LEGAL MORTGAGEE WHOSE MORTGAGE IS NOT REGISTRABLE

A legal mortgagee whose mortgage is not registrable can lose priority to a later mortgagee in limited circumstances only:

(a) By allowing the mortgagor to retake possession of the title deeds, thus enabling the mortgagor fraudulently to represent to a new lender that the property is not mortgaged. It seems, however, that this rule applies only if the mortgagee knew of the fraudulent intent, or where he was 'grossly negligent' in his caring for the title deeds (for example he left them lying around and enabled the mortgagor to 'steal' the deeds).

(b) If an earlier mortgagee prematurely endorses a receipt for the debt on the mortgage deed before he has in fact been repaid, and a later mortgagee therefore assumes the earlier mortgage has been discharged, the earlier mortgagee will be estopped from claiming priority.

32.3.2 POSITION OF AN EQUITABLE MORTGAGEE WHOSE MORTGAGE IS NOT REGISTRABLE

(You should remember that the old-fashioned, pre-1989 equitable mortgage by deposit of title deeds will fall into this category.)

An equitable mortgagee whose mortgage is not registrable could lose priority to a later mortgagee (legal or equitable) under the rules just discussed with respect to legal mortgagees.

In addition, you may recall that an equitable mortgage where the mortgagee **has** taken the title deeds is an example of an equitable interest not registrable as a land charge but still subject to the doctrine of notice. Therefore, such an equitable mortgagee could

theoretically lose priority to a later **legal** mortgagee who took his mortgage without notice of the earlier equitable mortgage.

Why is this risk of losing priority to a bona fide purchaser of a legal estate/mortgage a purely theoretical one?

If an equitable mortgagee remains in possession of the title deeds, the fact that the mortgagor does not have them will be notice to any subsequent mortgagee of the existence of the prior equitable mortgage.

32.3.3 MORTGAGES REGISTRABLE AS LAND CHARGES

If a registrable mortgage is in fact registered as a land charge then it is bound to have priority over subsequently created mortgages. If it is not registered, then by s. 4(5) of the Land Charges Act 1972, it 'shall be void as against a purchaser of the land charged therewith, or any interest in that land'. (This is the usual rule which operates when there is a failure to register **any type** of land charge.)

Applying the Land Charges Act rules, if X grants a registrable mortgage to A which A omits to register, and then X grants a mortgage to B, who will have priority?

B will have priority. Moreover it is crucial to realise that (applying the Land Charges Act rules) B has priority:

(a) whether B's mortgage is legal or equitable;

(b) whether B's mortgage is registrable or not;

(c) whether or not, if registrable, B's mortgage has been registered;

(d) whether B knew of A's mortgage or not.

32.3.4 SECTION 97 OF THE LAW OF PROPERTY ACT 1925

This provision creates a difficulty when considering the priorities between mortgages which are registrable as land charges. It provides:

Every mortgage affecting a legal estate in land . . . shall rank according to its date of registration as a land charge pursuant to the Land Charges Act.

Read literally, this appears to lay down a special rule for a series of mortgages all of which are registrable; viz. that priority depends upon the order in which the mortgages are entered onto the register.

Apply s. 97 literally to the following example:

1 April	**X grants a registrable mortgage to A, who does not register.**
1 May	**X grants a registrable mortgage to B, who does not register.**
1 June	**A belatedly registers.**
1 July	**B belatedly registers.**

Whose mortgage gets priority?

Applying s. 97 **literally**, you should have worked out that A gets priority.

Apply the usual Land Charges Act rule to the example just given.

Applying the usual Land Charges Act rule, B has priority. So here we have two statutory rules which produce conflicting results. Which is the correct rule? No one is sure, as there is no relevant case law.

32.3.4.1 Arguments for applying the Land Charges Act rule

Most commentators seem to think that s. 97 of the 1925 Act should not be construed literally. Where s. 97 says 'pursuant to the Land Charges Act', that phrase (it is argued) should be taken as incorporating the principles of the Land Charges Act, including s. 4(5).

If the literal interpretation of s. 97 were adopted, there would be a special rule for registrable mortgages operating by way of exception to the general rules for priority which apply to all other registrable interests. That could be very awkward.

32.3.4.2 Arguments for taking s. 97 literally

There are two arguments in favour of construing s. 97 literally:

(a) A literal reading of s. 97 produces a simple rule that 'first on the register is first in priority'. Moreover this rule is the one which (in effect) operates where the mortgaged land is registered title. (We will examine this point in **Chapter 33**.)

(b) If the normal Land Charges Act rules apply to priorities of mortgages, we could end up with a 'vicious circle' of priorities.

Try to apply the Land Charges Act 1972, s. 4(5) to the following example:

1 September	**Z grants a registrable mortgage to D, who does not register.**
1 October	**Z grants a registrable mortgage to E, who does not register.**
1 November	**D belatedly registers.**
1 December	**Z grants a registrable mortgage to F.**

Applying s. 4(5), you might conclude that D has priority over F, F has priority over E, and E has priority over D. This is clearly nonsense.

32.3.4.3   Will these problems ever be solved?

Do we construe s. 97 literally? If not, what do we do about the vicious circle just described in **Activity 142**?

These questions have now existed for about 70 years, and, despite the large number of mortgages of unregistered titles, the courts have never had to answer them.

Do you think that these questions will ever be answered? If not, why not?

My personal guess is that they will never be answered. I suspect that if these questions arise, the competing mortgagees (all commercial enterprises of one kind or another) choose to settle out of court rather than engage in expensive litigation where the costs are almost certain to exceed the amount at stake.

You should also remember that with the extension of registration of title, the chance of these problems arising is much reduced.

32.4 Priority of Mortgages Where the Mortgaged Property is an Equitable Interest

(This would occur, for example, where a life interest or an interest as tenant in common is mortgaged.)

Priority depends on the 'rule in *Dearle* v *Hall*'. (Nothing is to be gained from reading this case.) Under this rule 'first in time is first in right' is the prima facie principle. But a later mortgagee of an equitable interest will gain priority over an earlier one if:

(a) he took his mortgage without notice of the earlier mortgage; and

(b) he sent a written notice of his mortgage to the trustees, which was received by the trustees before they received a written notice from the earlier mortgagee.

The trustees to whom the notice must be sent are as follows:

(1) If the land is settled land, to the SLA trustees.

(2) If the land is held on trust for sale, to the trustees for sale.

(3) In any other case, the owner of the legal estate out of which the equitable interest is derived.

32.5 Tacking of Further Advances

(Note that the word used here, 'tacking', has nothing to do with sailing! Rather 'tacking' is used in this context in a sense similar to 'nailing together', or 'sewing together'. Under the 'tacking' rules, a mortgagee is allowed to join together two or more loans.)

Tacking is in effect a qualification upon the rules of priority already discussed. Tacking is of importance only where one person (call him A) has lent two or more loans secured on the same property, while some other person (call him B) has also lent money secured on the same property. If under the general rules for priority the order would be A–B–A, but the conditions for tacking are fulfilled, A can amalgamate his two loans, and thus gain priority for his second loan over that of B.

32.5.1 THE ECONOMIC SIGNIFICANCE OF TACKING OF FURTHER ADVANCES

A further advance is any additional loan secured on a piece of property made by a lender who has already lent money secured on that property. It is worth noting immediately that mortgagors often borrow money from an 'institutional lender' and then later go back to that same lender for a 'further advance' to finance (say) an extension to the house, or to raise money for a business enterprise or even to finance their education! Moreover, many modern mortgages are expressed in terms such as: 'This mortgage secures a loan of £X0,000 and any further advance which the mortgagee chooses to make.'

Consider how the current discussion applies to a secured overdraft.

The mortgage to secure the overdraft will always contain a clause similar to that just quoted. Every time the bank honours a cheque drawn on the overdraft it in effect makes a further loan (a 'further advance') to the customer.

The rules as to 'tacking' are thus important to institutional lenders, and absolutely crucial for banks.

32.5.2   WHEN CAN A FURTHER ADVANCE BE TACKED?

A further advance may be tacked:

(a)   where the intervening lender has agreed that the further advance should have priority; or

(b)   where the further advance was made without notice of the intervening mortgage (whether legal or equitable).

If the intervening mortgage was registrable, and has been registered, then as registration equals notice tacking is normally impossible. This is subject to the exception that where a mortgage is expressly made to secure not only the original loan but any further advance which may be made subsequently, the rule that registration of a land charge equals actual notice does not apply. The mortgagee is able to tack unless he has 'notice' of the intervening mortgage in the pre-1926 sense.

This special rule (Law of Property Act 1925, s. 94(2)) was enacted to benefit banks. If there were no such rule, a bank might have to search the land charges register every time it was considering honouring a cheque drawn on a 'secured overdraft' account.

32.5.3   MORTGAGE CONTAINING AN OBLIGATION TO MAKE FURTHER ADVANCES

Where a mortgagee is under an obligation to make further advances up to a given figure should the mortgagor ask for them, there is an **automatic right to tack** which cannot be lost by any form of notice of the intervening mortgage, provided that the total amount lent does not exceed the figure agreed on. This is another rule of importance to banks; banks often promise a customer to lend money up to an agreed limit, should the customer ask for the money.

Quentin executed a first legal mortgage of Blackacre in favour of his bankers, Bloggs Bank plc. The bank took possession of the title deeds. The mortgage is to secure Quentin's overdraft. The bank promised, in any event, to lend up to £40,000; the mortgage also secures 'any further overdraft facilities as the Bank in its discretion shall see fit'.

Suppose that six months ago the overdraft stood at £35,000. Quentin then took a further loan of £25,000 from Blue Dragon Securities Ltd secured by a legal charge on Blackacre.

Quentin is now in financial difficulties. His overdraft stands at £55,000. By agreement between the parties Blackacre has been sold, and the net proceeds after deducting the costs of sale are £60,000. To how much of that sum is the bank entitled?

Under the rule just discussed the bank can, in any event, claim £40,000 out of the proceeds of sale. Whether it can claim the other £15,000 (in whole or part) ahead of Blue Dragon will depend upon whether (rule (b) above) it had notice of the second mortgage before making further payments from the overdrawn account.

In a situation like that in SAQ 153, what should a lender like Blue Dragon do to preserve its priority against tacking of further advances by the bank?

It is not enough for Blue Dragon to register its mortgage as a land charge (Law of Property Act 1925, s. 94(2)). Blue Dragon should write a formal letter to the bank informing it of the second mortgage. Remember, however, that no action by Blue Dragon can prevent tacking up to £40,000.

32.6 Conclusion

I think you will agree that this chapter, while relatively short, has been full of complications. In one crucial respect (s. 97 of the 1925 Act) the law is in urgent need of clarification, either by the courts or by Parliament.

404 PRIORITY OF MORTGAGES OF UNREGISTERED TITLES

Unfortunately, the problems are unlikely to be resolved in the near future. However, and this is fortunate, they will gradually fade away with reduction in the number of unregistered titles.

CHAPTER THIRTY-THREE

MORTGAGES OF REGISTERED LAND

33.1 Objectives

By the end of this chapter you should be able to:

- explain the three ways of mortgaging a registered title;

- explain the priorities and tacking rules for mortgages by registered charge;

- appreciate the difficulties which surround an informal mortgage by deposit of the land certificate.

33.2 Introduction

Registered titles, and therefore mortgages of such titles, have existed for about 100 years (since the Land Registration Act 1897). Yet, as the recent case of *Mortgage Corporation* v *Nationwide Credit* demonstrates (see **33.5.3**), even institutional lenders can still experience difficulties with the legal requirements for such mortgages.

Mortgages of registered titles are really quite a different animal from mortgages of unregistered titles. I can illustrate this by referring back to the preceding four chapters. The only part of **Chapter 29** directly applicable to mortgages of registered title is the concept of 'legal redemption date' and 'equity of redemption'. **Chapters 30** and **31 do apply** to mortgages of registered titles, but **Chapter 32** (except for the short section on priority of mortgages of equitable interests at **32.4**) has **no application whatsoever** to registered land.

There are three types of mortgage of registered land, though one of them (mortgage using an unregistered form) must be very rare indeed. The other two forms, mortgage by registered charge and mortgage by deposit of the land certificate, are both very common.

33.3 Mortgage by Registered Charge

This is the standard way of mortgaging registered land, and is the direct equivalent of the 'charge by way of legal mortgage' used for unregistered titles. The mortgagor executes a deed charging the land; the land must be identified by reference to the register. (In practice the title number(s) is given.) While a nominal legal redemption date is not necessary for a mortgage by registered charge, old practices die hard, and one usually is inserted.

After the charge has been executed, the mortgagee presents the mortgage deed and the land certificate to the registry. The mortgage is registered; only on registration does the mortgagee acquire a **legal** charge. The land certificate is kept at the registry (not taken by the mortgagee) and the mortgagee is issued with a 'charge certificate'.

33.3.1 PRIORITIES OF MORTGAGES BY REGISTERED CHARGE

If there is a series of registered charges, they rank for priority in the order they are entered on the register, not in the order of creation.

(Compare the simple statement above (one sentence of 27 words) with the pages of discussion at **32.3** and **32.4**.)

33.3.2 TACKING

(Re-read the discussion on tacking at **32.5** and compare it with the discussion below.)

If a registered charge is expressed to secure further advances, the mortgagee has the usual right to 'tack' further advances on to the original loan. However, if there is any application by a third party to make an entry on the register with respect to the land (e.g., a third party applies to register a charge in his favour), the registrar must send a formal warning of this application to the mortgagee. Any further advances made after the date on which this warning notice should have been received do not have priority over the third party's rights, unless there is an obligation to make those further advances.

Where a mortgagee by registered charge is under an obligation to make further advances up to an agreed limit, the existence of this obligation should be made clear in the mortgagee's application to register his charge. Provided this has been done, the existence of the obligation will be entered on the register and the mortgagee can 'tack' up to the agreed limit; i.e. further advances up to the agreed limit will have priority over later entries on the register.

Please use the same example as in SAQ 153 and SAQ 154 at the end of the previous chapter, except that Blackacre is registered land and both mortgages are by registered charge. What should happen in the period immediately after the second mortgage executed in favour of Blue Dragon, and with what consequences?

Blue Dragon should apply to register its charge. The registry will send a formal warning to Bloggs Bank. The bank will no longer be able to tack further advances, **except** it can tack up to the agreed limit of £40,000, provided the existence of the obligation to lend up to £40,000 appeared in its application to register its charge. (In practice it undoubtedly would be included in the bank's application.)

33.4 Mortgage Using a Form Suitable for Unregistered Title

Such a mortgage is effective to create a minor interest in favour of the mortgagee. To preserve priority the minor interest must be protected by notice or by a caution. If the mortgagee wishes to exercise its remedies it will have to request the mortgagor to execute a mortgage by registered charge. (I imagine that this kind of mortgage can now happen only by mistake.)

33.5 Mortgage by Deposit of the Land Certificate

This form of mortgage is popular with banks and other similar lenders when granting short-term finance to trusted customers. Provided no need arises to enforce the mortgage, this form of mortgage is cheaper than a mortgage by registered charge. In particular, the bank avoids paying the fee required for a mortgage by registered charge.

33.5.1 PRE-1989

This form of mortgage was the (rough) equivalent to the pre-1989 equitable mortgage by deposit of title deeds. The land certificate was handed to the lender, and that created a 'lien' over the registered land. To preserve his priority the mortgagee entered a special 'notice of deposit' with the registry. Strangely, this special 'notice' gave the mortgagee only the protection given to someone who has entered a caution. (You have no doubt remembered that a caution merely gives the right to 14 days' warning of transactions with the relevant title.)

In practice a deposit of the land certificate was accompanied by a 'memorandum under seal' setting out the terms of the loan. The memorandum would include a clause whereby the mortgagor undertook to execute a mortgage by registered charge should the mortgagee so require. This clause was necessary because until a registered charge was executed the mortgagee could not exercise any of its normal remedies.

33.5.2 POST-1989

The mortgage by deposit of the land certificate can be still used, but will involve three stages:

(a) A written contract, signed by both parties, setting out all the terms of the mortgage. This contract will include a promise by the mortgagor to execute a mortgage by registered charge should the mortgagee so require. (This comprehensive written contract is necessary to satisfy s. 2 of the Law of Property (Miscellaneous Provisions) Act 1989: see **29.7.3**.)

(b) The borrower hands the land certificate to the lender.

(c) The lender enters a notice or caution (the 'notice of deposit' has now been abolished).

Despite the change in 1989, mortgages by deposit of the land certificate remain popular with the banks when lending to trusted customers. The banks save on the Land Registry fees. Some banks have, however, added a fourth stage to the process just outlined:

(d) The borrower on being given the loan immediately executes a formal registered charge which the bank **keeps in its vaults**.

What do you think is the advantage of this four-stage procedure?

If, but only if, the bank needs to enforce its security, it will take the charge deed out of its vaults and register it. Only then will it have to pay the registration fee. Thus the bank, unless the customer unexpectedly gets into financial difficulties, saves on Land Registry fees, but at the same time has the assurance that it can register its charge at any time.

33.5.3   A POTENTIAL DRAWBACK OF MORTGAGES BY DEPOSIT OF THE LAND CERTIFICATE

Read *Mortgage Corporation* v *Nationwide Credit Corporation* in *Cases and Materials* (33.1). You should notice that to solve this case the Court of Appeal had to resort to basic principles of property law.

In *Mortgage Corporation* v *Nationwide Credit Corporation* [1993] 4 All ER 623 X mortgaged a property to A by executing a charge. A did not register the charge or protect its rights in any other way. X then executed a charge in favour of B which protected its interest by entering an **ordinary notice**. Did A or B have priority?

If B had actually substantively **registered** its charge, B would undoubtedly have gained priority. But the Court of Appeal found that entering an ordinary notice, while guaranteeing that the mortgage binds **later purchasers or mortgagees**, does not give the mortgage priority over an earlier created right, even though that earlier right has not been protected by entry on the register. A had priority, applying the general principle of 'first in time first in right'.

It would appear that banks who rely on mortgages by deposit of the land certificate could find themselves in a situation similar to B's. A mortgage/charge executed by the mortgagor **before** the deposit of the land certificate with a bank would have priority over the bank, even if the earlier mortgage had not been protected by any entry on the register.

33.6 Conclusion

Compared with most of the other chapters in this book, I hope that you have found this one short and relatively straightforward. Mortgages of registered land is a good topic to end with, as it illustrates two important facets of English land law.

First, one of weaknesses of the English system of registration of title is that it still allows transactions (such as mortgages) to take place with 'registered' land which are not fully recorded on the land register, for example the mortgage by deposit of the land certificate. To lawyers from at least three of our partners in the European Union (Germany, Austria, and Sweden) this is totally absurd.

Secondly, for many purposes England (and Wales) has two systems of substantive land law; there is the unregistered title system and the registered title system. The first of these two systems will gradually fade away, but it will be a long time before it totally disappears.

33.7   End of Chapter Assessment Question

'The rules governing the priority of mortgages of an unregistered title are both complex and uncertain. The rules governing the priority of mortgages of a registered title are by comparison straightforward, though the recent case of *Mortgage Corporation* v *Nationwide Credit Corporation* does create a problem for lenders who take a deposit of the land certificate.'

Discuss.

See *Cases and Materials* (33.3) for a specimen answer.

INDEX